People Skills Handbook:

Action Tips for Improving Your Emotional Intelligence

Judy Aanstad

Pamela Corbett

Catherine Jourdan

Roger Pearman

Winston-Salem, North Carolina

Copyright 2012 Judy Aanstad, Pamela Corbett, Catherine Jourdan, and Roger Pearman

www.peopleskillshandbook.com

Printed in the United States of America

ISBN 978-0-9839955-0-0

Trademark Designations

The EQ-i® and MESCEIT® are registered trademarks of Multi-Health Systems, Inc., of Toronto, Canada. Type 360® is the registered trademark of Leadership Performance Systems, Inc. The Hogan Personality Inventory® is the registered trademark of Hogan Assessment Systems. The ECI® is the registered trademark of the Hay Group. The Myers-Briggs Type Indicator® is the registered trademark in the United States and other countries of the Myers Briggs Type Indicator Trust. The California Psychological Inventory® is the registered trademark of CPP, Inc. CCL® and LDP® are the registered trademarks of the Center for Creative Leadership, Inc. Choices Architect® is the registered trademark of Lominger International — a Korn/Ferry Company. Six Thinking Hats® is the registered trademark of the De Bono Group, LLC. Leadership Trust® is the registered trademark of the Leadership Trust, Inc. Post-it® is the registered trademark of the 3M Company. MBSR® is the registered trademark of Jon Kabat-Zinn.

Editorial, typographical and prepress services by
Acorn Abbey Books, Madison, North Carolina

Contents

Part 3 — Toolboxes
Tools for Applying EQ Competencies

Preface

People skills. Who doesn't need them? Who couldn't improve on them? We wrote this user-friendly guide to provide an easy, direct and practical route to being more effective, in just about every way that involves people, including your understanding of yourself. Effectiveness is accelerated by understanding emotions — yours and others' — and acting on emotions in ways that achieve outcomes — yours and others'. This is the value of increasing your emotional intelligence.

Greater understanding of emotions and how to manage them is the bridge to enhanced performance and to greater emotional intelligence. There's no escaping this simple fact: Emotions are central to your personal and professional life. How you use emotional energy is directly related to your effectiveness as partners, parents, friends, colleagues, and professionals.

Emotional intelligence is a big concept with several labels. "Emotional intelligence" also goes by "EQ" and "EI." "EQ" is a play on words, combining "emotion" with the more familiar "IQ" or intelligence quotient. So, "EQ" represents how emotionally smart you are. "EQ" is the term we will use interchangeably with emotional intelligence throughout this book. And we will occasionally remind you of that as we go along.

Emotions are central to your decision-making, problem-solving, and health. Developing the 54 EQ Competencies in this book can mean the difference between fulfillment at home and at work or frustration and disappointment. While there may be some critical debate about what is neurological and what is behavioral when it comes to emotional intelligence, our focus is on the behaviors associated with emotional intelligence. That's what you have control over. Throughout the *People Skills Handbook*, our use of the terms emotional intelligence and EQ is intended to refer to the 54 behavioral competencies that are proven to link emotional intelligence to effectiveness.

Emotional intelligence frameworks focus on how you are aware of and manage emotions, and how you acknowledge and work with the emotions of others. These elements combine to produce various personal and social behaviors that contribute to your effectiveness. These behaviors, skills, and perspectives are integrated into the 54 EQ Competencies in Part 2 of this book.

Evidence rules

This book is built on research studies that provide practical guidance for "what you need to do when" related to managing your emotions. In addition to this research, our professional experience has guided the suggestions in each of the 54 EQ Competencies in this book. Our desire is to be comprehensive and practical. Whether you want to become more effective in your personal life or in your work life, the competencies and perspectives provided on the following pages will help you each step of the way.

Four authors, four styles

Each of the authors of this book has a unique style and way of expressing ideas. You will notice that as a result of these four styles there may be subtle shifts from time to time. Because you, the reader, represent many different personalities and preferences, we are hoping that this will benefit you. Though we have established a standardized format and sought to create a cohesive and consistent book, we also believe that our four unique styles will allow us to speak to a wider range of people. Sometimes the writing will be more informal and personal, and at other times you will find it more to the point, matter of fact and instructive. We can say the same for you, our readers: Some of you tend to be more informal and personal, and some of you are more businesslike and matter of fact.

While we, the authors, have different writing styles, we do have much in common, including educational and professional backgrounds. As executive coaches, psychologists, training facilitators, and counselors, we have heard our clients ask again and again where they can learn more about how to develop compassion, or flexibility, or some other interpersonal trait or competency. Very often our clients are open to learning but don't know where to begin or how to determine their current skill level in an interpersonal skill that they hope to develop. Many of the skills or competencies for which our clients seek coaching or help fall under the category of emotional intelligence.

Especially in the last twenty years, much has been written about emotional intelligence, but we have yet to find a comprehensive book that lays out the behaviors and perspectives that comprise EQ, along with defining what they look like at the talented, skilled, and unskilled levels, and giving clear, concrete ideas for how to develop them. In addition, we provide the rationale for why these competencies are important in your personal and professional lives. We also give some additional resources for those who are motivated to continue their research or education in a particular EQ competency. Note that each competency in this book links EQ to personal and professional effectiveness and well-being.

This book is a beginning, not a destination

We hope this book will be a great starting point for your journey toward greater emotional intelligence in your life. When you use the suggestions and tips to develop a particular EQ skill, you will certainly benefit. When you follow up on the many resources offered, you will benefit even more. Use Chapter 4 (Part 1) to create a plan to add even greater value to your efforts and increase your chances of success. We believe you will see this book as a handy reference for personal and work-related challenges for yourself and others.

Organization of the People Skills Handbook

The book is divided into three parts. Part 1 provides the foundation for understanding and acting on EQ skills and perspectives. Part 2 gives you a detailed review of the 54 EQ Competencies and appropriate Action Tips to improve your effectiveness with those behaviors. Part 3 is made up of Toolboxes that give action links between the competencies and an array of important issues.

Part 1: Introduction to People Skills

■ Chapter 1: Why Read the People Skills Handbook?

In this chapter you will find a rationale for the book and suggestions for how you might benefit from reading it. Because EQ is used in your daily life — work, home, relationships — you will find scenarios and examples of emotional intelligence competencies that are used to make a positive impact.

■ Chapter 2: What Is Emotional Intelligence (EQ)? A Review of Frameworks and Perspectives

This chapter frames the key principles of EQ and provides a compelling argument for developing your emotional intelligence. It offers personal examples of how EQ can have a widespread impact not only on your life but also on the lives of all those with whom you come in contact. In addition it makes the case for how organizations and families can benefit when members develop their emotional intelligence.

■ Chapter 3: Learning to Be Your Emotional Best

In this chapter you are introduced to learning agility and how you can do what the best learners do to become more emotionally intelligent. Learning agility is arguably one of the most critical skills you will need in the 21st century, and it can make developing your emotional intelligence much easier.

Learning agility involves a variety of strategies and behaviors that allow you to learn more, learn better, and learn faster. Emotional intelligence and learning agility have much in common. They are both learnable, and because they share many behaviors, as you strengthen one you strengthen the other. Carl Rogers, a famed counseling psychologist, could not have captured it better than when he said, "The only person who is educated is the one who has learned how to learn — and change." This chapter, indeed this book, is about learning to be more emotionally effective.

■ Chapter 4: Create an EQ Action Plan That Works for You

This chapter gives you some guidance on next steps or developmental planning as you decide to move forward and put into action some of the ideas for growth and development presented in the EQ competency chapters. This is the chapter where you put it all together! We have made it easy for you to move forward and create an EQ Action Plan. Research tells us that people who have a plan of action and who establish target goals are more likely to succeed in the accomplishment of those goals than those who do not set specific goals for themselves.

■ Chapter 5: EQ Competencies and Clusters

In this chapter the 54 EQ Competencies are placed into user-friendly clusters, defined, and thoroughly outlined so you are prepared to get the most out of Part 2: The 54 EQ Competencies with Action Tips. The clusters organize the competencies into categories of self-awareness, self-regulation, and relating well with others. At the end of the chapter you will find a summary of the 54 competencies that will give you a thorough orientation to the information and action tips in the next part of the book.

Part 2: The 54 EQ Competencies with Action Tips

The 54 EQ Competencies that make up emotional intelligence are covered in this part of the book. Each EQ competency is clearly organized to help you get the information you need. Each competency description includes:

- A definition and illustrative quote
- Behavioral list covering Talented, Skilled, and Unskilled categories for self-evaluation
- A "Big Picture View" to provide a comprehensive look at the competency and its importance
- Barriers to Effectiveness for each competency
- Related EQ Competencies
- Quick Action Tips to help you quickly become more effective

with each competency

- Learning From Experience gives you specific activities to help you integrate your lessons about each competency into your daily life

- A Resources section lists books, web sites, and other media to aid with learning to use each competency more thoroughly

Part 3: Toolboxes: Tools for Applying EQ Competencies

The Toolboxes provide handy implements for using the competencies in a variety of ways. Select a Toolbox that meets your need: a personal or work relationship challenge, feedback themes, or linkages to assessments.

Toolbox 1: The 54 EQ Competencies and Definitions

The 54 EQ Competencies are listed and defined. The listing provides an easy check list, and the definitions provide a quick reference.

Toolbox 2: Career Stallers and Interpersonal Problems

This toolbox provides a quick connection between key challenges and EQ competencies that can help you meet issues head on. For example, if motivating your team to higher performance is a challenge, then you can look up the competencies that are essential to meeting that challenge. If improving communication with a teenager at home is a challenge for you, you will find guidance in this toolbox.

Toolbox 3: Personal and Work Challenges

This toolbox contains a list of problem behaviors that, if left unchanged, could become an issue in both career and personal relationships. If you have received feedback about a problem behavior that needs improvement, it may be found in this toolbox. Some example of problem behaviors you will find in this toolbox are: being arrogant, intimidating, judgmental, overly sensitive, or moody.

Toolbox 4: If You Don't Find What You're Looking For, Look Here

To be as comprehensive as possible, this toolbox provides a list of additional competencies and skills that you might be looking for in addition to the 54 EQ Competencies covered in Part 2. In addition to being a dictionary of synonyms, there are a range of skills and traits that we have linked to the 54 EQ Competencies to aid your understanding and potential developmental planning.

Toolbox 5: Linking EQ Competencies to Assessments

This toolbox shows how scales from different personality and multi-rater assessments relate to the 54 EQ Competencies covered in Part 2. Individuals familiar with instruments like the FIRO-B®, CPI 260®, MESCEIT®, and

EQ-i® will find it useful to link their results with the competencies for developmental planning purposes.

Toolbox 6: EQ Development Opportunities for the 16 Personality Types

The sixteen personality types are listed with those competencies that are typical areas of development for each type. These personality patterns are often identified by instruments such as the Myers-Briggs Type Indicator® (MBTI®), Majors Type Indicator, and others.

Toolbox 7: Identifying Emotions

This list of pleasant and unpleasant emotions can be used to enrich your identification of and use of emotions.

Toolbox 8: EQ Action Plan

This reproducible master is intended for multiple development initiatives over time. Once you have worked on one primary competency and integrated new behaviors into your life, you can use a new EQ Action Plan form to develop your next EQ enhancement.

With you in mind

We hope this book will help you connect with your ability to learn to use your emotions more constructively, with practical benefits — like learning to use math to balance your checking account. There are plenty of books to teach math but few that teach how your emotions work. This book provides practical information about what EQ is, why it matters, and, most important, how to develop it. This learning guide takes you from assessing your EQ to creating an action plan to raise your EQ. Each chapter, carefully planned, serves as a practical resource.

Provide us with feedback about how useful you have found the information in this book. You can write to us at info@peopleskillshandbook.com.

Thanks

A work of this magnitude invites expressions of gratitude to legions of colleagues, friends, family, and clients. Listing them would double the size of this book. We are deeply grateful for their support and encouragement during the long journey of ideas to the product that you are holding. A special thanks goes to David Dalton of Acorn Abbey Books, who has edited and patiently worked with our manuscript.

Judy Aanstad, Ph.D.
Pamela Corbett, M.A.
Catherine Jourdan, MA.Ed.
Roger Pearman, Ed.D.

Part 1

Introduction to People Skills

CHAPTER 1

Why Read
the People Skills Handbook?

What you will learn in this chapter

- The rationale for emotional intelligence at work and at home
- The definition of Emotional Intelligence (EQ)
- How EQ is demonstrated in your daily life
- The three areas of increased relationship and life effectiveness related to improved emotional intelligence

Why should you be concerned with emotional intelligence?

Our experience as leadership coaches, counselors and educators has shown us that the greatest personal and professional setbacks in the lives of people are directly related to a lack of adequate self-awareness and to poor interpersonal skills. There is an abundance of evidence to demonstrate what most of us know through our own observations — that intelligence, luck, education, ambition and money can go only so far in leading a person to success if that person lacks well-developed emotional intelligence. If you mistreat people or allow yourself to be mistreated, it will eventually catch up with you. As anyone in the trenches can tell you, people will go the distance for a leader, manager or person who inspires them, talks to them respectfully and honestly and recognizes their good intentions and efforts. But if you are known for leaving a trail of battered and bruised people in your wake, then eventually this fact will overtake you.

As experienced adjunct staff with the Center for Creative Leadership (CCL®), we are familiar with their research demonstrating the link between people skills and professional effectiveness. That research indicates that 75% of careers that come off the tracks or derail do so for reasons related to poor emotional competencies such as:

- Inability to effectively handle change or to elicit trust
- Poor team or group skills ("doesn't play well with others")
- Lacks interpersonal skills such as empathy, listening, openness to others [1]

Seventy-five percent! That gets your attention! On the personal side, we know that the divorce rate in this country is hovering at the 50 percent rate, and that is for first marriages. Second marriages crumble at a greater rate — 67 percent — and third marriages at a rate of 74 percent. John Gottman, Ph.D., who has studied the reasons that couples divorce, says that the two primary deficits in couples that split are poor communication skills and the inability to handle conflict. It is clear that people need help in managing their relationships both at work and at home. Emotions such as anger, fear, anxiety and the stress that accompanies them can wreak havoc in the best of relationships. Throughout the course of this book, you will find tips for handling the emotions that threaten to get out of control, increasing the possibility of long-term relationship damage.

In another study conducted by the Center for Creative Leadership in which emotional intelligence variables were measured and correlated with competencies used in the workplace, the results suggested that managers "who don't feel a responsibility to others, can't handle stress, are unaware of their own emotions, lack the ability to understand others, or erupt into anger easily are viewed as likely to derail due to problems dealing with other people."[2]

The Harvard Business Review (HBR) writes a yearly publication in which they take note of key business trends and events for the year. In their 2003 publication, they wrote about the importance of emotional intelligence in creating successful businesses. They point out the value of offering developmental opportunities to employees to assist in the improvement of their emotional intelligence behaviors.

"Executives who fail to develop self-awareness risk falling into an emotionally deadening routine that threatens their true selves. Indeed, a reluctance to explore your inner landscape not only weakens your own motivation but can also corrode your ability to inspire others."

Concluding on the subject: "If emotional obliviousness jeopardizes your ability to perform, fend off aggressors, or be compassionate in a crisis, no amount of attention to the bottom line will protect your career. Emotional intelligence isn't a luxury you can dispense with in tough times. It's a basic tool that, deployed with finesse, is key to professional success." [3]

What is EQ?

Emotional Intelligence (EQ) is a term born out of the research and observation of social scientists that describes a person's ability to know one's self well and to relate to others with skill and sensitivity. Daniel Goleman, who brought the concept of emotional intelligence to the general public through his many books and publications, has defined it as:

"[A] set of abilities such as being able to motivate oneself and persist in the face of frustrations; to control impulses and delay gratification; to regulate one's moods and keep distress from swamping the ability to think; to empathize and to hope." [4]

Different from IQ (intelligence quotient), EQ, or emotional intelligence quotient, is a set of perspectives and behaviors that allows you to navigate your way through the complex world of emotions and interpersonal challenges. EQ helps you to better understand your behaviors and yourself. In Chapter 5 you will find the 54 EQ Competencies defined, and in Part 2 we make a case for the value of each of the EQ competencies and offer a variety of suggestions for developing them.

Demonstrating high EQ means that you are a person who others enjoy being around because you express genuine concern for people, because you take responsibility for your own behavior and choices, and because you are open to feedback and learning about yourself. Those with high EQ take charge of their own lives. They set goals and pursue them while still being able to care about the people they meet along the way.

Why we wrote the People Skills Handbook

We wrote this book to help people like you (or your clients) become more effective in your personal and professional lives. Research and life experience have taught us that emotionally intelligent people are flexible and adaptable. They are able to meet problems head on and work to find solutions to the challenges of day-to-day life. They are healthier physically and interpersonally and are more successful in their life choices. Over the years we (the authors) have seen the need for a resource book that operates as a guide to assist those who are seeking to increase their understanding of themselves and others and as a result improve their relationships both at home and at work. We believe you will find *People Skills Handbook: Action Tips for Improving Your Emotional Intelligence* to be that resource.

A good way to think about someone with effective and well-developed emotional intelligence is to ask yourself the following question: *Who is one of the most impressive people in your life?* Who comes to mind? It's possible that you might recall the most academically brilliant person you know, someone whose brainpower is impressive. But chances are that someone's intellect or

IQ is going to be less impressive than their qualities as a person. Most people, when asked this question, describe someone they know who is genuine, trustworthy, and interpersonally skillful. The people you are likely to remember are those who have touched you deeply in a real and personal way, and who made you feel acknowledged and accepted. If you have remembered such a person, then it is likely that he or she has a high EQ. *In the same vein, who in your life has left the most negative impact on you?* Is it the person who lacks brainpower? Or is it someone who is insensitive, who is like a bull in a china shop, or who can't seem to connect with others in a meaningful way? Such a person is probably exhibiting low EQ or emotional intelligence.

Daily experience with EQ

Though you may never have heard of the term EQ or emotional intelligence, you certainly have experienced it every day of your life. You have interacted with those who employ it well and with those who don't. You have had your own good EQ days as well as your lousy ones! Emotions are part of everyday life. Your ability to effectively employ healthy emotional intelligence can help you to achieve strong, meaningful and honest relationships with family, friends and co-workers. That is our goal — to help you develop great people skills.

Emotional intelligence improves your capacity to better understand your internal motivations and yourself. Emotionally intelligent people examine their behaviors and intentions and are able to see how those behaviors affect other people. With some reflection, you can easily identify the dozens of times every day that you have an opportunity to use your EQ. The examples below occur in life all the time. Do any of them sound familiar?

- Struggles with your teenagers over school, friends, curfews, picking up their stuff (and a hundred other things)
- Conflict with your significant other over finances, sex, disciplining the kids, your in-laws (and a hundred other things)
- Challenges at work with a co-worker
- Your neighbor's dog barks all night long, and you've got to find a way to negotiate some peace and quiet without alienating the neighbor
- Motivating the Little League (or soccer or football or volley ball) team or getting the players' parents to cooperate and behave appropriately
- The need to sell an idea at work and get people on board with it
- Soothing a tense situation or calming a person in distress

This is just a small sample of the many things we experience daily where using emotional intelligence can help us handle the events of everyday life. If you have received feedback from a colleague or family member that your behavior is occasionally disturbing or upsetting to them, or that you sometimes appear clueless about your impact on others, then this might be the book for you. Our goal is to provide readers with clear, constructive information on how to improve or develop emotional intelligence — people skills — in order to live a more fulfilling and productive life.

A personal EQ experience from one of your authors

One day during the writing of this book I arrived at the gym about thirty minutes early for my Pilates class. Because I had time to spare, I took my mat to the exercise room to save my spot in the class and to work out while waiting for class to begin. When I entered the room, I noticed it was entirely dark, but the light from the hallway fell on a person lying on the floor. Thinking I had disturbed someone who had stayed behind after a previous class to relax, I quietly put down my mat and left the room. A few minutes later a man came rushing up to me and asked if I had just put my mat down in the exercise room. Before I could say a word he began yelling at me. "You are the rudest person in the world. You came in during the middle of our relaxation time. What you did was inexcusable," and on and on. Stunned and remorseful, I tried to apologize. I understood his distress. I too am annoyed when others are loud or disruptive when I am in class. But he wasn't interested in my apology. He was more interested in telling me off. As he ran down the hallway back to his "relaxation time," he continued this barrage, creating a disturbance among the people along the way. Sympathetic strangers soon surrounded me and were all apologizing for this hot-headed man, trying to comfort and assure me that I had not deserved this outpouring of anger and vitriol.

As I thought of this event, I felt sympathy for this man. Clearly he was reacting to a situation in an impulsive way. While he had a legitimate complaint, all he did was tell me off rather than achieving a real awareness of the problem. His behavior only succeeded in drawing negative attention to himself. Witnesses to his rage were more concerned about me as the victim of his anger than with the nature of his complaint. Perhaps this person is very smart, has an advanced degree, or makes a lot of money. But none of those things helped him on this particular day. He diminished his effectiveness by engaging in behavior that caused others to dismiss him rather than take him seriously. This is a story about someone who, at least in this situation, exhibited low EQ or poor people skills.

Postscript to this story: As the weeks went by, no opportunity to talk with this man occurred until a month or so later, when our classes were combined. We were students in the same class! One day after class I asked if I might talk with him. In my best effort to use some of the very EQ skills we present in the book, I briefly replayed the events of weeks before and said I had not had a proper chance to apologize and that I would like to do so now. He was for a few moments speechless. When approached in this nonthreatening way he was able to apologize for his own negative behavior, and we were able to have a constructive conversation. He was clearly embarrassed and apologized again and again for his behavior. Because he seemed open to it I was able to share with him the impact his behavior had on me — that his very legitimate complaint had been overshadowed by his angry outburst. The satisfying ending to this story was that we were both able to offer appropriate apologies and move forward.

Benefits from reading People Skills Handbook

Collectively, we the authors offer decades of experience as teachers, trainers, executive coaches and psychologists. This book also reflects the academic knowledge and research that we have studied as well as the insights we've gained from the practical experience of our own lives and working with our clients. There are plenty of books on the market that discuss the theory of emotional intelligence. But if you want a practical and down-to-earth guidebook — an EQ primer of sorts — then we believe you will be happy with what you find in the *People Skills Handbook*. It is our goal to provide you with a clear, concise explanation of each of the 54 EQ Competencies and actionable ideas for developing each one.

Each of the EQ competency chapters includes additional resources in case you wish to investigate that competency further. We also explain in Chapter 4 how to create an EQ Action Plan incorporating ideas you have gained from the competency chapters.

Who might want to read and use this book?

You and just about everyone else! If you are a parent, significant other, leader, manager, coach, teacher, clergy, counselor, friend — anyone who interacts with others — one or more of these might speak to you.

Ask yourself if …

- You want to improve your listening skills (or you've been told they could stand some improvement)
- You want to better understand how your behavior affects others
- You want to improve your self-confidence
- You feel misunderstood and angry a lot of the time

- You wonder why others don't take you as seriously as you would like

- You often find yourself saying "I don't know what got into me" or "I don't know why I did that"

- You feel adrift and lost with no particular aim in your life

- You become stressed at the smallest (as well as the biggest) things

- You want to feel more in control of your life

- You often get stuck in old ways of thinking about new situations and can't seem to break the pattern

- Your boss (spouse, partner, friend or sibling) has said you need to work on your people skills

- You want to improve your interpersonal skills and become a more effective person or leader

- You want to improve your creativity, flexibility or resilience

How does EQ make you more effective?

1. EQ helps you become more self-aware. Self-awareness is a mindset that is often mentioned as a cornerstone to effective EQ or people skills. Are you aware of your own behavior, why you behave the way you do, and how it affects others? Or do you have a blind spot preventing you from seeing the need to make important changes in your life? Are you sensitive to how others feel and to what might be going on with them? Do you have a realistic idea of your strengths and weaknesses or know what tends to stress you out? The various qualities of self-awareness help you answer all such questions.

Increasing your self-awareness starts by being open to the feedback that others offer regarding your behavior and the impact it has on them. You can increase your self-awareness by taking an assessment instrument such as the Myers-Briggs Type Indicator® or by engaging in a 360-degree feedback process through work. People who value self-awareness tend to read books, take classes and workshops, invite feedback from others and in general are seekers of self-knowledge and wish to understand what motivates them.

Awareness also is an important aspect of better understanding others and tuning in to what they might be thinking or feeling. Self-aware people are better able to notice what is going on in the people around them. Development of self-awareness can help improve your relationships and lessen confusion about your emotions. Some EQ competencies that assist in the development of self-awareness are: (3) Authenticity, (12) Emotional Maturity, (19) Independence, (23) Integrity and (38) Resilience.

2. EQ helps you control emotions and behavior. A very important aspect of good emotional intelligence is self-control (of your behavior) and self-regulation (of your emotions, temper, anxiety, etc). While self-awareness can tell you how you feel and what is going on with you, it is self-control that helps you convert unwanted behaviors and emotional outbursts into positive behavior and emotional expression. Management of your inner dialogue (you do talk to yourself, don't you?) allows you to respond to instead of reacting to situations. It also involves your ability to reprogram negative thinking patterns and to learn to approach situations and people with an expanded and healthy attitude. Here are some examples of EQ competencies that help increase self-control and self-regulation: (14) Emotional Self-Control, (18) Impulse Control, (28) Mindfulness, (36) Reframing and (51) Tolerance.

3. EQ helps you relate more skillfully to others in both your personal and professional life. The better you are able to "play well with others" and manage your relationships with the people in your life, the more enjoyable your life will be. Caring about others, relating to them, building trust and respect between yourself and others, and listening well facilitate personal and interpersonal satisfaction and happiness. Emotional intelligence also means being a productive and accomplished member of your community, whether in the work you do for pay or for your community and family. People with high EQ are focused, they set goals, they are good problem solvers, and they approach the world with a positive and focused attitude. Examples of EQ competencies in this category are: (2) Assertiveness, (4) Collaboration, (6) Conflict Management, (17) Group Savvy, (25) Interpersonally Skillful, (27) Listening Generously and (46) Social Intelligence. (Check out Table 1 in Chapter 5 for a complete list of the EQ Competencies organized by clusters or categories.)

We are social animals

The field of neuroscience is making some interesting and exciting discoveries about the human brain. David Rock, founding president of the NeuroLeadership Institute, writes in his article "Managing With the Brain in Mind" that scientists are discovering evidence suggesting that the need for connection with one's own kind has evolved in mammals because it is essential to our survival.[4] Many studies are concluding that the human brain is a social organ. We are wired to want to connect with others, and when exposed to isolation and a lack of human interaction the human brain floods with neurochemicals telling us "stop, this hurts!" It seems that emotional intelligence plays a critical role not only in our happiness but also in our very survival as a species.

Is there hope for changing your ways?

Yes there is! And not just hope. There is good reason to be optimistic. The good news is that EQ is something you can learn and improve. We wrote this book to help you, the reader, to develop your own emotional intelligence or perhaps to offer a resource for those you work with or know who also want to improve their EQ.

- Part 2 provides descriptions of the 54 EQ Competencies, Quick Action Tips to get you to the level of effectiveness you desire, and resources for further study.

- Chapter 3 helps you identify a personal learning strategy for learning a new skill or behavior.

- Use the development guide found in Chapter 4 to lay out the blueprint you need to move forward on your goals by developing your own EQ Action Plan.

Our web site also offers additional resources to support you in the development of your effective emotional intelligence. We hope you will visit us there.

www.peopleskillshandbook.com

Summary of key points

Emotional Intelligence has been demonstrated to have a profound impact on the success of leaders in organizations.

- 75% of careers are derailed for reasons related to lack of emotional competencies.

How EQ differs from IQ:

- IQ is one's intellectual quotient (how smart you are).
- EQ is a set of perspectives and behaviors that allow you to navigate your way through the complex world of emotions and the challenges of interpersonal relationships. EQ helps you to better understand your behaviors and yourself.

Why was the People Skills Handbook written?

- To help people become more effective in their personal and professional lives.

Research indicates that those who are talented in EQ skills are healthier, happier, more optimistic and more able to succeed in reaching their goals.

EQ helps you improve your effectiveness in 3 broad categories

- Self-Awareness
- Self-regulation/Self-control
- Relating to and working well with others

Research in neuroscience indicates that the human brain is a social organ. We seem to be wired for connection with others, and it is part of our survival instinct.

CHAPTER 2

What Is Emotional Intelligence (EQ)? A Review of Frameworks and Perspectives

What you will learn in this chapter:

- What are the roots of the various perspectives on emotional intelligence?
- How an EQ competency analysis using a real life case illustrates the framework
- What expert researchers say
- What behaviors can you learn to improve your emotional Intelligence?

Ever since professional groups began collecting data on the following topics, the trends have remained unchanged[1, 2]:

- 80 percent of employees who quit their jobs report that they leave managers, not jobs
- 90 percent of those who quit report that a lack of appreciation and respect leads to their decisions to leave
- 80 percent of all ethics complaints are about the harassment or abuse of others over the misuse of organizational resources
- 90 percent of the measured difference between high and medium performers in organizations is accounted for by qualities such as empathy, interpersonal skills, and social responsibility shown by the high performers

The behaviors or conditions that are identified by these statistics relate to the presence (or absence) of emotional intelligence. Among managers, research consistently shows that variables such as IQ, experience on the job, and educational level do not differentiate between the best and the worst. What is fundamental to being an effective manager is EQ, and those with high degrees of emotional intelligence consistently outperform those without it.

What are the roots of the various perspectives on emotional intelligence?

Charles Darwin's 1872 book *The Expression of the Emotions in Man and Animals* is the first scientific effort to document the role of emotions in everyday life.[3] While many aspects of the book are extraordinary, the use of carefully prepared illustrations to capture the universality of emotions is among the first in publication history. Darwin proposes that emotions are expressed in spoken language, body movement, and facial changes and that they communicate to others what is important to you. As other scientific trends unfolded in the study of human behavior after Darwin's work, the definition and measurement of general intelligence became a foremost topic of concern. This meant that the role of emotions took a back burner in scientific inquiry.

Researchers concluded that, while studying intellectual functioning seems possible, the role of emotions was too complex. The question was set aside until the 1980s, when a new breed of researchers took up the challenge of understanding emotions. Note that scientists hold that the roots of any kind of intelligence are related to perceiving information and purposefully using it. If you contrast emotional intelligence with the kind of intelligence used for doing math, where you can readily "see" the numbers or formulas to be used, you can understand the challenge of defining and measuring EQ. "Seeing" the information in emotions is somewhat more complex than "seeing" math information because you must rely on cues such as facial expressions or tonality in others' responses to reveal the underlying emotions. Even if you notice emotional cues in others, interpreting what those cues mean and what triggered the emotions behind them can still be a challenge.[4] Learning to do so, though, is necessary for effective interaction with others.

Learning to improve your emotional intelligence can be achieved through developing more complex people skills. This has many benefits, because emotions are interwoven into the fabric of daily life. Your emotions play a role in your effectiveness, health, achievement, and fulfillment — in all areas of life. The competencies detailed in Part 2 of this book provide insight into, and describe the effective behaviors which make up, our emotional intelligence.

The growth of studies of intelligences suggests that there are a number of intelligences on which we rely. To name a few:

- Kinesthetic — body movement in time and space
- Spatial — understanding of dimensions of space
- Linguistic — capacities to learn and readily use languages

- Mathematical and logical — understanding numbers and ordering of information

- Musical — understanding and using musical tools and instruments

- Interpersonal — capacities related to understanding and working with others

And you can now add "emotional intelligence" to the list because the scientific study of emotions has shown how central they are to your well-being and relating well with others. It is now apparent that there are very complex emotional linkages to our cognitive or psychological ways of dealing with life. Neurological scientists indicate that if our emotional center (amygdala) is damaged, then we cannot function at the most basic level of making a simple decision. Or, by contrast, when our emotions hijack our higher-order reasoning, our perceptions and reactions are under the influence of such emotional flooding.[5]

While Darwin made the expression of emotions a legitimate area of study, it wasn't until psychologists Mayer and Salovey (1989) proposed that specific capabilities of emotional intelligence are structured in much the same way as intellectual intelligence. For example, Mayer and Salovey identified the ability to perceive facial expressions, emotional moods and emotional intensities, along with the ability to interpret the emotions we experience and observe in others as emotional intelligence.[6] Building on this research, Daniel Goleman popularized the concept of emotional intelligence with his books published in the 1990s (*Emotional Intelligence* and *Working with Emotional Intelligence*).[7] Concurrent with this line of work was another approach to emotional intelligence which focused on emotions and behaviors rather than various capabilities.

The field of emotional intelligence has three schools of thought. These are:

School 1: Innate capabilities. This school proposes eight capabilities that make up inherent emotional intelligence. These eight areas are covered in Toolbox 5, where the concepts measured by the Mayer-Salovey-Caruoso Emotional Intelligence Test (MSCEIT) are linked to our competencies in Part 2.

School 2: Neurology. More researchers than can be listed here have studied how the neurological nature of emotions and cognitions affects behavior. Researchers with this approach argue that emotions are so wired into the neurons of human action that it is best to think of emotions as a part of a human energy which you might be able to understand and influence. These researchers are more interested in the neurology of emotions and how medicines can affect emotional states.

School 3: Behavioral effectiveness. Another school of thought argues that behaviors that factor in the use of emotions are more effective than others that ignore emotions. Effectiveness is based on the behaviors that reflect how well we manage our emotional experiences. The focus with this school is on behavior rather than innate capabilities or neurological wiring. Thus, the behaviors that are essential to personal success can be learned. The EQ-i, EQ MAP, and the Emotional Competence Inventory assessments all subscribe to this view (and are covered in detail in Toolbox 5).

We take the view that behavior tells the story. If you want to know how to improve, then you have to know what is possible to develop. The premise on which this book is based is that you can learn and grow in specific, targeted ways. These specific ways are what we refer to as competencies.

Even the smallest of interactions with your partners, friends, or work associates can have an enormous influence on how they perceive you and the relationships they have with you. Consider the following illustration as a reminder of the power of paying attention to the emotional quality of your interactions with others.

Examine Carla's Case

The everyday importance of these competencies is illustrated in the case of "Carla" (who is a real executive and with a different name). Everyone who works with Carla is excited by her leadership, which is based on sound emotional intelligence. Carla demonstrates emotional intelligence at its best, and all those who work with her are grateful for and influenced by her skills in relating to and leading people.

As 49-year-old Carla stepped out of her car, she noticed an employee was having trouble carrying a variety of bags from his car to the building. Carla approached the employee saying, "Good morning! I see that you've got your hands full. I've got a free hand, let me help." The employee was immediately grateful but declared that he would take care of it. Carla responded with, "At least let me take one of these bags to the front desk to save you some trouble." She picked up a bag and started walking with the employee to the front of the building. She casually noted, "Looks like a department party. Something special today?" The employee said, "Some new employees are starting today and the facilities staff wants to welcome them." "Great news," Carla said, "We're growing."

Carla left the bag at the front desk, and while walking to her office she spoke to each person she met along the way. Her comments included: "Hey Joe, I hear we'll get to see your project report later," and "Hey Diane, I haven't seen you for a while. I hope that everything is fine." As she made her way to her office, she interacted with every person, making each interaction brief and direct. Each time, she addressed the person by name, asked a supportive question, and often invited the individual to let her know how things were going.

Total time investment in each interaction is a few seconds. Return on effort: employee loyalty, trust, and a flow of information that every manager desperately wants and needs to make intelligent organizational and personal decisions.

Carla is the vice president of marketing in a $1.2 billion dollar financial services company. She is known throughout the organization as an attentive, energetic leader. Her stated philosophy is that the success of the organization is tied to the engagement of everyone employed. She believes that leaders have the responsibility to treat people with respect so that engagement can be invited, with productive results.

Carla exhibits many of the recognized emotional intelligence (EQ) competencies, or people skills, in her life at work and at home. She understands that relationships are built through micro-interactions and the emotional content they contain. Each interaction has multiple possible outcomes, but, in general, she knows that people experience her as either warm or cold.

Over time and numerous interactions, people experienced as cold are usually thought of as self-absorbed and disinterested in others or their contributions. On the other hand, individuals seen as warm are experienced as inviting and interested in others and their ideas. This second group of individuals more easily gains others' cooperation and is usually granted more latitude when working with others. They are invested in others and recognize that their own success is tied to the work of others in the organization — or at home. Everyone feels like they are in the same boat, pulling together and in the same direction.

To be sure, in the world of work, success is a combination of vision, business smarts, persistence, and the ability to realize the vision through people's efforts. The single most important, and for some the simplest, aspect of success is working with others and getting their commitment — not just their compliance — to work on agreed-upon goals and objectives.

Being emotionally intelligent means making the most of every interaction, no matter how small it may appear to be at that time. It means using each interaction as an opportunity to recognize others, communicating to them that they are significant to you. Asking inviting questions shows you have some confidence in what they think. Offering to help others communicates that you see them as worthwhile.

At the end of the day, Carla sent an email to the manager of facilities: "I heard you had a welcoming party today. I hope it went well and that the new members of the team are excited to be here." Is there any wonder why everyone we interviewed in this company made the opening statement: "Now about Carla, I would walk through hell for that woman. She's the most remarkable business person I've ever worked with."

Effectiveness in reaching your goals is achieved through building productive and satisfying relationships. And just like a brick house, these relationships are built one brick (one interaction) at a time. How strong is your relationship house? How attentive are you to the emotional qualities of your interactions? This is the cement that holds the house together.

What makes Carla so effective?

The short answer is Carla's behavior. How Carla chooses to behave is what makes her so very effective. As you read Carla's story and link her behaviors with those of the 54 competencies identified in Part 2 of this book, you will see that she skillfully uses these competencies. For example, let's look at the opening of this story with reference to the competencies:

As 49-year-old Carla stepped out of her car, she noticed an employee was having trouble carrying a variety of bags from his car to the building. Carla's awareness of another individual's situation reflects (45) Situational Awareness.

Carla approached the employee saying, "Good morning! I see that you've got your hands full. I've got a free hand, let me help." Carla greeted the individual, assessed the situation, and offered to provide assistance which reflects (2) Assertiveness, (15) *Active* Empathy, (25) Interpersonally Skillful, (13) Emotional Problem-Solving, and (47) Social Responsibility.

The employee was immediately grateful but declared that he would take care of it. Carla responded with, "At least let me take one of these bags to the front desk to save you some trouble." She picked up a bag and started walking with the employee to the front of the building. While making an offer and being respectful of the individual's request, Carla took the initiative to provide some assistance to a point that she read as acceptable. This reflects (2) Assertiveness, (3) Authenticity, (19) Independence, (24) Intentionality, (25) Interpersonally Skillful, (33) Personal Power, and (46) Social Intelligence.

She casually noted, "Looks like a department party. Something special today?" The employee said, "Some new employees are starting today and the facilities staff wants to welcome them." "Great news," Carla said, "We're growing." Carla noted the unusual nature of the supplies and showed interest. She also responded to the information with positive encouragement which reflects her use of (21) Initiative, (31) Optimism, (34) Perspective-Taking and (35) Reality Testing along with those already mentioned above.

So within the first few moments of the example, Carla exhibited aspects of at least fifteen EQ competencies which contribute to the quality of this interaction.

As many interviews with those who work with and for Carla revealed, this one story is typical of Carla. The overwhelming feeling among staff is that Carla is the person to work for and to be with because she communicates regard, understands others' needs, and is genuine.

What expert researchers say

Experimental researchers in emotional intelligence would say that Carla uses the central capabilities that make up emotional intelligence:

- Perceiving her own emotions and those of others
- Identifying appropriate responses to constructively channel those emotions
- Managing her responses in ways that both reflect the emotions and leverage energy for constructive action
- Using an array of interpersonal skills to engage constructively with others

There is information in people's emotions.[8] Carla paid attention to her emotions and those of others and the information they contained. For example, the emotional reaction of seeing an individual who may need assistance (many bags out of the car, walking to the building) prompts the thought, "If I were in that situation, I would appreciate some help." This emotionally empathetic (15) response provides the information on which you can then act to provide assistance, whether by taking initiative (21) or not taking initiative or doing the socially responsible (47) thing (or not). Note that the numbers in the parentheses indicate which of the 54 EQ Competencies relate to this behavior.

What behaviors can you learn to improve your EQ?

You start with a basic set of capabilities including natural gifts and many productive behaviors. Throughout your daily life, you encounter opportunities to apply and develop these capabilities. One of the most important capabilities is that of learning from experience. Here is the premise of this book: By using the strategies and tactics described in *People Skills Handbook*, you can develop behavior that is more emotionally intelligent. There may be limits on some behaviors due to your inherent capabilities but, on the whole, you can develop and demonstrate every competency in this book. Learning to be more effective in your relationships enhances your well-being and overall satisfaction and increases your sense of fulfillment and contribution to others and to the world.

A rose by any other name

Carla provides an example of how effective emotional intelligence works. She has integrated some key behaviors into her approach to others that build stronger relationships. Emotional intelligence requires being able to accurately perceive the emotions that people are experiencing in a situation, to select an appropriate response and to implement it in a way that produces a constructive outcome.

Some would describe Carla's behavior as "just good sense." Regrettably, too many people do not seem to demonstrate that quality. In survey after survey, people report that they do not feel heard or recognized — in their organizations and often at home. When relationships falter, the issue, remarkably, is more related to how each person in the relationship felt he or she was treated rather than to issues of money or personal wants.

Summary of key points

- Emotional intelligence — whether defined by innate capabilities, neurological patterns, or behavioral effectiveness — matters. And it is our view that since behavior can be seen and developed, there is no better place to expand your personal effectiveness than to focus on the things you can learn.

- Different frameworks of emotional intelligence are based on different research approaches — traditional capabilities that make up innate intelligence, neurological, and behavioral models yield complementary frames on EQ.

- Though the scientific study of emotional intelligence is 141 years old, beginning with Darwin's initial study, only in recent years has more substantial empirical evidence confirmed the interactions among emotions, aspects of thinking, and demonstrated behavior.

- The case of Carla illustrates how interpersonal behavior can be understood through the lens of emotional intelligence.

- The behaviors that make up emotional intelligence can be learned and used with greater effectiveness.

CHAPTER 3

Learning to Be
Your Emotional Best

What you will learn in this chapter:

- What is learning agility?
- Why does learning agility matter?
- What does learning agility have to do with emotional intelligence?
- How do you learn?
- What is your learning style?
- How can you use learning agility to accelerate your EQ development?
- What does the profile of a learning-agile person look like?
- What are some examples of learning agility tactics?

What predicts success better than intelligence or technical skills? Studies show that learning agility is a better predictor. How can that be? Agile learners learn more, learn better and learn faster. This is not because they're intellectually superior. It's because they know how best to learn, and they're intentional about it. If you want to become more emotionally intelligent, learning agility can get you there — smarter, better and faster.

How well you manage your emotions and interactions with others accounts for more of your success on the job than IQ. According to an article in the Harvard Management Update, "Studies indicate that your emotional intelligence or emotional quotient (EQ) accounts for 15%-45% of your success on the job. Your IQ, by comparison, is said to account for less than 6%."[1] Stephen Covey, author of *The Seven Habits of Highly Effective People*, seems to agree. He points out that, "Research shows convincingly that EQ is more important than IQ in almost every role and many times more important in leadership roles." [2]

EQ or emotional intelligence is what makes you smart about how you get along with others. People who develop the behaviors associated with emotional intelligence enjoy more satisfying relationships. They are better able to bring out the best in others, and they more easily gain others' commitment.

While employing learning agility tactics will accelerate your development of emotional intelligence, it is important to remember a common barrier to learning. As a creature of habit, you tend to repeat what has worked for you in the past. But what worked before is not always the best choice. Learning agility is a willingness and intent to learn from the effort, sometimes going against the grain. That is what gets you around that barrier. Learning agility is a skill set that you can develop, teach to others and use to build your emotional intelligence.

Emotional intelligence is made up of many behaviors. Developing or changing behavior can be difficult. But if you look at those who have grown and changed over time you will notice that they share a common practice — they are active learners. This quality of being an active learner — learning agility — is the bridge that will get you from where you are to where you want to be.

Learning is a gradual process. Developing emotional intelligence is too. For many people, however, learning takes longer and is made more difficult than necessary. Those who are good at it — the learning agile — have figured out how to learn more, learn more effectively and in less time. They are better able to size up and respond effectively to first-time situations and changing conditions. How do they do it?

1. They use a wide variety of learning strategies
2. They think about when to use which ones
3. They intentionally reflect on and learn from their experiences
4. They apply what they learn

Developing learning agility offers benefits that reach well beyond emotional intelligence. In technical studies, for example, one half of what a student learns in her first year of college is outdated by her third year.[3] Learning agility is quickly becoming one of the most critical skills in the 21st century. It is the great multiplier. Learning agility can make you better at learning just about anything. People and organizations that don't sharpen their approach to learning put their futures at risk.

What is learning agility?

Learning agility is how smart you are about *how* you learn, not how *smart* you are. It is not about academic performance, book knowledge, cognitive intelligence or IQ. It is about using a variety of tactics to learn from your experiences and putting those lessons to work for you. Learning agility is being open to doing something different based on what you're learning. That requires flexibility. Being flexible doesn't come easily for everyone. It involves changing behavior and possibly doing something outside your comfort zone. Some people operate on automatic pilot. Some don't want to make the extra effort to think about doing something different. And still others want to avoid the anxiety that comes from the unknown and unfamiliar. (If this sounds like you, then you might want to pick up a copy of *Who Moved My Cheese*, a quick and fun read, maybe even life-changing). 4

In the movie Miss Congeniality, actress Sandra Bullock plays an FBI agent on the trail of a murderer who turns out to be connected with a beauty pageant. To get inside the pageant, Bullock goes undercover as a beauty contestant. Strikingly beautiful, she looks the part, but, like most other FBI agents, she is suspicious and confrontational. Beauty contestants, on the other hand, typically are charming and gracious as they seek favor among pageant officials. Michael Caine is hired to coach Bullock on the "softer" qualities necessary to be taken seriously as an aspiring beauty queen. Bullock is transformed, gradually (and humorously), before your eyes, demonstrating what learning agility looks like, especially the flexibility on which it depends.[5]

The transformation Bullock undergoes occurs because she is open to new information, willing to try new behaviors and learn from them while encountering new and changing situations. She is also willing to go against the grain of her FBI agent training and what comes naturally to her given her personality. Learning-agile people are simply among the most effective at *whatever* they do. You can be too.

Remember, learning agility is learnable. Unlike IQ, or cognitive intelligence, which can *not* be appreciably improved, learning agility, like EQ, *can be*. That is what this chapter is about. Are you open to learning? Are you willing to be flexible? *"There are no mistakes, save one: the failure to learn from a mistake."* If you agree with Robert Fripp, then this chapter is for you.

Agile, lazy or blocked learner — which are you?

It is estimated that between 20 and 30 percent of the population of the United States are learning agile. How about the rest? What kind of learners are they? About 40 to 50 percent are random or lazy learners — they actively learn from their experiences, but only occasionally, often to avoid the pain of repeating some mistake. Their learning experience is uneven, and it fails to capitalize on compounding growth over time. The remaining 20 to 30 percent are known as "blocked learners." They are an entirely different group altogether. Ask any one of them and they will tell you, "I already know what I need to know," in effect saying, "there's nothing new for me to learn." These are often very bright people, who have achieved some rank or wealth. But when confronted with a development need or a blind spot, they can become defensive, sometimes offensive. And they rarely budge from this position unless a highly skilled external coach intervenes.

Why does learning agility matter?

Learning agility makes you a better learner, and it's learnable. You can use it to learn many things. Becoming more learning agile will prompt you to be more reflective, intentional and flexible — the very behaviors that contribute to effectiveness generally, and emotional intelligence specifically.

What about technical skills? Remember, central to learning agility is the ability, the willingness and the intent to learn from your experiences. Whether you are an engineer, a medical technician or a web designer, being learning agile helps you keep your skills current. Practice learning-agile behaviors and you will become more comfortable with change and experimentation. Learning agility involves thinking more critically about your experiences and your best next steps. Rather than keeping your head down absorbed in the task, a learning-agile mindset encourages you to be alert to changing circumstances, to figure out how best to address them and to be flexible enough to adapt.

Remember, agile learners learn more, better and faster, not because they're intellectually superior, but because they know *how best* to learn, and they're *intentional* about it. They select experiences that challenge them to learn, grow and change. So can you. They pay attention to the new information those experiences offer. So can you. They demonstrate a better ability to *adapt* to shifting demands than others. So can you. They are willing to push the envelope of their comfort zones by going against the grain. So can you.

According to the Bureau of Labor Statistics, the average worker changes jobs every four years. How is learning agility important to job-seekers and potential employers alike? If learning agility predicts success, it should be what every employer looks for and what every employee needs to be. This is also true for emotional intelligence. Savvy executives know that selecting learning-agile and emotionally intelligent candidates will lead to building successful teams. Two often repeated rules of thumb for hiring are:

1. Hire people you like (you can teach them the rest)
2. If you can select for only one thing, make it learning agility.

What does this mean for you? Whether you are job hunting or want to be the top contender for a promotion, learning agility will enable you to demonstrate how quickly you will become productive in the new position. If you are job hunting, you will have the advantage of being able to handle the interview questions with ease. Being intentional about your learning will help you to respond naturally, and comfortably, with the kind of answers interviewers are looking for.

What does learning agility have to do with EQ?

Learning agility and emotional intelligence have much in common. Both rely on being aware, being open to new information, understanding what matters in that information, and being flexible enough to adapt behavior based on what was just learned. Learning agility strengthens many skills and capabilities (the great multiplier), but especially emotional intelligence. Since emotional intelligence depends on many of the same behaviors and practices that go into building learning agility, if you build learning agility you build emotional intelligence as well. And this is in addition to how learning agility can help you as you develop specific competencies that make up emotional intelligence. Conversely, building emotional intelligence contributes to the component skills that drive learning agility. But what is most important is that both learning agility and emotional intelligence are learnable. So, as you become more learning agile, there's a really good chance that you also will become more emotionally intelligent.

What is your learning style?

There are different approaches to, or styles of, learning. And within each style there are multiple tactics. Think about some recent experiences when you learned something new or worked to improve a particular skill. Maybe you learned a new golf swing, how to use a new technology or piece of electronic equipment. Or perhaps you brushed up on some academic material, developed patience or got better organized. How did you do it?

> *There are multiple ways to learn: taking action, reflecting, managing emotions and involving others.*

A number of models of learning have been proposed by researchers, including David Kolb, Ph.D.[6]; Kerry Bunker, Ph.D.; the Center for Creative Leadership[7]; and Lominger, Inc., a Korn-Ferry Company.[8] Each model presents an array of learning styles, and within each style a variety of tactics.

For this discussion we will focus on four common learning styles.

- *Action-oriented* tactics emphasize jumping in and seeing what happens, including trial and error, teaching others and going against the grain.

- *Thinking-oriented* tactics emphasize reflection, analysis and envisioning. These include reflecting on past experiences, comparing current with historical events and mentally rehearsing.

- *Feeling-oriented* tactics to manage emotions when they interfere with learning rely on your being emotionally self-aware. Examples include asking yourself what you're feeling, challenging assumptions underlying counterproductive emotions and identifying factors that influence how open you are to new experiences.

■ *People* tactics involve seeking the advice of others when facing new situations. Some *people* tactics include consulting with
experts, brainstorming with others and attending courses.

It is important to understand what your learning preferences are so you can
build on them. Do you employ primarily one style or several? Just a few
tactics, or many? Experiences and challenges vary, and so do the best ways to
deal with and learn from them. People armed with the most learning choices
are more likely to have the ones that are best suited to the challenges at hand.
Said another way, learning-agile people typically employ the broadest array of
learning tactics. And they are best at figuring out which tactic best matches
the experience. Tip: Stretch beyond what is familiar and comfortable for you
so you can expand your toolbox of learning tactics.

Using learning agility

Anyone can become a better learner. Your biggest obstacle will be reluctance
to try something new or to go against the grain. It is human nature to keep
doing what you already know how to do and what you do well. It is logical
to repeat what has worked in the past. You have good reason to believe that
it will work again. It is familiar. It seems predictable. But what if the circumstances are slightly different? Will you stop long enough to consider whether
there is a better approach? Doing something new or different can take longer,
is often uncomfortable and might risk failure. It may threaten feelings of
competence and confidence. But being open to trying something new is critical to becoming more learning agile and more successful. The best learners
try out and adopt different learning strategies, enough so they can choose
which ones are likely to work best. And they are flexible enough to choose
something different if what they're doing isn't working.

To build learning agility, let's identify some of the necessary behaviors. They
include self-awareness, which comes from seeking feedback and being open
to it, taking on challenging experiences and learning from them, and finding
ways to quickly apply those lessons. These behaviors interact with and enhance each other. Each is a step in the process of learning to be more learning
agile. Each is a step in the process of learning to be more emotionally intelligent. Part 2, the heart of this book, contains 54 competencies that contribute
to emotional intelligence. Use these steps to develop them.

Step 1: Increase self-awareness. Self-awareness — being objectively alert about
yourself and the impact you have on others — is fundamental to both emotional intelligence and learning agility. It makes sense if you think about it.
Knowledge of your strengths and weaknesses, and how others react to you,
allows better choices. When it comes to learning agility, knowing your preferences for learning will help diversify your options. Doing a formal assessment
is one approach. See footnotes 6, 7 and 8 for some organizations offering

formal assessment. If you have access to human resources professionals, they may have or could recommend a learning assessment. There are also a variety of web sites offering information and assessments about learning styles and learning tactics. Research them and choose two or three that you don't typically use but that look interesting. Practice using them. In the process, you will be exercising your "learning muscle" and developing your learning agility.

You also can do an informal self-assessment. As suggested earlier, think about a recent time when you successfully learned something new or improved a skill. How did you do it? Describe what you did that worked, the sequence of steps, and what might work even better next time. Think about a time when you successfully handled one or more challenges that were first-time situations for you. How did you evaluate what was needed? What approaches did you attempt? What happened? What did you learn? How did you later use what you learned? Use these same questions to enhance your learning as you put into practice the Quick Action Tips from Part 2.

Step 2: Seek feedback. Ongoing feedback is critical to both emotional intelligence and learning agility. Conduct an informal survey among people who work and live around you. Do others see you as open to learning — as someone who invites input from others, learns from mistakes and demonstrates flexibility? Write out a description of an agile learner that includes some of the associated behaviors and perhaps some examples. Distribute the description and ask others to compare your behavior with this description. Ask for suggestions that might improve your learning agility.

Step 3: Take on challenging experiences. Learning-agile people deliver results in "first-time" situations, that is, situations that are new to them. By stepping up to a first-time situation, you accept the risk that comes with it — dealing with the unfamiliar and the potential for failure. But it is exactly this kind of experience that offers the greatest learning and development opportunity. Be on the lookout for first-time experiences or potential assignments that involve capabilities you need to develop. Stretch yourself to take on one such assignment, and be intentional about learning from your experience with it.

Apply this approach to developing your emotional intelligence too. Identify which EQ competency from Part 2 of this book that you want to work on. What assignment, experience or volunteer position would challenge you to get better at it? For example, if you want to work on your influencing skills — (20) Influencing Others — you might volunteer for a fundraising role or take the lead in persuading the senior management team to make a change in the product line. The assignment's development value rides on how difficult or important the assignment is and how much the assignment depends on the competency you're working on.

Stretch yourself to take on such an assignment, and set up ways to maximize your learning from it. Experiment with different learning tactics (see a sampling of learning tactics later in this chapter). Choose learning tactics that will best help you size up this particular challenge and what it will take to resolve it. (Some examples of learning tactics you might consider are: recruit a learning partner, interview a role model or research influencing strategies.) Plan how you will evaluate your results and apply what you learn going forward.

Do you have a difficult interpersonal situation that you should deal with, but are avoiding? Many people do! This might be a great opportunity to work on your emotional intelligence. Which EQ competency would be most helpful in this situation? For example, (2) Assertiveness, (7) *Effective* Confrontation,(15) *Active* Empathy, (42) Self-Confidence. Consider approaching this situation instead of avoiding it, and practicing some new behaviors. This is your opportunity to learn and grow.

Step 4: Learn from experience and apply the lessons. This is the most often overlooked step, but it may be the most important step. Take time to reflect on your experience to identify what you've learned. Some questions you might ask are: How did you initially assess the problem or challenge? How did you figure out what to do and whether to involve others? What was your plan? How did you evaluate your progress as you went along? How did you feel, and how did you manage your emotions? Did you make adjustments or bring others in? Most important, if you had a do-over, what would you do differently? When is the next opportunity to try that out? Make sure you build in the time necessary to reflect and extract the lessons as you go. Apply those lessons as quickly as you can, and test your assumptions. This is intentional learning. This is learning agility. Be sure to work learning agility into your EQ Action Plan (available in Chapter 4) when you choose which EQ competencies from Part 2 you want to work on.

Experiences that make you stretch offer the best learning opportunities. As you set goals to develop emotionally intelligent behaviors, remember to reflect on the experiences as you have them. What are you learning? How can you apply what you've learned, sooner rather than later? Consider finding a learning partner, someone to discuss your experiences with, someone who will support and challenge you, someone who asks great questions that trigger insight. Above all, be intentional. As you consider which of the 54 EQ Competencies in Part 2 you want to develop, think about how to build your learning agility, and use it to help you build your emotional intelligence.

Profile of a learning-agile person

Learning agile people value change. Instead of settling on the first option considered or focusing on what is obvious, they push — themselves and others — to look beyond the obvious for different and better ideas. They manage negative feelings and take setbacks in stride, which allows them to experiment and take risks more readily. They zero in on what is important, then step back to see how it connects to the bigger picture or other observations. They use multiple strategies to read situations and use that information to adapt what they're doing to get their desired results.

What does this look like when it all comes together? Consider the following illustration: Jo Ellen comes from a technology and banking background. Today she serves as the executive director of a nonprofit community leadership organization. She interacts with nonprofit, government and corporate leaders, donors, volunteers, and a class of leader-participants drawn from a wide swath of the community. She has many bosses, multiple customer groups and just two part-time direct reports. Although her board is a working board, it is made up of senior level community and corporate leaders who juggle multiple competing demands. This is no different, really, than what most nonprofit executive directors contend with.

In a recent board meeting, members were struggling with a pivotal decision. Before them was an opportunity that would both improve the organization's sustainability and broaden its community leadership role. However, it required significant funding from reserves, some of which could not be itemized until the decision to move forward was made. As one might imagine, the decision to spend money "blindly" was very uncomfortable for some. While she probably wanted to say more, Jo Ellen limited her input to answering questions. By a very slim margin, the motion to spend the money passed. What happened next was a lesson in learning agility. Just as the meeting was about to wrap up, Jo Ellen asked a simple, but crucial, question: What needed to happen for the dissenting board members to support the decision?

Why was asking this question crucial? The question gave those who objected an opportunity to express their feelings, and in the direction of *supporting* the decision. It also produced information that could be acted on, and by doing so, broaden the commitment to the decision.

By observing people over time, Jo Ellen learned when and how to involve board members to leverage their talents and gain their commitment. She knows when and how to push the board beyond the status quo to embrace change and growth. By reading what was behind the opposition, she used the question "What would it take?" to create flexibility in people's positions. She was willing to go off script and risk revisiting the discussion and, potentially, the favorable decision. Jo Ellen knows when to probe and when to stand back, when to lead and when to let others take the lead and when to be practical and when to be strategic. Jo Ellen reads situations well. She possesses an array of capabilities to approach them. And she uses what she has learned from previous experiences to flexibly deploy that skill set. Jo Ellen is learning agile.

Can you see why and how learning agility can fast forward your success? Learning-agile people learn, grow, and change across time. Consequently, they develop new skills, not just enhance what they already know. The next section offers a variety of action ideas to help you become more learning agile. Consider including some of these strategies in your development plan (available in Chapter 4) when you choose which EQ competencies in Part 2 you most want to develop.

Where does learning agility fit in?

Continuous learning, like emotional intelligence, is rapidly becoming the price of admission to meet the challenges of the 21st century. The best way to develop both is simply to *plan* to develop both. Most people are short on time and are too busy to fit one more thing into their schedules. Perhaps the only way to ensure growth is to plan for it. Create a development plan that, where possible, incorporates and leverages what you're already doing. Think about which lessons emerge from which assignments (on and off the job). Align your assignments (whether personal or work-related) with your goals. Chapter 4 will help you custom design a plan that will accelerate your progress in reaching your development goals.

There has been considerable research into the learning tactics of those who learn best what they need to learn to be effective. In fact, a number of studies that focused on which skills differentiated high potential executives who were successful from those who derailed actually turned up valuable information about how the most successful actually *learned* those skills. So, not only did they discover that emotional intelligence differentiates successful executives from those who derailed, their learning strategies also were discovered.

Listed below is a sampling of the learning tactics used by these successful executives. Remember, having many and varied learning tactics is what will make you learning agile. As with any toolbox, you want more than just a wrench and a screwdriver. You need several different types of wrenches and screwdrivers to fit the various situations you might encounter.

Expand your choices by selecting tactics that are new to you. Practice them until you become comfortable using them. When you encounter a specific problem or challenge, you will find that you are better able to select one that best suits it, especially important when it is a first-time situation.

As you adopt new learning tactics, make sure you weave them into your plan for developing emotional intelligence.

Learning agility tactics: a sampling

Taking action tactics

- Experiment with different roles
- Experiment with new approaches, observe impact
- Take specific learnings and identify specific situations in which you can apply them
- Make a plan, adjust as needed

- Learn and practice something new
- Observe others' reactions and make small changes
- Use trial and error, test new behaviors
- Teach someone else how to do something
- Learn from mistakes and failures, decide where and when you can apply what you learned

Reflecting/exploring tactics

- Reflect on your experiences, ask yourself lots of questions, identify lessons learned
- Keep a learning journal
- Encourage curiosity (see EQ competency (54) Understanding Others)
- Explore beyond the obvious, what seems complex or ambiguous
- Find similarities and contrasts, patterns and historical parallels
- Reframe, imagine different circumstances and outcomes
- Develop rules of thumb
- Think through problems and potential solutions from different angles or perspectives of others
- Explore hunches, imagine future possibilities, define ideal
- Mentally rehearse how you might approach a problem situation
- Speculate about what the ideal person would do in a given situation

Managing emotions tactics

- Notice your own feelings, their triggers and impact; consider strategies to manage them
- Observe self in action; reflect on feelings and attitudes
- Set aside a time to consider your feelings
- Anticipate stressors and plan strategies to diffuse them
- Look for value emerging from conflict to decrease avoidance
- Pay attention to which feelings energize you
- Notice what motivates you
- Keep a journal; make connections between current and earlier experiences
- Go against the grain, take a risk, and find ways to develop increased comfort doing so

Involving others tactics

- Get feedback and input
- Debrief successes and failures
- Recruit a learning partner
- Find ways to support others with their challenges
- Identify role models and subject matter experts; interview them for strategies and emulate their behaviors
- Engage with others with different perspectives
- Build an ad hoc advisory group
- Interview others who have faced similar challenges

Summary of key points

- Emotional intelligence (EQ) creates a more rewarding interpersonal life and more successful work life. With a little effort and practice you can get better at it and make it work for you.

- The bridge from where you are to becoming more emotionally intelligent is learning agility.

- Learning agility is using a variety of practices to size up and deal effectively with first-time situations, extracting the important lessons from your experiences and putting those lessons to work for you.

- Agile learners learn faster and learn more than most others. They do so not because they're intellectually superior, but because they know how best to learn, and they're intentional about it. Learning agility and EQ have many behaviors in common. As you become more learning agile you also become more emotionally intelligent.

- There are multiple ways to learn: taking action, reflecting, managing emotions, and involving others. The secret to learning agility is being skillful with multiple styles and varied tactics within each style.

- The critical components of learning agility are: self-awareness, seeking and being open to feedback, choosing and learning from challenging experiences and applying what was learned.

- Both learning agility and EQ are learnable. Put a development plan together in the next chapter and you are on your way to becoming better at both.

CHAPTER 4

Create an EQ Action Plan That Works for You

What you will learn in this chapter:

- Why set goals?
- How can you begin your action plan?
- Should you work on your weaknesses or further develop your strengths?
- What is a learning goal?
- How is a learning goal different from an outcome or performance goal?
- What is "SMART" and how can it help you write a better goal?
- You've set a learning goal, now what can help you achieve it?

The power of setting goals

Have you ever wondered whether goal-setting is worth the effort? Then consider:

- Research studies over the last 35 years involving more than 40,000 participants and over 100 different tasks show that specific, challenging and self-defined goals increase performance and do so more than easy goals or goals based on "try your hardest". [1]

- Research suggests that individuals can achieve an improvement in work performance by as much as 20 to 25 percent simply by using goal setting. [2]

You, too, can harness the power of setting goals.

Starting your plan

Changing any behavior requires effort and focused attention. Ask a friend who joined a gym and doesn't use it or a co-worker who has trouble getting work completed on time. Old habits can be strong habits. So before you set a learning goal for yourself, consider what motivates you to want to improve your emotional intelligence (EQ) skills in some way. Why do you want to put energy into development?

In our experience there are three main reasons why you might have picked up this book:

1. You know what you want to change and are looking for ideas
2. You have a key challenge that demands new skills
3. You have received feedback from others that suggests developing new skills or behaviors might make you more effective

Which of these three approaches sounds like you?

Approach 1: You know what you want to change

You probably knew what you wanted to work on when you picked up this book. You are perceptive enough to be aware of one or more issues in your life that you want to manage more effectively. Below are some of the many statements we have heard from coaching clients that prompted us to write this book about improving emotional intelligence. If you have had any of these or similar thoughts, then you are ready to take action:

- I need to better influence my teenage son without alienating him
- I wish I had more confidence than I do
- My spouse says I never listen to her (him); I think I do
- Things are constantly changing at work, and I feel overwhelmed
- There are things I want to try, but I am afraid I will fail
- I know I need more patience; how do I get some?
- I want a closer relationship with my kids
- I want to better motivate my team members at work
- I got feedback at work that suggests I need to improve my interpersonal skills

Do any of these statements sound familiar? These are just a few of the issues that have led others like you to investigate emotional intelligence. Author David Campbell once expressed a great deal of wisdom in the name of his book: *If You Don't Know Where You're Going, You'll Probably End Up Somewhere Else.*[3] You do know where you want to go.

What change do you most want to see in yourself over the next six months? Below, write it in the form of a positive action statement, such as "I want to be more comfortable meeting new people."

_____

_____

_____

As you look at what you most want to change in your life, which of the emotional intelligence competencies might be stepping stones to get you there? Look at the list of competencies and their definitions on page 48 and list below the ones that seem most relevant. Another source of ideas is the list of typical challenges and related competencies in Toolbox 3: Personal and Work Challenges.

1. _____

2. _____

3. _____

4. _____

5. _____

6. _____

Approach 2: You have a key challenge that demands new skills

A second possible starting point is to consider the key responsibilities and challenges that you are facing in your profession or personal life that are crucial to your success or happiness. For example, Jim is an accountant for a small firm, and recently he decided that he wants to start his own business offering accounting services to other small business owners. He knows that, to be successful, he needs to find ways to meet potential clients and influence them to consider him for their accounting needs.

Or consider Susan, who just volunteered to run for president of the Parents Association of her son's school and was elected. She knows that she needs to be able to engage other parents to achieve the goals of the Parents Association and also manage conflict when inevitable differences of opinion arise among the parents. You also may have taken on new responsibilities or challenges that require you to stretch. You may need some ideas to help you be successful.

List one or two responsibilities or challenges that you currently or soon will face:

_____

_____

_____

Which emotional intelligence competencies seem most relevant to those challenges or responsibilities? Use the list of emotional intelligence competencies and their definitions on page 48 to help you make these choices. Below list those that you want to read for ideas.

1. _____

2. _____

3. _____

4. _____

5. _____

6. _____

Approach 3: You have received feedback that you need to address

A third way to use this book for your own development is to start with feedback that you have received from family, friends, colleagues, a multi-rater assessment at work, or performance evaluations.

List up to three strengths that others have used to describe you and up to three developmental challenges that others have pointed out.

Strengths

1. _____

2. _____

3. _____

Developmental challenges

1. _____

2. _____

3. _____

Do you want to start with maximizing your strengths or improving your areas of challenge? Research suggests that developing and maximizing your strengths may make the most difference to your career or personal success. For over 30 years, the Gallup Organization has researched how to best develop a person's potential and has found that "each person's greatest room for growth is in areas of his or her greatest strength." [4] If you choose to upgrade talents that are valued by your organization and needed for your position from average to strong or even outstanding, then you are likely to find further visibility and opportunities. With this in mind, choose one to three areas in which you already are skilled that you want to develop into top strengths. Then use those for goal setting.

Fred has always been the "go to" person on his team when team members needed to get cooperation from other parts of the organization. Fred seemed to know the right person to approach, and he had a style that seemed to make others want to help him. Fred decided to build on this talent by further developing his influence skills and his collaboration skills, which may lead to more opportunities in his organization. So Fred may want to look at the competencies of (4) Collaboration and (20) Influencing Others. He may also want to look at the Toolboxes to see if there are other related competencies with action tips that could help him develop these skills.

It also is crucial to minimize any potential barriers to success by bringing weaknesses that may affect your performance at least up to average levels. So if a lower-rated competency could block your career or jeopardize your job situation, then you may want to include that in your goal setting. Consider the situation of Joan, who works at a customer call center for a major technology firm. She has always received great performance reviews until this year, when she was promoted to the head of second shift. During her latest performance review, Joan was told that she is seen as unfair by some of her associates and doesn't seem to take them seriously. Joan wants to find a way to address these issues before her ratings become a problem. Joan decided to work on the emotional intelligence competencies of (15) *Active* Empathy, (25) Interpersonally Skillful, and (53) Trustworthy in order to improve her relationships with her direct reports on second shift. When she looked at Toolbox 3, Personal and Work Challenges, she thought "Teamwork is lagging and team members seem unmotivated" also fit, so she read the competencies recommended there.

Look at the preceding list and star the *strengths* or *challenges* that are important for your success. List below the emotional intelligence competencies that seem most related to those *strengths* or *challenges*. Use the list of competencies and their definitions on page 48 to help you make these choices.

1. _____
2. _____
3. _____
4. _____
5. _____
6. _____

Use learning goals

Now that you have identified a direction for your goal setting and some related emotional intelligence competencies, you need to consider how to write your learning goal(s) to ensure success. Most of our experience is with outcome goals rather than learning goals.

Outcome goals are performance goals. They encourage you to reach a higher level of performance or effectiveness by using your present skills. Stretch outcome goals are a common strategy to focus and energize action. Examples include:

- I want to spend twice as much time with my colleagues to improve those relationships
- I will raise $1000 for the Humane Society by Christmas
- I will spend quality time with each of my children once a week

Learning goals

Learning goals are important for you at this point since you are most likely to either be developing new behaviors and perspectives or else practicing ones that are difficult for you to use on a consistent basis. To create a plan for learning and practicing these new behaviors, you first may need to problem solve and use trial and error to identify the most effective ways for you to learn. Learning goals might begin with issues like these:

- I want to listen more effectively to my spouse.
- How can I delegate so that my direct reports take ownership for the work?
- How can I influence others when I don't have direct authority over them?

We all learn differently, so what works for you may not be as helpful for me. An example of a learning goal might be "identify five strategies for improving my listening skills and practice them over the next two months with my spouse and children," or "learn at least three ways I might influence without authority and try them out with Jim and Joyce in our cross-functional project meetings this month." A learning goal allows for discovery while focusing you on specific skills that can increase your effectiveness in areas that matter to you. Revisit Chapter 3 for additional ideas about learning strategies and tactics.

Be SMART in setting your goals

SMART is an acronym that provides a means of remembering five characteristics of a well-defined goal that will greatly increase your chances of being successful.

S — specific
M — measurable
A — achievable
R — relevant
T — time-limited

S — specific

The first step to remember as you write your goal is to be specific. Research shows that people who have specific goals that are within their reach are more motivated to achieve those goals than those who have no goals, vague goals, or overly ambitious goals. A specific goal provides both a challenge and also a way to know how well you are doing. Reaching a specific goal leads to a feeling of satisfaction. A goal like "I will listen better" is admirable, but not specific. "Identify five ways to improve my listening skills and practice the three ways that seem to work best for me at least once a week for a month" is specific. You can make that goal even more focused after you research and identify the ways to improve your listening that offer you the most potential. You can then write your goal to include specific listening skills, with whom you will practice these listening skills and in which situations you will practice. "I will use the skills of asking open-ended questions and confirming what I hear at least twice each during staff meetings on Mondays with my direct reports." "For the next month I will ask my son an open-ended question about school (how was school today, what was your favorite part of school today, etc.) as we drive home and not interrupt as he responds."

M — measurable

Research overwhelmingly shows that when progress toward goals is measured, goals are more likely to be completed. Elementary school teachers who put gold stars on a poster for completed arithmetic assignments understand this principle. If you start with specific goals, this step is much easier. A measuring technique can be as simple as noting on your calendar at the end of the day if you did what you planned to do. It is important to measure often to keep you honest. Because you have good intentions, you may think you are practicing the behaviors and attitudes associated with the competency you want to develop more than you are. Find an easy way to measure or keep track of your progress either online, in your daily calendar, or some other easily accessible place to make notes.

A — achievable

For you to be successful, your goal must be one that you both believe is doable and for which you can access the resources you need. Learning goals especially allow you to take on challenges that seem daunting at first, but problem solving and planning can enable you to succeed. Years ago this author wanted to work on her Ph.D. but put off making that commitment because she felt overwhelmed and inadequate at the thought of writing a dissertation. Only a comment by a close friend that "You don't need to know how to do a dissertation before you start — it is a learning process," enabled her to proceed. She did know that she could learn and move ahead one step at a time.

R — relevant

A fourth characteristic of a good goal is that it is important to you, that it matters to you. If the goal doesn't have real value for you, then many other demands and commitments in your life will take priority. Take the time now to choose a goal that matters to you. As a coaching client wisely told me, "Timing in my life is now right for me to set goals with myself in mind. Up until now, my focus has been on my children and establishing my career. Now it is my turn." This person then went on to set specific and meaningful goals for next steps in her life based on what she personally enjoys and values.

T — time-limited

Finally, you need to establish a time frame for completing your goal. Without a deadline or time frame, it is easy to put off action steps toward your goal or even to forget your goal altogether in the midst of other pressures or pleasures in your life. Set a specific time and deadline to take action. "By Saturday I will read the competencies that seem most related to my goal of handling the stress in my life better and list three actions I will take to help myself improve."

Use the EQ Action Plan at the end of this chapter to write your goals. It will prompt you to use the information found in each competency section relevant to your goal to help you formulate some of your action steps. Make additional copies of the EQ Action Plan form in Toolbox 8 as you need them.

Strategies for reaching your goals

Write a SMART goal and put yourself on the road toward success. Use the following strategies to help you to stay motivated and productive on your learning journey. Now is also a good time to review Chapter 3 for additional in-depth insights about how to increase your learning agility.

I. Find role models, books and articles, and training opportunities. Research suggests that one important way to jump-start your learning is by observing someone who is good at the skills you want to learn. Select someone you know, then watch how they handle situations that are difficult for you. What exactly do they do, don't do, or do differently from your tendencies? Tim decided to work on his EQ competency (27) Listening Generously, especially in meetings with his direct reports, so he identified a colleague, Louise, who seemed good at listening. He asked to observe her in a team meeting. When Tim watched how Louise ran the team meeting, he noticed how she engaged everyone at some time during the session by asking them to share their thoughts. She also used open-ended questions to focus discussion on key issues while indicating she was interested in ideas from the team. At the end of the meeting she summarized decisions made. Tim was excited because he decided he could practice these three specific skills when he next met with his direct reports. Other ways to get started building your emotional intelligence competencies include reading books about the skill area important to you or finding a course or training opportunity that fits your purpose.

2. Set short-term goals. Using short-term or sub-goals is an effective strategy to keep you motivated. Not only do short-term goals build in time for you to get progress checks to be sure you are moving in the right direction, but they also give you a means of feeling successful as you take small steps in the right direction.

3. Ask for feedback. Asking for and receiving feedback about progress toward your goal dovetails nicely with setting short-term goals. Feedback is crucial to your success in reaching your goals because it enables you to change strategies and modify your behavior if needed. Getting feedback on short-term goals means that you don't waste time doing the wrong thing. The power of feedback might be understood with an example. Imagine you are learning how to play tennis and need to improve your serve, but there is a curtain at the center court line so you can't see anything on the far court. Whenever you hit a serve, you have no idea whether the ball went over the net or even if it remained within the boundaries. How long would you practice with no feedback? Probably not long. We also need to know the effects of the behaviors we practice that are meant to improve our emotional intelligence related to our goal. Feedback helps us know if we are improving our skills and gives us the motivation and energy to keep practicing. Take the time to identify a few people whom you trust to ask for specific feedback. Fill them in on your goal and identify a situation that they might observe to use for giving you feedback. Be sure to thank them. They are important to your success.

4. Use practice sessions. A visitor to New York City was walking along the streets of Manhattan when he saw a man rushing along with a violin under his arm. Late for a concert, he stopped the man to ask how to get to Carnegie Hall. The musician paused briefly to tell him, "Practice, practice, practice."

Many of us are involved in busy lives full of commitments to others such as meeting production or sales goals at work, needing to be at school by 2:15 to pick up a son or daughter, planning meals and buying groceries, or engaging a team to solve a critical problem by the end of the day. It can be difficult to both remember a goal you have set and to make time for this personal and professional development. Try using one or two "practice sessions" which you will select and put on your calendar Monday morning. These are specific times when you are still involved in your everyday commitments, but you also use those times to focus on practicing the behaviors that will help you reach your goal.

For example, you may want to improve your patience by waiting for others to respond when you ask a question instead of quickly answering for them or completing their thoughts. To practice, you may choose a business meeting on Tuesday afternoon and dinner with your family on Thursday evening as practice sessions. Everything else goes on as usual at those times, but your particular goal is to practice asking at least three open-ended questions and then pausing for an answer and using silence to allow space for others to respond. The only way to increase your comfort with new behavior, more emotionally intelligent behavior, is to make time to practice those behaviors you choose that will help you reach your goals.

5. Identify your cheering section. Another key to reaching your goals and developing new skills is to identify those people you care about and respect at home or at work that you can ask for support — people with whom you can share your commitment and goals while knowing that they want you to do well. These are people with whom you can celebrate successes and ask for ideas when you feel stuck. These are people who can help hold you accountable for practicing the changes you want to make. We all need friends, family, and colleagues to help, so identify those people you want to enlist in your cheering section. Keep them in the loop with regular updates about your progress. Feeling responsible to them can help keep you committed when your own motivation is sagging.

6. Choose meaningful and challenging experiences. As you read in Chapter 3, learning from experience is your most powerful teacher, even responsible for up to 70 percent of successful development. So as you set your own goals, use or adapt suggestions made in the *Learn from Experience* section of the competencies. Be sure to choose longer-term commitments that both fit with your lifestyle and that will challenge you in meaningful ways. John wanted to improve his ability to collaborate with others, so he decided to volunteer with Habitat for Humanity once a month for a year. By working with a group of other volunteers on a project that mattered to him, he was able to practice asking for help, making suggestions, and not taking offense if no one agreed with him. He found that this experience allowed him a safe environment to practice his skills in collaborating with others and that it translated into an increased ability to work well with others on the job and better give-and-take with his family members.

Write Your EQ Action Plan

Now is the time to write your emotional intelligence learning goal. A clear goal will enable you to make the behavior changes you want for added success in your personal life and career. Start with what behavior changes you want to make, what challenges you are now facing, or what feedback you want to address that is related to improving your emotional intelligence. Use the 54

EQ Competencies in Part 2 as a resource for ideas to help you design your personal EQ Action Plan. You will find a reproducible copy of the EQ Action Plan in Toolbox 8.

I. State your goal

1. What specific behaviors are you doing, not doing, or overdoing that you wish to change?

_____

_____

_____

2. What is the EQ goal or outcome you wish to achieve?

_____

_____

_____

3. How will achieving this goal benefit you?

_____

_____

_____

II. Make it happen: Action steps

4. List any of the 54 EQ Competencies that might be related to your goal.

_____

_____

_____

5. Read the competencies you listed above. Use the *Quick Action Tips* and *Learn from Experience* sections to identify action steps that are most relevant and useful for achieving your goal. Later, star (*) the ones that work best for you and continue to use those.

Action step 1. _____

_____Timeframe/target date: _____

Action step 2. _____

_____Timeframe/target date: _____

Action step 3. _____

_____ Timeframe/target date: _____

Action step 4. _____

_____ Timeframe/target date: _____

6. Who might be a role model you can learn from?

_____

7. List at least three resources (books, courses, web sites, etc.) that you will investigate to better understand the skills needed to reach your goal. Later, star (*) the most helpful.

_____ Target date:_____

_____ Target date:_____

_____ Target date:_____

_____ Target date:_____

8. How will you get ongoing feedback about your progress?

_____

_____

_____

9. Who will you ask to be a learning partner to hold you accountable and to support you as you work on your goal?

_____

_____

Additional copies of this EQ Action Plan are available in Toolbox 8.

Summary of key points

- Knowing what prompted you to want to develop emotional intelligence competencies is the place to start. Most of us find one of these to be primary:
  - You know what you want to change
  - You have a key challenge that demands new skills, or
  - You have received feedback from others suggesting development opportunities which might make you more effective

- Maximizing your strengths may make the most difference for your career or personal success unless you have poor skills in a competency that could block or jeopardize your career or personal life. If that is the case, start by bringing that competency up to at least average.

- A learning goal begins with understanding how to successfully perform either new behaviors or personally difficult behaviors and then developing a plan to make those skills part of your everyday actions. Most likely you will be setting a learning goal to build your emotional intelligence competencies.

- You are more likely to reach your goal if you write it so that it is:
    - Specific
    - Measurable
    - Achievable
    - Relevant
    - Time-limited

- Strategies to help you achieve your goal include:
    - Find role models, books and articles, and training opportunities
    - Set short-term goals
    - Ask for feedback
    - Use practice sessions
    - Identify your cheering section
    - Chose meaningful and challenging experiences.

CHAPTER 5

EQ Competencies and Clusters

What you will learn in this chapter:

- How do the competencies interconnect?
- What is the organizing structure of the 54 EQ Competencies?
- Why do the 54 competencies matter?
- How to get the most out of the competency descriptions
- What are the 54 competencies and their definitions?

Competencies are interdependent

Your circulatory, skeletal, neurological, and muscular systems work inter-dependently so you can live. Each serves a distinct purpose and yet must rely on the workings of the others to be viable. In the same way, our emotional, behavioral, and cognitive systems are interdependent at personal and interpersonal levels. For example, it is impossible to distinctly and uniquely separate emotions from ways of thinking. It is important to realize that the competencies covered in Part 2 are interdependent in how they are learned and used in everyday life.

No single emotional intelligence competency can stand alone. The 54 EQ Competencies work best when applied together. For example, if you are trying to develop the EQ competency (6) Conflict Management, then you must do so while keeping (15) *Active* Empathy in the front of your mind, as well as (34) Perspective-Taking, (30) Openness to Others or (2) Assertiveness. All are important companions when demonstrating talented (6) Conflict Management skills. You will see those connections as you take note of the clusters in Table 1 on page 47. Excellent people skills or emotional intelligence involves the interface of different EQ competencies with one another. One competency may link or partner with a complementary EQ skill. Just as an excellent athlete may have the physical skills to be a prolific scorer, unless he also has the ability to relate well to his or her teammates, to demonstrate leadership, to work hard and to be open to feedback (coaching), his athletic prowess alone is not enough to guarantee effectiveness.

You will find that while working to enhance one competency you elevate your effectiveness in several others. Further, you will find that the competencies "organize" themselves in various ways. In the analysis of all aspects of emotions and emotional intelligence that resulted in this book, a structure of "clusters" of how the competencies relate emerged. This structure provides a way of considering behaviors to enhance your emotional balance and effectiveness.

What is the organizing structure of the EQ competencies?

After analyzing the research literature on the perspectives and behaviors related to emotions that lead to personal and professional effectiveness, we settled on 54 competencies that could be defined, analyzed, developed, and used in productive ways. We found the evidence far and wide to support the 54 EQ Competencies and their role in personal and professional well-being. The competencies naturally cluster into three large arenas of behavior: awareness of self, self-regulation, and relating to and working well with others.

As we developed the material for each of the competencies, we noted patterns in the relationships among them. First we identified three larger groups which we called clusters. Within each cluster we were able to create smaller groups of competencies which were more closely related. We called these groups families. The relationships among the three Clusters, 11 Families and 54 Competencies are illustrated in Table 1.

Why the clusters matter

You have different strengths and life experiences which serve you in various ways. You most likely also vary in your ability to use the 54 EQ Competencies. By using Table 1 as a quick self-assessment of where you understand your key strengths and development challenges to be, you can begin your thinking about next steps for yourself. Identifying patterns of how your strengths and weaknesses group among the three Clusters and 11 Families of Competencies allows you to more easily begin your EQ Action Plan, which is explained in Chapter 4.

Emotional intelligence — like all forms of intelligence — is a useful lens through which to scrutinize your everyday life. The focus through this particular lens is on understanding and managing emotional energy for greater personal effectiveness and fulfillment. To enhance individual effectiveness, learn how to use the 54 EQ Competencies which are described in detail in Part 2 of this book. As you review the competencies in Part 2, keep in mind

Table 1:   EQ CLUSTERS

EQ Cluster 1	EQ Cluster 2	EQ Cluster 3
Awareness of Self	**Self-Regulation**	**Relating to and Working Well with Others**
Knowing Self (12) Emotional Maturity (40) *Accurate* Self-Assessment (41) Self-Awareness (42) Self-Confidence (44) Self-Regard	**Self-Management** (11) Emotional Expression (13) Emotional Problem-Solving (14) Emotional Self-Control (18) Impulse Control (43) Self-Disclosure	**Dealing with Others** (2) Assertiveness (4) Collaboration (20) Influencing Others (21) Initiative (25) Interpersonally Skillful (33) Personal Power (37) Relationship Savvy (53) Trustworthy
Integrated Self (3) Authenticity (8) Congruence (19) Independence (23) Integrity (39) Self-Actualization	**Approaches to Experience** (1) Adaptability (16) Flexibility (30) Openness to Others (31) Optimism (51) Tolerance	**Building Relationships** (5) Compassion (15) *Active* Empathy (27) Listening Generously (29) *Reading* Nonverbal Communication (32) Patience (52) Trusting (54) Understanding Others
Coping Perspectives (38) Resilience (49) Stamina (50) Stress Hardy	**Complex Thinking** (10) Creativity (22) Insightfulness (24) Intentionality (26) Intuition (28) Mindfulness	**Working with Conflict** (6) Conflict Management (7) *Effective* Confrontation (9) Constructive Discontent
	Managing Perceptions (34) Perspective-Taking (35) Reality Testing (36) Reframing	**Dealing with Social Context** (17) Group Savvy (45) Situational Awareness (46) Social Intelligence (47) Social Responsibility (48) *Managing* Social Space

that these work synergistically together and often in a dynamic relationship with each other. For example, (15) *Active* Empathy in combination with (2) Assertiveness and (19) Independence enhances relationships, while (15) *Active* Empathy without the balance of (2) Assertiveness and (19) Independence may lead to unhealthy relationships and interpersonal discomfort.

Tips for using this material

As a practical matter, you are encouraged to use the list of Talented, Skilled and Unskilled behaviors for each competency as a self-assessment. Using these behavioral cues, you can begin to identify those competencies that are relevant to your success. You may also ask others for feedback using these lists of behaviors. Underline the competencies in Table 1 which are your strengths and draw brackets around those that need further development.

For those competencies you want to develop, carefully read the Quick Action Tips in Part 2 and identify the actions steps that are likely to benefit you. Use them to create your EQ Action Plan as outlined in Chapter 4.

What are the 54 competencies by number and definitions?

The competencies are listed here in alphabetical order with the exception of a few titles in which the first word is italicized. For example, *Reading* Nonverbal Behavior is with the "N" group as the focus is on Nonverbal Behavior; *Managing* Social Space is listed under the "S" group as the focus is on Social Space and so forth.

1. Adaptability (page 54) Responding effectively to multiple demands, ambiguity, emerging situations, shifting priorities, and rapid change

2. Assertiveness (page 60) Standing up for your rights; expressing your feelings, thoughts and beliefs in ways that respect yourself and others

3. Authenticity (page 68) Being honest with yourself and transparent with others, even when it is difficult to do so

4. Collaboration (page 74) Working with others toward shared goals — willingly

5. Compassion (page 80) Understanding, caring about, and responding to the needs of others

6. Conflict Management (page 86) Identifying tension or disagreement within yourself or with others and promoting solutions that are best for all

7. *Effective* Confrontation (page 94) Addressing behaviors or decisions that are negatively impacting you or others in ways that are understood and lead to action

8. Congruence (page 102) Behaving in ways consistent with your feelings, values, and attitudes as demonstrated by decisions and actions; walking your talk

9. Constructive Discontent (page 108) Expressing dissatisfaction, frustration or displeasure in a way that others can hear and respond to; finding a creative way to bridge differences

10. Creativity (page 114) Generating, envisioning and getting excited about ideas that depart radically from current thinking

11. Emotional Expression (page 120) Recognizing your emotions and expressing them directly, appropriately, timely, and thoughtfully

12. Emotional Maturity (page 126) Choosing how you react to your emotions so that your responses are both appropriate and productive

13. Emotional Problem-Solving (page 132) Understanding a problem and its possible causes while taking emotional components into consideration, then generating the best possible solutions

14. Emotional Self-Control (page 138) Controlling and restraining your emotionally based actions; demonstrating self-restraint

15. *Active* Empathy (page 146) Understanding how and why others feel the way they do and conveying it effectively

16. Flexibility (page 154) Remaining open and responding effectively to new, different or changing information or circumstances

17. Group Savvy (page 160) Reading and adjusting to group dynamics to promote an intended impact or to motivate the group to act

18. Impulse Control (page 166) Recognizing emotional triggers as a signal to slow down, think before acting and choose a constructive response

19. Independence (page 174) Thinking for yourself and making decisions based on personal values and beliefs while considering, but not being overly influenced by, the feelings, needs and desires of others

20. Influencing Others (page 180) Conveying a message in a manner that moves people towards commitment to it

21. Initiative (page 188) Taking a proactive, action-oriented approach

22. Insightfulness (page 194) Seeing beyond the obvious and discerning the true nature of a situation or the hidden nature of things

23. Integrity (page 202) Behaving consistently with your values, principles and motives; being trustworthy, truthful and candid; doing the right thing even when no one is looking

24. Intentionality (page 208) Acting with purpose, direction and clear will toward a specific outcome or goal

25. Interpersonally Skillful (page 216) Using a wide range of skills to effectively communicate with, relate to and get along well with others

26. Intuition (page 224) Tuning in to your "gut feeling" or inner wisdom and checking it against something more tangible to help in decision-making and creativity

27. Listening Generously (page 232) Being completely attentive and accurately responding to what the speaker says and means, and also to what might be behind the words

28. Mindfulness (page 240) Focusing on the present moment and suspending both internal chatter and also external distractions to allow clarity and composure.

29. *Reading* Nonverbal Communication (page 248) Observing and interpreting nonverbal messages expressed by body language and how a message is conveyed

30. Openness to Others (page 254) Being receptive to others' feelings, thoughts and ideas

31. Optimism (page 260) Expecting that things will turn out well, that good will triumph; finding positive meaning or perspective in any situation

32. Patience (page 266) Waiting your turn. Enduring hardship, difficulty or inconvenience without complaint and with calmness and self-control; the willingness and ability to tolerate delay

33. Personal Power (page 272) Demonstrating authority, control and confidence in ways that influence action, command attention or gain agreement on how to get something done

34. Perspective-Taking (page 278) Considering various points of view or assumptions about a situation; seeking alternative options and choices

35. Reality Testing (page 284) Understanding and reacting to the way things are rather than responding to the way you wish, fear, imagine or assume them to be

36. Reframing (page 290) Seeing situations in a new light by considering different meanings, intentions or consequences to elicit more positive and productive responses

37. Relationship Savvy (page 298) Relating well and creating relationships with all kinds of people, even those you may not particularly like, to accomplish goals

38. Resilience (page 304) Bouncing back from difficult events and stressful situations by employing effective strategies to maximize well-being

39. Self-Actualization (page 312) Pursuing activities that lead to a personally meaningful life; becoming more of your best self

40. *Accurate* Self-Assessment (page 318) Knowing your strengths and limits

41. Self-Awareness (page 324) Knowing your own emotions, thoughts, motives, tendencies to react and their impact on others

42. Self-Confidence (page 332) Believing in your worth — your abilities, qualities and judgment — and behaving accordingly

43. Self-Disclosure (page 338) Sharing information about yourself with others, appropriately and in the face of risk or vulnerability

44. Self-Regard (page 344) Behaving in ways that reflect how good you feel about yourself; accepting yourself, warts and all

45. Situational Awareness (page 350) Being alert and informed about your environment; reading patterns of interactions among individuals and observing what may be unique about the setting

46. Social Intelligence (page 356) Sensing, understanding and reacting effectively to others' emotions and the interactions with and between people; getting along well with others and getting them to cooperate with you

47. Social Responsibility (page 364) Cooperating with and contributing to the common good of your community or social group by acting out of a basic concern for others and putting them first

48. *Managing* Social Space (page 370) Recognizing and maintaining the physical and emotional distance needed to interact comfortably with others

49. Stamina (page 378) Persisting in the face of difficulties, obstacles or disappointments

50. Stress Hardy (page 384) Maintaining performance, positive mood and commitment to goals in spite of adversity

51. Tolerance (page 392) Listening to and appreciating differing perspectives and ideas; valuing diversity

52. Trusting (page 398) Believing that an individual or entity will do the right thing and act in the best interest of others

53. Trustworthy (page 406) Behaving so that a large and diverse circle of people respond to you with belief and confidence

54. Understanding Others (page 412) Being curious about and understanding motivations, feelings and moods that underlie behavior — yours and others'

Summary of key points

- The 54 EQ Competencies have a relationship to one another and can be clustered into three large arenas of behavior:
    - Awareness of Self
    - Self-Regulation
    - Relating to and Working Well with Others

- A listing of the 54 EQ Competencies and their definitions

- Emotional Intelligence can be learned and improved upon

Part 2

The 54 EQ Competencies With Action Tips

| ADAPTABILITY

Definition

Responding effectively to multiple demands, ambiguity, emerging situations, shifting priorities, and rapid change

It is not the strongest of the species that survives, nor the most intelligent that survives. It is the one that is the most adaptable to change.

—Charles Darwin

Talented

❏ Sees ambiguity and shifting priorities as opportunities and responds by bringing people together to share perspectives and strategize

❏ Focuses on key issues and strategic goals to keep up in a complex, fast-paced environment

❏ Helps others adapt to new systems and procedures

❏ Easily adapts responses and tactics to fit changing circumstances; will search for alternatives to meet the needs of those around them

❏ Monitors his or her stress level and is adept at managing it

Skilled

❏ Problem-solves and manages well when facing a crisis

❏ Sets priorities and realistic expectations on a daily basis in the midst of upheaval and change

❏ Recognizes when change is coming and is relatively capable of managing through it

❏ Applies procedures and policies to meet objectives in a flexible manner under most circumstances

❏ Deals with stress by strategies such as regular exercise

❏ Uses social networks for brainstorming ways to address challenges

Unskilled

❏ Feels uncomfortable or overwhelmed dealing with a crisis, rapid change or uncertainly

❏ Needs closure on one issue before tackling the next

❏ Uses a familiar approach to problem solving and decision-making regardless of changes in circumstances; thinks his or her approach is the "right" one

❏ Rigidly adheres to policies and procedures or sticks to what has worked before

❏ Experiences high levels of stress during ambiguity or rapid change that may lead to physical or emotional issues

Big Picture View

A paradox of living effectively is that strength is found in being clear, resolute and determined and also in being able to adapt and adjust when circumstances call for it. In a world of fast and constant change, an emotionally intelligent person needs to rapidly read what is happening now, to be genuinely willing to understand other points of view, to modify his or her approach, and to move quickly forward. Acting in the face of changing circumstances, shifting priorities, and new frustrations takes courage and often the willingness to operate outside of one's comfort zone. Those who are adaptable anticipate challenges and opportunities by staying up to speed on technological changes, world events, and local news. They easily engage others in determining responses to new demands and changing circumstances. Since change usually is accompanied by the stress of dealing with the new, the different and the unexpected, adaptable people incorporate effective ways to manage their stress levels.

Barriers to Effectiveness

❏ Going off in too many different directions; becoming unfocused and divided in your attention (too adaptable!)

❏ Expects that life can be controlled, that there is a "right" way to do things, and that your opinion is correct

❏ Failing to utilize the abilities of others who may be good at adapting

❏ Thinking that change is a one time event

Quick Action Tips

1. Tend to freeze in a crisis? Some people are energized by a crisis while others are overwhelmed. When faced with a crisis, start by evaluating how urgent and serious the crisis is using a scale of 1 (lowest) to 10 (highest). If it rates an 8, 9, or 10, you might need to drop other priorities and focus on it. Gather those involved and available to share information and brainstorm options. Select the best one with the least downside, and then proceed.

2. Never take the time to consider what upheavals may be around the corner? Some changes and crises in our lives drop down out of the blue, but others can be anticipated if we are willing to do so. Make time in the next month to do a trend analysis of your career or home situation so that you aren't blindsided later on. Ask yourself: If things continue as they are, what challenges might you be facing in five years? For example, if your organization is losing market share, what might be the consequences in five years, or even next year? What can you do now to prepare for that eventuality or what can you do now to change that trend? Maybe taking that class in Excel can give you additional skills to increase your value. Maybe you have great customers right now, but taking time to reach out to new ones might help if some of your customers decide to change to internal sources for what you offer. If your oldest daughter will be applying to colleges in five years, what costs might you be facing then and what can you and your daughter do now to be ready?

3. Are you someone that loves closure? While striving for closure can give energy for finishing projects, sometimes the demands of life are too complex for quick decisions or immediate closure. Identify a friend or colleague who is comfortable balancing several projects at once. Ask for tips. Try using a time line on a whiteboard for each ongoing project to provide a sense of control and planning, even when the issue remains ongoing. List small steps for each project on your time line and check off actions as you move forward. Revisit as priorities and information change.

4. Do you tend to want to stick to your guns even when circumstances change? Take time to step back and review new information or circumstances and how they might affect your project. Tell yourself that there may be several ways to respond, and brainstorm what those might be. Engage those around you who also are involved, and listen to their thoughts. Do a list of pros and cons of doing nothing differently or responding to a change in circumstances with new actions. If the benefits outweigh the cons, choose the best approach for the moment even if it means regrouping. It's better to face reality now than to continue on a path that no longer makes sense.

5. Feeling stressed much of the time? Ask yourself what expectations might be creating that discomfort. Do you assume that you should be fully in control and know the right answer? Are you frustrated with lack of direction from others? Are you worried about the impact of changes on colleagues or customers? Remind yourself that you may not be able to control all the circumstances around you but that you can control your response and do your best. Take a "one step at a time" problem-solving process with the concerns you identify.

6. Don't tend to take care of yourself? Be sure that you have incorporated several stress management strategies into your lifestyle. Regular exercise is basic, along with using a support network to talk out any problems you face. Avoid viewing things as either "good" or "bad;" most circumstances and responses have some of both. Create a positive attitude by mentally listing two or three positive accomplishments each day as you leave work. Leave the challenges you are facing at the door when you leave work; you can pick them up again when you arrive in the morning. Use deep, slow breaths several times a day to return your body to a relaxed state. If you have physical concerns, consult a physician. In fact, as each new year begins, be sure to schedule your regular yearly physical, twice a year dental checkups, and an eye exam.

7. Do you get sidetracked during a day with lots of interruptions? Use a time management technique each morning when you arrive at work by writing down the one or two most important tasks or goals you have for that day. Return to those after each interruption to help you stay focused. Build into your expectations for the day an acceptance that interruptions are natural and will happen. Staying focused around these interruptions is a choice you can make and practice to be adaptable without going off track.

Related Competencies

(13) Emotional Problem-Solving (16) Flexibility (34) Perspective-Taking
(36) Reframing (38) Resilience (50) Stress Hardy

Learn from Experience

Work

❏ Ask for an opportunity to manage a situation with a lot of initial ambiguity and stakeholders from a broad range of backgrounds, such as a new task force or a visible startup project. Ask for feedback from colleagues about your ability to adapt and their perception of your progress.

❏ Interview someone who has successfully managed a large turnaround project and ask what strategies helped deal with changing circumstances and multiple or conflicting demands.

❏ Offer to take over responsibilities for a colleague who is going on leave.

Personal

❏ When faced with a problem, come up with at least two approaches to handling it; note the pros and cons of each and choose one. Later review how creative your solutions are.

❏ On a Saturday morning, look through the newspaper and choose some event to attend that usually doesn't appeal to you. Go with an open mind, plan to enjoy the event and see what you can learn.

❏ Volunteer at a nonprofit agency that works with immigrants, helping them adjust to a new country.

Resources

Books

Peters, Tom. *Thriving on Chaos*. New York: HarperCollins, 1985.

Ryan, Mary Jane. *AdaptAbility: How to Survive Change You Didn't Ask For*. New York: Broadway, 2009.

Gurvis, Joan, and Al Calarco. *Adaptability: Responding Effectively to Change*. Greensboro, NC: Center for Creative Leadership, 2007.

Internet

www.FindArticles.com. Search for "Personal Adaptability at Work." Journal of Leadership and Organizational Studies. Nov. 26, 2011, by D.J. O'Connell, E. McNeely, and D.T. Hall.

American Management Association. Search for "Agility and Resilience in the Face of Change," a webcast. Ed Reilly, Jay Jamrog, and Nick Horney. www.amanet.org

Classes and training

Mindworks. Research their course offerings on emotional intelligence. www.mindworkscorp.com

2 ASSERTIVENESS

Definition

Standing up for your rights; expressing your feelings, thoughts and beliefs in ways that respect yourself and others

I live by the truth that "no" is a complete sentence.

—Anne Lamott

Talented

❏ Builds confidence and a sense of personal power by taking small, meaningful risks to speak up, take on responsibility, and ask for what he or she wants

❏ Uses effective nonverbal communication to strengthen the impact of a verbal message

❏ Sets limits, says no, and disagrees when it is important, without damaging relationships

❏ Skillfully engages others in a group setting

❏ Enthusiastically pursues personally meaningful goals

❏ Responds in the moment by clearly and directly sharing ideas, feelings, and thoughts

Skilled

❏ Sets limits, disagrees, and says "no" to take care of self but with some discomfort or hesitation

❏ Knows what he or she wants and usually asks for it

❏ Sets and works toward personal goals but may sometimes get distracted or give up

❏ Expresses thoughts and feelings tactfully; listens to others

❏ Asks open-ended questions to explore what others think and want

Unskilled

Unassertive or passive behavior:

❏ Goes along with what others want just to keep the peace; is reluctant to set limits or say no

❏ Is unclear about own wants and needs

❏ Fails to set and act on personal goals

❏ Undermines own confidence by not taking actions or risks necessary to succeed

Aggressive behavior:

❏ Acts in overbearing, demanding, or caustic ways that leave others feeling resentful and alienated

❏ Insists on having his or her own way, sometimes to the detriment of others

❏ Interrupts and talks over others

❏ Criticizes others in derogatory or sarcastic ways

Big Picture View

Assertive, unassertive and aggressive are three basic styles of communication you most likely use in varying degrees and at various times. Consider:

▪ Being assertive means being able to express yourself clearly, ask for what you want, say no, and set limits in a way that shows respect for yourself and others.

▪ Unassertive or passive behavior allows others to make decisions for you that are rightly yours to make. Unassertive behavior such as bottling up your feelings and thoughts instead of speaking up can lead to a loss of confidence and loss of respect from others.

▪ Aggressive behavior, such as pushing others into doing what you want regardless of their feelings or needs, is both insensitive and a good way to lose colleagues or friends.

Low confidence and poor assertiveness skills can be part of a common circular pattern: In order to get along with others or preserve the peace, you may be unassertive (passive) and let others make all of the decisions. Eventually frustration or resentment can set in, leading to aggressive behavior such as criticizing, demeaning or pushing others away. Guilt then sets in, causing a relapse into being unassertive. Communicating assertively by taking responsibility and ownership for what you want and think without putting other people down or embarrassing them is a key way to avoid this pattern.

While some of us are more naturally assertive than others, we all can build our confidence and improve relationships by practicing being assertive in small ways or with safe people and then take on more difficult challenges. Clearly asking for what you want greatly increases your chances of having your needs met.

Barriers to Effectiveness

❑ Believing no one cares what you think

❑ Not asking for feedback to reinforce positive changes in assertive behavior

❑ Lack of self-esteem and poor self-awareness

❑ Confusing the difference between being assertive and aggressive

❑ Being insensitive to others; the bull in the china shop

❑ Not knowing how to be assertive

❑ Fear of the reactions of others

Quick Action Tips

1. Lack confidence expressing your thoughts? Worry about handling the reactions you might get? Build confidence by first asking for what you want or expressing your ideas in low-risk situations with trusted friends or colleagues or in small groups. Outline your thoughts before going into a meeting, practice presenting them to confidants ahead of time, and ask for feedback to improve the clarity of your message. Speak up early in a meeting so others see you as a contributor. Take small steps and give yourself credit for when you do share your thoughts. Remembering a time when you did express yourself well and received a good response from others can also help build your confidence as you face new situations.

2. Worry about handling someone with a strong personality? Afraid of personal attacks on you? Be sure you have collected your facts. Keep the discussion focused on objective facts and ideas, not personalities, by asking questions such as "Who have you talked to about this problem?" "Is there any downside to trying this approach?" Redirect personal criticisms by making statements such as, "This isn't about me; let's consider how we might solve this issue." Stop a steamroller approach by comments like, "This is too important to decide without additional reflection and information." Redirect the focus away from a dominant personality in a group by asking others for their ideas on the issue. Use procedural suggestions such as, "Let's list the pros and cons of the various alternatives we have identified." Or, "Let's go around the room to get a brief reaction from everyone to the ideas that have been mentioned."

3. Feel like others take advantage of you? Don't automatically say yes. Don't let yourself be bulldozed. Respond to questionable requests by giving yourself time to consider whether you want to take on a project by saying something like "Let me get back to you about that request later this afternoon." Then decide if you want the responsibility and can manage it or not. Say no sometimes. When you take on new projects, be clear with those involved what you consider to be reasonable deadlines and how the new commitment changes your priorities. Negotiate what you can and can't reasonably accomplish. Remember that, when you make commitments, you may be affecting the lives of other people close to you. If you agree to volunteer at a homeless shelter on Saturdays, you may need your spouse to take your son to soccer practice. If you agree to lead the cost reduction committee at work, a colleague may need to attend a weekly project meeting in your stead.

4. Not sure how to respond to others who are attempting to take advantage of you? Use the DESC method described by Sharon and Gordon Bower to respond assertively with these steps:

- *Describe* the behavior or actions that are bothering you in concrete, specific terms ("You said this car repair would cost $100 and now you are giving me a bill for $220).

- *Express* how you feel about the situation or what impact others' behavior is having on you or the situation ("I'm unhappy because this bill is significantly higher than what I agreed to.")

- *Specify* or ask for a different, specific behavior ("I want you to readjust my bill back to the original estimate unless you can clearly justify these additional charges.")

- Spell out in concrete language what the *consequences* are for changing that behavior. Ideally use natural consequences or a positive consequence. ("If you do, I will continue to recommend your auto works to all of my friends.")

Use these steps the next time you don't feel respected or think others are taking advantage of you. Write out what you will say ahead of time and practice if needed. Who do you know who is good at standing up for herself or himself? What do they do or say to manage difficult situations? Watch them if possible and try the approach they use.

5. Think that you are not making the impact you wish to make? Feel like others are not hearing you in a group? Ask for feedback from trusted friends or colleagues. If they agree, ask why you might not be heard. Be sure you are using helpful nonverbal cues such as a strong voice, good eye contact and gestures that fit your message. Speak to the dominant member of the group by name. If you get the attention of that person, others will also listen. Keep your comments clear and to the point. Be sure your body language conveys the conviction of your intentions. If appropriate, build on the ideas of others by name so that you gain their buy-in. If you feel more comfortable one on one, talk to opinion leaders ahead of a meeting to share your ideas and to ask for their feedback and support.

6. Do you know what you want? Sometimes we are so caught up in our work that we fail to stop and determine what our own needs, feelings, and goals are. What do you want to achieve? Where do you want to be in five years? Make time for a career conversation with your boss. Ask for the opportunities you want. Consider who in the organization you might ask to mentor you. Talk to your spouse or significant other. Are you satisfied with the direction of your life? Any changes you wish to make? If you don't know what you want, no one else will.

7. Do others seem to avoid you? Find that you are not included in casual conversations? It may be that you are behaving in an aggressive manner — interrupting or talking over others, showing little interest in the ideas of others, monopolizing air time, criticizing others, or demanding that things be done your way. Stop and consider how you can show others as much respect as you want for yourself. Share air time, ask what others think, value the time of your friends and colleagues, be willing to take "no" for an answer, let others have their way. In the long run you will succeed by uplifting others.

8. Are you unsure what you have a right to expect from others? We all have these basic rights among others:

- To be treated with respect
- To have and express your own feelings and opinions
- To be listened to and taken seriously
- To set your own personal priorities
- To ask for what you want
- To get what you pay for
- To say no without feeling guilty

The next time you hesitate to speak up, consider whether you have a basic right to say what matters to you. Do so in a manner that respects others. Own your own feelings, needs and thoughts by speaking up for yourself.

Related Competencies

(3) Authenticity   (6) Conflict Management   (11) Emotional Expression
(20) Influencing Others   (25) Interpersonally Skillful   (42) Self-Confidence

Learn from Experience

Work

❏ Represent your department in a cross-functional problem-solving group. Speak up to express the interests of your department while listening to other perspectives. After a meeting of the group, ask someone you trust for specific feedback about how clearly you expressed your ideas, what positive contributions you made, and what you could do differently.

❏ Handle an employee problem that you have ignored up to now.

❏ Fill in for your boss presenting to upper management. Practice ahead of time with someone who knows you and can give you specific feedback about your impact.

Personal

❏ Over a week's time identify situations in which you tend to be assertive, unassertive or aggressive. What patterns do you see? What are you telling yourself that may keep you stuck in one style of behaving? Set a goal of practicing being assertive in one or two situations that are important to you, such as speaking up at a parent-teacher conference about the level of homework your son has each night.

❏ Identify someone you know who is assertive in a way you admire. Watch that person to see how he expresses himself and how others respond. Write down two or three specific behaviors that are part of that person's assertive communication, and practice using those actions.

Resources

Books

Alberti, Robert E., and Michael L. Emmons. *Your Perfect Right: Assertiveness and Equality in Your Life and Relationships* (9th ed.). Atascadero, CA: Impact Publishers, 2008.

Bolton, Robert. *People Skills*. New York: Simon & Schuster, 2003.

Bower, Sharon A., and Gordon H. Bower. *Asserting Yourself: A Practical Guide for Positive Change* (Updated 2nd ed.). Reading, MA: Perseus Books, 2004.

Paterson, Randy J. *The Assertiveness Workbook: How to Express Your Ideas and Stand Up for Yourself at Work and in Relationships*. Oakland, CA: New Harbinger, 2000.

Internet

Psychology Today. Search for "assertiveness." www.psychologytoday.com

Classes and training

American Management Association, www.amanet.org. Search for "assertiveness training."

Ed2go. Search for "assertiveness training."

2

3   AUTHENTICITY

Definition

Being honest with yourself and transparent with others, even when it is difficult to do so

No man can wear one face to himself and the other to the multitude without finally getting bewildered as to which may be true.

— Nathaniel Hawthorne, in *The Scarlet Letter*

Talented

❏ Lives and speaks with emotional honesty and self-awareness

❏ Demonstrates genuineness and sincerity while being direct; gets to the point

❏ Behaves congruently with spoken words, values, and purpose

❏ Offers opinions so that others know where they stand

❏ Communicates in an open and transparent way

Skilled

❏ Demonstrates basic honesty, but under stress varies words and behavior to fit in or to be accepted

❏ Displays nonpretentiousness; what you see is what you get

❏ Acts with good intentions but is not fully aware of own motivations and feelings.

❏ Takes responsibility for behavior when outcomes contradict good intentions

❏ Puts best foot forward, sometimes camouflaging the warts

Unskilled

❏ Says one thing and does another

❏ Tries too hard to please others; is chameleon-like, trying to fit in

❏ Loses touch with what really matters by trying to fit in

❏ Manipulates the truth. Spinmeister!

❏ Fakes feelings, pretends to be someone or something different, exaggerates the truth

Big Picture View

Authenticity is found in leaders and individuals who live according to their values and beliefs. Achieving authenticity depends on knowing yourself and then acting with integrity and consistency when sharing your thoughts, feelings and opinions with others. Whatever your role — leader, parent, manager or friend — as you communicate with honesty and genuineness, others will find you authentic. In the classic children's book, *The Velveteen Rabbit*, when the stuffed bunny asks what it takes to become real, he is told, "It doesn't happen all at once. You become. It takes a long time. That's why it doesn't happen often to people who break easily, or have sharp edges, or who have to be carefully kept." Authentic people are resilient: they can be honest with themselves and others, even when it is difficult to do so. Being authentic is being truthful — to self and others — which, ultimately, better serves all involved.

Barriers to Effectiveness

❏ Tries too hard to be liked, sacrificing truth and honesty

❏ The need to control; uses one's position or power to influence

❏ Tries too hard to please others, undermining self-knowledge

❏ Poor communication skills; being untruthful, or unclear

❏ Lack of independent thinking

❏ Self-critical, low self-esteem

Quick Action Tips

1. Find it difficult to deliver honest but tough news? Do you hesitate when you have difficult feedback or information to give? Most people find it annoying or disappointing when you fail to be up front with them. When delivering tough news, the research indicates that people who are honest, clear and direct about the message, even when it is bad news, are more respected and believed. Remember though, you can be honest, clear and direct with tough news and show compassion. Make a commitment to speak the truth and to refrain from saying anything when you cannot be truthful. Spend some time being very intentional and examining your motives and behaviors. As you drive or ride home from work each day, think through your major interactions: Did you say what you needed to say? Were you clear, kind and direct? If not, why? What interfered with your honesty? Look for ways to be more honest and genuine in your interactions with others. If you have tough news to deliver, then deliver it in a way that you think will be useful to the other person.

2. Do your words and your behaviors match up? Are colleagues or friends sometimes confused about what you really mean? Do you say you would be glad to help a friend move, but you don't follow up on the details? Do you say a report looks great, and then later make many corrections to it? If you have received feedback about how your words and actions don't appear to align, you may be lacking in vital authenticity. Make sure that your verbal and nonverbal behaviors are congruent. Ask a colleague who is in the same meeting or group gathering with you to observe you and later to give you feedback about how you came across in that setting. Ask for observations on the consistency of your words and your actions. Many organizations offer leadership training that includes a module in which your interpersonal interactions with others in coaching or simulation exercises are recorded for the purposes of learning. Such opportunities, which provide feedback from a professional or from peers, can help you better understand how you are perceived by others.

3. Do you believe it is always important to show strength? Although authority and strength are viable leadership qualities, if those qualities are not tempered by authenticity, then people might not be inclined to follow. Jim Collins in *Good to Great* talks about the paradox of personal humility and ambition. Make sure you don't abandon your true self in favor of wanting to appear strong or more knowledgeable. Learn to say, "I don't have the answer to that, but I can get it," or, "Let me find the help you need." People will respect your honesty. If you are uncomfortable with not having all the answers, this might be a good time to examine why that is. No one has all the answers. If you are making any assumptions that suggest otherwise, here is an opportunity to let yourself off the hook.

4. Don't know what it means to be authentic? Sometimes, when authenticity is mentioned, people don't know what it means or how to develop it. A good place to start is to read the biographies of well-known and highly respected people to get a glimpse into lives of authenticity (examples, Gandhi, Martin Luther King, Mother Teresa, Abraham Lincoln). Silently begin observing the people in your life you most admire for their authenticity. What behaviors or actions convey that this person is true to him or herself? What do they do that impresses you as authentic? Do their behaviors appear lined up with what they feel, believe and value? Which of these behaviors can you adopt or do more of? Personal growth workshops and retreats also are great opportunities to learn more about yourself and to experiment with some different behaviors.

5. Have you lost touch with your passions? Turned a deaf ear to your inner voice? Revisit the passions and goals of your youth and ask yourself, "Where did they go?" or "Where did I go?" Have you made more and more compromises over the years? If you've lost sight of your passions, how might you revisit them? Consider writing or talking with someone who knows you well, or taking a long walk and using this time to focus on your passions and dreams. Are there parts of these passions you can fast forward and make a priority in your life today? How about the smaller preferences in life? Do you honor or ignore them? On a daily basis, think about what you actually prefer. Consider making your preferences known, like where you want to go for lunch, which movies you prefer, or how you want to spend your down time. You may not always get your way, but you and others will become much more aware of what's important to you. That matters, or it should, in any relationship you have. As you go about your daily activities, think about how you might prefer to use your time. Are you doing what you prefer to be doing, all things considered? If not, how might you do more of what you want, less of what you don't want, and still maintain your responsibilities and commitments?

6. Are you impeccable at keeping your word? Do you follow through with your promises? It is important to take your words and your promises seriously. Think twice before you offer a promise or commitment to someone. It is far better to avoid such a promise than to make it but then be unable or unwilling to keep it. If you've dropped the ball more than once, a good practice might be to keep a record of the promises that you make. Examples include telling an employee you will talk to human resources about their potential promotion, or promising your son you will take him to the baseball game. Keeping a record will help you to be conscientious about such promises and to remember to follow through. Do you have a tendency to overpromise or overestimate what you can do and underestimate what it will take to deliver? Recording your promises will also shed some light on your promise-making behavior and how realistic it is. In today's world of electronic calendars and smart phones, tracking your commitments is easy to do.

7. Ever find yourself saying yes when you really mean no? Or are you afraid to ask for something for fear of being rejected or of being an imposition? Being authentic means showing up and doing so in an honest and sincere way. Many of us are uncomfortable turning down requests or telling someone no when they have asked something of us. When we agree to something that we don't really want to do, it's likely that our reluctance will be conveyed in some way to those around us. Our words might say, "Yes, I'm happy to do that," but our demeanor may convey a lack of enthusiasm. The flip side of the coin is the importance of speaking up and asking for a favor or help when needed. To do so is an example of being authentic, of honestly expressing yourself in a sincere and genuine way, rather than beating around the bush or hinting at something — or worse, feeling bitter or resentful when those around you can't guess what you want. Resolve to speak up and give your honest response to a request, whether yes or no, as well as to ask for feedback or help when it is needed.

Related Competencies

(8) Congruence   (23) Integrity   (39) Self-Actualization

(41) Self-Awareness   (52) Trusting   (53) Trustworthy

Learn from Experience

Work

❏ Look at a speech or PowerPoint presentation you've made and check it for inflated language that is more designed to impress than to reflect your genuine opinions or beliefs. Replace it with basic, simple words that best reflect your true meaning.

❏ Ask to take a 360 degree assessment instrument. Feedback increases self-awareness, and self-awareness enables increased authenticity.

Personal

❏ Volunteer at a local homeless shelter or soup kitchen. This can often restore your perspective and help you see what is important to you in life.

❏ Think of a situation in which you were not entirely honest or didn't tell someone the truth about your feelings (we've all been there!). If prudent and useful, consider going to that person now and telling that person the bigger truth. It may be difficult or awkward, but it may bring resolution and perhaps some peace to you both — the peace that comes from telling or hearing the rest of the story.

Resources

Books

Arbinger Institute. *Leadership and Self Deception: Getting Out of the Box.* San Francisco: Berrett-Koehler, 2010.

Collins, Jim. *Good to Great.* New York: HarperCollins, 2001.

Hudson, Russ, and Don Riso. *The Wisdom of the Enneagram: The Complete Guide to Psychological and Spiritual Growth for the Nine Personality Types.* New York: Bantam Books, 1999.

Katie, Byron. *Loving What Is: Four Questions that Can Change Your Life.*

New York: Three Rivers Press, 2002.

Peck, Scott. *The Road Less Traveled.* New York: Touchstone, 2003.

Raiten-D'Antonio, Toni. *The Velveteen Principles: A Guide to Becoming Real.* Deerfield Beach, FL: Health Communications, 2004.

Ruiz, Don Miguel. *The Four Agreements: A Practical Guide to Personal Freedom.* San Rafael, CA: Amber Allen Publishing, 1997.

Internet

Harvard Business Review. "Managing Authenticity: The Paradox of Great Leadership" by Rob Goffee and Gareth Jones. December 2005, www.hbr.org

People Skills Handbook web site: www.peopleskillshandbook.com

The Authentic Happiness web site of Dr. Martin Seligman. www.authentichappiness.com

Classes and training

The Enneagram Institute, classes for personal, spiritual and interpersonal development. www.enneagraminstitutue.com

The Work by Byron Katie: classes to increase self-awareness, personal growth and living authentically. www.thework.com

4 | COLLABORATION

Definition

Working with others toward shared goals—willingly

The end result isn't mine or yours — it's ours.

— Anonymous

Talented

❏ Promotes seamless partnerships by sharing plans, information, expertise and resources

❏ Values and solicits others' input

❏ Effectively finds common ground

❏ Spots and nurtures opportunities to foster a friendly and cooperative climate

❏ Holds self and others accountable regarding commitments

Skilled

❏ Cooperates with others' efforts to work together but initiates these efforts only occasionally

❏ Neglects to seek input but actively listens when it's offered

❏ Negotiates with a bias for own position

❏ Focuses more on task than relationships

❏ Values hierarchy and the majority opinion more than facilitation and consensus

Unskilled

❏ Fails to clarify goals, ground rules and resources needed

❏ Avoids sharing information and resources (turfism)

❏ Lapses into individual efforts over collective efforts to achieve goals

❏ Clings to previous plans over adjusting and compromising

❏ Competes for control or resources

❏ Misses milestone commitments when they compete with personal gain or other demands

Big Picture View

Collaboration depends on joint effort, a sense of belonging, a sense of urgency and commitment. Also necessary to achieving common goals are mutual trust and shared ownership, resources, information, influence and decision-making. As with any team, complementary and diverse backgrounds can enhance the outcome but also raise the possibility of conflict. When it works, partnering with others to achieve goals can be rewarding, even exhilarating.

Great in theory, collaborating can also be a challenge to implement, sometimes painful. For a collaboration to achieve its promise, you may have to sacrifice some personal ambition and independence.

Barriers to Effectiveness

❏ Distrust (yours or others')

❏ Competitive personality

❏ Ineffective communication

❏ Fragmented, inconsistent or passive leadership

❏ Emerging fears around loss of autonomy, control and rewards

❏ Reacting to pressure of workloads and tight deadlines

❏ Strong leaders, superstars or coaches whose presence or style upset the balance of shared responsibility and ownership

❏ Overlooking or avoiding conflict

Quick Action Tips

1. **Tempted to start solving a problem before you clarify the goal?** When a group of people come together to do some work, they often dive right into the task, sometimes without clarifying the goals and how to reach them. A team must set goals that everyone understands and can get behind. Common purpose unites and energizes a group, and goals provide focus. At the same time the group needs to determine the talent they have and the talent they need. What other resources are needed? (See Quick Action Tip #2 below.)

2. **Do you remember to take stock of what resources are needed and what resources are**

available? You can save much time, effort and resources if you assess, value and use the talents that team members bring to the table — their perspectives, experience, knowledge, expertise, ideas and skills. Create a list of the talents, interests, strengths, and weaknesses of each team member before assigning tasks. Teams that know their collective strengths enjoy greater team pride and optimism. Equally important, they are better positioned to tackle tasks effectively and fairly. Deciding who has what talent to carry out certain tasks might be easier than getting others who are less talented or less interested to take on those tasks. How will these decisions be made? Will there be a point person to follow up and coordinate communications? However the tasks are delegated, it needs to be done in a way that makes the person taking on the task feel valued, motivated, and able to contribute.

3. Prefer to do it yourself? Does it just seem easier, or faster? When focused on a task or venture, many find it easier or preferable to pursue it alone. True, involving others in a task may take more time or effort, at least initially. But it is also true that "all of us are smarter than any of us." Many tasks are more effectively accomplished in teams. And the more complex or large in scope a task is, the more necessary collaboration becomes. If you are resistant to collaborating, reflect on why that might be. Some factors could be very high standards, the pressure of workload or tight deadlines, need for control, introversion, habit, or limited options. Want to become more collaborative? Invite two or three other stakeholders to join you on a project. Experiment with several tips found here and in the resource section. Afterwards, examine what worked, what didn't and what you will do differently in the future.

4. Are the group's efforts being derailed by individual agendas, rigidity or disagreement? Begin any collaborative effort with setting and agreeing on the ground rules. Settle on how information and resources will be shared, how conflicts will be handled and how team members will be accountable. Talk about how and when compromise should be considered. When working with a team, it is impossible for everyone to get their way, so compromise is imperative. Find ways to recognize team members for resisting the urge to get their own way and for helping the group do the same.

5. Are conflicts (overt or hidden) sabotaging the group's efforts? Anticipate conflicts, spot them early, and confront them. Brainstorm with the team where potential problems could arise. Pinpoint what is likely to cause them, and brainstorm how to prevent them or to deal with them should they arise. Periodically review these strategies and agreements about how conflict will be handled.

> ■ *Clarify commitments.* A sure indication of conflict or resistance
> is unmet commitments. Make sure everyone is clear about what
> is going to be done, by whom and when. Consider sending out
> summaries with agreed-upon assignments after every meeting.
> Create a system to ensure that commitments are met and, if not,

what steps will follow.

- *Effective communication* improves your chances of keeping inevitable problems from escalating. Pay attention to others' feelings and motivations. Sometimes feelings and motivations are not expressed, but, you can be sure, they always affect the outcome.

- *Effective collaboration* depends on open communication about ideas, experiences and opinions. And open communication depends on trust and safety. In groups where hierarchy is present, it can block the free flow of communication. If you suspect this might be the situation, then consider creating communication channels that are confidential until issues involving trust or safety can be addressed.

6. Dealing with emerging egos or competitive zeal? It is hard to collaborate when you feel competition within the group. Competition for power, position, being right or having a specific idea adopted all get in the way of collaborative success. With clear purpose and goals, people can be refocused on what they are trying to accomplish and how to serve the team's success, not individual (or departmental) success. Having set clear ground rules early provides support for team members to confront these disruptive behaviors.

7. Is a formal leader needed? Rotate leadership where you can. Although there may be a formal leader, greater collaboration will occur if everyone feels some responsibility for the team's results. Where different team members can step up to take a leadership role or take the lead in making something happen, that sense of personal responsibility grows. Most collaborative groups have leaders, but you want a team in which all the members have a sense of responsibility.

8. Is team participation spotty or tepid? Build relationships and team spirit. Make collaboration rewarding, even fun. Schedule team-building activities to strengthen relationships and collaboration skills. Be relentless about building relationships. The classic Bell Labs studies of very large and complex project teams made up of very smart scientists demonstrated that a network of collegial relationships outside the team is what differentiated those teams that were the most successful.

9. Or is it you? Are you the one who is inflexible, competes for resources or fails to deliver on commitments? Being a reliable team-player is highly valued in today's work environment. However, doing so can sometimes collide with what you need to do to accomplish your individual goals. You may be faced with having to choose between what will help the team and what will move your agenda forward. Start with what is important to you. What are you trying to accomplish, in the bigger picture? How will your choices today impact your longer term goals? What reputation are you developing? Is it possible that you are sabotaging your own longer-term goals by failing to adapt, compromise or deliver as promised? If you're getting feedback, overt or subtle, that your choices or behavior are interfering with the progress of a team-based project, it may be time to take a fresh look at what you are doing and how it is likely to play out. You might also want to enlist someone else in an honest conversation about this.

Related Competencies

(6) Conflict Management   (9) Constructive Discontent (17) Group Savvy

(27) Listening Generously   (29) *Reading* Nonverbal Communication

(45) Situational Awareness.

Learn from Experience

Work

❏ Plan the launch of a new product, process or software conversion.

❏ Participate in implementing a move or a change in where or how people do their work.

Personal

❏ Coach a children's sport team.

❏ Volunteer to lead a fund raising event with multiple subcommittees.

❏ Facilitate a citizens' meeting dealing with a community crisis.

Resources

Books

Sawyer, Keith. *Group Genius: The Creative Power of Collaboration*. Cambridge, MA: Basic Books, 2007.

Glaser, Judith E. *Creating We: Change I-Thinking to WE-Thinking and Build a Healthy, Thriving Organization*. Avon, MA: Adams Media Corporation, 2005.

Covey, Stephen. *The Speed of Trust: The One Thing That Changes Everything*. New York: Free Press, 2008.

Hansen, Morten T. *Collaboration: How Leaders Avoid the Traps, Create Unity, and Reap Big Results*. Boston: Harvard Business School Press, 2009.

Tamm, James W. *Radical Collaboration: Five Essential Skills to Overcome Defensiveness and Build Successful Relationships*. New York: Harper Paperbacks, 2005.

Internet

Harvard Business Review. Search for "How Bell Labs Creates Star Performers." The Magazine, 1993. www.hbr.org

www.leader-values.com. Under "Article themes," select "Knowledge" and then "Learning Organization."

Speedoftrust.com. For a free online 360 survey go to www.whotrustsyou.com

Ted Talks. Howard Rheingold: "The new power of collaboration," February 2005. www.ted.com/talks

Classes and training

Wharton Executive Education. Search for "Building Relationships That Work." www.executiveeducation.wharton.upenn.edu

Find Your Genius. Once on their web site, search for "collaboration." www.training-classes.com

5 COMPASSION

Definition

Understanding, caring about, and responding to the needs of others

Compassion automatically invites you to relate with people because you no longer regard people as a drain on your energy.

— Chogyam Trungpa

Talented

❑ Expresses empathy to those in distress

❑ Reads the emotions of others and responds in a caring manner

❑ Demonstrates concern with intentional acts of support

❑ Reacts to and connects with an individual in distress before most others realize there is a problem

❑ Finds a way to show compassion for needs in the community

Skilled

❑ Expresses sympathy more than empathy

❑ Acknowledges others' emotions

❑ Offers to be available to help though doesn't necessarily take the initiative to follow up

❑ Gives active support for a short period of time

Unskilled

❑ Fails to identify or acknowledge others' emotions or reactions

❑ Displays and expresses discomfort with others' emotions and is unable to discuss them

❑ Avoids dealing with sensitive issues

❑ Seems inattentive and unresponsive to others' needs

Big Picture View

Compassion can be learned by developing an eye and ear for another's emotional reactions to things. Part of compassion is being attentive and open to how you would experience what another person is going through. Being compassionate does not mean giving permission to do something you may not approve of. Be compassionate first and problem-solve second, unless someone's well-being is at risk. You can enhance compassion by thinking about the needs of those involved, expressing concern, asking how you might help, and acting to support them in meaningful ways. A challenge with developing compassion is balancing the needs of others with your own needs, time and energy.

Barriers to Effectiveness

❏ Confuses compassion with giving approval

❏ Hiding your emotions or not responding to the emotions of others will hinder the expression of compassion.

❏ Lack of comfort with your emotional reactions

❏ An inability to experience empathy

❏ More concerned with your own needs than those of others

❏ Overdoing compassion may lead to not considering your own needs.

Quick Action Tips

1. Are you unsure about what emotions you see or hear from those around you? To be more aware of others' emotions, look at their faces for signs of pleasure, discomfort, or bewilderment. Understanding the emotions another person is experiencing in a situation enables you to react with compassion. Learn to identify your emotions and the emotions of others. Emotions are negative, neutral, or pleasant, and each emotion serves a purpose. Some common emotions are anger, sadness, joy, curiosity, and embarrassment. Confirm the feelings you see, express concern or caring if appropriate, and ask how you might help.

2. When others show the emotions of anger or hurt, do you quickly change the subject? Quickly remember when you were angry or hurt last time. Having that acknowledged rather than ignored is an act of compassion. Try being a nonjudgmental witness to others' emotions. Learning that emotions are a natural part of how individuals respond to various life events or challenges can allow you to simply "sit with" the other individual while they express their feelings.

Often some simple words can be used, such as, "You seem angry right now. Anything I can do to help?" These kinds of comments show caring about and responding to the needs of others. If you sometimes change the subject when others are expressing emotions, consider whether you do so because you are uncomfortable or unsure how to respond effectively. Take a deep breath and listen.

3. Confuse compassion with sympathy? Sympathy is when you express that you are sorry about another's experience because you imagine how upset or disappointed you might be if you were having the same experience. Empathy is understanding and appreciating the emotion. Expressing sympathy because someone is sad is not the same thing as appreciating how the other person may be experiencing sadness. Compassion is understanding the emotion and taking action to address the needs in the situation. Perhaps the woman who usually cleans your home has a car accident. With sympathy you tell her how sorry you are that happened to her. Empathy allows you to ask how her son is handling it, how it must be difficult for her as a single mother to not be able to work, and ask how she is doing. Compassion leads you to send her a card with the money you would have paid her for the morning she was unable to work. Identify one situation in your life where you might express compassion, then act on it.

4. Understand the situation but fail to act? Part of being compassionate is knowing what the needs of another person are and acting on that insight. Simply knowing but not acting is missing the importance of (or opportunity for) compassion. A question like, "How can I help you deal with that?" is a question that moves you toward compassion. If you are trying to think of a solution to the situation, you have bypassed compassion and moved to "fixing" the problem. The action in compassion is acknowledging the situation and offering the support or assistance that the individual needs.

5. Afraid that an initiative to reach out and help will be misinterpreted? There is always a risk in any communication that the person you are talking to will misinterpret your behavior. Fear of how others might respond to your effort may be rooted in a sense of not knowing how to help. Acknowledge what you see, what the person shares, and how they respond to your offer to assist — even if it is just being an ear to listen to their worry. Offer to provide assistance, and be patient as they decide what they want to do.

6. Want to show more compassion, but not sure how? Sometimes when compassion is mentioned people don't know what it means or how to develop it. A good place to start can be to do some reading or to attend a personal growth workshop or retreat on the subject. Reading the biographies of well-known and highly respected people who are known for their compassion can offer glimpses into what compassion looks like. Silently begin to observe the person in your life you most admire and who you feel is compassionate. What are the behaviors that demonstrate that compassion? Are those behaviors that you can cultivate in yourself? Is there a current situation where you might practice some of these behaviors?

7. Listening not your strength? Even when you feel compassion for someone, listening to them may not be easy for you. Some factors that can interfere with listening include: impatience, focusing on your agenda, thinking about your own similar experience, ideas for solution, interrupting the other person, critical thoughts, and daydreaming about where else you'd like to be. Staying focused on the other person requires intention and discipline. You need to tune in to hear the thoughts, feelings and reactions of the person who may need your compassion. Talk with an excellent listener to get hints and suggestions for becoming more effective. Check out some of the YouTube videos on listening behavior to see examples of the kind of behavior to emulate.

8. Have a tendency to overlook the nonverbal behavior of others? To be talented in being compassionate, you need to recognize others' needs as early as possible in an interaction. Learn to notice others' body language, such as eye contact, tone of voice, body posture and facial expressions. These are often clues to what's going on inside the other person and can help you develop empathy or understanding of the other person's needs. Create opportunities to observe the behaviors of others while you are waiting at the airport or standing in a grocery line, notice someone's posture and imagine how they might be feeling. Begin to make real-time observations about the nonverbal behaviors of those with whom you interact — co-workers, family, friends, or neighbors. Keep a notebook with your observations. Confirm whether or not your observations and guesses were accurate with data collected later.

9. Expressing your feelings — no problem, right? Do you find it difficult to express your feelings clearly, appropriately and assertively? Put simply, assertive behavior is saying what you want (or need) to say, when you want to say it, in a nice way. Some occasions where that can be difficult include: when delivering bad news, when confronting someone where a negative emotion is anticipated or when asking for help. There are generally two blocks to assertive behavior: fear of the reaction you might get and simply lacking the skill. Either can interfere with expressing compassion, as well as being assertive. Start with sharing how you feel about the situation and ask how the other person feels.

10. Find it hard to balance compassion with getting the work done? You may be quite good at identifying others' feelings and knowing when to ask if you can be of assistance — when you feel you have the time. Sometimes it is difficult to see that the compassionate act is sometimes an effective time management strategy. If your colleague or associate needs support and is not getting it, they are not likely to be as effective and pleasant to be around. If you are the boss, being compassionate may feel like you are giving permission to be less productive. Think about the balance of energy a colleague or employee may give when they experience support compared to the absence of support. Make a list of the times when a small act of compassion would have made the difference in your focus and productivity. Identify the lesson for you given the insight that comes from making your list.

Related Competencies

(2) Assertiveness   (3) Authenticity   (12) Emotional Maturity

(15) *Active* Empathy   (27) Listening Generously   (34) Perspective-Taking

Learn from Experience

Work

❏ Lead a company-wide sponsorship of a community service.

❏ Volunteer to represent the company on a board serving underserved populations.

❏ Ask to mentor a new employee who you determine has a great deal of potential.

Personal

❏ Volunteer for the local soup kitchen or for the Big Brothers/Big Sisters program.

❏ Become involved in Hospice.

❏ Identify those who have been compassionate to you and emulate them.

Resources

Books

Barasch, Marc I. *The Compassionate Life: Walking the Path of Kindness*. San Francisco: Berrett-Koehler, 2009.

Dalai Lama XIV. *An Open Heart: Practicing Compassion in Everyday Life*. New York: Back Bay, 2001.

Gyatso, Geshe K. *Universal Compassion*. New Delhi: Motilal Banarsidass, 2002.

Ladner, Lorne. *The Lost Art of Compassion: Discovering the Practice of Happiness in the Meeting of Buddhism and Psychology*. New York: HarperCollins, 2004.

Wilson, Amy L. *Compassion: Thoughts on Cultivating a Good Heart*. Nashville: Abingdon Press, 2008.

Internet

Ted Talks. Daniel Goleman on Compassion, March 2007.
www.ted.com/talks

The Compassion Fatigue Awareness Project: www.compassionfatigue.org/

Classes and training

The Center for Compassion and Altruism Research and Education, Stanford University. Search for "Companion Cultivation Training."
www.ccare.stanford.edu/cct

The Greater Good. Research their courses in developing compassion.
http://greatergood.berkeley.edu/

6   CONFLICT MANAGEMENT

Definition

Identifying tension or disagreement within yourself or with others and promoting solutions that are best for all

I argue very well. Ask any of my remaining friends. I can win an argument on any topic, against any opponent. People know this and steer clear of me at parties. Often, as a sign of their respect, they don't even invite me.

—Dave Barry, humorist

Talented

❑ Actively looks for win-win solutions to difficult situations

❑ Uses effective negotiation and process skills with intent to recognize and respect all involved

❑ Recognizes the value of acknowledging conflict and skillfully works through it

❑ Acknowledges feelings and reactions in others as well as self

❑ Knows and uses a variety of techniques for managing conflict

Skilled

❑ Seeks ways for all parties to be heard during conflict

❑ Acknowledges the basic facts of a conflict situation but may miss the subtle emotional issues

❑ Responds to conflict appropriately when it is pointed out by others

❑ Knows when conflict is brewing, tries to eventually resolve it

❑ Cares about others and their viewpoints but seems to care more about his or her own viewpoint

Unskilled

❑ Ignores or dismisses feelings — others' and own

❏ Acts defensively, critically and aggressively in conflict situations

❏ Tries to win at all costs

❏ Avoids conflict and leaves things unattended so long that it increases problems

❏ Yields to others, is too accommodating, and always wants to "keep the peace"

❏ Fails to find common ground or consider the viewpoints of others

Big Picture View

Conflict typically occurs between people when their goals, hopes, decisions, preferences or need for resources compete. When conflict management goes well, the opposing people or groups examine the choices before them. They take responsibility for their own behaviors, owning up to what they're doing that is helping or hindering the process. They seek resolutions that work for all. To effectively manage conflict, you must engage in communication that involves give and take and a willingness to listen to the thoughts and feelings of others. While such efforts might not always lead to the resolution of the conflict, at the very least these behaviors should lessen the conflict while increasing the respect among those involved.

Another goal of effective conflict management is to improve the relationship between the clashing parties, to free the relationship of any destructive threat, whether physical or emotional. Life is full of tensions and conflicts. The goal is not the absence of conflict but rather to become skilled at handling it well before conflicts escalate to an unmanageable level. Learning to listen well to others, to find common ground, and to give up the need to win or always be right are some of the ground rules of effective conflict management. These essential communication skills will help improve relationships at home and at work by preventing the buildup of resentment and enhancing honesty and openness between you and others.

Barriers to Effectiveness

❏ Being defensive; resistant to taking responsibility for own actions

❏ Easily flies off the handle — triggers to anger are close to the surface

❏ Conflict avoidant

❏ Looks for a winner and loser to every conflict — overly competitive

❏ Holds feelings in

❏ Poor negotiation skills

Quick Action Tips

1. **Do friends or colleagues get angry when you try to talk about a conflict and your reactions?** Do you use "I statements" which help you take responsibility for your own feelings, thoughts and opinions ("I am not happy with this plan," or "I am irritated that you borrowed my lawn mower without asking first.") Or do you use "you statements," telling others how they feel or what their problem is, or blaming them for your own negative experience? ("You created a terrible plan." Or, "It was irresponsible of you to borrow the lawn mower without asking first.") Learning how to send a clear and responsible "I message" regarding your thoughts and feelings will improve your ability to talk about a conflict. For example, a "you message" might be, "You are so mean and thoughtless, you really hurt me by doing that." Instead try an "I message": "I am very hurt and angry with your behavior and would like to discuss it with you." Think of a recent conflict and identify one or two "I statements" that might express your feelings or concerns. Ask a friend or colleague to hear your statements and judge if they are clear without assigning blame to the other person.

2. **Do friends or colleagues complain that you don't seem to be listening?** Good listening involves paying attention to a person's reactions, thoughts or opinions when they are speaking. Paraphrasing or acknowledging the other person's point of view demonstrates active listening. Empathic listening is tuning into the Feelings, Issues, Needs and Expectations (FINE) behind their words. Try summarizing the message of the next person who approaches you for a serious conversation or discussion. Here are a set of paraphrasing stems you can use when seeking to better listen to and understand another person: Are you saying... Let me see if I understand you... Sounds like you... If I understand you correctly.... For example: "If I understand you correctly, you are angry that I made the decision regarding the final budget numbers without first consulting you." In the competency (27) Listening Generously you will find many more tips for improving your listening skills.

3. **Do you let others run over you and take advantage of your good nature?** You do not have to respond to intrusive questioning or become everyone's best friend. You have the right to say no or to, at the very least, say, "I need more time to think about that." It is important to establish healthy boundaries by communicating your limits and expectations of others. If this is new behavior for you, practice can help. Identify a current low-stakes situation where you want to set limits, say no, or even change your mind about something you agreed to, perhaps under duress. Think through what you want to say. Try stating what you are willing or not willing to do, and see how it works.

4. **Have you left a trail of broken or damaged relationships?** Most people prefer friendly relations over animosity and strained relationships. It is emotionally intelli-

gent to focus on the positive aspects of your relationships and work to resolve problems in a timely fashion when they arise. This requires that you know yourself and know the hot buttons that trigger your feelings of hurt, anger or resentment. If you are critical of the behavior of friends or colleagues, try using "I messages" as described above in Quick Action Tip #1. Do you tend to be defensive? When a conflict or problem is being addressed, examine carefully your actions for any potential contribution to it and, where appropriate, accept responsibility. In this way you can begin to repair the damage in your relationships. The skill of apologizing and making amends is crucial to restoring relationships damaged by conflict. To whom do you owe an apology?

5. Do you insist upon having your own way? It is important in relationships to find common ground. Challenge yourself to see situations from different perspectives in order to find where you might be in agreement. Being able to say, "I can see your point," or, "I'm willing to talk about it some more," is an essential conflict management tool, especially if the conflict is with someone you care about and with whom you want to remain friendly. Learning to let yourself be influenced by, and open to, another person is another skill that helps in dealing with conflict. Next time you find yourself in conflict with someone close to you, invite that person to express himself or herself. Try suspending any internal chatter defending your position so you can hear and consider the opposing view more clearly. Listen closely and validate the other's position before expressing your own. Who do you know that you can try this with? Identify one person and take the initiative to ask, listen and confirm.

6. Do your nonverbal behaviors get you in trouble? If you have a tendency to roll your eyes, sigh heavily, cross your arms or point your finger, these behaviors are more likely to fuel a conflict rather than to diminish or resolve it. Whether or not you are aware of your own nonverbal behavior, start with observing others in conflict — in real life, the movies or on TV. List those behaviors that you think might antagonize or provoke a negative reaction. Next, mark which behaviors you think you might display at times. Who is someone you trust to give you good feedback? Ask that person to indicate which of these behaviors he has observed you doing. If in doubt, ask your closest friend or your partner — they will surely know! Compare your list with theirs. Stay open to the feedback. Then pick one behavior you wish to change and identify a more open and friendly behavior that you want to replace it with. Make a daily effort to avoid the negative behavior, replacing it with the open and friendly one.

7. Do you get hijacked by your emotions, speaking before thinking? Think of the conflicts that could have been avoided! "Count to ten," or "sleeping on it" can be useful tools. If you have a tendency to open your mouth and say something before you've had a good chance to think about it, then institute a practice for a month in which you will refrain from being the first person in a group to speak. Pause before speaking if you are in a tense situation. Taking time to reflect upon something or to sleep on it keeps you from making an impulsive decision or one you might regret. Impulsive behavior is often fueled by stress, so by better managing the situations in your life that contribute to stress you can help prevent impulsive behavior you'll later regret. See the competencies (38) Resilience, (49) Stamina and (50) Stress Hardy for ideas on how to reduce stress.

8. Don't know the difference between constructive and destructive conflict? The Center for Conflict Dynamics describes seven aspects of constructive conflict and eight aspects of destructive conflict. Look them over and ask yourself: Of the destructive responses, which are you most prone to make? And which of the constructive responses could you most benefit from employing? Then do it!

Seven constructive responses to conflict:

- Perceptive-taking: Put yourself in the other's shoes

- Creating solutions: Look for win-win opportunities

- Expressing emotions: Explain how you feel

- Reaching out: Show a desire to make amends and take responsibility

- Reflective thinking: Stop, reflect, think before acting

- Delay responding: Take a break when needed. Calm yourself

- Adapting: Be flexible

Eight destructive responses to conflict:

- Winning at all cost: Argue fiercely for your position

- Displaying anger: Use harsh, angry voice

- Demeaning others: Putting others down, being judgmental

- Retaliating: Getting even

- Avoiding: Backs away from conflict

- Yielding: Gives in, too accommodating.

- Hiding emotions: Hesitant to express self

- Self-criticizing: Lacks confidence, doubts self

9. Do you close down or withdraw when you feel hurt or angry? There are many models for giving feedback to a person when you feel hurt or concerned by their behavior. Here is a short outline of one example of how to frame such a message:

- Describe the problem behavior in the most objective terms, using only behavioral and factual descriptors (without judgment or criticism or interpretation)

- Indicate the impact this behavior had on you including your feelings
- If appropriate, request a change in behavior

Think of a situation that is causing or has caused conflict in your life. Describe your experience using this model. Read it in front of a mirror, then practice with a trusted friend or colleague. Get some feedback before actually delivering it in person.

Related Competencies

(2) Assertiveness   (7) *Effective* Confrontation   (15) *Active* Empathy

(25) Interpersonally Skillful   (27) Listening Generously

Learn from Experience

Work

❏ Ask to sit at the negotiation table with representatives of a labor union (if your organization has one).

❏ Take the lead in dealing with a dissatisfied customer.

Personal

❏ Volunteer as an assistant coach on your child's soccer team (or baseball, or basketball etc.). Offer to take the lead in handling the concerns of parents.

❏ Attend a course in mediation. Often they are offered through nonprofit organizations.

Resources

Books

Bolton, Robert. *People Skills: How to Assert Yourself, Listen to Others and Resolve Conflicts.* New York: Simon & Schuster, 1997, 2003.

Chapman, Gary and Jennifer Thomas. *The Five Languages of Apology: How to Experience Healing in All Your Relationships.* Chicago: Northfield Publishing, 2006.

Covey, Stephen. *Seven Habits of Highly Effective People.* New York: Free Press, 1989, 2004.

Dale Carnegie Training. *The Five Essential People Skills*. New York: Fireside, 2009.

Fisher, Roger, William Ury, and Bruce Patton. *Getting to Yes: Negotiating Agreements Without Giving In*. New York: Penguin Books, 2011.

McKay, Matthew, Martha Davis, and Patrick Fanning. *Messages: The Communication Skills Book*. Oakland, CA: New Harbinger Publications, 2009.

Conflict Guidebook series published by the Center for Creative Leadership, www.ccl.org (includes: *Managing Conflict with Peers*; *Managing Conflict with Direct Reports*; *Managing Conflict with Your Boss*).

Internet

The Ombuds Office at the University of Colorado, Boulder. "The Power of Apologies." www.ombuds.colorado.edu

Conflict 911: Resources on conflict management. http://conflict911.com/

Leadership Performance Systems: Offers a wide array of training in many areas: www.leadership-systems.com/

Harvard Business Review: "Leading Through Conflict." August 2006 Podcast with Mark Gerzon. www.hbr.org

Classes and training

Becoming Conflict Competent. Center for Conflict Dynamics; offers training and resource materials. www.conflictdynamics.org

Becoming a Conflict Competent Leader. Center for Creative Leadership web-based seminar. www.ccl.org

Franklin-Covey Training. Based on *Seven Habits of Highly Effective People*: "Seek First to Understand; Then Be Understood." www.franklincovey.com

Mediation Training Institute: Training, certification, and consulting in workplace conflict management and mediation. www.mediationworks.com

6

7 | EFFECTIVE CONFRONTATION

Definition

Addressing behaviors or decisions that are negatively impacting you or others in ways that are understood and lead to action

When we're angry with our enemies, we are giving them power over us: power over our sleep, our appetites, our blood pressure, our health, and our happiness. Our anger hurts them not at all, but it turns our own days and nights into turmoil.

—Dale Carnegie

Talented

❑ Anticipates situations that might result in tension, using effective interventions to avert potential problems

❑ Approaches confrontation boldly, with confidence, understanding the value of addressing a tense situation in a timely fashion

❑ Confronts in a specific, clear and descriptive way, avoiding generalities or vagueness

❑ Responds to being confronted with openness, honesty and a desire to understand the feelings of the confronter

❑ Combines effective feedback with empathy and active listening when confronting others

❑ Speaks up in a way that invites discussion of issues when disagreeing with others

Skilled

❑ Responds to conflict once it is detected, unless taken by surprise

❑ Understands another point of view better when confronting than when being confronted

❑ Manages own emotions and defensiveness during a confrontation

❑ Attempts to be clear when confronting unwanted behavior

❏ Notices when disagreements or conflict occur and participates in discussion of issues

Unskilled

❏ Complains or gossips about others rather than dealing honestly and directly with them

❏ Avoids confrontation, believing it will yield negative consequences

❏ Remains silent when frustrated or angry

❏ Challenges others in ways that people find offensive, aggressive or unpleasant (for example, critical or contemptuous)

❏ Waters down the message with too much explanation, rationalizing or softening of the message

Big Picture View

Effective confrontation is demonstrated by standing up for your rights or confronting someone when they have done something harmful or hurtful, and doing so in a way that achieves positive change with little or no damage to the relationship. When promises are broken, commitments missed, or you are treated rudely it is important to find a way to hold the other person accountable and to express your feelings by giving effective feedback. Effective confrontation can help to restore harmony and balance in your relationships and to avoid future problems caused by the buildup of unresolved conflict. Social scientists have long recognized that people who effectively confront damaging behavior experience more relationship satisfaction. Effective confrontation, a form of honesty, stimulates communication, promotes personal growth in each individual and increases the affection and respect between people.

The countless ways to go wrong when confronting someone generally fall into two categories: avoiding it (too passive) or overdoing it (too aggressive). Effective confrontation is a skill that develops over time and with practice. Courses in assertiveness, conflict resolution, and the art of giving useful feedback provide many tools that contribute to effective confrontation.

Barriers to Effectiveness

❏ A hot temper

❏ Conflict avoidance

❏ Tendency to stew

❏ Fear of negative reprisals

❏ Inability to tune in to others and understand their points of view

❏ Desire to win or get one's own way

❏ Complaining or gossiping

❏ Passive-aggressive behavior tendencies

Quick Action Tips

1. Do you like winning at all costs? The problem with winning is that someone has to lose. And that someone might not like working in the future with the person who contributed to their losing. An effective confrontation attempts three important goals:

- Achieve the desired outcome
- with the least damage to the relationship and
- with the least damage to the other person's self esteem

This can be accomplished by:

- Approaching each confrontation with the intent to understand the other person's perspective
- Employing active listening — a skill that involves paraphrasing or stating the main points made by the other person. Advanced levels of active listening include validating a person's experience (understand and state why they might feel that way, whether you agree or not). At the most advanced level you are able to empathize with that person by putting yourself in their position and imagining their feelings and emotions.
- Responsibly sharing your own feelings without criticizing, judging or interpreting the other's point of view. Keep your comments brief, factual and descriptive, without blaming the other person.

2. Are you aware when you feel offended, hurt or angry? Being aware of your internal state of mind and emotions is essential to successful confrontation. Without clear awareness of what you are experiencing, your ability to openly and appropriately share your feelings with another person is difficult if not impossible. Additionally, repressing feelings of anger, hurt or frustration can result in physical problems such as insomnia, headaches, anxiety, tension and other stress-related problems. Develop insight into your internal state of mind by keeping a stress management and emotional reaction journal. For a week, list any event that causes you to feel a strong emotion, positive or negative, but especially when offended, hurt or angry. What about that event led to your emotional response? How did you handle your reaction? Looking back, what might you have said in the actual situation to better accept responsibility for your own feelings? Consider the benefits of seeking out the other person or persons involved and, when appropriate, sharing your reactions with them.

3. How are your listening skills? Confronting others effectively requires that you also listen to them. Although your goal is to communicate how their behavior is affecting you, it can be very helpful to tune in to their thoughts, feelings and reactions. Understanding their perspective can help move the discussion toward a productive conclusion. If someone confronts you, you also will need to listen carefully to that person's concerns, paraphrasing or stating back to them the main points you hear them saying. This is an excellent skill to have, practice and strengthen. It not only offers greater understanding of those around you and their concerns, it also forces you to slow down to really hear the other person, and it lets that person know you heard what they are trying to tell you. Listening carefully and sincerely to another is a simple yet profound way in which you can contribute to solving problems between yourself and others.

4. Don't know where to start an effective confrontation? The first three Quick Action Tips lay out important suggestions for undertaking an effective confrontation. They are summarized below in a step-by-step process for addressing a bothersome situation with another person rather than allowing it to fester.

1. Clarify the outcome you wish to accomplish as a result of the confrontation or conversation you are contemplating. What is your positive intention? Start there.

2. Be clear and specific about the problem behavior. Describe the behavior, avoiding judgments, opinions and blame.

3. Describe the impact the behavior had on you, others or the situation in which it occurred.

4. Be sure to take responsibility for your feelings by using "I" messages (I feel ... , I was hurt, I'm confused, etc.)

5. Ask for a change in behavior or for the other person's ideas about how to reach a meaningful solution to the problem.

6. Emphasize the benefits of making the requested changes to the relationship between the two of you.

These steps also incorporate the EQ competencies of (2) Assertiveness, (27) Listening Generously and (41) Self-Awareness, so check these competencies for additional ideas.

5. Do you have trouble achieving common ground? To successfully move a confrontation forward, listen to what matters to each person. Identify and clarify outcomes acceptable to all. Find the key points that you and others agree upon and learn to negotiate through the differences. Make it a point to ask, "If we successfully work through our differences what would that look like? What do you see as an acceptable outcome for us?" Stephen Covey's fourth habit in his book *The Seven Habits of Highly Effective People* is "seek first to understand, then be understood." Identify a current situation involving differences. Practice looking for common ground, an outcome important to all. Try building on that to reach agreement.

6. Do you get hot during a confrontation? Whether or not you are known as a hothead or someone who cannot maintain his or her cool during difficult situations, it will benefit you to learn effective ways of managing your emotions. Assertiveness training or a stress management course can provide some guidance. Relaxation training, meditation, anger management and yoga are especially helpful for those who routinely lose their tempers. Research conclusively demonstrates that those who engage in routine exercise several times a week have reduced stress and anger levels. The important thing here is to recognize any tendency to over-react and then to do something about it for your sake and for others in your life.

7. Often find you feel insulted by others? Sometimes this is about being hypersensitive and seeing offense where none is intended. If this is true for you, then ask yourself, "What evidence supports my belief that others intend to be offensive toward me?" Check out your assumptions (or beliefs that you have not yet confirmed) rather than immediately acting on them. Approach the person involved and ask if you can have a few minutes of their time. Ask, "May I check something out with you? I want to make sure I understood you what you said." Be sure to listen to their response and avoid the temptation to disagree with their perception of what was said or done. What you may learn is that their intention was different from what their words suggested, and much more positive. Doing a reality check can help clear the air by learning if you misheard the comment or misjudged their intention. A field of psychology that has proven to be particularly helpful is called Cognitive Behavioral Psychology (CBT). Its approach rests on challenging irrational beliefs that cause self-defeating emotions and behavior, similar to the example above. If you have received feedback that you sometimes overreact to a situation, or are behaving irrationally, it would be helpful to check out CBT resources.

Related Competencies

(2) Assertiveness   (6) Conflict Management   (15) *Active* Empathy

(18) Impulse Control   (27) Listening Generously   (34) Perspective-Taking

(36) Reframing   (41) Self-Awareness

Learn from Experience

Work

❏ Have you had a showdown or avoided being honest with someone at work? Write out what you want to say using a clear and concise description of that person's behavior, how it has affected you and your request for a change. Consider using this as a preparation for a conversation with that person.

❏ Serve on a task force in your organization requiring you to assess the viewpoints of various constituencies and find solutions to competing agendas.

❏ Volunteer to work with HR in implementing or strengthening a sexual harassment training module to include how to effectively confront inappropriate behavior.

Personal

❏ Take a course or training in relationship enrichment. Such courses emphasize honest communication and techniques for providing feedback in emotionally charged situations.

❏ Look for opportunities to serve on a local nonprofit board, a committee in your community, or a political endeavor. All will develop your skills in finding common ground and learning to confront others in respectful ways.

❏ Check out the Guardian Ad Litem program in your community: a guardian ad litem is appointed by the court to protect the interests of a minor or a disabled adult in situations requiring legal intervention. There would be plenty of opportunity to develop a number of skills including effective confrontation skills in this role.

Resources

Books

Burns, David. *The Feeling Good Handbook*. New York: Penguin Books, 1999.

Covey, Stephen. *The Seven Habits of Highly Effective People*. New York: Simon and Schuster, 2004.

Davis, Martha, Elizabeth Eshelman, and Matthew McKay. *The Relaxation and Stress Reduction Workbook*. Oakland, CA: New Harbinger Publications, 2000.

Fisher, Roger, William Ury, and Bruce Patton. *Getting to Yes: Negotiating Agreement Without Giving In*. New York: Penguin Books, 1991.

Mckay, Matthew, Martha Davis, and Patrick Fanning. *Messages: The Communication Skills Book*, Oakland, CA: New Harbinger Publications, 2009.

Patterson, Kerry, Joseph Grenny, Ron McMillan, and Al Switzler. *Crucial Confrontations: Tools for Resolving Broken Promises, Violated Expectations, and Bad Behavior*. New York: McGraw-Hill, 2005.

Patterson, Kerry, Joseph Grenny, Ron McMillan, and Al Switzler. *Crucial Conversations: Tools for Talking When Stakes are High*. New York: McGraw-Hill, 2002.

Stone, Douglas, Bruce Patton, Shiela Heen. *Difficult Conversations: How to Discuss What Matters Most*. New York: Penguin Books, 1999.

Feedback Guidebooks from The Center for Creative Leadership: www.ccl.org

- *Feedback That Works: How to Build and Deliver Your Message* by Sloan R. Weitzel

- *Giving Feedback to Subordinates* by Raoul J. Buron and Dana McDonald-Mann

- *Ongoing Feedback: How to Get It, How to Use It* by Karen Kirkland and Sam Manoogian

Internet

Harvard Business Review: "How to Overcome Communications Fear" blog by J.D. Schramm. September 2010. www.hbr.org

Classes and training

American Management Association: Research conflict management and confrontation training. www.amanet.org

Career Builder Institute Training Programs: Investigate their offerings on Conflict and Confrontation: www.careerbuilderinstitute.com

Fred Pryor Training Seminars: Search on subjects such as dealing with difficult people, stress management, dealing with emotions in the workplace. www.pryor.com

7

8   CONGRUENCE

Definition

Behaving in ways consistent with your feelings, values, and attitudes as demonstrated by decisions and actions; walking your talk

Only the truth of who you are, if realized, will set you free.

—Eckhart Tolle

Talented

❑ Gives the sense of being present in the moment and emotionally focused on the matter at hand

❑ Knows and acts in accordance with deeply held values

❑ Communicates powerfully by aligning words, nonverbal and emotional expression

❑ Expresses underlying ideas, attitudes and feelings consistently across audiences even when to do so is inconvenient

❑ Lives life in an emotionally honest and consistent way; what you see is what you get

Skilled

❑ Aligns statements and actions

❑ Keeps verbal and nonverbal messages in sync most of the time

❑ Expresses underlying values, attitudes and feelings consistently across audiences when convenient to do so

❑ Realizes when the alignment between intentions and outcome aren't quite what was hoped for

Unskilled

❑ Appears insincere or easily distracted while talking to others

❑ Says one thing and does another

❏ Confuses others by words, nonverbal cues, and emotional expressions not matching

❏ Makes personal decisions that suggest values and preferences are unclear or unimportant

❏ Says what people want to hear even if bending the truth

Big Picture View

Personal congruence develops over time as you reflect on and clarify key values and beliefs and then use those to make decisions and to set goals for how you live your life. Congruence isn't always easy, since there can be many forces that pull you away from your own values, beliefs and goals. These include what colleagues and loved ones want you to do, pressures from society and the media, opportunities for money and fame, and lack of confidence in your own abilities. Congruence between what you believe and how you live your life leads to being perceived as trustworthy, honest, and reliable. The alignment of personal values, beliefs and goals with the choices you make in life can give extra power and conviction to your life and leadership. On the other hand, dissatisfaction with life, or stress or personal turmoil, may be an indication that you aren't living a congruent life. In the fast pace of life, personal misalignment can sneak up on you. Those who value congruence use personal turmoil as a wake-up call to get back in touch with what matters most and to use that as a personal compass to realign actions.

Barriers to Effectiveness

❏ Fear of how others may react if you were true to yourself

❏ Lack of self-knowledge and values

❏ Need to impress others may cause overdoing behaviors

❏ Taking the easy route rather than remaining true to self

❏ Lack of self-confidence

Quick Action Tips

1. Catch yourself saying something you don't truly mean? What are your top five personal values and your top five professional values. Under what circumstances do you act at odds with your beliefs and values? To say things you don't believe generally leads to a loss of credibility at some point down the road. What does it cost you to be true to your values and beliefs? What are the consequences or personal costs of not being true to your values? Consider the coming week and plan how to remain true to your beliefs in the situations

that may be most challenging.

2. Are you expecting others to meet standards that you don't follow? Do you preach quality and then take shortcuts yourself? Criticize others for lack of commitment and then leave early on Friday through the back door? Urge your kids to do their homework before checking in with their friends on Facebook while you check your smartphone during dinner? Co-workers and family are quick to notice when your actions and what you expect of them are incongruent. If you aren't living the standards you ask of others, make a few concrete changes to your own behavior.

3. Others don't believe what you say? People will react to your nonverbal expressions and visible emotions in spite of the words you say if you lack a consistent message. Ask for feedback when you present to a group or team about what they see and whether it fits with your verbal message. If you are enthused about a new quality-control program at work, do your tone of voice, facial expressions, word choice and gestures convey positive energy? Does your audience believe you are supportive of the new program? Practice a presentation ahead of time and ask for suggestions about what you might do to enhance your credibility. We all tend to get comfortable with a personal range of emotional expression, so you may need to practice using more emphasis. Identify someone who shows a wider range of emotions and enthusiasm. What actions, behaviors and nonverbal signs do they use to add credence or punch to their words? Try some of them in low-risk situations to increase your comfort with a wider variety of expression.

4. Do others assume all is well with you when you don't feel as satisfied as you once did? Perhaps you have changed over the last several years without realizing it. A role that was once satisfying to you is now old hat, or interests you once had are calling to you in a new way. Or maybe your job has become all-consuming at the expense of your personal interests and life. Perhaps you are moving into a new stage of your life. If so, now is the time to look at how satisfied you are in each of life's major arenas: work, family, hobbies, interests, volunteering, spiritual, and friends. What does success in the whole picture look like to you? How can you live a more congruent and satisfying life in all you do? Replacing old habits or activities with ones that are more personally satisfying can make all the difference in your happiness.

5. Do you say one thing and then do another? Are you telling direct reports that you have an open-door policy and then not turning away from your computer when someone comes into your office? Do you tell your son you love him, but never seem to get home in time for his soccer game? Giving incongruent messages to those around you can sometimes happen without full awareness (you really may mean well, but you get caught up in the pressures of the day). People on the receiving end, however, are usually more interested in what you actually do. Lack of consistency and poor follow-through with commitments leads to distrust and disappointment by those who may mean the most to you and perhaps help you succeed. Examine the commitments and promises you make to be sure you are willing to stand behind your word. Don't make promises you can't keep. Sometimes you may have good intentions, such as, "I love my kids and want them to do well, so I push them hard when they get poor grades to encourage them to do better." Or, "I tell my direct reports how to handle a challenge so they will succeed." Although your intentions may be positive, your impact may not be what you hoped for. Your kids may feel criticized and your direct reports may feel micromanaged. Ask for feedback from those around you to help you recognize if you need to own up to inconsistent behavior or change your behavior to have the impact you want.

6. Afraid that speaking from the heart could cost you your job, your friends, or your life partner? Sometimes we all hold back feelings or thoughts that others close to us might not like. You may not want to jeopardize people and positions that are important to you. And certainly it is wise to reflect how to best express strong emotions or concerns rather than to blurt them out. At the same time, if you hold back too often or rarely get around to sharing ongoing concerns, differences of opinion or strong feelings, then you may find yourself living a lie. If this sounds like you, then make a list of important issues or people in your life. How are you feeling about them — honestly? Write what you might say in language that:

- Describes specifically what you are reacting to in nonjudgmental behavioral words
- Expresses the feelings or concerns you have including your reluctance to speak up if appropriate
- Asks for what you want or don't want
- Invites discussion

An example might be if your spouse spends more than he or she makes and has ongoing credit charges. You might say, "I've noticed our credit card balance has grown over the last year to an amount that has me worried. I have been reluctant to speak up because I know you work hard, but I would like for us to come up with a strategy to pay off the balance by the end of the year. What do you think?"

If you are reluctant to take a first step to communicate something that matters to you, consider consulting a close friend, coach or counselor.

7. Living the life you intend? People are busy; spare time is scarce. But a worthwhile exercise is sorting through a list of values (check the Internet for such lists), choosing the five to seven that are most important to you. Then consider what two to four behaviors you can do that would reflect each value. How does your customary behavior compare? Choose one important value and practice behaviors that fit that value this week.

Related Competencies

(3) Authenticity   (9) Constructive Discontent

(11) Emotional Expression   (12) Emotional Maturity   (23) Integrity

(41) Self-Awareness   (43) Self-Disclosure

Learn from Experience

Work

❑ Champion an organizational change where you must present a consistent message to various departments and levels within the organization. Speak from the heart and listen sincerely to concerns.

❑ If you find yourself distracted by personal concerns during the workday, keep a list of what you need to do later and refocus on the issue at hand. Others maybe benefit from your positive energy if you do so.

Personal

❑ Talk with your spouse or close friend about what you want to do in retirement. What will make that time in your life meaningful?

❑ Volunteer with an organization that fits with your values

Resources

Books

Cloud, Henry. *Integrity: The Courage to Meet the Demands of Reality.* New York: Harper Paperbacks, 2009.

Kegan, Robert, and Lisa Laskow. *How the Way We Talk Can Change the Way We Work.* San Francisco: Jossey-Bass, 2001.

Rogers, Carl, and Barry Stevens. *Person to Person: The Problem of Being Human.* London: Souvenir Press, 1994.

Internet

Chandler Leadership and Development. CoreValue training. http://www.corevaluetraining.com/

Classes and training

Qualifying.org. Choice points certification program. www.qualifying.org

Movies

"Forrest Gump," Paramount Pictures, 1994.

9   CONSTRUCTIVE DISCONTENT

Definition

Expressing dissatisfaction, frustration or displeasure in a way that others can hear and respond to; finding a creative way to bridge differences

Those who expect moments of change to be comfortable and free of discontent have not learned their history.

— Joan Wallach Scott

Talented

❏ Articulates in nonjudgmental ways the assumptions, needs, and desired outcomes of all sides in a situation where discontent is present

❏ Uses questions to explore possible solutions

❏ Identifies discontent that may exist in a situation and helps all parties involved to share feelings, aspirations, and expectations

❏ Demonstrates patience and calm with discontent while working to find a solution

❏ Channels energy from dissatisfaction toward creating new options

❏ When discontent is evident, expresses optimism that a constructive outcome can be found

Skilled

❏ Encourages the group to work together to find a constructive solution

❏ Suggests ground rules for productive discussions when participants are discontent

❏ Invites stakeholders to discuss possible creative options

❏ Persists in spite of personal discomfort dealing with discontent for prolonged periods of time

❏ Shares own assumptions and perspectives openly

Unskilled

❏ Uses judgmental and emotional terms

❏ Fails to facilitate a discussion, especially where emotions are running hot

❏ Communicates that discomfort when working toward goals is inevitable so "just live with it"

❏ Behaves in ways that trigger more emotional reactions from others

❏ Ignores or fails to respond to what people need

❏ Assumes that discontent is not resolvable so leaves it alone

Big Picture View

If you pull a rubber band between two points, the energy in the band can be used in a variety of way — to pop the person next to you snoring in the movies, perhaps, or to motorize a small child's toy. The energy builds up because the band is stretched between two points. By parallel, psychological energy builds up when something is stretched between two points: differences in goals, differences in visions about how to move forward, or just plain differences in the way something is seen. That tension is the psychological discontent you feel when there is pull between two or more situations. The associated energy can be used constructively or not so constructively. The emotionally intelligent response is to use that energy to push for more and better ideas, constructively resolving the points of difference.

For some individuals, this discontent may feel destructive, annoying, or at least uncomfortable, and may seem like a barrier to productive problem-solving. The tension created by the discontent, however, can be a source of creativity. Individuals who consciously acknowledge their differences and work together to bridge the tension created by those differences create opportunities. To do so requires a willingness to work with competing views. Ignoring discontent can lead to relationship troubles, so it is generally worth the time required to reach out and talk about the sources of discontent and attempt to identify ways to work constructively together. When this is the approach taken, discontent can produce ideas and improved quality that would otherwise not have been achieved.

Barriers to Effectiveness

❏ Presumptive thinking

❏ Rigidity

❏ Inability to express emotions in constructive ways

❏ Right or wrong mindset

❏ Aggressive competition

❏ Pessimism

❏ Unwillingness to acknowledge that the discontent is present and is a possible source of energy for productive outcomes

❏ Inability to see value in discontent

Quick Action Tips

1. Confused about the difference between being judgmental and nonjudgmental? In discontent, emotions are not always immediately apparent. Often the issues that prompt the discontent are more evident in the language you use or hear others use. Judgmental statements such as "you are ..." or "you did ..." rather than "I sense that ..." or "I observed ..." can accelerate emotional reactions. By using statements such as, "When I asked you about that, I sensed that you were very irritated," you can open discussions to examine the discomfort. Another example is, "I'm trying to understand your position, and a couple of things are unclear to me. Can we explore these things?" Most of the time when an individual feels judged and thinks that there is no recourse, he or she will come out fighting. By framing observations with "I sense," or, "It seems to me," or, "I'm confused about," you are being more tentative and less declarative, thereby reducing the emotional heat. This opens up a way to manage the different views more productively. Discontent does not need to be a source of negative interactions, but getting to the constructive use of the discontent is much less likely if people feel judged.

2. Unsure how to use your emotions related to dissatisfaction or frustration with what is happening? Emotions contain information that can be useful. When you have an emotional response, consider what your emotions are conveying. For example, anger can stem from a number of things, but some common reasons for anger include an agreement that has been breached, a barrier has unfairly put in your way of achieving a goal, or one of your key principles or values has been violated. Discontent generally is accompanied by a general feeling of tension, ambivalence, anticipation and confusion. Exploring a deeper layer of meaning to your discontent sometimes leads to finding a solution to the issue. Discontent often is rooted in differences of perspective, expectations, aspirations or preferred outcomes. If so, identify differences and the associated reactions of those involved. Ask questions such as, "What is your perspective about this?" "What are your thoughts for managing the differences we have discussed?" "How might we reduce the frustration you are feeling by a degree or two?"

3. Not sure how to best leverage discontent when it emerges? Often in situations where individuals are experiencing frustration and dissatisfaction with a process, they will stop offering productive ideas, especially if they feel no progress is being made. You can be helpful at this point if you keep the discussion going with open-ended questions. A yes or no question is a dead-end — especially in conflict conversations, because these questions often sound adversarial. Turn yes or no questions into facilitative questions by asking, "Tell me more about that," or, "I'd like to understand about those assumptions or the information you are using." These kinds of questions are designed to facilitate exploring information, perspectives, and possible solutions. Constructive discontent begins with the proposition that the source of the discontent may be quite valuable to all involved and that with proper facilitation better answers or more suitable understanding can be achieved.

4. Does discontent keep you from shifting perspectives? Begin by asking, "What is the desired outcome of this interaction?" If you are not clear that you want the other individual to feel as satisfied as you, then a solution is unlikely to be found. In short, you have to begin with the end in mind even when working in an interaction with discontent. If the individuals involved simply can't find any common ground and yet they must work with each other, then the most constructive "end" is to create a mechanism for interaction that keeps emotions neutral and the focus on finding ways to work collaboratively. For example, if you are working with an individual whose personal behavior is totally unacceptable to you, yet they are fully competent in their work, then create ways to work with the capabilities the person brings to the table. The discontent of having to work with someone you find objectionable in their personal behavior should not keep you from doing your best.

5. Tend to push your ideas and fail to grasp the ideas of others? Constructive discontent is best used when all parties involved feel heard and that their perspectives are valued. Whether you are a leader of the group or a group member, you can use active paraphrasing to create the conditions in which individuals feel heard and valued. The goal of constructive discontent is to use the energy created by the discontent to find better ideas. If discontent exists, then those involved really care about the situation and have ideas about how things could be better or more effective. That positive intent of pursuing an ideal can be used to find a way to work with two approaches. Ignoring this basic element of discontent will result in a stalemate of tension that drives individuals away from the situation rather than engaging in finding a workable outcome. By paraphrasing what you are hearing and seeing, and inquiring about how people are feeling and how they would like to work together, this tension can be used creatively.

6. Have difficulty seeing things from different perspectives? Experiment with different points of view. Ask yourself how another stakeholder might see the same situation (or idea or object) that you're looking at and about which you are experiencing some discontent. Ask yourself how this might look in 10 years, or in 100 years. Break the areas of difference between you and others down into smaller components and examine just one from multiple angles. For example, if the difference is something tangible, then you might use a copier or computer to enlarge small components or shrink big ones. Make a collage to visibly show different perspectives about a situation where discontent is being experienced.

7. Impatient with trying new approaches? Discontent may both generate and be generated by new approaches. If you are impatient with change, then it may work against creative management of the issue at hand. Experimentation can lead to new information, but you need to be open to the opportunities that might emerge. When things don't go as expected, angst and frustration often follow. Possibilities that are promising but less obvious may be overlooked. Pausing, stepping back and taking a different view of things can open the door to new possibilities. The ice cream cone emerged in just such a circumstance. Temperatures were so hot at the 1904 World's Fair that a stall selling ice cream was quickly running out of dishes. The stall next door, offering wafer thin waffles from Persia, couldn't give them away. The vendors were able to take a different view of their products and, by rolling the thin waffles into cones, introduced the first ice cream cones.

8. Do you discount your feelings of discontent, hoping they will go away? You might be suffering from magical thinking or conflict avoidance. Magical thinking is believing that something will happen without any real effort on your part. This is normal thinking in children, but it is self-defeating in adults. Constructive discontent is a prompt to use innovative or creative thinking strategies. If you are feeling stymied by a situation where you think there could be a better approach, then try to consider how you can use your discomfort in in a productive way. It may require reframing the issue, soliciting advice or brainstorming strategies to keep the focus on constructive courses of action. Acknowledge your feelings of dissatisfaction and lack of comfort with how things are going to others involved without blaming them. Perhaps they also are not as satisfied with the present direction as you thought they were. Together reconsider assumptions, opportunities and options. Prioritize what is most important to all concerned. Identify more possibilities until one that is acceptable to all is found.

Related Competencies

(10) Creativity   (17) Group Savvy   (20) Influencing Others

(22) Insightfulness   (27) Listening Generously   (30) Openness to Others

(34) Perspective-Taking   (35) Reframing

Learn from Experience

Work

❏ Work with an unhappy customer to find a solution to his or her complaint.

❏ Ask a peer who manages conflict very well to share his or her strategies for finding constructive answers.

❏ Identify a mentor who is effective at keeping a positive psychological climate around him or her during difficult times; ask how they do it.

Personal

❏ Volunteer to serve on a community board which handles specific agency or service problems.

❏ Seek out community mediation training.

Resources

Books

Adams, James. *Conceptual Blockbusting: A Guide to Better Ideas.* Cambridge, MA: Perseus Books, 2001.

Buzan, Tony. *The Power of Creative Intelligence: Ten Ways to Tap Into Your Creative Genius.* London: Thorsons, 2001.

Claxton, Guy, and Bill Lucas. *The Creative Thinking Plan: How to Generate Ideas and Solve Problems in Your Work and Life.* London: BBC Books, 2007.

De Bono, Edward. *Lateral Thinking: A Textbook of Creativity.* London: Penguin Books, 1990.

Harper, Gary. *The Joy of Conflict Resolution: Transforming Victims, Villains, and Heroes in the Workplace and at Home.* Gabriola Island, BC: New Society Publishers, 2004.

Internet

VoiceAmerica.com. "Constructive Discontent: Rocking the Boat – Moving Ahead." February 23, 2011. Hosted by Esther Orioli.

Classes and training

American Management Association. "Responding to Conflict: Strategies for Improved Communication." For this and other training courses: www.amanet.org

10 CREATIVITY

Definition

Generating, envisioning and getting excited about ideas that depart radically from current thinking

"Creativity comes from trust. Trust your instincts. And never hope more than you work."

Rita Mae Brown

Talented

❑ Generates multiple original ideas

❑ Sees connections, perspectives and possibilities others don't, or sooner than most

❑ Connects seemingly unconnected or contradictory ideas in ways that eventually make sense

❑ Goes against the grain to consider and propose untried or unconventional approaches

❑ Translates novel thinking into broadly understandable and compelling concepts

❑ Advocates for and supports innovation in the organization

Skilled

❑ Builds on the novel ideas of others more often than initiates new ideas from scratch

❑ Accurately tracks complexity but may not always see connections or relevance

❑ Is open to but does not readily seek novel approaches

❑ Takes risks, but cautiously

❑ Responds favorably to others who are innovative

Unskilled

❏ Struggles to think beyond what already exists

❏ Fails to see new opportunities

❏ Seems to miss or ignore underlying complexity of situations or how things connect

❏ Favors more conventional solutions

❏ Appears impatient with experimentation

Big Picture View

Creativity blends your experiences, the novel ideas that emerge from these experiences and your strategies for applying them. Creativity seems to be one of those characteristics that rely more on our hard wiring than others. And some people embrace and demonstrate creativity more readily than others. But for most, there is untapped potential that is available to be developed. You can strengthen and stretch your creative thinking by exercising it. Creativity, along with strategic thinking, intuition and innovative problem-solving, are thought to be right-brain functions. So, if you strengthen any one of them, you build capacity among the others.

Barriers to Effectiveness

❏ Overly analytical, concrete or linear in your thinking

❏ Anxiety

❏ Creature of habit, including ways in which you see the world

❏ Prefers to stick with what you know or are comfortable with

❏ Underestimating your ability to think creatively; assuming others are more creative

❏ Expediency — choosing the first idea generated

Quick Action Tips

1. **Stuck in a rut using tried and true approaches to solving problems?** A tendency to conform, to follow the rules or maintain the status quo — all hamper creative breakthrough. Do you find yourself saying, or agreeing with others when they say, "We've always done it this way?" Exercise your flexibility muscle and step out of your comfort zone. Do things differently. Take an everyday habit and turn it on its head, like beginning the day with dinner and ending it with

breakfast. Consider using outdoor furniture inside. Cook more regularly if you usually don't. Explore new and unusual spices that you've never used. Use the smells and tastes to guide you. Sign up for a course at your local community college in a subject that differs from your usual interests.

2. Have difficulty seeing things from different perspectives? Experiment with different points of view. Ask yourself how another stakeholder might see the same situation (or idea, or object) that you're looking at. Ask yourself how this might look a year from now, in 100 years, from a different country or generation, or using different assumptions or information. Break this entity down into smaller components and examine just one component from multiple angles. For example, use a copier or computer to enlarge small objects and shrink big ones. Make a collage. Change or remove one factor and take a fresh look.

3. Find it hard to visualize what is not there? Don't worry, many people do. Practice taking things apart and reassembling them, differently than before. Consider how two or more ideas might relate and can be combined, how two or more processes or features from different products might work together. Take a card or board game and change the rules. Change them again.

4. Quick to see how an idea won't work? Are you quicker to assume that a novel idea won't work than to assume that there must be a way to make it work? Do you recognize the power of your assumptions? Become aware of which of your assumptions fosters creativity. Play the "what if" game. Give yourself permission to think freely. Practice keeping ideas alive rather than shutting them down with, "That can't work," or, "That's impractical." If an idea seems silly, then it might very well be. But digging for silly responses pushes you to think with your right brain, the seat of creativity. Tap into your curiosity, optimism or flexibility to stretch your thinking. Apply that thinking to planning a vacation similar to the one you dreamed of as a child but never experienced. Offer to set up a fun experience that abandons the ordinary for your team at work, a group of friends or your family. Or challenge yourself to identify several different ways to tackle a project, at home or at work. Pass on the first idea that occurs to you, and try out the second or third idea.

5. Impatient with or fearful of trying new approaches? Experimentation can lead to new information, but you need to be open to the opportunities that might emerge. When things don't go as expected, angst and frustration often follow. So much so that less obvious, but promising, possibilities can be overlooked. Remind yourself that being creative requires taking risks. Risk, by definition, involves the potential for mistakes, failure and even looking foolish. Pause, step back and take a different view of things. It can open the door to new possibilities. The ice cream cone emerged in just a circumstance. Temperatures were so hot at the 1904 World's Fair that a stall selling ice cream was quickly running out of dishes. The stall next door, offering freshly baked wafer thin waffles from Persia, couldn't give them away. Both vendors were sweltering and panicking when one came up with the idea of rolling the waffles into cone shapes and popping the ice cream on top. More than 100 years later we're still licking ice cream that melts down the side of our cones! Next time things don't go as planned, look for less obvious ways to accomplish what you're doing and for the potential benefits. For example, a team was on deck to present the plan for a product launch to senior leadership when the lead presenter got stuck at an airport. The presentation was reconfigured to focus on implementation instead of expected results and to involve the leadership team in planning it. This approach not only introduced a more effective collaboration, it also exposed potential problems in time to prevent them.

6. Do you tend to take things at face value and not look beyond what is obvious? Both conscious and unconscious assumptions can limit creative thinking. Challenge the assumptions you know about and uncover others that you are only barely aware of. Pick a topic and jot down two or three assumptions you already have about this subject. Now, using the Internet, research the topic. Find at least three new facets about this topic that you didn't know. How does this new information affect your assumptions? Play a game where you use a search engine to explore a topic, but, instead of following the links based on related information, take the first letter of the link and pursue another topic beginning with that letter. See what random and amusing sites you find.

7. Hard to keep track of all the moving parts in a complex situation? Complexity is inherently challenging and, sometimes, confusing. Like a chess game, dealing with complexity requires that you anticipate others' needs and reactions, potential future moves, and alternative strategies. In fact, learning chess and improving your game will exercise the very thought processes that are involved in managing complexity. Other games of strategy also provide you with opportunities to stretch your thinking, to look for underlying patterns and to consider how choices might play out.

8. Don't have the time to be creative? The over-worked and over-stressed person finds it particularly difficult to think objectively, much less creatively. Stress, especially working under tight time pressures, reduces the quality of all mental processes. It's counter-intuitive, if all you can think about is the looming deadline, but this is when taking a brief time out can really help. Changing your focus or internal (physiological) state reduces stress, improves energy and outlook, and refreshes your perspective. Have you ever had the experience of working on something so hard that you became blocked in your efforts? Sure, we all have. The common recommendation of walking away offers a gift of wisdom. Invariably, upon returning, ideas and answers emerge, almost magically. Can you spare five minutes? Sure you can! Take a walk around the building — inside or out. Change your location. Take up thinking in a different space. Do you have an iPod, smartphone or some other music source with headphones? Change your state with music that makes you more productive. Talk with someone about what you're working on, if you're more extroverted. Sit quietly and concentrate on your breathing for a few minutes if you're more introverted.

9. Do you over-rely on logic? Logical thinking is a left-brain function, while creative thinking is thought to take place in the right brain. That's why many groups start their brainstorming by first engaging in playful activity or relaxation. It loosens them up and helps them to "get out of their heads," so to speak. What do you do to relax or become more playful? Try one or more of those activities the next time you're seeking creativity. Or you might read something humorous, or doodle or draw, or write an affectionate tribute to someone you love or appreciate, or listen to a brief musical interlude.

Related Competencies

(16) Flexibility   (22) Insightfulness   (26) Intuition

(34) Perspective-Taking   (36) Reframing

Learn from Experience

Work

❏ Lead a task force charged with solving a business problem in an unrelated field or area of expertise.

❏ Renovate or redesign a workspace.

❏ Manage a new service or product from concept to marketplace.

❏ Seek out opportunities to work on short-term projects with individuals who are very different from you.

Personal

Start up something small that is new or hasn't been tried before where adjusting to new information is crucial. Some examples:

- Organize a neighborhood association or committee
- Initiate a group supporting a cause
- Lead a committee charged with a new initiative
- Create a process for collecting, storing and/or using information
- Develop something entirely new that has commercial potential

Resources

Books

Von Oech, Roger. *A Whack on the Side of the Head: How You Can Be More Creative*. New York: Business Plus, 2008. There also is an associated pack of cards, the "Creative Whack Pack."

Gryskiewicz, Stan, and Sylvester Taylor. *Making Creativity Practical: Innovation That Gets Results*. Greensboro, NC: Center for Creative Leadership, 2003.

De Bono, Edward. *Six Thinking Hats*. New York: Back Bay Books, 1999.

Cameron, Julia. *The Artist's Way*. New York: Tarcher, 10th edition, 2002.

Michalko, Michael. *Thinkertoys*. Berkeley, California: Ten Speed Press, 2006.

Internet

The Artist's Way. www.theartistsway.com

Classes and training

Cornell University eLearning site. Online Course — Leading Through Creativity. www.ecornell.com

EMOTIONAL EXPRESSION

Definition

Recognizing your emotions and expressing them directly, appropriately, timely, and thoughtfully

Those who don't know how to weep with their whole heart don't know how to laugh either.

— Golda Meir

Talented

❏ Knows his or her hot buttons, understands the whys, and proactively manages situations that might lead to strong emotional reactions

❏ Expresses emotions taking into account timing and possible impact on others or the situation; listens to understand how others feel

❏ Understands that emotions are not good or bad but that how they are expressed can have positive or negative consequences

❏ Articulates a wide range of emotions in real time

❏ Takes responsibility for expressing emotions

Skilled

❏ Knows some hot buttons and often manages emotions related to them

❏ Uses sensitivity to the situation to effectively express emotions

❏ Recognizes a variety of emotions, but tends to judge them as good or bad

❏ Expresses a variety of emotions, sometimes after the fact

❏ "Catches" him or herself before reacting emotionally to a situation

Unskilled

❏ Reacts to hot buttons with anger, frustration and poor self control

❏ Expresses emotions without considering the possible impact on others; doesn't listen to how others feel

❏ Is aware of and can name only a few basic emotions

❏ Uncomfortable with or fearful of experiencing emotions

❏ Finds it difficult to understand, express or describe emotions

❏ Blames others for his or her own emotions

Big Picture View

Emotions are a rich and meaningful part of life for us all, although we vary in how comfortable we are expressing them and how able we are to learn from our emotions. Emotions span a range from pleasant emotions such as love, joy, and caring to unpleasant emotions such as anger and fear. Feelings are energy that range in intensity from mild to very strong. The better you are able to identify emotions in yourself and others, understand the context of emotions at a given time, and appropriately express emotions, the healthier you and your relationships will be. Emotions are your personal response to how you feel about what is happening in your world or in your head. Your emotions may be related to the actions of others, but emotions and feelings are based on how you interpret or judge what is happening (this may happen internally very quickly). You can't control feelings, but you can choose how to react to them and how to express them. Mature emotional expression includes identifying an emotion, naming that emotion, sorting out the context of that emotion, and choosing how to express it or act on it.

Barriers to Effectiveness

❏ A lack of role models or poor role models (parents, family, co-workers) for expressing and responding to emotions and feelings

❏ Poor self-awareness and a lack of understanding of your reactions, feelings and behaviors

❏ Criticism from significant others when you have expressed your feelings

❏ Being part of a culture or social group that devalues feelings

❏ Little practice expressing emotions

Quick Action Tips

1. Got a blind side when it comes to how your behaviors affect others? Being a bull in the china shop of emotions can lead to trouble unless you find ways to tune in to how others are reacting. Identify someone you trust that is skilled at reading feelings and emotions and ask that person for insights after a stressful meeting; compare the emotions you read in others to what they saw. Ask what

cues they noticed that signaled those emotions. Try naming the feelings you sense in others ("You left our conversation in mid-sentence. Are you feeling frustrated with how things are going?") Acknowledging the feelings of others can tone down a potentially heated conversation. Seek to understand what others are thinking that led to their feelings. Sometimes misunderstandings, faulty assumptions or jumping to conclusions leads to needless frustration and anger that you can clear up by listening and acknowledging feelings.

2. Do you often think about what you should have said after a tense situation is over? Rather than worrying or pushing it out of your mind, stop and consider what emotions you, and perhaps others, were feeling. Practice expressing those emotions with someone you trust, and ask for feedback. Once you have thought through what you were feeling and practiced expressing that, approach the person or persons involved and ask for time to discuss the situation. Share your feelings by owning them as your reaction. Use the feedback model:

- In this situation _____
- When you did or said _____
- I felt _____

Ask for reactions from those involved and listen to their feelings. Use good listening skills to confirm their feelings without judgment. Clearing the air can make a huge difference in how you and those close to you get along.

3. Do you find yourself overreacting to certain situations? We all have hot buttons or topics that tend to quickly lead to anger or frustration. These are as varied as we are. To help yourself prepare to deal effectively with these situations, start by making a list of your personal "hot buttons" such as someone questioning your competence, being ignored in a meeting, or being repeatedly interrupted. Once you identify your top five, come up with two or three thoughtful ways to respond to each hot button if (or when) it happens. Using the model for responding in tip 2 may help you be clear about your reaction to that hot button without over reacting. Practice when the situations arise and ask for feedback from a trusted person who also is present. Use their feedback to refine your responses.

Another factor that can lead to emotional eruptions is when you feel bothered by something, but you hope it will not happen again. For example, your friend signs you up for a fund-raiser that you don't want to attend, but you don't complain and go. The third time your friend commits you to something without first checking, you may blindside your friend by yelling and complaining that he or she has no right to take advantage of you. Tune in to your emotions regularly to keep yourself honest with those you care about by speaking up when you feel unhappy or bothered. Better now than later.

4. Uncomfortable expressing emotions? Get a list of emotions (see Internet resources listed below) and check those you feel comfortable expressing, those you are uncomfortable expressing and those you never express. Sometimes just reminding yourself of the names of emotions helps expand the number of ones you feel comfortable using. Practice naming and expressing your emotions when you experience them in conversation; start with people you know well and trust. Expand the emotions you are comfortable expressing through use. Listen for others using the language of emotions. You may know a few people who are good at communicating their feelings and can expand your comfort with emotions by observing them.

5. Wonder how you might energize those around you to work harder or reach goals? Emotions are energy. When was the last time you expressed excitement, enthusiasm, or satisfaction at a team success? Practice expressing these emotions with words and nonverbal expression. If this feels uncomfortable for you, practice in small steps. By including more feeling words in your communication with those around you, you may convey more of the enthusiasm you actually feel inside but tend to not express. Your family members or direct reports may feel energized in response. If you are a sports fan, remember the last exciting game you attended or watched on television with friends. Probably you were expressing a lot of excitement along with the other fans around you. Access some of that same energy and enthusiasm to generate momentum for challenges at work.

6. Do you tend to explode and alienate those close to you when you get angry or frustrated? It may not be the anger, frustration, or disappointment you feel that pushes others away, but how you express these feelings. If you tend to explode, most likely you have been building that head of steam before the moment you began raising your voice, calling someone names, or using statements such as, "You never help me…," or, "You don't give a …." When you feel your anger rising, take a time out, maybe by walking around the office or building. Then identify what you are angry about. Write it down. Sometimes when we are angry we start statements with the word "you" and use absolute words like "never," such as in "You never listen to me." Both habits tend to lead to defensiveness in others. Try using nonjudgmental language to describe what set you off. Take responsibility for how you are reacting by using statements that start with "I" as in "I felt upset when you left without talking to me." Ask how the other person sees the same situation and listen. There are often two sides to an issue, and you need to know what the other side is to move forward in a productive manner.

For example: "Yesterday we agreed you would get me the figures I needed for the year end report. When I told you I was up against a deadline, you assured me you would have them here by 5 p.m. When you didn't show up, I called, but you had left and I was late with my report. I am frustrated that you didn't get me those figures and didn't call. What happened?"

Depending on the response in the situation above, you may be able to either appreciate why your colleague failed to get the figures to you on time or agree on how the two of you will handle a similar situation in the future, both better outcomes than exploding and alienating those whose cooperation you need to be successful.

7. Ever use the phrase "You made me feel..."? For example: "You made me feel upset when you missed my birthday." Or, "You made me feel embarrassed when you laughed so loud at that joke." While you may have the feelings mentioned, others usually don't respond well when it seems they are being told they forced you into some feeling. The discussion may then become about you blaming them instead of talking about what happened and how you feel. Try changing the wording to change the reaction you get. Own your feelings as a reaction you had to something said or done. "When you forgot my birthday, I was upset and not sure how to say so." "I felt embarrassed when you laughed so loud at the joke Fred told." Your feelings are your own reaction and give clues about what matters to you.

Related Competencies

(2) Assertiveness   (12) Emotional Maturity (14) Emotional Self-Control
(22) Insightfulness   (54) Understanding Others

Learn from Experience

Work

❏ Think of a difficult conversation you need to have, such as talking to a direct report who is not performing to expectations, and plan how to begin it. What are the fears you have that keep you from having it? Talk to someone you trust about how to approach the situation and express your reactions and feelings. Make time to listen to the reaction and feelings the other person may have.

❏ Celebrate a success within your work group by expressing positive reactions and feelings.

Personal

❏ Practice at home or with friends expressing a few feelings each week in real time.

❏ At the next social gathering you attend, listen for how others express their feelings. Try responding with feeling statements of your own.

Resources

Books

McLaren, Karla. *The Language of Emotions: What Your Emotions are Trying to Tell You.* Boulder, Colorado: Sounds True, 2010.

Orloff, Judith. *Emotional Freedom: Liberate Yourself From Negative Emotions and Transform Your Life.* New York: Random House, 2009.

Pearman, Roger R. (2007). *Understanding Emotions.* Winston-Salem, NC: Leadership Performance Systems, 2007.

Pearman, Roger R. *Emotions and Leadership.* Winston-Salem, NC: Leadership Performance Systems, 2007.

Internet

Helpguide.org. "Emotional awareness: Managing and dealing with emotions and feelings." www.helpguide.org

About.com. "Men Expressing Emotion." www.menshealth.about.com

Psychology Today. Once on the web site, search for "emotional expression." www.psychologytoday.com

Classes and training

Helpguide.org. Emotional Skills Toolkit.
www.helpguide.org/toolkit/emotional_health

12 EMOTIONAL MATURITY

Definition

Choosing how you react to your emotions so that your responses are both appropriate and productive

Maturity: Be able to stick with a job until it is finished. Be able to bear an injustice without having to get even. Be able to carry money without spending it. Do your duty without being supervised.

— Ann Landers

Talented

❏ Appears aware of own emotions and thoughtfully expresses them

❏ Seeks win-win outcomes when responding to emotions

❏ Shares credit for success, learns from criticism and failure, admits mistakes and apologizes when appropriate

❏ Demonstrates courage and grace under fire

❏ Considers other people's ideas and dissent

Skilled

❏ Expresses awareness of own emotions and their potential impact on others when prompted

❏ Shares emotions appropriately but struggles to do so under stress

❏ Shows an ambitious or competitive side that interferes with effectiveness from time to time but isn't known for this

❏ Postpones tough conversations in the interest of harmony at times

❏ Attempts to remain receptive to opposing ideas, often successfully.

Unskilled

❏ Lacks awareness of own emotions as they occur and their impact on self and others

❏ Has difficulty knowing when, where or how to express emotions

❏ Over-reacts emotionally

❏ Becomes defensive or sidesteps responsibility when facing failure

❏ Handles conflict poorly or avoids it altogether

❏ Focuses more on own ideas, wants and needs than on those of others

Big Picture View

Think about people you know who resist indulging their whims, who are able to leave unsaid the wrong thing at the tempting moment. Compare them to those who exhibit temper tantrums, prolonged pouts, rapidly changing moods or easy frustration. People who show resilience, patience, good judgment, trustworthiness and grace under fire are emotionally mature. They have learned to tolerate experiences that test their emotions. They use these experiences to learn how to deal with emotions — theirs and others' — more effectively. It is this incremental, often intentional, process that leads to emotional maturity. Their relationships tend to be stable, and they are often looked to for guidance during crises. Emotionally mature people develop the capacity to endure uncertainty and discomfort and to be patient with themselves and others. As a consequence, their self-confidence grows. Because they are self-confident and less likely to take things personally, there is a degree of level-headedness about them that contributes to effective decision-making, healthy relationships and simply getting things done.

Barriers to Effectiveness

❏ Low self-esteem or feeling inadequate

❏ Being defensive, resistant to feedback

❏ Staying on the move, and avoiding reflection

❏ Impulsive reactions to challenging events

❏ Sidestepping disagreements, conflict and challenges from others

❏ Ignoring stress, its impact and strategies for reducing it

Quick Action Tips

1. **Wear rose-colored glasses?** Do you see people and situations as they are or as you'd like them to be? Do you become disappointed later and react negatively? The ability to read people objectively, sooner rather than later, allows you to make better people decisions and navigate relationships with fewer surprises. Good judgment is sizing up people and situations accurately and

making sound decisions with what you discern. Judgment improves over time as you test your assumptions and reflect on the soundness of your decisions. To test your assumptions and generalizations, you first must determine what they are. How did you arrive at them? Do they correlate with other information you have? Bring someone whose opinion you respect into this testing process as a sounding board. Bounce your thoughts off them. Over time you will refine your thinking process and see people and situations more clearly.

2. Do certain relationships or issues trigger automatic reactions in you? Some experiences leave a lasting emotional impact and can interfere with good decision-making. If you react emotionally, more strongly than warranted, and it is putting your effectiveness at risk, consider these steps:

1. Sort out first what you're feeling.
2. Then sort out what's driving those feelings.
3. Ask how those feelings relate to the situation facing you today.

It may be helpful to do this with a trusted friend or advisor who can ask questions that you might not ask yourself. Talking with another person can help deepen your understanding of what is going on. Consider exploring the forces that shape your thinking and actions. Some include: the rules, values and beliefs you were raised with; biases inherent among the various groups you identify with; and rules of thumb learned in the school of hard knocks (your personal experiences). Perhaps not well understood, they need to be tested periodically to insure that they connect rationally with the choices you are making. Take time to reflect on your experiences, perhaps in writing (journals are commonly used to facilitate reflections). Examine your decisions and what went into them. Consider what you would do differently if you had the opportunity. Notice any patterns? Missed opportunities? Changes you'd like to make?

3. Find the expression of emotions — yours or others' — intimidating? Many people avoid expressing their emotions directly because they fear what will happen if they do. Some sit on their feelings until they cannot do it any longer, but then the timing, delivery or intensity are likely to mismatch the message. The objective here is to practice saying what you want to say, when you want to say it — in a nice way — when the emotional intensity and the stakes are low. One simple approach is to describe the situation and behaviors that triggered your emotions — just a brief factual description to ensure everyone is talking about the same thing. Then describe the resulting emotional impact on you.

- Use empathy if you anticipate a strong emotional response, defensiveness or resistance. Acknowledge the other person's feelings or position (empathy) first, then present your feelings or position followed by your request, suggestion or idea, if you have one.
- Practice. Behavioral rehearsal improves delivery and outcome. Role

playing with someone else offers valuable practice, feedback and ideas for fine-tuning.

- Assertiveness training courses teach the benefits of assertive behavior, the differences between passive, assertive, and aggressive behavior, and how to remain assertive even in high-stakes situations.

4. Tend to suppress strong emotions and impulses when you experience them? Or do you acknowledge and deal with them? If not, here are some action tips that can help:

- Put your feelings in perspective by recognizing that feelings are messy, that mistakes are made, that relationships are complex, and that life doesn't stand still. Remember, any one feeling or event is but a point in time. Later it will look different.

- Confront guilty feelings We all make mistakes. Take responsibility for them, verbally express your regrets, take your lumps and whatever action is needed to make amends. Then, move on.

- Embrace change and uncertainty. Learn to tolerate anxiety because suppressing it, paradoxically, is likely to make it worse. "What you resist, persists." Acknowledge it, talk about it, examine the rationality of what's driving it, exercise it, relax it or meditate on it.

5. Dismiss, ignore or undervalue other people's ideas? Do you look for what you like, think will work or will fit with other ideas under consideration? Or, do you tend to see what's wrong or missing? Emotionally mature people recognize that focusing on the positive brings out the best in others, while the critical view is better focused on tasks, not people. Use your next meeting to get better at this. First, zero in on your expectations. What about the upcoming meeting has value for you? Next, as the agenda unfolds and people speak, listen for what you like, think has potential, or would like to know more about. After the meeting, capture the best ideas and contributions and communicate that to those responsible. It's easy to spot the spectacular idea. But seeing beyond the obvious to spot an idea's value that is not apparent to most people is what sets really astute people apart. Try it. The very next discussion that you're in, suspend your judgment. Practice finding what you like about others' ideas. Ask questions. Ask what about the proposed idea was appealing, how it might work or offer superior value. Practice finding ways to build on others' ideas. See the connections between your ideas and those of others. Look for synergies.

6. Slow to own your decisions and behavior or their contribution to mistakes and failures? Learning to own your mistakes is a critical aspect of developing emotional maturity. Mistakes are unavoidable and are part of the development process. When you make one, own it, offer the appropriate response (apologize, make amends, whatever makes sense), learn from it, be patient with others as they deal with it, and move on. Reflection will help you to learn from and deal with mistakes. Ask yourself these important questions as you take responsibility for yourself and your actions. What is the important lesson from this experience? Does this experience remind you of or connect with others you've had? Is there a pattern? What rule of thumb might you take forward from this experience? How can you put what you're learning to work in the near future? Make a plan to apply what you've learned, and execute the plan.

7. Do you wait for problems to solve themselves or for bad situations to improve on their own? You might be suffering from magical thinking. Magical thinking assumes that something did or will happen without any real effort on your part. This is normal thinking in young children, but self-defeating in adults. Be clear about what you want and what your goals are. Here's a common example. "If I work hard and do a good job, others will notice and my boss will promote me." What is the goal? Promotion. Replace the magic thinking with a more rational, and dependable, approach. Explore what you need to do to reach this goal and what has prevented it so far. What assets or strengths do you bring? How will you and others benefit? How will you discuss this with your boss rather than waiting for him or her to guess this is what you want? The key to overcoming magical thinking is to plan and act on your goals. Include:

- A clear, measurable outcome
- Strategies for leveraging your strengths and overcoming the barriers
- Time lines and deadlines, and
- Indicators of success. Invite the help of partner, someone who will give you ideas, cheer you on and hold you accountable.

8. Disoriented by uncertainty, ambiguity or chaotic change? Facing uncertainty or the unknown is stressful. Some people become less effective while others rise above the uncertainty and channel their energy into helping themselves and others around them deal with the situation. To increase a sense of equilibrium in these otherwise uncertain situations, consider the following: 1. Recognize that situations sometimes simply don't go as planned but always produce useful information that can be used to make adjustments. 2. Some factors simply cannot be predicted, so predict their unpredictability (and feel more in control). 3. Some planning simply has to await the results of earlier plans that are unfolding. Patience and flexibility work well here. Learning flexibility is your best hedge against becoming disoriented by change, ambiguity and uncertainty.

Related Competencies

(2) Assertiveness   (14) Emotional Self-Control   (30) Openness to Others

(32) Patience   (34) Perspective-Taking   (38) Resilience

(42) Self-Confidence

Learn from Experience

Work

❏ Lead a task force charged with improving results with reduced resources. Stay motivated, optimistic, energized and productive.

Personal

❏ Volunteer to serve an agency providing help to those affected by an economic downturn. Find the balance between understanding the situation your clients are facing and staying objective enough to help them.

❏ Interview people who have demonstrated resilience in the face of adversity, and identify their strategies.

❏ Read about Nelson Mandela, Anne Frank and Mother Teresa.

Resources

Books

Lerner, Harriet. *The Dance of Intimacy.* New York: Harper Paperbacks, 1990.

Morler, Edward E. *The Leadership Integrity Challenge: Assessing and Facilitating Emotional Maturity.* Sonoma, CA: Sanai Publishing, 2nd expanded edition, 2006.

Seligman, Martin E. *Learned Optimism: How to Change Your Mind and Your Life.* New York: Vintage, 2006.

Covey, Stephen R. *The Seven Habits of Highly Effective People.* New York: Simon and Schuster, 1989.

Internet

Stephen Covey or Franklin Covey web sites: Search terms: maturity continuum. www.stephencovey.com and www.franklincovey.com

The Authentic Happiness web site of Dr. Martin Seligman. www.authentichappiness.com

Classes and training

The Seven Habits of Highly Effective People Fundamentals Workshop (One-Day) www.franklincovey.com

13 EMOTIONAL PROBLEM-SOLVING

Definition

Understanding a problem and its possible causes while taking emotional components into consideration, then generating the best possible solutions

It is wise to direct your anger towards problems — not people, to focus your energies on answers — not excuses.

— William Arthur Ward

Talented

❏ Solves problems through collaboration or win-win methods

❏ Looks for own part in a problem by recognizing own counterproductive thoughts, feelings or behaviors

❏ Identifies and manages emotions triggered by a problem

❏ Talks about how emotions and their impact factor into problems and their solutions.

❏ Recognizes and acknowledges the emotional components of a problem and explores the personal feelings of those involved

Skilled

❏ Effectively analyzes problems but may miss the emotional implications

❏ Generally manages interpersonal components of a problem

❏ Reacts emotionally but works to keep emotions from interfering with effective problem-solving

❏ Uses emotions as information in problem-solving but may underestimate their impact

❏ Seeks to involve all stake holders in problem solving

Unskilled

❏ Gets paralyzed emotionally by problems

❏ Fails to see that many problems are a result of negative emotions or irrational thinking

❏ Blames others for problems

❏ Analyzes to an excessive degree; lives in head too much

❏ Fails to consider the impact on people and relationships when developing solutions to issues; overly analytical

❏ Seeks to solve problems by getting own way

Big Picture View

Problems provide opportunities to sharpen not only your critical thinking skills but your EQ skills as well. Using emotional intelligence and valuing the information that emotions give ensures that the human element is taken into account when we solve problems. It involves integrating the wisdom of the mind with the compassion of the heart. By viewing each problem as an opportunity for positive change and growth, you increase the chances of a beneficial outcome for others and yourself. Research indicates that those who are optimistic— who view problems as opportunities — tend to be healthier, happier and more positive about their lives.

Since people and their emotions are inherent in any problem, the failure to effectively manage them — in self and others — is unproductive. For example, feeling paralyzed by fear or overwhelmed by possible negative outcomes can derail decisions. Recognizing the situations in your life, or in the lives of those important to you, that cause emotional distress, empowers you to proactively plan to avoid problems or to deal effectively with those that do happen. Elegant solutions to challenges are elegant because they go the extra step to incorporate emotions to solve problems.

Barriers to Effectiveness

❏ Easily overwhelmed when faced with problems

❏ Selfish, wants own way

❏ Analysis paralysis or its opposite, impulsivity

❏ Discounts, neglects or misses emotional factors

❏ Overemphasizes emotions, wears heart on the sleeve

Quick Action Tips

1. Do you panic when faced with a looming problem or deadline? Begin by taking a step back from the problem and try looking at it with calmness and focus. Count

to ten or take a few minutes to calm down, breathe and relax. Ask yourself: Am I over-reacting? Have I been irresponsible? Could I have handled myself with greater calm and focus? Am I being rational? You might find help in re-visiting how you have handled problems in the past. Remember a time when you were successful solving a problem. What were some of the attitudes, behaviors and skills you used then? Are there any that might be helpful now? Remember, while problems are different, they have many elements in common. Once you find effective strategies for problem solving, you can apply them in most situations. Be sure to recognize your emotional response and find ways to take care of yourself as you manage difficult issues. Deal with stress by employing regular exercise, calming practices such as yoga, gardening or meditation, or talking with a close friend. Take your emotional responses seriously. Maybe that bad feeling in the pit of your stomach is telling you to not take that "wonderful" promotion with a 1000-mile move. Identify any irrational beliefs that may be affecting your emotions such as, "I must be perfect in everything I do," or, "Everyone must like me." These irrational beliefs can add angst to any problem. Counter them with reasonable thinking: "No one is perfect, we all make mistakes." "Of course not everyone is going to like me or everything I do."

2. Is your problem-solving handicapped by irrational thinking? Do you wonder if you have a belief system that gets in your way of effectively solving problems? Identify one problem in your life that you want to resolve. List the beliefs you have around this issue, such as, "I must find a solution that everyone likes." Or "I am responsible for the happiness of all involved." If your answers indicate a pattern of irrationality or anxiety, then you may want to start your problem solving by being more realistic about your expectations. Experts in the area of refuting irrational beliefs offer the questions below as a way to overcome fear and anxiety when facing difficult problems. Look these questions over and see if they might help you examine the beliefs that influence your thinking.

- Does this belief encourage personal growth, emotional maturity, independence of thinking and action, and stable mental health?

- Is this belief one, which, if ascribed to, will result in behavior that is self-defeating for you?

- Does this belief assist you in connecting honestly and openly with others, in a way that promotes healthy growth, engendering positive connections in your interpersonal relationships?

- Does this belief assist you in being a creative, rational problem solver who is able to identify a series of alternatives from which you can choose your own personal priority solutions?

- Does this belief stifle your thinking and problem-solving ability to the point of immobilization?

3. Do you tend to ignore your emotions when faced with a problem? You are not alone! It is easy to believe that emotions are irrelevant and a bother. Walking the line between rational analysis and your emotions can be challenging, but you need to listen to both. Recognize and deal with emotions related to the problem at hand first, before seeking a solution. You will avoid stress and unexpected emotional challenges later. When others are involved, hear them out by acknowledging their feelings and strong sentiments before working toward a successful solution. When appropriate, share the strong emotions you have that relate to a problem and seek to understand the feelings of the others involved as well.

4. Aren't sure how to promote your ideas or your point of view? Problem-solving often involves some kind of negotiation — sharing and listening to each other's thoughts, feelings and preferences and finding an acceptable solution. Some people tend to capitulate or give in without adequately representing themselves and their ideas and needs. Failing to speak up for your ideas or needs puts both in jeopardy. You risk losing the respect of others as well as your own. You risk developing resentment toward those who always seem to get their way. To improve the presentation of your ideas, practice a succinct statement of what you think and why in advance of your meeting. Be prepared to offer additional details if appropriate. Ask people who support you for their reactions. Talking with key people ahead of a meeting may get them on board with you or give you an understanding of issues important to them. After the meeting, ask a colleague for feedback about whether your message was clear and had an impact.

5. Any chance you are a bully when trying to influence the problem-solving process? The opposite of giving in is imposing your will in a problem-solving process or negotiation. It calls to mind the adage, "win the battle, and lose the war." While you may win the current decision, it may be at the expense of a later, more important, decision or relationships in your life. Take time to consider the long-term consequences of your behavior (if you tend to be forceful). Practice being open to the viewpoints of others involved in the problem. A win-win approach to problem solving builds trust and improves your chances of future success when negotiating and problem solving with others. Another adage worth keeping in mind is, "Choose your battles." All problems are not equal. If you have a strong personality, choose which problems you want to take on, thereby limiting the impact of your strong personality on others. If you force your will on others too often, then you risk having to face and solve the problem again, in addition to having to handle the feelings that have festered in the interim.

6. Do you neglect to hammer out the details of any achieved resolution? Collaborative problem solving is very effective at finding a solution that works for all parties because people and emotions are factored into the process. Quick Action Tip 7 below describes the steps involved, including the one to work out the details of "who, what, when, and where." If you stop short of clarifying the details, you've got a vision without a plan. Conflicts or problems are likely to emerge when the details do come into play and misunderstandings come to light. Make sure that you have established clear expectations and that all involved have agreed on the implementation phase.

7. Wonder how to approach problem solving? Which step to take first? Below is a six-step model of problem solving adapted from the work of Dr. Thomas Gordon (and Gordon Training International). Look at the six steps and think through how you might apply them to a problem in your life.

- Define the problem in terms of needs and emotional factors, not solutions

- Brainstorm possible solutions

- Select the solution(s) that will best meet both parties' needs (including emotional), and check possible consequences

- Plan who will do what, where and by when

- Implement the plan

- Evaluate the problem-solving process and, at a later date, how well the solution turned out

What makes this method so effective is that it uses so many aspects of emotional intelligence. You are encouraged to acknowledge your own needs and the needs of others, to be creative, open-minded, a good listener and skillful at considering all viewpoints when seeking mutually acceptable solutions to the problem.

Related Competencies

(2) Assertiveness   (12) Emotional Maturity   (14) Emotional Self-Control

(22) Insightfulness   (34) Perspective-Taking   (35) Reality Testing

(41) Self-Awareness

Learn from Experience

Work

❏ Ask to serve on an organizational task force. There will be many opportunities to assess the needs of various constituencies and to engage in collaborative problem solving.

❑ Seek an opportunity to work with a customer (internal or external) in which there is a conflict of needs. Practice tough negotiation skills to resolve the problem.

Personal

❑ Volunteer for a community organization that is in the midst of a reorganization or redefining its mission (church, library, or neighborhood pool).

❑ Organize the family vacation or holiday event. There will be plenty of opportunities to practice your emotional problem-solving skills!

Resources

Books

Bolton, Robert. *People Skills: How to Assert Yourself, Listen to Others and Resolve Conflicts*. New York: Simon and Shuster, 1979, 1986.

Davis, Martha, Elizabeth Eshelman, and Matthew McKay. *The Relaxation and Stress Reduction Workbook*. Oakland, CA: New Harbinger Publications, 2000.

Gordon, Thomas. *Leadership Effectiveness Training: Proven Skills for Leading Today's Business Into Tomorrow*. New York: Penguin Putnam, 1977, 2001. (Look for the other books in the Effectiveness/Gordon model, such as Teacher and Parent Effectiveness Training.)

Dale Carnegie Training. *The Five Essential People Skills: How to Assert Yourself, Listen to Others and Resolve Conflicts*. New York: Simon and Shuster, 2009.

Welch, David A. *Decisions, Decisions: The Art of Effective Decision Making*. Amherst, NY: Prometheus Books, 2001.

Internet

Resources for refuting irrational beliefs. Here are a few:

> www.Psychcentral.com
> www.livestrong.com

www.ezinearticles.com. Search for an article entitled: "Problem-solving Process with Emotional Intelligence" by William R. Murray.

Classes and training

Gordon Training International: The Conflict Resolution Workshop (CRW) teaches the six step collaborative problem-solving model. www.gordontraining.com

14 | EMOTIONAL SELF-CONTROL

Definition

Controlling and restraining your emotionally based actions; demonstrating self-restraint

Self-reverence, self-knowledge, self-control; these three alone lead one to sovereign power.

—Alfred Lord Tennyson

Talented

❑ Links emotional reactions and assumptions about the situation at hand to moderate responses

❑ Expresses emotional energy in constructive ways, such as problem-solving

❑ Shows a calm and patient demeanor in the face of challenges

❑ Promotes healthy long-term outcomes by controlling emotional responses in the moment

❑ Provides an even-handed approach to challenging emotional situations.

Skilled

❑ Expresses insights after reacting emotionally, such as, "I just realized what made me upset."

❑ Uses insights about emotional reactions to modulate subsequent behavior.

❑ Views emotions as a natural part of interpersonal interactions and tries to share them appropriately

❑ Explains but does not defend how emotions fuel reactions

❑ Shows distress on his or her face but is able to calm down and react to situations in a positive or neutral tone

Unskilled

❑ Loses temper easily; has few healthy outlets for emotions

❏ Expresses anger or frustration in volatile ways

❏ Emotions are unacknowledged

❏ Appears unaware of how one's thoughts about a situation affect emotions and related behaviors

❏ Shows no awareness of the effect of emotional expressions on others

❏ Reacts impulsively to others' behavior without any apparent effort to understand

Big Picture View

Your emotions are entirely your own — no one makes you feel a certain way. Language such as "you made me feel" is neither accurate nor helpful, as it suggests someone else is in control of your emotions. The first step toward self-control is to understand that your emotions are your response to what you think is happening around you and to you. In other words, your interpretation of events leads to your emotions. Change your understanding of what is happening and you change your emotional response. You can do this by checking out what you think others are saying to you, what you think is happening, and what your concerns about events are. Then how you express your emotions is up to you. Often we don't realize that we have choices about how we express our feelings, but we do. This choice opens the window to emotional self-control. If you are angry, you can choose to yell at someone, stomp out of the room, or ask to sit down and talk about what concerns you. The choice is yours. Use it wisely. Uncontrolled expression of emotions usually leaves a lasting negative impression on those around you.

Barriers to Effectiveness

❏ Poor stress tolerance and lack of resilience

❏ Failing to explore how emotions are connected to meeting personal needs

❏ Failing to identify emotions and their underlying meaning

❏ Unwilling to accept or discounting the consequences of negative emotional reactions on others

❏ Impatience

❏ No role models for healthy expressions of feelings

Quick Action Tips

I. Fail to recognize or understand the "information" in emotions? You can decode the information that emotions provide. Emotions serve a purpose to alert you to something that you should attend to in your environment. Pleasure lets you know that you like what is occurring; the emotion of interest stimulates exploration. Anger might mean that you feel violated in some way, that an unnecessary barrier has been put in your way, or that an agreement has been broken. Once you understand the probable "meaning" of an emotion — yours or someone else's — you can confirm what needs to be addressed to improve a difficult situation. For example, if you reflect on why you are angry, and you come to the conclusion that it is about unmet expectations, then you now have the option to explore and adjust expectations to produce a more satisfying situation. The same is true when understanding the emotions of others: You can ask a question or share an observation to create greater understanding of the emotions of others.

2. Notice when you are irritated, you aren't as effective as you need to be? Thirty years of neurological research has uncovered vital links between emotion and decision making and problem-solving. For example, when we are irritated, our problem-solving is impaired; emotional comfort increases our ability to generate solutions. You have probably had the experience of getting so annoyed during a conversation that you were unable to really listen or even contribute to the discussion. Passion also can work in your favor to enable you to work hard on a challenge until you succeed. In other words, finding ways to use your emotional energy can help you be more effective. Emotions affect decision-making and problem solving — both of which can be improved with managing your emotions. When your emotional temperature seems to be getting in the way, ask, "On a scale of 1 to 10, how upset am I?" And then ask, "What can I do to lower that temperature a couple of notches?" These questions can help you, or someone you want to help, control emotions and their impact. The mere fact that you anchor the degree of the negative emotion and then begin to articulate how to move forward reduces the impact of negative emotions in decision-making.

3. React first, think later? Showing passion and enthusiasm is important in most relationships. However, in a conflict-related situation, some emotions can be negative and destructive. If you find yourself in a conflict and your emotions are rising, try one or more of these strategies: Count to ten (to yourself), focus on simply listening and confirming what you hear (you don't need to agree) to let the other person feel heard, or take a time out by rescheduling to continue your discussion later. Use the time to cool down and consider how you want to respond. Reframe the way you see the situation by asking yourself what may be the likely positive intent of the other person with whom you dealing. Are there any assumptions the other person might be making about you or your actions based on what they said? If faulty assumptions on their part might be contributing to their anger, check it out when you get together again. When you meet, start by sharing your positive intention of sorting out any differences or problems and finding a mutually satisfying solution. Ask open-ended questions, then listen. Share your perspective without attaching blame to the other person. Ask what might work for both of you.

4. Haven't made the link among mindsets, feelings, and behavior? Some call this the classic chicken and egg problem because the three are so interrelated. Evidence from a host of neurological studies reveals that mindset is the fertile soil in which feelings and behavior grow. In general, a "mindset" is the perspective and attitude we take about a situation. For example, you have a certain mindset about how to get your work done or how work relationships should be managed. To develop greater emotional control, you need to become a student of your mindset, the mental maps you use to evaluate situations. Learning to adjust your mindset about people and situations will move you closer to emotional self-control. For example, reflect on a situation in which you have had several bad experiences with a peer or colleague. It is likely that when you approach that person now you have these previous experiences in the back of your mind, and you may begin the conversation with the assumption that the same or a similar outcome is likely to occur. The statement, "Given my experience, I know…" is a common mindset that implies that your experience is comprehensive and that the knowledge you gained from it is certain. Consequently, if that knowledge is challenged, you may feel defensive. Engage in greater self-control by checking your assumptions and your perceptions. Challenge your mindset about what could happen in the next interaction. Create a log with five columns with the following labels: specific situation or event, thoughts/attitudes/mindset, emotions, actions taken, and thoughts to change. Keep the log for six weeks, leaving the fifth column blank. After the sixth week, identify what needs to change in the fifth column to shift the emotional and behavioral reactions.

5. "Why did I say (or do) that! I know better; what is the matter with me?" Sound like you? We all at times find our words leaving our mouths before our brain engages. And, if you are smart, you will realize that you need to be able to defer reacting emotionally when it makes sense to do so. Feelings are messy, mistakes are made, relationships are complex, and life doesn't stand still. Any one feeling or event is but a point in time. Later it will look different. Consider putting your feelings in perspective. Reflect on a time when you saw your feelings differently after a period of time. What feels intense now will probably not feel that way later.

6. Do strong emotions ever lead to mistakes and subsequent feelings of regret or guilt? Consider facing them. And give yourself a break: We all make mistakes. Make time to talk with anyone you may have offended, express your regrets, ask for forgiveness, and take your lumps. Undertake whatever action is needed to make amends. Then, move on.

7. Does change or uncertainly throw you for a loop? Does change make you anxious?

It might help to learn some strategies to help you tolerate anxiety. Start by acknowledging how you feel. Suppressing your anxiety, paradoxically, is likely to extend or exacerbate it — "what you resist, persists." This can lead to fearing that you may feel anxiety, a state referred to as anticipatory anxiety. Pushing through the anxiety puts you in control of it. It's sort of like working out with weights. When they get heavy, your arm gets tired and you experience the urge to put the weight down. But if you push through the fatigue, you strengthen your muscles and feel more energized and in control. Other emotions also may be heightened during change and uncertainty because of the underlying anxiety about what it all means.

8. Ever reacted too quickly and felt like you made matters worse? Emotions are a powerful part of your makeup, and sometimes they override your better judgment. Rather than reacting impulsively to events and people around you, learn to slow down and choose constructive ways to act, to use the impulse rather than being at its mercy. Start by keeping a log for a couple of weeks: What preceded your impulsive reaction, what were you thinking at the time you responded, what did you do, and did you get the constructive results you really wanted? Track your findings. Any surprises? See any patterns? What ideas occur to you now about what you could have done differently that would have been more constructive, or gotten you closer to your desired results? What will you do differently in the future? One of the secrets of emotional control is to use the impulse as a cue to push the pause button, take a broader perspective, ask for clarification, and push yourself to identify at least three constructive responses. Practice choosing a constructive response and notice the difference in your effectiveness.

9. Are you getting better at managing your anger and frustration? While these emotions aren't good or bad, how you express them can be destructive. One way to help manage how you act on these emotions is to track when you feel angry, irritated or frustrated and how you express yourself. Whether you use an electronic device (for example, a smartphone) to keep up with your experiences or a printed calendar, make notes about your efforts to manage these emotions. Note the who, what, where, and when of emotional reactions and make a note of what you said or did. Often just collecting these data points provides tremendous insights about the emotional triggers that lead to anger or frustration. Are there particular people or situations that often trigger these emotions in you? Are there ways to avoid them, change the situation, or prepare yourself to manage them more effectively? Be sure to give yourself credit when you do so.

10. Fail to listen fully and over-react? Have you ever reacted and later learned that had you paused long enough to listen fully, you would have had a different, more productive reaction? Perhaps you know how to listen effectively but have difficulty taking the time to do it. If so, you've probably underestimated the value of listening. "If speaking is silver, then listening is gold," according to a Turkish proverb. Not only do you learn more from listening than talking, but it's also the quickest and easiest way to warm up any interaction and, potentially, the relationship. But it is a skill you have to practice to be good at it, especially when you need it in emotionally charged situations.

Related Competencies

(12) Emotional Maturity	(18) Impulse Control	(24) Intentionality
(27) Listening Generously	(32) Patience	(36) Reframing
(41) Self-Awareness		

Learn from Experience

Work

❑ Work with a politically sensitive task force or committee

❑ Identify an activity that requires a great deal of focus to get the job done

❑ Ask for feedback from individuals in different contexts about your degrees of emotional reactivity; journal the feedback to identify patterns of time and place when self-control seems more problematic

Personal

❑ Seek to resolve a personal conflict with someone in the neighborhood or community

❑ Take Tai Chi to learn overall emotional, physical, and mental self-control

Resources

Books

Berfelo, Usha. *Is Your World Flat?: Experiencing Emotional Awareness in an Upwards-Moving Cycle.* Bloomington, IN: iUniverse, 2006.

Gerzon, Robert. *Finding Serenity in the Age of Anxiety.* New York: Bantam, 1998.

McKay, Matthew, Martha Davis, and Patrick Fanning. *Thoughts and Feelings: Taking Control of Your Moods and Life.* Oakland, CA: New Harbinger Publications, 2007.

Nagy, John S. *Emotional Awareness Made Easy: Uncommon Sense About Everyday Feelings.* Tampa Bay, FL: Promethean Genesis Publishing, 2008.

Internet

EQ toolbox: Emotional intelligence exercises. www.eqtoolbox.org

Helpguide.org. "Improving emotional awareness: Learning to handle intense emotions" article by Segal, Smith and Jaffe. www.helpguide.org

Classes and training

Talent Smart. Emotional intelligence public workshop. www.talentsmart.com

Leadership Performance Systems: Emotional Intelligence (an e-learning class) www.leadership-systems.com

15 | ACTIVE EMPATHY

Definition

Understanding how and why others feel the way they do and conveying it effectively

Walk a mile in my moccasins and you will know my journey.

— Saying from the Cherokee Nation

Talented

❏ Demonstrates deep sensitivity to others' feelings, needs and goals through generous listening

❏ Makes fine distinctions in the verbal and nonverbal communication of others (tone of voice, eye contact, word choice)

❏ Asks open-ended questions designed to better understand others and their feelings

❏ Sits comfortably with someone in silence when appropriate

❏ Identifies emotions in others and is able to convey that to the person

❏ Defuses emotional situations by respectfully identifying the emotions involved

Skilled

❏ Cares about others and tries to understand them

❏ Senses the feelings and thoughts of others but may not always be able to convey it

❏ Recognizes the nonverbal cues of others and tries to respond

❏ Demonstrates attentive body language when listening to others

❏ Portrays attentiveness through effective listening and patience

Unskilled

❏ Confuses trying to solve another person's problems with empathy

❑ Recognizes emotional reactions from others but responds by justifying, defending and explaining

❑ Shows no real concern with the feelings and emotions of self or others

❑ Focuses on the task rather than the emotional impact on those involved

❑ Clashes with others and lacks understanding of their concerns or view-points

Big Picture View

Empathy is the ability to tune in to another person, often allowing a personal and meaningful connection. By taking the time to understand what is important to another person and why, you can enrich your personal relationships and even begin to improve relationships where there is conflict.

Empathy is a skill that can be developed. A genuine concern for and interest in other people is a prerequisite to empathy. Empathy is your ability to accurately read the feelings of another person — their feelings, not yours. To empathize is to enter the other person's world and to imagine what it must be like to be in their shoes. The ability to tune in to another person, to their feelings, improves your ability to relate to them and can increase intimacy and understanding between you and them.

You demonstrate empathy if you notice how stressed a colleague appears, acknowledging and trying to understand how she feels, or if you take the time to listen to your partner and value his emotions and point of view. Empathy does not mean that you necessarily agree with or like what a person is saying but that you are willing to try to understand what matters to that person. Empathy involves the temporary suspension of your own concerns and feelings as you listen to and value another person's feelings and experience. Being empathic reduces conflict, increases understanding and assures a more relaxed home and workplace.

Barriers to Effectiveness

❑ Self-centeredness or insensitivity to others

❑ Defensiveness

❑ Inability to relate to diverse people or populations

❑ Dominating conversations, failing to engage others

❑ A determination to get across your own point of view

❑ Trying too hard to help, "save," or rescue others

Quick Action Tips

1. **Find yourself apologizing for failing to listen to the key people in your life?** Do you know the importance of listening but need help with the more basic tools of communication? Empathy emerges as the natural outcome of using the basics of good communication skills, the ability to *paraphrase, acknowledge,* and *empathize.*

- To *paraphrase* involves listening and then summarizing the content of the speaker's message by using sentence stems such as, "If I hear you correctly...," or, "Sounds like...," or, "Are you saying...?" Effective paraphrasing asks that you suspend your internal chatter and the need to express your thoughts and opinions. To do otherwise derails your ability to truly hear the message of the speaker.

- When *acknowledging* someone's message you are saying, "I can see that you feel angry," or, "You seem upset that happened." Being able to paraphrase and acknowledge the feelings of others does not necessarily mean that you agree with them, but rather that you have made the effort to listen and to understand their thoughts and feelings.

- The groundwork for *empathizing* is set when you, as the listener, have done a good job of summarizing the speaker's content and acknowledging the speaker's point of view. You are now able to tune in to the person's feelings, imagining what they are experiencing by trying to put yourself in their position. This is empathy!

2. **Do you overlook your own feelings, needs and motivations?** Emotional self-awareness is a critical component of empathy. If you are unaware of your own feelings, you will not be able to accurately reflect upon and recognize the feelings in others. If talking about your feelings is not your custom, consider going against the grain and doing it more often. Processing your feelings with others increases your emotional self-awareness and raises your sensitivity to emotional cues in others. Maintain a journal of your personal experiences and your emotional reactions to them. Note your emotions, any physical changes such as racing heart, sweaty palms, or fuzzy-headedness, and write about it in your journal. Explore the possible connections between emotions and each physical event. You can also take a deeper dive into a very intentional effort at self-awareness by taking a personal growth workshop such as the Landmark Forum or by becoming a student of a personality system such as the Enneagram. It can also be helpful to do a daily review, perhaps while you drive home from work or walk the dog, as a way of increasing self-awareness.

3. Do you tend to shut down communication by asking the wrong questions? Do you tend to get yes or no answers to questions when you had hoped for more detail? Empathy involves getting to know what's going on inside a person to better understand their situation. Open-ended questions seek answers beyond a simple a yes or no response. Ask questions designed to learn more about the person, their situation, their thoughts, feelings, expectations, needs and hopes. If this does not come naturally to you, write questions on an index card, or post them to your iPod or smartphone. Use them as reminders when going into a meeting at work, talking with your kids or attending a social gathering. For example — instead of, "Did you have a good day at school?" try, "What was the most interesting part of your day?" Instead of "Is that report finished?" try "How is it going with the report?"

4. Are you an interrogator or an inquirer? Do you show impatience or judgment when talking with others? The art of inquiry is related to the ability to remain open to what others have to say. If you tend to be aggressive in your questioning, then you risk shutting doors to a deeper conversation. Watch for the presence of "should, ought to, can't, shouldn't" in your language as well as a tendency to criticize or judge another's situation or feelings. These are sure to put a damper on the conversation and certainly prevent empathy. Create a list of "inquiry questions" to use when you want to better understand the point of view of your co-worker, child or partner, and then try using them over the course of the next few weeks. Be sure to pause after a question and listen thoughtfully to the response. Take note of the difference it makes in your communications with others. Examples: "How did you arrive at that conclusion?" "Tell me more about that." "What are your thoughts about…?" "I'd like to better understand that decision, so could you please share your reasoning?"

5. Wonder how you can walk a mile in someone else's moccasins? Empathy is an ability that is enhanced when you put yourself into another person's situation. By understanding the emotions being experienced by that person you are opening the door to empathy. Do you tend to monopolize the conversation? Do you leave a gathering realizing that you haven't learned anything about your companions? Do you know how the reorganization in your company is affecting your co-workers? Make it a point to get to know your colleagues, discovering their interests, learning about their families or their ideas for an upcoming project in the department. You can develop greater empathy by spending time with someone who is different from you with the intent of understanding him and his perspective. This might involve talking to someone whose opinions about work, politics, or parenting are different from your own, which will require you to temporarily suspend your own thoughts in order to tune in to theirs.

6. Do you find it hard to read someone's body language, missing important cues about

what is going on? Do others seem to notice what's happening with a colleague or friend before you do? If it doesn't come naturally to you, prompt yourself to notice a speaker's nonverbal (body) language, such as eye contact, tone of voice, body posture and facial expressions. These are often clues to understanding another person — the basis for empathy. Create opportunities to observe the behaviors of others while you are waiting at the airport or standing in a grocery line. Notice someone's posture and imagine how they might be feeling. Observe the nonverbal behaviors of those around you — co-workers, family, friends, neighbors — and when appropriate check the accuracy with them about what you think they are feeling.

7. Does your anger, disappointment or frustration with others get in the way of your noticing their feelings? Negative feelings can be a major impediment to empathy. Negative emotions can subvert your attention and prevent you from getting the distance from your own experience that you need in order to see things from another person's perspective. Emotional challenges are common. If you don't deal with those emotions or if you don't have the capacity to put your emotions on hold, then your ability to relate to others is hampered. A great strategy for processing, then parking an emotional experience is "the unsent letter." If you are carrying around residual negative emotion related to a recent interaction, consider writing the "unsent letter," in which you pour out all your negative feelings and thoughts. This frees you up emotionally to focus on the person with whom you want to actively empathize. An additional benefit to this strategy is the path it creates to resolve a pending conflict. Don't send the letter — let it sit for a while. Come back to it later, and, if there still remains a need to communicate your feelings, then revise the letter to meet this goal. Get your point across, with the least damage to the person and the relationship. If feasible, read the letter to your recipient rather than sending it, so that you both can discuss it.

8. Limited horizons? Do you tend to associate with the same people, do the same activities and avoid people and experiences that represent a different culture or approach from your own? Exposure to other cultures, nations, religions and viewpoints has the potential for broadening and enriching your perspective. Expanded awareness enables you to better relate to people whose lives are different from yours, thereby helping you to experience greater empathy. Not everyone has the ability to travel to foreign countries, but you can gain exposure to different viewpoints through books, plays, movies, and community cultural events. Do you avoid talking to someone because you perceive them to be different from you? Notice if and when that happens and consider exploring what about that difference is important to you. Absent that, choose a segment of your community that you know little about. Participate in events such as multicultural festivals or other ethnic celebrations or organizations. Put together a plan to broaden your knowledge and extend your horizons.

9. Do you mistake advising for listening or giving an opinion for support? If you find yourself wanting to advise, provide solutions, question or analyze others, then you are probably in a communication rut. Thomas Gordon, Ph.D., a psychologist, developed an excellent communication and training program for parents, leaders and teachers. In it he describes 12 roadblocks to effective communication. Read through the list below and ask yourself if any of these sound uncomfortably familiar to you. Pick one or two roadblocks to work on overcoming. By working to eliminate or reduce these roadblocks, you increase the possibility of expressing empathy for another and are better able to make a meaningful connection with the people you care about.

- Ordering, directing: "Get over it and move on..."
- Warning, threatening: "You'd better stop worrying or..."
- Moralizing, preaching: "Pray about it..." "Tune in to your wiser self"
- Advising, giving solutions: "What I would do is...", "Why don't you..."
- Persuading with logic, arguing: "Logically speaking…"
- Judging, criticizing, blaming: "You are not thinking clearly..."
- Praising, agreeing: "But you're so great!"
- Name-calling, ridiculing: "You jerk!"
- Analyzing, diagnosing: "What's wrong with you is..."
- Reassuring, sympathizing: "Don't worry." "Everything will be OK."
- Questioning, probing: "Why..." "Who...?" "What did you...?"
- Diverting, sarcasm, withdrawal: "Let's talk about pleasant things..."

Related Competencies

(12) Emotional Maturity   (25) Interpersonally Skillful   (26) Intuition

(27) Listening Generously   (34) Perspective-Taking   (41) Self-Awareness

(46) Social Intelligence

Learn from Experience

Work

❏ Job exchanges or job shadowing can be useful for improving empathy.

Ask to shadow someone or trade jobs for a day to increase your understanding of their job.

❏ Plan a team-building workshop or program for your immediate work group that involves exercises to increase understanding and communication among team members.

Personal

❏ Sit in a crowded place like an airport or the local shopping mall and develop your observational skills by watching people and imagining what they might be feeling.

❏ Dinner table conversations: At dinner with your family or others, experiment with asking open-ended questions and responding with paraphrasing and acknowledgment. Make it your goal to refrain from opinions or judgment.

❏ If your religious institution or community has a social justice committee, consider serving on it. Volunteering at the soup kitchen or running a Stop Hunger Now initiative will provide many opportunities to practice empathy as you will find yourself interacting with those whose lives can be heartbreaking and challenging.

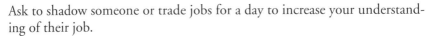

Resources

Books

Covey, Stephen. *Seven Habits of Highly Effective People*, New York: Simon and Shuster, 1989. (Read the chapter for Habit 5: "Seek First to Understand Then Be Understood.")

Davis, Martha, Kim Paleg, and Patrick Fanning. *How to Communicate Workbook: Powerful Strategies for Effective Communication at Work and Home*. New York: Fine Communications, 2004.

Gordon, Thomas. *Leadership Effectiveness Training*. New York: Berkley Publishing Group, 1977, 2001.

Gordon, Thomas. *Parent Effectiveness Training*. New York: Three Rivers Press, 1970, 2000.

Gottman, John, and Joan DeClaire. *Raising an Emotionally Intelligent Child*. New York: Simon and Shuster, 1997.

Stein, Steven, and Howard Book. *The EQ Edge: Emotional Intelligence and Your Success*. Toronto: MHS, 2000.

Stone, Douglas, Bruce Patton, and Sheila Heen. *Difficult Conversations*. New York: Penguin Books, 1999.

Patnaik, Dev. *Wired to Care: How Companies Prosper When They Create Widespread Empathy*. Upper Saddle River, NJ: FT Press, 2009.

Internet

Harvard Business Review: "Social Intelligence and the Biology of Leadership" by Daniel Goleman and Richard Boyatzis, Sept 2008. www.hbr.org

Enneagram Institute: www.enneagraminstitute.com

Landmark Forum Education Group: www.landmarkeducation.com

Classes and training

"Getting the Love You Want" workshop. Course which emphasizes communication skills and empathetic listening. www.gettingtheloveyouwant.com/

Gordon Training International: Search for courses in active listening. www.gordontraining.com

16 FLEXIBILITY

Definition

Remaining open and responding effectively to new, different or changing information or circumstances

Adapt or perish, now as ever, is nature's inexorable imperative.

—H. G. Wells

Talented

❏ Looks for new and varied ways to address current challenges and changing conditions

❏ Thrives on change: reacts and responds exceptionally well to unforeseen change and is often energized by it

❏ Stays productive when pulled in many different directions at the same time

❏ Easily varies behaviors and approaches to achieve desired outcomes

❏ Seeks a variety of ideas, perspectives and approaches to challenges and problems

Skilled

❏ Tolerates ambiguity, shifting priorities and changing circumstances

❏ Displays variable levels of motivation when confronted with ongoing change or multiple competing demands

❏ Considers different ideas, perspectives, methods and practices when presented by others

❏ Changes mind or stance when circumstances are compelling

Unskilled

❏ Chooses status quo over change

❏ Ignores indicators of the need for change

❏ Digs in heels when opposed

❏ Seeks to bolster position rather than to enlighten it

❏ Seems to think there's just one right answer or solution

❏ Becomes resistant, defensive or argumentative in the face of change

Big Picture View

The individual with the most choices wins. The more choices you have in responding to any situation, the more likely you are to have at least one that will work well. Flexible people are intrinsically open to different ideas and different ways of doing things, and they more easily embrace both. As a result, they have more choices when faced with decisions that can range from dealing with a problem to choosing a career. Having multiple options improves health — emotional and physical. Recognizing that you have choices helps you to feel more in control. By taking ownership of your experience you lower your stress and make better choices.

Barriers to Effectiveness

❏ Overly dependent on consistency, predictability or expediency

❏ Fear; avoidance of risk

❏ Fatigue

❏ Tight deadlines

❏ Inexperience

❏ Conviction that there is only one right solution or perspective

Quick Action Tips

1. Uncomfortable with change? Most people are comfortable with what is familiar and, conversely, uncomfortable with what they don't know. Some seek the unknown, but usually on their own terms. One way to offset discomfort with the unknown or unfamiliar is to gain experience with it. Make the unknown more familiar by experimenting with it. Identify one or two habits (like the route you drive to work, what or where you eat lunch, where you usually shop for groceries or how you spend your weekends) and make a change. For example, take the backroads, pack a lunch and eat at the park, visit an ethnic grocery, get three new ideas for weekend activity from your friends and try one. If you don't have any friends with new ideas, start with finding some new friends. Take the time to connect with people you don't normally spend time with.

2. Go with the flow — easier said than done? Change can be stressful and is often accompanied by uncertainty and little control. Learning to be flexible in the face of change is a skill that can ease the stress of changing circumstances. Change happens, so finding ways to work with it is less stressful than fighting it.

What follows is a four-step strategy for becoming more flexible:

- First, identify two or three past experiences where you were flexible, where circumstances changed and you successfully changed with them. What did you notice that led you to consider doing something different? How did you feel? How did you convince yourself to shift direction or method? How did you feel after convincing yourself to make the change? This is your natural strategy for dealing with change.

- Next, think of others around you who seem pretty flexible. What are their strategies for coping with change? What are their thought processes? How do they manage the discomfort that sometimes comes when having to abort a preset plan?

- Third, determine the next opportunity where remaining flexible might be more useful than sticking with a plan. Remind yourself of how you became more flexible in the past and put that strategy into play. Or borrow strategies you've learned from others. Anticipate conditions that might tempt you to relapse into old habits and plan how you will override them.

- And last, plan, practice, and mentally rehearse. Then do it. Afterwards, review what worked, what didn't, and congratulate yourself for your efforts!

3. Values and standards are forever, aren't they? Values and standards are like most decisions, in that once you've given it reasonable consideration and reached a conclusion, it ought to be final, right? If only it were that easy. Values and standards often start out as the product of the environment in which you grew up. But do they remain fixed? Try this:

- First, think of a value that you hold dear, one that you've subscribed to most of your adult life.

- Next, think of a behavior that would be the opposite of that value.

- Last, think of at least one circumstance in which you would choose that behavior, a behavior that is the opposite of the value that is important to you. Now, this is an extreme example, but it serves to point out the value of flexibility.

4. Stubborn? Reluctant to change your mind? Learning to be flexible in your thinking and open to new information or points of view will help you be more successful in relationships and work. Once people form opinions, they often cling to them in spite of competing information, which they either ignore or dismiss. The reasons vary, but if you're one who is reluctant to change your mind once it's made up, then consider the following: One definition of intelligence is the capacity to entertain two opposing concepts at the same time. Remaining open to new information leads to more options, flexibility, better problem-solving and better decision-making. Consider this example: You don't like your boss, and it's causing problems in your work relationship. Try this: Shift your perspective (for example, five years from now) or focus on a different aspect of your boss' behavior (what does she or he do well?) until you notice a change in your feeling. Or what would you need to believe in order to feel differently? What additional information might help? Tap into your curiosity; seek more information to gain a better understanding. Shift your attention to information that results in a different, more productive, feeling.

5. Prefer to do what worked before? As creatures of habit we tend to do what worked last time even when the circumstances may have changed. The problem is that we don't pause long enough to consider other possible options. Research has shown that the best solution to most problems usually falls between the second and third solution generated. When making a decision, make it a practice to push beyond the first idea. Consider two more and explore the benefits of choosing one of them instead. Before responding automatically, ask yourself what outcome you want and what other actions might achieve it as well or better. Encourage the habit in yourself and others to push beyond the first idea. Remember, to a hammer, most things look like nails.

6. Over-rely on the plan? Are you working a plan or process that has been in place for a long time without being re-evaluated? Take a look at the Continuous Improvement movement, Six Sigma, Lean Manufacturing or TQM, where efficiency and quality are emphasized. They all rely on ongoing evaluation and making necessary adustments. From Continuous Improvement comes the P-D-C-A model which stands for Plan, Do, Check, Act. Make a plan, do it on a small scale, check the impact and, if successful, activate it more widely. Otherwise restart at the "plan" step and adjust it. Consider one of these models to experiment with doing things differently.

7. Frustrated when people change their minds? The Law of Requisite Variety, when paraphrased, says that the person with the most choices (or options) is the most powerful or influential. Said another way, the person with the most options available to deal with a given situation is in the best position to have the best choice available to him. Have you ever worked with someone who knew how to size up situations accurately and to quickly sort through multiple approaches to figure out what needed to be done? Find those who are among the most flexible and interview them for their strategies for dealing with change. Consider making one of these folks your learning partner. Match their strengths to your weakness and vice versa. Use each other as mentors, confide in each other and serve as sounding boards for one another.

Related Competencies

(1) Adaptability   (10) Creativity   (22) Insightfulness

(30) Openness to Others   (34) Perspective-Taking   (36) Reframing

Learn from Experience

Work

❏ Consider an assignment working with someone more senior who is either notably talented or notably deficient in a skill necessary to the task, requiring you to read the situation accurately and find the best way to adapt to it.

❏ Accept the leadership of a rapidly changing team, unfolding challenges or business expansion.

❏ Participate in an assignment where you will be working with others who have strong opinions or styles that are different from yours.

Personal

❏ Volunteer to tutor a child or coach a children's sport team. Seek advice from several who have done this well in the past and identify two or three of their strategies that are new to you to practice.

❏ Volunteer for projects that are new and different from what you volunteer for normally or projects where existing policies and practices do not apply.

❏ Identify someone you know who (in your view) is very good at being flexible. What do they do that makes you think they're "very good" at being flexible? Which of these behaviors can you do more often? Interview them for their strategies.

Resources

Books

Johnson, Spencer. *Who Moved My Cheese: An Amazing Way to Deal with Change in Your Work and in Your Life.* New York: Putnam Publishing Group, 1998.

Hersey, Paul. *The Situational Leader*. Upper Saddle River, NJ: Prentice-Hall, 1985.

Gladwell, Malcolm. *The Tipping Point*. New York: Little, Brown and Co., 2000.

Internet

Check out these web sites on maintaining mental agility and flexibility.

> The Franklin Institute: Resources for Science Learning. Do an internal search with key word: brain. www.fi.edu/learn/brain/
>
> Happy Neuron: www.happy-neuron.com/
>
> National Institutes of Health—Kids: exercises to increase brain flexibility. www.niehs.nih.gov

Classes and training

SocyBerty.com: Top 10 web sites for brain training. www/socyberty.com/psychology

Karl Albrecht web site: Check out the thoughts and ideas of someone known as a visionary and big thinker. www.karlalbrecht.com/

Lumosity — Reclaim your brain. Training site to improve brain health and performance. www.lumosity.com

16

17   GROUP SAVVY

Definition

Reading and adjusting to group dynamics to promote an intended impact or to motivate the group to act

> *Never doubt that a small group of thoughtful, committed people can change the world. Indeed. It is the only thing that ever has.*
>
> — Margaret Mead

Talented

❏ Identifies and articulates how group members are relating to each other

❏ Runs effective meetings; engages all group members in conversation, decisions and plans

❏ Manages the ebb and flow of discussions with facilitating questions and process suggestions

❏ Responds effectively to all levels of group membership regardless of position, demographics or ethnicity

❏ Spots opportunities to leverage naturally occurring dynamics to move the group toward desired outcomes

Skilled

❏ Knows the primary interests and talents of group members but may miss those that are more subtle

❏ Understands that some group discussions take time but isn't always patient

❏ Creates group processes that encourage members to participate

❏ Shows warmth and openness with group members

❏ Facilitates discussions when topics are easy or not controversial

❏ Creates teams that are effective at achieving goals

Unskilled

❑ Seems oblivious to group dynamics

❑ Makes no effort to listen or show interest in others' needs in the group

❑ Needs to control or else appears uninvolved in the group conversation

❑ Misses opportunities to use a team approach

❑ Demonstrates a disdain for group activity

❑ Fails as a team leader to motivate others, manage conflicts, or consistently achieve goals

Big Picture View

You deal with groups all the time — work teams, families, social groups and community organizations. Groups are an important part of your life. Understanding how groups function and how to work effectively through groups or teams can mean the difference between success and failure, especially within complex organizations. It helps to remember when working in groups that interpersonal relationships are crucial and that all interactions are compounded — that is, there is you and me, what I thought of our interaction, what you thought of the interaction, and how these reactions affect not only us but other group members. Group savvy means knowing how to initiate contact with all group members, gauge their interests and needs, identify and understand the various dynamics among group members, facilitate discussion around group expectations, manage conflict as it arises (and it will) and use the unique energy and creativity that emerge in groups to accomplish team goals while ensuring that all members feel satisfied and committed.

Barriers to Effectiveness

❑ Failing to balance the importance of building relationships with accomplishing the task

❑ Lack of experience working in groups

❑ Ignoring and failing to deal with group conflicts, however subtle

❑ Failing to understand team dynamics

❑ Impatient when group ideas diverge from yours

❑ Not seeking help when you are in over your head with a poor functioning team

❑ Self-centered

Quick Action Tips

I. Forget to check in with others, or to find out what interests them? Developing group savvy is an incremental process — first one person, one interaction at a time, then several people and multiple cross interactions at the same time. As you spend time with people, make observations and develop rules of thumb. Make it a point to have a regular conversation with group members about their interests and plans. Explore the kinds of things that are important to group members. Watch for these plans, needs and interests to play out during group interactions. Be sure to have some sense of their personal lives and how being in this group meets their needs. The more you know about what individuals want and need, the greater your chance of reading accurately their behaviors and working effectively with them. Also, you may learn the expectations that individuals bring to the group and how you can help them find satisfactory outlets for their interests. The more you know about group members, the easier it is to read their needs and wants.

2. Unsure about how to get the best creative problem solving possible from your team? Try using these three team strategies: (a) brainstorming, (b) posting, and (c) small group idea generation. Brainstorming starts with a clear problem statement including all information that is known and then asks for all possible ideas to be shared with no expressed judgments. Once all ideas are listed, the group may evaluate them to choose the best opportunity with risk and expenses that they can live with. For posting, all individuals get Post-it® pads to use to write down as many ideas or solutions to an issue or problem as they can generate, one idea per Post-it page. The team leader or facilitator then collects the Post-it notes and organizes the ideas on a large easel into themes and patterns for the group to discuss and build on. Small group idea generation uses small groups to create their ideal lists of options that they then present to the rest of the larger group. Choose one strategy and try it the next time you want to involve your team in creative problem solving. Your goal is to motivate the group to act, and one of these three tactics will help you engage group members and gain commitment.

3. Know how to avoid a group going rogue? When with a group of people, you need to: inquire, share information, summarize, demonstrate warmth and openness, initiate — especially with those who are not engaged. Creating a dialogue among all present helps to create comfort. Keep in mind that the interactions should be like tossing a ball back and forth — sharing ideas and information. A group may exist for simple social reasons or to provide solutions to complex problems. No matter what the primary reason, when human beings are involved, there is a need to keep a constant flow of information so that everyone understands what is happening and what they signed up for. And a sure way for a group to go rogue is for individuals to be confused about the reasons for a change of course or what is being asked of them. Make sure you ask what group members want to get out of the time together, then facilitate movement toward a common objective.

4. Do you feel compelled to control the conversation? There are few better ways to keep a group from being productive or enjoyable than being an absolute bore. If you are talking all the time, interrupting others with your opinion, or simply ignoring the fact that you are taking up all of the air time, then you can be sure that the group you are with — family, friends, or work colleagues — will find plenty of ways to avoid the next gathering. Next time you are with a group, make sure that you keep quiet and see how others respond. Replace your talking with asking thoughtful open-ended questions to encourage others to share their ideas. Notice who is quiet and ask for their thoughts. Try summarizing a couple of main points you hear. Ask for suggestions about how to proceed. You may shock your colleagues with the change in you!

5. See the group as an impediment to achieving your goals? Organizations are made up of groups of people working to reach personal and organizational goals. The value of group savvy is that you use your emotional intelligence to help move the group along toward the desired outcomes. Rather than seeing the group as an impediment, start thinking of group members as untapped sources of energy to work on important objectives. A well functioning group can generate more productive ideas and make better decisions than one individual. A group that works well together can take on big and complex tasks, sometimes for the pleasure of the challenge. Shift your thinking from "a group is too complex to deal with" to "a group offers more opportunity."

6. Prefer to do the work yourself rather than use a team approach? Some individuals simply do not like any group with more than two members. While it is true that groups usually do take more time to accomplish simple tasks, complex organizations have complex challenges that often demand involvement from a variety of people and perspectives to be successful. Understanding group dynamics and processes is a crucial leadership skill. Groups have natural cycles where issues of inclusion and support need to be addressed for the group to move forward. Pick a team that you are part of and identify the stage of development for that team. What is needed to move that team forward? You can also respond appropriately to the group's behavior by asking others about their needs or expectations. Who do you know that is effective when working with teams? Ask for tips that might help you continue to develop your own group savvy skills.

7. Do you shy away from taking group leadership or facilitating group conversations? Practice leading a small group — three or four people whom you do not know well — on a basic task. Choose a group outside of your work setting such as neighborhood get-togethers, volunteer work, or your kids' activities. Take the initiative to introduce yourself to new people with three sentences explaining who you are. Increasing your connections with others by sharing and soliciting their perspectives will help facilitate greater understanding of group dynamics and your confidence in initiating group leadership.

8. Find it difficult to manage a group that has members in different time zones, countries and cultures? The world economy is increasingly doing business via conference call and video conferencing. Effective communication, clear meeting management and strong relationships remain key to working with cross-cultural groups. Since most of these group conversations are by phone or other telephonic means (e.g. Skype), a triple action approach is required — interact with individuals before the meeting, facilitate during the meeting by laying out an agenda and procedures, and a follow-up to see how members perceive the meeting went. Try writing down the names of each individual in the conversation and making a note of their apparent level of engagement and openness. This will enhance your reading of the group's energy and help you identify who may need additional follow-up.

9. Find it hard to read people's reactions? To be group savvy, you need to read people. Are you good at reading and responding to others, intuitively? Notice facial expressions, body language and voice qualities. Then relate these cues to how people report they are feeling and, eventually, learn to "read" these people. You can learn to be more attentive to these clues through practice and by being fully present with others. Start by observing people, their actions and reactions. Begin exercising your "social cues" muscle by speculating about what you observe about others. What emotions are they feeling? What matters to them? What are they likely to do next? What other ideas occur to you? Make a note of these speculations, because that's all they are until you get some confirming data. Continue to observe and stay on the lookout for information that might relate to your speculations either to confirm or refute your hypotheses. Notice how many of your guesses prove accurate. And remember, you can always consider checking in with the person you're observing for a self report. Learning to be more observant will help you facilitate understanding between group members and move the group toward a common goal.

Related Competencies

(15) *Active* Empathy   (16) Flexibility   (20) Influencing Others

(22) Insightfulness   (25) Interpersonally Skillful   (26) Intuition

(29) *Reading* Nonverbal Communication   (30) Openness to Others

(45) Situational Awareness

Learn from Experience

Work

❑ Volunteer to lead a product launch involving others from a variety of functional areas.

❑ Offer your services to HR to train or orient a group. As you prepare the content, also plan how you will study the group's dynamics.

❑ Build a coalition. Identify a cause and recruit support for it. What do you observe when talking to groups of two or more about it?

❑ Enroll in a workshop focusing on group facilitation, team building, or running effective meetings.

Personal

❑ Volunteer to organize meetings for a political campaign

❑ Become an observer of groups: identify patterns of interactions

Resources

Books

Levi, Daniel. *Group Dynamics for Teams*. Los Angeles: Sage Publications, 2010.

Webne-Behrman, Harry. *The Practice of Facilitation: Managing Group Process and Solving Problems*. Charlotte, NC: Information Age Publishing, 2008.

Scholtes, Peter R., Brian L. Joiner, and Barbara J. Streibel. *The Team Handbook*. Madison, WI: Oriel Incorporated, 2003.

Internet

Research educational institutions offering programs in Organizational Development and Behavior. Most will offer courses or research that study team building and group dynamics. Go to: www.gradschools.com/search-programs/organizational-studies

www.leader-values.com. Go to "Themes"; go to "Knowledge"; go to "Learning Organizations (Part 2)"

Classes and training

American Management Association. Search term: Building effective teams. www.amanet.org

18   IMPULSE CONTROL

Definition

Recognizing emotional triggers as a signal to slow down, think before acting and choose a constructive response

> *Nature is at work. Character and destiny are her handiwork. She gives us love and hate, jealousy and reverence. All that is ours is the power to choose which impulse we shall follow.*

—David Seabury

Talented

❏ Uses emotional triggers as a prompt to think before responding

❏ Converts negative emotional urges into constructive actions

❏ Before responding seeks clarity and weighs alternatives

❏ Anticipates situations that trigger emotional reactions and takes pre-emptive action to avoid them

Skilled

❏ Recognizes impulses and is aware of how they affect behavior but is inconsistent in managing them

❏ Apologizes after realizing that a reaction offended or hurt someone

❏ Resists knee-jerk reactions in provocative situations

❏ Demonstrates a few strategies to manage impulses

❏ Delays responding to gain time and composure

Unskilled

❏ Reacts without regard to consequences

❏ Speaks before thinking through situations

❏ Uses alcohol, substance abuse, overeating or angry outbursts to cope with anxiety or frustration

❏ Fails to recognize how impulses may limit choices and behaviors

❏ Acts without regard to how impulsive reactions damage relationships

Big Picture View

Impulse control is what you choose to do between an immediate internal reaction you have and your next behavior. You get a bad review at work and want to quit. What do you do? Your spouse is struggling with depression and you want to just walk out. What do you do? Impulse control is important to your functioning and is a major contributor to effectiveness. What you do with your impulses is often the best predictor of how successful you are going to be interpersonally. Those who go quickly from being annoyed to action usually make a bad choice. Learning about situations in which you tend to be impulsive, naming them, and gaining clarity about what you want to have happen will lead to greater impulse control. Much of your behavior is automatic; one challenge of maturity is knowing how to use your impulses for productive ends. Your impulses let you know you are alive; however, when they interfere with long-term goals they can be damaging. Impulse control starts with awareness of when you tend to act impulsively, pressing the pause button, and choosing to delay your response to give you time to consider how to best respond or act.

Barriers to Effectiveness

❏ Poor coping skills for managing stress

❏ Pushy; interrupts to "get things done"

❏ Unclear goals and objectives, making it difficult to use emotional impulses constructively

❏ Lack of self-awareness

❏ Lacking empathy or compassion for others

❏ Being around others who fail to use good impulse control

Quick Action Tips

I. **React too quickly, resulting in negative interactions or comments you later regret?** Many people have impulse control challenges. While there are lots of impulses that guide your behavior, those most relevant to emotional intelligence are tied to your emotions. Impulses serve as a reminder about your personal needs and wants when faced with difficult situations or challenges. You can learn to react constructively (to use the impulse) rather than being used by the impulse. Keep an impulse log for a couple of weeks: What did you do, what were you thinking at the time you responded, and did you get the constructive results you really wanted? One way to develop impulse control is to use the impulse as a cue to step back, get perspective, ask for clarification before you react, and identify at least three constructive responses instead of your typical reactive response. Use the impulse as a clue to see an emotional STOP sign and respond in constructive ways.

2. When overwhelmed or stressed, do you tend to react impulsively? The combination of high stress, poor stress management tactics and lots of impulse control challenges is a formula for emotional distress and over-reaction. You may have been in less stressful situations when a particular event or statement by someone doesn't prompt much of a reaction at all. Later, the same comment by another person prompts an immediate negative reaction. The only difference was your stress level. Fortunately, we can learn stress management tactics which will lower our distress and increase our abilities to manage our impulses. Typically, stress management tactics involve physical activity, perspective reframing, social connections, and spiritual or philosophical reflection on the situation at hand. If you make it a point to walk 20 minutes a day, park as far from your office as possible, and take the stairs rather than the elevator, you will enhance your physical well-being. To reframe situations when you are upset with someone, ask yourself, "What is the individual's positive intention?" If you haven't recently listed your top ten values, then do so, and identify how you demonstrate these values in your interactions with others. Evaluate which of these tactics you might use more often and then practice them.

3. Would it be news to you if someone said, "Stop interrupting me!"? One indication that you have impulse control challenges is how often you interrupt others, dominate the discussion, discount what someone is saying to you before hearing them out, or answer questions before the speaker has finished. If you've never received this feedback before, you may not have an impulse problem. However, it could be that people experience you as so domineering that they are afraid to call you on the behavior or don't think you would take kindly to feedback. In other words, don't take the absence of this kind of feedback as necessarily good news. Check it out by asking a colleague or friend for specific feedback about the behaviors listed above. Practice letting others finish before commenting. Allow a few seconds to pass before responding. Replace a tendency to interrupt with asking open-ended questions and confirming what you hear. Create a reminder to put on your desk or computer screen to slow down and listen.

4. Are you "had" by your past? No one likes to be "had" — to feel out of control in some form. Yet, when you respond quickly out of your personal history which has not been reflected on and understood, you are being "had" by it. For example, say that you find yourself dealing with someone who is just like an irksome family member. If you respond to them like you would to the family member, you are being "had" by your past. Instead of responding to the individual in front of you with attention to the present, you are responding as if this person were your relative. In other words, rather than being in the present, you are acting out of "old tapes" from the past. If you occasionally feel that you are becoming your mother or father in your responses, then you are acknowledging that your reactions may be driven by things you learned from your parents. Any time you find that your automatic reactions can't be readily understood by the facts in front of you, you probably are responding out of events in your past. Reflect on your reactions to situations and what about your reactions may be based on childhood events or lessons from your parents. Use these lessons to help you respond more productively.

5. Find that there are often words you wish you hadn't said? Your expressions display (or betray) your true reactions. Your reactions are based on your point of view and tacit assumptions about what is going on. You may need to create an external cue such as a piece of tape on a daily log, journal, etc., to remind yourself to wait to hear the whole story before reacting. You will also find it helpful to analyze previous situations in which you wish you had said something different. What would be the alternative words or phrases you would use that would facilitate a constructive outcome? Make a list of the words that you would like to change when talking with others and identify a constructive option for each one. Strive to use the constructive term such as in this example: "Who dropped the ball here?" can be better said as, "Let's list all of the things that went well and then the things that didn't go as well with an eye to correcting them."

6. Do you know what emotionally hijacks you and why? Impulses may serve needs that come from a deep place inside of you. To grapple with your impulses, identify previous reactions and what you wish had happened in retrospect. List those things that get you "hot" under the collar. Notice any trends or patterns. You may find that you are irritated by individuals who move at a different pace than you, or who focus on the outcomes before you want to, or who violate in some way values you hold dear. By knowing your hot buttons, you can develop a plan for circumventing them. Establish some ground rules with others to use these clues. Ground rules might be, "No interruptions when one person is talking," "share potential solutions when you identify a problem," or "ask before you tell."

7. Do you easily get discouraged and lose momentum? When frustrated, do you tend to give up on completing tasks, leaving things unfinished? If you have projects that are still gathering dust around the house or work responsibilities not completed on time, this may be an important challenge for you to address. One approach to managing your impulse to give up is to acknowledge your good intentions around starting things, but slow down your actual commitment to starting. Give yourself time to decide if that project is really where you want to spend your time and resources. Sure it would be wonderful to put a hand railing up along the stairs to the basement, but before you go to the home improvement store, give yourself a few days to think about what else you need to accomplish in the next month. If the hand railing is still a priority, go for it. Sometimes, however, we don't get to set our priorities. Then developing strategies to motivate yourself when you don't much feel like moving ahead can be very useful. When have you felt motivated before? What triggered that feeling? Can you use that same motivator again? Or how can you reward yourself for pushing through and getting the job done when you don't feel like it? What moves you to move mountains? Is there a higher purpose or value that you can invoke to give you what you need to cross the finish line? Can you break the mountain down into hills you are more likely to walk over? Whom can you ask to support you and hold you accountable as you make progress? Choose a project you need to complete, choose one of these strategies, set a small goal, and try it out.

8. Alienate people you care about? Often when impulse control issues are present such as constantly interrupting others, you will find that people important to you keep their distance. No one wants to be around a blasting furnace all the time — meaning, do you constantly put out critical, emotional energy? Consider the number of times you have held your comments until others have finished theirs. If you need to work on being more patient, ask for assistance from others around you. In other words, sign up some accountability partners. Those who care about you are more willing to tolerate your interpersonal challenges, and they will appreciate even more your declared willingness to work on what you say, and when and how you say it, when dealing with them. Another impulse control challenge is risky behavior (e.g. drinking too much), which can push people away. If others feel that you may not be in as much control as you should be in words and deeds, then you can benefit from becoming more aware of how your responses affect those around you and what you may need to do to slow down your responses before you react.

9. Find yourself in dangerous or difficult situations because you failed to consider possible consequences? Every decision has consequences. For example, the direction you take when you step out of a restaurant in a large city may unintentionally send you to a dangerous neighborhood while you are looking for a taxi. If you ignore your surroundings and simply act without consideration of the situation, your impulse to keep moving is overriding your need to strategize about safety, especially in large cities or new neighborhoods. If you don't have a system for alerting you to potentially risky scenarios or consequences, create one. Whether it is a night out or an important team meeting, begin with the end in mind. Identify any special considerations and specific actions you need to take to get to that end point with physical and psychological safety as part of the process.

10. Wish you had stayed in school to complete that degree? Youth is known for its impulsivity. Too many do not complete their degrees — they prefer to spend their time and energy on other things. If this is true of you, then reflect on what you spent your time on rather than the books or going to class and what the long-term consequences have been or may be. Use this as a lesson from which to learn how fulfilling immediate impulses more often than not has limited benefits. Fortunately, you can correct this particular situation with night school and distance learning programs. Importantly, what decisions are you now facing that can have long-term implications (e.g. car purchases, career related decisions, etc.)? These might benefit from a very careful cost-benefit analysis. Write down the issue, all of the options you can think of, and ask others for their advice. Identify the pros and cons of each option, select key criteria for desirable outcomes (such as financial return), rate the options, and begin to implement what appears to be the best choice. Each time you have the impulse to quit, change, or ignore your goal, revisit your notes about the benefits of making this choice. If you have new information, then redo the cost-benefit analysis.

18

Related Competencies

(12) Emotional Maturity   (14) Emotional Self-Control   (24) Intentionality

(27) Listening Generously (32) Patience   (33) Perspective-Taking

(36) Reframing   (41) Self-Awareness   (50) Stress Hardy

Learn from Experience

Work

❏ Take on a task force or organizational challenge that addresses an issue you feel passionate about and which needs a long-term solution.

❏ Negotiate a highly sensitive deal that has significant financial consequences for the organization, a deal that requires careful, well planned interactions with key stakeholders.

❏ Interview a senior leader in your organization who has shown significant impulse control when dealing with key issues or challenges.

Personal

❏ Engage in a hobby that requires *extensive* use of skills or abilities that you do not have and that will require focused attention to learn and adjust.

❏ Interview politicians on how they manage negative ads.

❏ Ask emergency response professionals how they manage the pressure of crises and their techniques for keeping calm during the "storm."

Resources

Books

Davis, Martha et al. *The Relaxation and Stress Reduction Workbook* (New Harbinger Self-Help Workbook). Toronto: New Harbinger Publications, 2010.

Grant, Jon, S. W. Kim, and Gregory Fricchione. *Stop Me Because I Can't Stop Myself: Taking Control of Impulsive Behavior.* New York: McGraw-Hill, 2004.

Grant, Jon, Christopher Donahue, and Brian Odlaug. *Overcoming Impulse Control Problems: A Cognitive-Behavioral Therapy Program*, Workbook (Treatments That Work). New York: Oxford University Press, 2010.

Spradin, Scott E. *Don't Let Your Emotions Run Your Life: How Dialectical Behavior Therapy Can Put You in Control* (New Harbinger Self-Help Workbook). Toronto, Canada: Raincoast Books, 2003.

Internet

Skillpath.com. Skillpath seminars: 'Managing emotions and thriving under pressure." www.skillpath.com

Neuro-Sculpting Training Studio. Click on Brain Fitness Blog—Impulse Control Training. www.neuro-sculpting.com/brain-fitness-blog

Do a search to locate impulse control or emotional self-control workshops in your community. They are often offered through continuing education programs in community colleges or mental health centers.

Classes and training

The Resilience Institute. Resilient leadership. www.resiliencei.com

18

19 INDEPENDENCE

Definition

Thinking for yourself and making decisions based on personal values and beliefs while considering, but not being overly influenced by, the feelings, needs and desires of others

Our ultimate freedom is the right and power to decide how anybody or anything outside ourselves will affect us.

— Stephen Covey

Talented

❑ Stands alone if needed when important values and beliefs are at stake; says "the emperor has no clothes" when appropriate

❑ Conveys clear opinions while engaging in good give and take in conversation and in working with others

❑ Takes the initiative to accomplish significant endeavors

❑ Learns from success and failure to move forward with confidence

❑ Collaborates with others, realizing that when all contribute the whole is greater than the sum of the parts, thus achieving synergy

❑ Creates interdependent groups to achieve success

Skilled

❑ Steps back to consider whether the current path works

❑ Speaks up for beliefs and values, but gives up in the face of strong criticism or pressure

❑ Consults others but usually trusts own judgment to make decisions

❑ Sets personal goals and generally works toward them without getting distracted

❑ Takes risks confidently

Unskilled

❑ Buys into the prevailing thought without question

❑ Seeks to be on the winning side or the powerful side regardless of what that side represents

❑ Curries favor vs. being able to stand alone

❑ Seeks approval before acting or speaking

❑ Acts like a lone wolf, failing to collaborate with others

Big Picture View

Personal effectiveness depends on a blend of being both independent and assertive while also being able to cooperate and collaborate with others. The successful blend is often a dance which depends on the situation, organization culture, expectations and your personality. Some people seem naturally independent. For others, a road to increased independence starts with taking small risks to make decisions, question what is happening, offer suggestions or express ideas. Small risks that lead to success (others listen and consider what you say or your decision pays off) can build increased self-confidence and a greater emotional independence. Good emotional independence means operating from an internal locus of control by taking credit for what you make of your life, including your relationships, accomplishments, satisfactions and fun rather than feeling like forces outside of you are in control. Being independent means listening to your own voice while caring about others, giving to and receiving from others without losing your own way. It also means collaborating with others while honoring your own boundaries and needs and honoring those of others. The ultimate independence means acting from self-confidence and self-respect while collaborating with others to create synergy and accomplish more than what can be accomplished alone. This is also called interdependence. Independence overdone, on the other hand, can leave you feeling alone and unconnected.

Barriers to Effectiveness

❑ Negative internal self talk and exaggerated fears

❑ Overly concerned about others and their needs, leading to an erosion of confidence and independence

❑ Low self-confidence, leading to defensiveness around others

❑ Being overly independent to the point of failing to take others into consideration when making decisions or charting a course of action

Quick Action Tips

1. **Get stuck when others challenge or disagree with your decisions?** Take time to understand how your colleagues feel about the decision facing you. Ideally, disagreement well stated can help you create a stronger plan. Weigh their considerations along with your own thoughts. Incorporate what you can. Assess the risks of going ahead with your ideal decision; if there is more to be gained than lost, take action. Ask yourself what is the worst that can happen. Plan how you might deal with that. Take a small risk first to build your confidence. Who do you know that manages disagreement well? Observe how that person handles challenges and disagreements and try out the tactics you see them use.

2. **Are you your own worst critic?** If you often over-focus on the negative and what wasn't accomplished or what you should have done, you may need to practice stopping the critical "tapes" in your head. Substitute positive statements. The "self talk" you do is often a habit that you can change with effort and practice. While driving home after work, remind yourself of three successes you had that day. Use positive thoughts to encourage yourself when you start new projects ("I have the know-how I need to be successful." "I am resourceful and can solve problems when they arise.") Listen to positive feedback you get from others instead of discounting it. Become your own encouraging mentor.

3. **Prefer that others make tough decisions for you?** Reflect on any patterns of repeatedly asking others for advice or wanting others to make tough decisions for you. Do you turn to close friends or co-workers for support or advice much more than they come to you? Practice making your own decisions once you have the information and buy-in from others you might need. To involve others in decisions and plans can be very helpful. But abdicating your right and responsibility to set your own goals and make your own decisions is self-defeating. Is there a difficult decision you have been putting off, such as seeking a promotion that would mean a move? Get as much information about the possibilities as you can; list your own pros and cons, including your feelings about the options; ask for input from those the decision would affect such as your partner or children and add that input to your pros and cons; consider the tradeoffs inherent in the decision and go with what makes the most sense given what you know. Remember, no one has all of the information or knows how a decision will turn out. You can only do the best you can with what you know now.

4. **Wish you had more friends and people you could count on?** Sometimes a need for success and independence leads to a series of life decisions that fail to value the impact you are having on those around you. If you usually stay late at work and work most weekends, when do you invest time in the relationships

that most matter to you or build friendships that will be there for you? If job opportunities are your only criteria for making geographic moves, with whom will you celebrate your success? Working hard and moving for a job don't need to come at the expense of having deep relationships. But if autonomy is a driving force in your life, considering how to balance that with an investment in caring relationships may be important for your overall happiness.

5. Are you independent only when you "know the right answer," but hold back if you are working outside your area of expertise? You are not alone in feeling more confident and independent when you are the expert. Unfortunately, being expert may mean that you fail to listen to others who might have good ideas. It might also mean that you fail to offer your own possibly helpful ideas when they are outside your field of expertise. One of the challenges for leaders moving from being a technical or individual contributor to supervising others is to do less while coaching and delegating more. Another challenge is to shift focus to solving broader organizational challenges. Consider ways you might foster the independence of your direct reports by delegating the work you used to do and holding them responsible. Develop your own self-confidence by contributing to the solution of broad organizational problems even if it means stepping out of your comfort zone.

6. Do you sometimes overdo independence? Confidence in your own ideas and the ability to initiate and take action is valuable. Too much independent action, however, might cause you to be seen as a lone wolf or someone who does not work well with others. In this fast-paced and complex world, no one can be successful without the support and help of others at work or home. Build a network of people you can count on by asking for what you need in specific, clear, and manageable ways. Be gracious and thank those who respond to your requests. Offer to help others when you can, especially when you have the time, know-how or resources they need. Network with those in your neighborhood and at work to find common ground and ways you might add value. One neighbor may be happy to feed your cat while you are on vacation. That person in accounting might be able to quickly explain how to fill out a new form required for purchases. Just ask.

7. Find that you often let others take the lead in conversations or discussions? Do you wait to share your ideas until you are asked? Even this small habit or style of interacting can communicate a lack of confidence or independence to those around you. Plus, you may undermine your own feeling of confidence. This week, practice taking the initiative to speak early in a meeting or discussion. Prepare, if necessary, before a meeting that has an agenda so you can contribute early. Start conversations with your spouse, children or colleagues by either sharing something you have done or read or heard. Ask an open-ended question to start a conversation. Notice how you feel when you initiate or take the lead in interactions. You may need to practice this action to feel comfortable and develop a new pattern of behavior.

Related Competencies

(2) Assertiveness   (3) Authenticity   (4) Collaboration

(41) Self-Awareness   (42) Self-Confidence   (44) Self-Regard

Learn from Experience

Work

❏ Take an expat assignment to a foreign country or a short-term assignment to another location.

❏ Get a meeting agenda ahead of time and prepare to present your own ideas on one key issue. After the meeting, ask a colleague for feedback about how well thought out and clearly presented your ideas were.

❏ Join a project team that is championing a new approach.

❏ Assemble a task force from various disciplines to address a common problem.

Personal

❏ Take a trip by yourself, making choices that please you.

❏ Attend a city council meeting and express your viewpoint about an issue before them that is important to you, such as a greenway, billboard ordinances, or rezoning requests close to your home.

Resources

Books

Adams, Jane. *Boundary Issues: Using Boundary Intelligence to Get the Intimacy You Want and the Independence You Need in Life, Love and Work.* Hoboken, NJ: John Willey & Sons, 2005.

Covey, Stephen R. *The Seven Habits of Highly Effective People.* New York: Free Press, 2004.

Davidson, Margaret. *I Have a Dream: The Story of Martin Luther King.* New York: Scholastic Paperbacks, 1991.

Beattie, Melody. *Choices: Taking Control of Your Life and Making It Matter.* New York: HarperCollins, 2002.

Internet

Center for Creative Leadership: "Leadership Skills and Emotional Intelligence," Research Synopsis #1, 2001. (Once on the site you will notice other articles on subjects such as empathy, authenticity, emotional intelligence and many other topics as well as programs to develop leaders and managers.) www.ccl.org

PicktheBrain.com. Five Ways to Develop Independent Thought." Tom O'Leary, 2005.

Six Thinking Hats.® Do an Internet search and you will find many sites offering information about this approach for problem-solving and independent thinking.

Classes and training

Broxburndrive.com. Search for interdependent manager workshop.

Movies

"Norma Rae," 20th Century Fox Film Corp., 1979.

19

20 INFLUENCING OTHERS

Definition

Conveying a message in a manner that moves people towards commitment to it

If your actions inspire others to dream more, learn more, do more and become more, you are a leader.

— John Quincy Adams

Leadership is influence.

— John C. Maxwell

Talented

❑ Understands that people make decisions based on what matters to them

❑ Recognizes that timing is important to consider when making an appeal

❑ Accurately reads what motivates different people and uses that to gain their commitment

❑ Expresses ideas and requests in ways that inspire groups as well as individuals

❑ Creates events and presentations that effectively shape opinions

Skilled

❑ Recognizes that people are motivated in different ways

❑ Expresses interest in what drives behavior — in self and others

❑ Attempts to persuade using straightforward methods

❑ Tries different approaches to influence people and projects

❑ Gets people to agree but not always to act

❑ Relies more on logic and less on emotions and relationships to influence outcomes.

Unskilled

❏ Displays limited awareness of what is important to self and others

❏ Assumes that everyone thinks the same way and is motivated by the same things

❏ Uses logic alone to influence

❏ Misses nonverbal cues signaling resistance

❏ Discounts others' points of view or values

❏ Pushes harder, louder or longer in the face of opposition

Big Picture View

People are moved by many things, and not all of them are conscious. You are shaped by values and experiences, by what others think or taught you, and by human nature and biological instincts. Decisions are often made with emotions and justified with logic. Deploying effective tactics for persuasion depends on your ability to suspend what's important to you and see situations from other people's perspectives and in terms of what matters to them. People with well-developed influencing skills recognize that the key to understanding others is to first understand yourself. Understanding where you are coming from and how that can differ from where others are coming from enables you to read your audience more accurately, what motivates them, where the similarities and differences are and to find common ground. Effective influencers employ an array of influencing tactics that are linked to the emotional drivers of their audience. Building trust and a broad network of relationships are additional tools that enhance the ability to influence others.

Barriers to Effectiveness

❏ Habit — sticking with what is familiar

❏ Egocentrism — seeing things only from your point of view

❏ Underestimating the power and role of emotions

❏ Zeal for your own agenda or position

❏ Impatience

❏ Groupthink (when decisions value harmony or consensus more than a realistic evaluation of choices)

❏ Over reliance on authority or intimidation

❏ Lack of self-confidence

20

Quick Action Tips

I. Think most everyone thinks the way you do? A common assumption is that everyone is motivated by the same things. You might be surprised to learn that as long as a fair wage is being paid, money is not a top motivator. Take the time to discover what motivates others. Compare that with what motivates you. The list below, drawn from research, indicates a sampling of the most powerful motivators for on-the-job satisfaction (Renwick and Lawlee, 1978):

- Doing meaningful work (ranked No. 1)
- Opportunity for growth and advancement (ranked No. 4)
- Participating in making decisions (ranked No. 10)
- Pay (ranked No. 12) and benefits (ranked No. 16)
- Working conditions (ranked No. 18)

People make decisions based on what matters to them. Find out what matters to those you want to influence by paying attention to their behavior, especially sudden changes in behavior. Some behavior examples include: becoming animated, sitting forward in the chair, establishing or intensifying eye contact and other changes suggesting increased attention or interest. Reflect on what might have prompted this change and what might be important to the person reacting. Listen for what this person asks about, volunteers to do, expresses interest in, supports or opposes. Look for and note patterns.

2. Puzzled about how best to influence others or what to look for? Gary Yukl, who has studied leadership and sources of influence, describes three potential outcomes to attempts to influence others: resistance, compliance and commitment. Of the three, commitment is the most desirable; it produces the most reliable, motivated and highest quality effort. Persuasion strategies most likely to produce commitment come from someone who is perceived as either highly credible or is highly admired, therefore able to engage others emotionally. (Yukl, 2009.) Consider who might be the best person to make the appeal. An emotional appeal might speak to the person's pride or self-image by expressing confidence in their ability to do what is being requested. For example, "You are among the best I know at making complexity easy to understand. We need your talent."

3. Do you depend too much on logic to influence others? Those who influence skillfully use both the rational appeal to logic *and* the emotional side of the argument to gain commitment. The best strategy, then, is to couple emotional appeals with the logical approach. Curt Grayson, who developed the "Head, Hands, Heart" influence model describes several emotional ("heart") tactics that lead to commitment. Some examples are: arousing enthusiasm, aligning requests with values or self-image, creating a compelling vision, and constructing cause and effect relationships between requests and improved well-being. They are effective because they link to a person's values, goals, self-regard and ideals, all containing an emotional component.

4. Slow to notice the nonverbal reactions you get when attempting to influence others? You can get a better read of how well your approach is working if you pay attention to the body language of your audience. The information conveyed in nonverbal behavior is less intentional or consciously driven, so it is likely to be more revealing. For example, nodding, smiling, remaining attentive — all suggest a favorable reaction ... so far. Looking down, away or (heaven forbid) at one's watch, fidgeting, sighing deeply, frowning — all might suggest that your current approach might not be working, regardless of how favorable the verbal response may sound. Practice looking for nonverbal behavior in low-stakes situations. Choose some occasions with your family or friends to speculate what their behavior might suggest about how they're reacting to some event. Confirm your impressions with them to sharpen and refine your skill at deciphering body language. Try watching TV with the volume turned down. What behaviors do you notice? What do they imply? Turn up the volume. How accurate were you? This is a skill that can be improved but only over time and with practice.

5. Overlook the importance of how others see things? Do you forget to think about or listen for the other person's perspective or values? Being curious about what other people think, value and feel is very useful when it comes to getting better at influencing others. Develop a habit of mind that puts you into the shoes of others. Be curious. Speculate about what you think is going on with others, then check it out. Create space for others to spontaneously speak up and tell you what's on their minds. Failing that, ask them what they're thinking, how they're reacting, and what is important to them. If you are trying to enlist the help of someone you know is eager to get ahead, your approach might be, "Join us on this project. It would be a great chance for you to learn new skills as well as to gain some visibility." If you are seen as someone who, above all, wants to add value, be helpful, and not just sell an idea, then people will usually pick up on that and be more open to your efforts to influence them.

6. Eager to get agreement or need help quickly? Efforts to influence others depend upon whom they like and trust. Impatience can derail your effort to get the cooperation or help you may need. Rather, exercising patience in building relationships, and the trust that comes with them, predisposes people to want to help. This is demonstrated in the famous Bell Labs studies (see reference in Resources section) focused on teams of exceptionally smart scientists tackling very large and complex projects. They found that the single factor that best predicted success was having networks of relationships, already in place, from whom the scientists could get the help they needed *when* they needed

20

it. Build your network of relationships before you need anything from any-one. Assess your current network and where you want to grow it. Reach out by offering help, sharing knowledge, making introductions and becoming a trusted colleague or friend.

7. In the face of opposition, do you push harder, louder or longer? Ever resort to in-sistence or a pushy approach to get your own way? When people use a con-trolling or forceful style to get what they want, or just push ahead without considering the impact they're having, they may achieve a short-term gain but a long-term loss. The undeniable benefit of being task-focused is that things get done. Added push might get the job done sooner, but at what cost? Being fixed on achieving the goal risks ignoring how the process is going or, worse, missing early signals of problems. Does "driven" describe you? Consider set-ting up an early warning system. Stipulate milestones that, if not reached when expected, will alert you to the possibility that something else is going on that was neither expected nor wanted. Schedule interim meetings to audit the process — multi-level meetings to collect broad input on specific parameters and suggestions for process improvement. Find ways to reward people for being continuously alert to ways things can be done better. Create accessible and safe methods for people to register their concerns and to get ideas for improvement on the table.

8. Underestimate the power of emotions? Emotions can be contagious. When ex-pressed clearly and intensely, other people will "catch them." While remain-ing authentic, persuasive people express the emotions that they want others to experience too. These emotions, in turn, can drive behavior. For example, positive emotions generally improve performance in the workplace. Yet joy, happiness, and excitement are the least directly expressed emotions in the workplace. Look for opportunities where these positive emotions can be ex-pressed.

Assess what emotions motivate you. Are you more motivated by positive emo-tion that draws you toward a goal or by negative emotions that motivate you to move in another direction? Think about the same emotional motivators while taking into account your audience. What attracts them or demotivates them, and which is stronger?

9. The magic of charisma ... not among your talents? Two former American presi-dents are often described as gifted communicators and as powerful connec-tors with their audiences — Ronald Reagan and Bill Clinton. Whether you agree with their politics or not, almost everyone they turned their "charm" on reported the profound impact it had on them. Some elements their ap-proaches had in common are elements you can practice. They quickly found common ground. "Where are you from? Tampa, Florida? My cousin lives in Tampa. One of my favorite places growing up...." Listen carefully for what you might have in common with others. Common ground establishes rapport. If intentionally establishing rapport is new to you, practice with friends, family, neighbors, people you meet at your favorite haunts. Practice will improve your comfort with this tactic and sharpen your ability.

Presidents Reagan and Clinton conveyed interest. They listened and asked questions. They wanted to know such things as the people you spend time with, about your happiness, your pain points and about your life. If interest in people doesn't come naturally to you, think about what you are curious about. What do you spend time learning more about? What captures your attention in conversations? What subject matter featured in TV shows, news stories or articles do you find interesting? Find ways to steer conversations to those topics until you hit upon a common interest. Then pursue it with questions.

Related Competencies

(15) *Active* Empathy   (16) Flexibility   (27) Listening Generously
(34) Perspective-Taking (54) Understanding Others

20

Learn from Experience

Work

❏ Sell an idea to your boss or upper management

❏ Partner with another department to achieve a common goal.

❏ Mediate a conflict.

Personal

❏ Recruit volunteers for a large commitment.

❏ Raise funds for a pet project.

❏ Interview persons leading donor relationships for a large university for their rules of thumb and successful strategies.

Resources

Books

Cialdini, Robert. *Influence: The Psychology of Persuasion.* New York: Harper, 2006.

Baldwin, David, and Curt Grayson. *Influence: Gaining Commitment, Getting Results* (Ideas Into Action Guidebooks). Greensboro: Center for Creative Leadership, 2004.

LaBorde, Genie. *Influencing With Integrity: Management Skill for Communication and Negotiation.* Bancyfelin Carmarthn, U.K.: Crown House Publishing, 2003.

Lieberman, David. *Get Anyone to Do Anything.* New York: St. Martin's Griffin, 2001.

Renwick, Patricia, and Edward E. Lawler. "What You Really Want From Your Job," Psychology Today, May 1978.

Yukl, Gary A. *Leadership in Organizations.* Upper Saddle River, NJ: Prentice Hall, 2009.

Internet

Discovery Learning Center. Influence Style Indicator. www.discoverylearning.com or www.influencestyleindicator.com

The Grayson Consulting Group. Influence tactics assessment. www.graysonconsultinggroup.com

Influencing Tactics Assessment. Take the instrument at www.ccl.org/leadership/pdf/community/InfluenceTacticsAssessment.pdf

Harvard Business Review. www.hbr.org. search for: "How Bell Labs Creates Star Performers." The Magazine, 1993.

"How to Influence When You Don't Have Authority," by Harold Scharlatt in Forbes.com, Jan. 3, 2011. (This article references Curt Grayson and David Baldwin's work on influencing with head, heart and hands.) www.forbes.com

Use Tactics. www.cathybolger.com/usetactics

Classes and training

Training Registry: a directory of various training programs. www.trainingregistry.com/influence_training.html

Center for Creative Leadership. Offers several leadership development programs all designed to increase self-awareness and knowledge of leadership and influencing skills. www.ccl.org

20

21 | INITIATIVE

Definition

Taking a proactive, action-oriented approach

Life is what we make it, always has been, always will be.

— Grandma Moses

Talented

❏ Takes the lead in creating alliances in order to achieve meaningful results

❏ Acts decisively after gauging the risks and rewards of possible pathways to success

❏ Recognizes a need and moves confidently and quickly to organize a response

❏ Inspires and motivates others to be part of an effort or process with ease

❏ Creates opportunities to make the company, a product, a process, or relationships better; is strategic

Skilled

❏ Makes things happen; meets deadlines

❏ Takes action when asked; usually is reliable

❏ Works well with others; responds to direction (though may not be the source of inspiration or direction)

❏ Seizes opportunities and makes things happen when encouraged to do so

❏ Comes up with good ideas, but may not act on them

Unskilled

❏ Procrastinates when unsure or risk is involved; doesn't follow through

❏ Waits for others to take the lead

❏ Fails to muster the support needed to follow through with a plan

❏ Reacts to events as they happen

❏ Operates in continual crisis mode

Big Picture View

The ability to take initiative depends on knowing yourself and being self-motivated to make a difference in those arenas that are important to you. Having a vision or being farsighted about where there are opportunities that others may not see opens the path for initiative. For example, being enthusiastic about a project at work and having thoughts about how it might provide a breakthrough in a problem your team is facing sets the stage for taking initiative. Seeing ways you might make a difference in your community sets the stage for taking initiative. Successfully taking initiative also depends on having the organizational and planning skills and discipline to set and accomplish a goal. When goals are complex and need the efforts of others, being able to motivate and mobilize others towards an end also is important. Finally, some calculated risk-taking is needed to step off the known trail to blaze a new path. Lack of self-confidence may inhibit some from taking initiative. While we all vary in the level of confidence we possess, one way to build confidence is by taking initiative in small matters and building on success.

Barriers to Effectiveness

❏ Good at starting projects, poor at following through or finishing them

❏ Impulsive; jumps in with action on a project before doing the necessary homework

❏ Fearful about taking action; lacks self-confidence

❏ Lacks the discipline and motivation to create or follow through on plans

❏ Unable to stand up to resistance from others

❏ Failure to gain the political support needed to support a project

❏ Poor timing

Quick Action Tips

1. Do you enjoy initiating projects, but hate the follow through? Some of us tend to be better at innovation, seeing the big picture, and creating opportunities to solve problems rather than managing the project and people needed to complete an endeavor. If this is true for you, try partnering with a colleague or friend who shines in managing the details, tasks and people once the project is started. Be sure to include him or her early, and use his or her ideas

to create shared ownership. Share credit with all who are involved. If follow through and project management are expected of you, consider finding a class or training opportunity to develop your project management skills, and therefore comfort, in that area. Community endeavors such as building a new playground work the same way; you might get neighbors excited about the idea and partner with someone who enjoys seeing the project through to completion.

2. Have great ideas for new ventures, but can't seem to muster the support to make things happen? Be sure you understand your boss's strategic plans and goals for the organization. Talk with your boss and colleagues about challenges that are facing them. Do your ideas fit the political climate of the organization or help solve problems that matter to those around you? Which departments and projects are getting resources? Link what you want to do with the strategic imperative. How are you selling your idea? Talk with decision leaders about what you are interested in, and ask for their ideas and feedback. Determine who would be affected by your initiative and talk with them. Enlist partners for your initiative who can help you take the first steps. Can you start with a trial run or limited scope version of your initiative to gain some momentum and show results? Be realistic about whether now is the appropriate timing for your initiative.

3. Want to make a difference, but have trouble coming up with a good idea or fresh approach? Not all of us are gifted at creativity. Try bringing together a team or group of colleagues or friends who are familiar with the problem or issue you want to address. Use good brainstorming techniques with the group by first sharing all the information known from various perspectives, then listing all possible approaches and ideas without judgment. Encourage group members to build on each other's ideas. When all ideas are on the table, assess the pros and cons of each possibility and choose an approach that seems to hold the most promise with manageable risk. Your initiative will show as you create an environment to address an issue and provide a process to do so.

4. Do others seem to beat you to the punch? Maybe you are waiting too long to start your analysis and planning process for an initiative. Maybe you tend to wait for others, such as your boss or spouse, to ask for your help or to delegate a challenge to you. Prime your own pump by scheduling 15 minutes on your calendar once a week to step back from your day-to-day responsibilities to ask yourself questions like:

- "Are there reoccurring problems that I might address once and for all so I can stop spending time putting out the same fires?" For example, maybe every time your product planning department comes up with a new product, the sales department later complains about it. How can you arrange to get all stakeholders involved sooner?

- Are there procedures and processes that we might change to save us time or money?

- What trends in our industry might affect us? If you don't have answers, attend a convention or industry meeting to learn about best practices. Are there any that might pay off for your organization?

- What good ideas have I heard lately? What might I do with those ideas? What incentives do we have to encourage employees to share good ideas?

Use your insight or answers to these and other thought-provoking questions to begin a meaningful initiative. These same questions may apply in your personal life. If you have had a few roof leaks when it rains, maybe it is time to put on a new roof rather than patch around the skylights.

5. Does fear of failing get in the way of your taking on projects or initiatives? It is important to remember that the road to success usually includes some failures along the way. Thomas Edison tried hundreds of possible filaments in his light bulb before finding that tungsten worked. Develop a tenacity of spirit that allows for learning from your failures while continuing your efforts. Experiment and use short feedback loops to make improvements. Engage others from diverse backgrounds in your project to increase the level of innovation possible. Take time to ask for and listen to their perspectives and experience before deciding on a plan of action. Take the time to understand the real problem or issue before trying to solve it in order to reduce your risk of failure.

6. Can't seem to find the steam to even think about that large project? Sometimes we all feel overwhelmed by that large project waiting in the wings of our lives such as doing our taxes or writing that year-end report. We feel guilty but keep putting it off. One way to help yourself start is to use the "Swiss cheese" method described by Alan Lakein. Tell yourself that you will take just 5 or 10 minutes to start your project, perhaps by pulling out last year's tax return and beginning to collect your information for this year's taxes. Once you take that first small first step, the project won't feel quite so overwhelming; inertia will work in your favor as you feel you are making progress. You have made that first hole in your Swiss cheese, and you can see how to make the second hole, chipping away at it, one hole at a time.

7. Does your motivation seem to go into hiding when facing a challenging project or long-term goal? To keep yourself going in the face of setbacks and problems, try giving yourself short-term and intermediate action steps that are doable. Give yourself credit for achieving these small steps toward your larger goal. Use the energy of success to keep yourself going when you hit barriers. If you are putting off making that cold client call, start with a first step of listing three people you want to call. Find the phone number of each person. Try out what you plan to say with a colleague and ask for feedback. Give yourself credit for making progress, and use the energy and confidence to make your calls. Focus on any positive response you get and use positive self talk such as "I have something of value and just need to find clients who want it" to keep yourself motivated to continue. You are in control of your own motivation.

Related Competencies

(2) Assertiveness   (20) Influencing Others   (33) Personal Power

(42) Self-Confidence   (53) Trustworthy

Learn from Experience

Work

❏ Offer to lead a team meeting. Afterwards ask for feedback about how you did and incorporate any suggestions for the next meeting.

❏ Ask to present the results of a project you are working on to some of your peers. Engage them in a discussion about the project and how it might affect them.

❏ Offer to help take a new product to market; specify which aspect of the process you would like to handle.

❏ Lead a quality improvement initiative.

Personal

❏ On Saturday morning, look around your home and pick out a project that you might have put off, such as cleaning out a closet, then do it. How does that success feel? See if it leads to other initiatives over the weekend.

❏ Decide what you want to do for fun next Saturday night and invite several friends to join you.

Resources

Books

Burkhard, Gudrun. *Taking Charge: Your Life Patterns and Their Meaning.* Edinburgh, UK: Floris Books, 1998.

Lakein, Alan. *How to Get Control of Your Time and Your Life.* New York: Penguin Group, 1973.

Nelson, Bob. *1001 Ways to Take Initiative at Work.* New York: Workman, 1999.

Robinson, Bryan. *The Art of Confident Living: Ten Practices for Taking Charge of Your Life.* Deerfield Beach, FL: Health Communications, Inc., 2008.

Smith, Douglas K. *Taking Charge of Change: Ten Principles for Managing People and Performance.* New York: Basic Books, 1997.

Internet

"Taking Initiative: The Options are Endless," by Bob Nelson, 1999. Do an Internet search for the title and you will find the article at inc.com or the Retention Connection web site.

Health Money Success web site. "Who Else Wants to Know the Benefits of Taking Initiative?" 2009. Search for the title at www.healthmoneysuccess.com

Classes and training

Development Dimensions International. Personal empowerment: taking initiative. www.ddiworld.com/learninglinks

21

22   INSIGHTFULNESS

Definition

Seeing beyond the obvious and discerning the true nature of a situation or the hidden nature of things

The key to understanding others is to first understand yourself.
　　　　　　　—Unknown

Talented

❏ Suggests new perspectives, ideas and connections before others see them

❏ Asks lots of questions that had not occurred to others

❏ Sees clearly and intuitively into the nature of complex persons, situations or subjects and wants to know more

❏ Offers wisdom and perceptive views to help others learn about life

❏ Displays avid curiosity

❏ Detects what cannot be seen directly

❏ Accurately hypothesizes cause and effect in behavior by noticing similarity of conditions under which behavior occurs

Skilled

❏ Asks questions about people, situations and topics once they are introduced

❏ Recognizes connections between events and reactions but may miss their significance

❏ Compares body language cues with verbal language and spots contradictions

❏ Detects emotional undercurrents and asks questions to better understand their causes and impact

❏ Typically responds to and adjusts for unspoken negative reactions

Unskilled

❏ Makes observations that are predominately obvious, superficial, simplistic, concrete or literal

❏ Neglects to consider that things might not be as they appear

❏ Appears disinterested in underlying causes of events and behaviors

❏ Describes events as discrete rather than seeing the relationships among them

❏ Describes limited experience from which to draw insights

Big Picture View

Insightfulness comes from being curious and intuitive. It requires you to be reflective and relentlessly honest with yourself. Curiosity motivates you to notice the world about you. Being reflective leads you to notice your reactions as well as others' to the world and to hypothesize about the implications of those reactions. The intuitive piece of this equation takes you beyond what's obvious. It invites you to speculate beyond the concrete evidence. And when practiced frequently enough, insightfulness becomes sharper and more accurate.

Barriers to Effectiveness

❏ Disinterested

❏ Overconfident

❏ Lack of curiosity

❏ Analytical to a fault

❏ Discomfort with conflict and ambiguity

❏ Defensive or opinionated

Quick Action Tips

1. **Not a people watcher?** The best way to develop insightfulness is to practice making observations about people and situations. Speculate what might be behind what you're observing. Then seek regular and objective feedback from various sources that will reflect on the accuracy of those observations and predictions. (In the beginning be sure to keep some notes to check the accuracy.) As time goes by, you are not only sharpening your intuitive skills but also your insight into connections, motivations and how events are likely to play out.

2. Concrete or literal? We all have gifts and limits. And typically there are upsides and downsides to any attribute. Being concrete (real) or literal (actual), for example, promotes accurate measurements and observations, a trait that is very helpful in certain engineering and investigative occupations. The downside, though, is missing what is beyond the obvious, the meaning behind the words or inconsistencies when they exist. Do you frequently misread people, get surprised by how things turn out or sense that circumstances are not what they seem, but you cannot put your finger on why? Try the action tip above (Quick Action Tip 1). At least once a day, reflect on an interpersonal experience where there might have been more going on than was obvious or stated. Describe what actually happened. Then make some guesses about what was left unstated — outcomes, assumptions, motives or feelings — anything that might have been experienced internally. Were there any surprises? How might you explain them? These are just guesses until you get confirmation, but they prime you to pay attention to details that you might otherwise overlook. Challenge yourself to explain why events turned out the way they did. Now pose a second but less obvious explanation, maybe even a contradictory one. So now you have one description (literal, actual) and two explanations that are just guesses. Make a note of them so you can come back later and evaluate your guesses. As time passes, notice when "concrete" information sheds light on the accuracy of your guesses. You might even discuss these experiences with others who might have more information or are known to be insightful. Compare your perceptions and guesses to theirs. As above, your guesswork will become increasingly insightful.

3. Don't readily notice the responses you get? Insightful behavior is sometimes evidenced by how quickly you notice whether the response you're getting is not the one you want, and how quickly you adjust until you do get the response you're looking for. Start by paying attention to and valuing the responses others have to your behavior. What will motivate you to do that? If you are not one to notice others or care much about their reactions, what would it take to stimulate that interest? One of the quickest ways to create that interest is to pair your attention to people and their reactions with something that naturally attracts your interest. What intrinsically matters to you? If you cannot quickly answer that question, think about experiences you've enjoyed. What about them appealed to you? Recall conversations you found interesting. What was it that interested you? Identify at least three topics that matter to you. Pursue those subjects when interacting with others. By staying on the lookout for these subjects, you're training yourself in a new habit — noticing the responses you get.

4. Narrow or limited experience? Sometimes, a lack of skill in certain areas is more about lack of experience generally or lack of the experiences that would test and build a particular skill. An example might be an accountant who works with individual clients and whose personal life doesn't include much volunteer activity. With a focus that is mostly solitary, this person may have had little opportunity to experiment with and develop insight into other people and groups. One remedy for this is to find opportunities where insightfulness is needed and can be practiced — maybe an assignment at work, a volunteer role or a family challenge where using insight can offer significant benefit. Insight also comes from reflection. Thinking about why you do what you do, as well as hypothesizing about the emotions and actions of others, will help you learn about yourself. As you get to know yourself, you will become more perceptive about others. Practice reading yourself and others. Find someone with whom you can discuss your observations and what sense you make of them. Over time, you will find that your insights will become more accurate. Insight and intuition have much in common. Check out competency (26) Intuition for other ideas.

5. Internally focused? For some people, paying attention to the people and situations around them doesn't come as naturally as it does to others. To get the experience you need in order to develop and to trust your "insights," you need to intentionally focus outwardly, toward the external world of people and their behavior. One way to motivate yourself to develop this habit is to think about the benefits. How might it help you to be more aware of the people around you? Some possible benefits are improved relationships and more accurate assessment of people — their strengths, motivators and likely actions and reactions — leading to better people decisions. That's improved emotional intelligence, for sure! Some people report that being more aware of others has helped them engage more comfortably in "small talk" in social situations. Remind yourself of the benefits that matter to you as a way to encourage yourself to be more focused on others.

6. Get stumped by complex challenges? Complexity can be, well, challenging. This is especially true if you haven't had much experience dealing with complex projects, problems or situations. Or you might be one of those people who prefers things to be more straightforward or black and white. Regardless, everyone can learn to deal more effectively with complexity. And insightfulness is a tool that can help get you there. Try this the next time you're confronted with any issue with some complexity:

1. First, gather all the relevant information. What question are you trying to answer and what kinds of information will you need? Use these criteria to winnow down the information.

2. Then, sleep on it. Yes! Sleep on it. Your conscious mind is limited, but research has documented the vast potential that your unconscious can bring to complex challenges via expanded insight. Conscious processes often disturb unconscious processes,

so you need to distract your conscious mind. Sleep accomplishes that.

3. Back test your thinking. Verify any concrete data necessary to evaluate your insight. The unconscious mind reportedly is less precise and less agile with concrete or literal information. So, use your conscious (rational) mind to perform this check. This is especially true if you're new to partnering with your unconscious.

Going to sleep isn't always an option. You can substitute going for a run or walk, listening to music, or doing any other task that gives your brain a break. Afterwards, notice whether one option feels better than the others. If it makes it through the back test step, you have brought new insight to your decision-making. So, while complex challenges seem to warrant hard and sustained thought, the science suggests otherwise. Taking a mental break produces better decisions.

7. Lazy learner? Becoming more insightful is not exactly like becoming a better listener or becoming more flexible. It is a cognitive or mental process that you are developing, and it might be more difficult. But, one of the best ways to learn anything is to borrow strategies from those who do it well. Practice those that you think will work for you, then teach them to someone else. Who do you know who qualifies as expert in insightfulness? What do they do that looks and sounds insightful to you? Interview them about how they developed those skills and behaviors. Which behaviors can you do more of? Which ones will you start doing? What help do you need? You now have a learning partner — use him or her as a coach or mentor. As you gain competence through practice, find a way to teach this to someone else. Consider assembling a learning group of three or four people (learning partners), including you. Choose topics you want to learn about and teach. Use each other as subject matter experts. In addition to getting smarter, you get a group of friends, maybe for life.

8. Reluctant to consider others' points of view or ideas when they conflict with yours or interfere with getting what you want? You might be suffering from egocentricity or a conviction that the way you see things is exactly the way things are, which is pretty convenient when the way you see things serves your purpose. Egocentricity, however, blocks critical thought, truth and objectivity. If egocentricity is the problem, insightfulness is the cure. Developing insightfulness may start slowly when it means giving up a perspective that is self-serving. It requires that you open your mind and listen carefully to other perspectives. It requires that you reflect honestly on your reasoning and behavior, make your beliefs explicit, challenge their objectivity and change them when in error. Insightful people apply the same standards they have for others to themselves.

Related Competencies

(15) *Active* Empathy   (34) Perspective-Taking   (41) Self-Awareness

(46) Social Intelligence   (54) Understanding Others

Learn from Experience

Work

❏ Mediate a conflict and learn to identify hidden feelings, issues, needs and expectations.

❏ Accept an assignment involving a task you hate to do and learn more about how to motivate yourself.

Personal

❏ Visit a foreign country, ask lots of questions and record what you learn. Reflect on the meaning of what you observe and discuss it with others.

❏ Engage in one new learning activity each year.

❏ Make peace with an enemy and notice what you learn about yourself that can help you in the future.

❏ Choose someone you know who seems especially adept at picking up on background dynamics. How do they do it? What do they notice? Observe them in action and interview them later to find out.

Resources

Books

Wyman, Pat. *Three Keys to Self-Understanding: An Innovative and Effective Combination of the Myers-Briggs Type Indicator Assessment Tool, the Enneagram, and Inner-Child Healing.* Gainesville, FL: Center for Applications of Psychological Type, 2002.

Pearman, Roger and Sarah Albritton. *I'm Not Crazy, I'm Just Not You.* Boston: Nicholas Brealery Publishing, 1997, 2010.

Tieger, Paul D. *The Art of SpeedReading People: How to Size People Up and Speak Their Language.* Boston: Little, Brown and Company, 1999.

Internet

Suite101.com. "Mindfulness Training for Self-Awareness" by Jerry Lopper, on the work of Jon Kabat-Zinn. August 2009. www.suite101.com

Project Implicit Mental Health. At PIMH you are invited to experience

modern methods of assessing evaluations that may exist outside of conscious awareness or conscious control.
www.implicit.harvard.edu/implicit/user/pimh

Classes and training

The Leadership Trust.® "Impacting Relationships to Impact the Bottom Line." Trains leaders with a highly personalized, self-awarness focus. www.leadershiptrust.org

The Silva Method. Offers training and material "to awaken the potential in everyone." www.silvalifesystem.com

23 INTEGRITY

Definition

Behaving consistently with your values, principles and motives; being trustworthy, truthful and candid; doing the right thing even when no one is looking

> *Have the courage to say no. Have the courage to face the truth. Do the right thing because it is right. These are the magic keys to living your life with integrity.*
>
> —W. Clement Stone

Talented

❑ Acts ethically and honestly, even in private matters

❑ Admits mistakes, learns from them, takes responsibility for them, and encourages others to do so without penalty

❑ Articulates best practices, personal values and a code of ethics; sets an example of adhering to them

❑ Creates an environment where all may raise ethical concerns which are fairly investigated

❑ Is respected for honesty, takes risks to be candid and honest

❑ Creates an environment where being candid and honest is valued

Skilled

❑ Keeps promises; is honest

❑ Expresses personal values and acts accordingly

❑ Makes decisions and takes actions at work that reflect the best interests of the organization

❑ Acts within general ethical guidelines and laws

❑ Does the right thing without being asked

Unskilled

❏ Inconsistent in keeping promises or confidences ("Psst, don't tell anyone, but...")

❏ Self-serving and self-promoting; acts more in service of personal interests than the stated organizational values

❏ Shows little tolerance for challenges or inquiry into questionable behavior or decisions

❏ Behaves in such a way as to give the appearance of impropriety, often acting in ways contrary to the "greater good of all" or the best interests of the organization

❏ Cannot be relied upon to the tell the truth; may lie by omission when the truth is inconvenient

Big Picture View

Integrity is one of the necessary conditions for effective leadership and relationships. Without it, a person is building his or her house on sand. Even if acts of dishonesty or malfeasance are not noticed by others, living a life which lacks integrity is soul and character damaging. Ideally the importance of integrity is learned early in life when the consequences of lapses of honesty are less severe. Maintaining integrity is much easier than rebuilding a besmirched reputation, especially for individuals in very visible positions. If a person is perceived to lack integrity, the reasons must be determined and addressed. To regain a reputation for integrity can have all the challenge of Humpty Dumpty in the nursery rhyme:

> *Humpty Dumpty sat on the wall*
> *Humpty Dumpty had a great fall*
> *All the King's horses and all the King's men*
> *Couldn't put Humpty Dumpty back together again*

Re-establishing a reputation for integrity probably will take longer than anticipated. It helps to apology for previous missteps, make amends if possible and show consistent actions that reflect integrity going forward over time. Integrity is enhanced by self knowledge, open communication, courage, clear personal values, and open relationships with others.

Barriers to Effectiveness

❏ Expedient with ethics when under time pressure

❏ Failing to learn personal responsibility at an early age

23

❏ Justifying integrity breaches as situational; the ends justifies the means

❏ Failing to realize that current behavior is inconsistent with previous statements

❏ Valuing personal gain more than integrity

Quick Action Tips

1. Not sure if you meet the standard of integrity? Are you clear about your own values? In the rush of life and accomplishing challenges at work, you might not stop to understand what integrity means to you. Take time to write your top ten personal and professional values and share them with your work group, friends or family. What are the key values of your immediate group at work? Top family values? Identify them and discuss how your group or family acts on them day to day. Connect the dots between values and your behavior. For further exploration, try taking an online values clarification inventory. Several possibilities are listed in the Resources section at the end of this chapter.

2. Do you keep sensitive information others share with you in confidence? Ask up front if unclear whether information can be shared with others. Speak up if you are not able to maintain a confidence due to ethical or legal reasons. Ask others to not share confidences if you don't think you can maintain their trust. Check with close colleagues or friends to see if they have any questions about how you maintain confidential information.

3. Do others know where you stand on important issues? If not, what keeps you from speaking up? If it seems risky to do so, consider the risks and downside of not speaking up. Try telling a few trusted colleagues or friends your thoughts and ask for feedback. Take responsibility for your thoughts using "I" messages such as "This is important to me," or "I feel strongly about this," rather than assuming there is only one way to approach a problem or issue. Self-disclosure is an important way to deepen our relationships and to allow others to understand our values.

4. Are you giving others credit for their work? To recognize and reward the contributions others make to a project generates trust and commitment. Include contributors in final presentations of results to higher levels; let them present if appropriate and give them credit. If you seem to be taking credit for the work of others, you may lose your reputation for integrity.

5. Do you share all relevant information with your colleagues and help them as needed? Too often we see peers or those in other parts of the organization as competitors for promotions or influence and seek an advantage by holding our cards close to the chest. To withhold information may seem dishonest to others and lead to an unwillingness on their part to work with you. Share what you know willingly. Seek out ways to work fully and openly with colleagues.

6. Does your organization have a code of ethics? Find out and read it if your organization does have one. Consider whether you and your work group are honoring it and the intentions behind it. Share it with your group and discuss whether any changes need to be made by the work team to be seen as demonstrating integrity.

7. Have you been dishonest, even in small ways? Start with acknowledging to yourself if you have cut corners, taken advantage of the system, stolen the property of others, lied, or cheated. Now is the time to turn over a new leaf by setting a higher standard for yourself. Make amends if you need to do so. Confess or apologize if appropriate. How will you keep from making mistakes that might undermine your reputation for integrity in the future? Decide if you need to seek a mentor or coach for support.

8. Do you respect others? How would your spouse, children, direct reports and neighbors answer that question? A person of integrity treats others with respect and dignity, demonstrates compassion when necessary and takes the needs of others into consideration. Integrity is enhanced by knowing yourself and acting in a consistent manner. Whom have you failed to treat with full respect this past week? While you may not have intended to interrupt someone, give an order rather than engage, or act in a demeaning manner, reflect whether you did so. Whom do you want to treat better going forward? How will you do so? How will you check yourself to know if you are living up to your commitment to do so?

23

Related Competencies

(5) Compassion   (39) Self-Actualization   (41) Self-Awareness
(44) Self-Regard   (47) Social Responsibility

Learn from Experience

Work

❏ Create an "integrity" taskforce to identify best practices for employees in your organization.

❏ Create a space for employees to confidentially share concerns about behaviors and actions that might reflect on the integrity of the organization.

❏ Check out the professional code of ethics for those professional organizations to which you belong. Share them with colleagues at work.

Personal

❏ Check with your spouse, children or close friends about any times you may not have kept a promise to them. Discuss it to fully understand the other person's point of view. Apologize and make amends if appropriate.

❏ Take a values clarification inventory as a way of examining your values and key motivators (See Resources section below.)

Resources

Books

Carter, Stephen L. *Integrity*. New York: Harper Perennial, 1996.

Cloud, Henry. *Integrity: The Courage to Meet the Demands of Reality*. New York: Harper Paperbacks, 2009.

Lavenia, John. *Integrity Is Everything: Regain Your Natural Ability to Get Everything You Want*. Charleston, SC: BookSurge, 2009.

MacArthur, John. *The Power of Integrity: Building a Life Without Compromise*. Wheaton, IL: Crossway Books, 1997.

Simons, Tony. *The Integrity Dividend: Leading by the Power of Your Word*. New York: Jossey-Bass, 2008.

Internet

AllBusiness.com. "Do you need integrity to be a successful leader?" Nancy Lane, 2005. www.allbusiness.com

Centre for Business and Public Sector Ethics, www.ethicscentre.org

Life Values Inventory. Free online assessment of personal and career values. www.lifevaluesinventory.org

Applied Psychology Resources Life Values Inventory. www.appliedpsychologyresources.com/life-values-inventory

Your Soul at Work, Five Steps to a More Fulfilling Career and Life. www.yoursoulatwork.com/values

Classes and training

The University of Pennsylvania: The Wharton School, Executive Education Leadership Development Programs. Explore programs such as "High-Potential Leaders: Accelerating Your Impact"; and "Building Relationships That Work." www.executiveeducation.wharton.upenn.edu

Center for Creative Leadership. Webinar, "The Pillars of Successful Executive Leadership: What We Know About Senior Leaders and What It Means for Your Development." www.ccl.org/leadership/community/pillarsWebinar.aspx

23

24 | INTENTIONALITY

Definition

Acting with purpose, direction and clear will toward a specific outcome or goal

Our vitality is as great as our intentionality.

— Paul Tillich

Talented

❑ Speaks clearly and acts consistently with goals and personal objectives

❑ Solicits help and support to achieve personal goals

❑ Adapts action plans as conditions change to get the desired outcomes

❑ Articulates the actions being taken and how these are aligned with intent and outcomes

❑ Stays focused even when competing interests or projects arise

❑ Approaches each day's schedule with energy and enthusiasm

Skilled

❑ Develops missions, goals and plans but doesn't always follow through

❑ Seeks feedback to better align intention, behavior and desired outcomes

❑ Communicates plans and goals with others

❑ Identifies and seeks out the resources needed to accomplish personal goals

❑ Expresses commitments consistently

Unskilled

❑ Approaches life challenges in an ad hoc fashion with no clear goals

❑ Rarely considers whether efforts are having the desired impact

❑ Seems uninterested in setting ambitious goals; rarely initiates projects or activities

❏ Expresses disinterest, boredom or confusion with life's current direction

❏ Appears aimless

❏ Lacks enthusiasm — for anything

Big Picture View

Intentional people know what they want. They figure out how to make it happen, and they turn their purpose-driven energy toward getting results. Purpose is about values, and values are emotionally driven. If you can figure out what purpose lines up with your values, both your emotions and your energy will carry you across the goal line. Whether it's choosing a career or another life direction, it's important to assess how it lines up with what is important to you. Only then will your choices, actions and enthusiasm all point you in the same contented direction.

You can be as intentional about situations as you plan to be. If you want to be seen as being intentional in your choices, then you have to learn the habit of asking yourself, "What do I want from this interaction or situation and how can I accomplish my goal without harming others?" To do this consistently requires that you make time to reflect on what matters to you, what you want to achieve, and what talents you possess or need to develop to be successful. Pull this together in a development plan and take action. You are showing intentionality when you express confidence and show excitement about choosing and creating the life you want. When you formulate an idea or expectation about a situation, you are thinking intentionally. When you identify a goal and specific action steps required to get there, you are planning intentionally. When you act on what you say, you are being intentional.

Barriers to Effectiveness

❏ Fails to set personal goals or to even consider what you want from your relationships

❏ Ignores feedback from others that might encourage a behavior change

❏ Not making time for reflection on the alignment of your behavior with desired outcomes

❏ Obsessively concerned with things that haven't worked or focusing on events that cannot be changed

❏ Lack of self-esteem or lack of a belief in self; depression

❏ Narrow life experience

❏ Lack of self-discipline

Quick Action Tips

1. See little value in creating a personal plan? Your intentionality is directly related to the energy you put into planning for the future. If you know you are working toward a particular outcome, then you tend to organize activities and direct energy toward that goal. A plan is a statement of intention, and if the plan is actively created and maintained, then it changes as situations require adjustment. Goals need to be specific (e.g., lose five pounds each week for six weeks versus "lose weight"). Activities or actions toward each goal need to be measurable. And for a plan to have long-term value, you need to record progress and have an accountability partner who can check in with you from time to time. Write your goals in a place you look every day. In a sense, the way you live your life shows a map of what you feel is important. Would you rather have this happen by intention or by accident?

2. Don't solicit feedback from others to know if your behaviors are supporting the desired intent? The only way to know for sure that your behavior is having the desired outcome with others is to ask them. Intentionality is affirmed when you are clear about the alignment of behavior and outcomes which feedback can provide. Find ways to ask others with whom you work and live for insight about how your behavior affects them. While you can ask for feedback in formal ways, often paying careful attention to how others are responding to you is feedback enough to know that you are achieving your relationship goals. At a minimum you need an accountability partner who you invite to remind you about your goals and who can give you feedback regularly.

3. Forget to monitor progress on personal goals? Whether you use an electronic device to keep up with your schedule or a printed calendar, you can make notes about your efforts on your goals. You are more likely to put energy — intentional effort — behind reaching those goals you monitor. It is important to set up benchmarks related to your goals and to mark achieving them. In fact, some "micro" celebrations for reaching various benchmarks is a good thing to do. A "micro" celebration could be calling a friend to just connect or to share good news about achieving a goal.

4. Feeling bored or disconnected? When we aren't intentional about what we want to achieve, even in small things, it is easy to feel bored. Begin with small but personally important goals. Think about a few situations in which you want a certain outcome. As you gain more experience with the link between your intentions and your outcomes, try it out on bigger life goals. For example, on a piece of paper create four columns and label them as follows: goal statement, desired or intended outcome, specific behaviors to get there, and measures of how it is achieved. Fill in the columns for a personal relationship, personal health and professional or work situation.

5. Ambivalent about what is worth doing? Sometimes you may not be directed or intentional because you are ambivalent about what you want to do. Ambivalence can exist for a number of reasons — too many options, unclear options and choices, and simply not having either enough or the right information about your choices. At the root of ambivalence is a lack of commitment to priorities. Having too many options to prioritize can be as debilitating as over-analyzing choices. To break through the ambiguity, make a list of your top five values and ask what your priorities are, given those values. Make a goal list with priorities, and plan accordingly.

6. Not sure how to start? Being intentional about what you want to achieve and how you want your life to be lived begins with clarity about what is important to you and how you like to spend your time. This is not about changing the world or taking on huge tasks; this behavior is about tapping into your purpose in life and living consistently with that purpose, whatever that may be. As you identify those experiences and events that mean the most, reflect on what you learned and what you did that mattered the most. Create a personal mission statement, and list the five main goals you need to achieve to realize that mission. For example, "My mission is to provide a safe, satisfying, and secure life for my family. To achieve this I need to...." Identify the strengths you will use to reach those goals. Prioritize what you have discovered and ask how you can recreate those satisfying and meaningful experiences for yourself today and tomorrow.

7. Haven't considered yourself as someone with the personal power necessary to achieve goals? You have to begin to recognize that you have as much personal power as everyone else — you don't need a special title to assume you are personally significant. Your life experiences, your personal choices, and the path you have taken are sources of wisdom that you can use to motivate yourself to achieve your personal and professional goals. One way to focus on your goals is to realize that "if it is to be, it is up to me." Each goal deserves a plan of action that specifies what you are going to do by when and whom you are going to use as an accountability partner to keep you on track.

8. Need to motivate yourself or build confidence to develop a plan and act on it? Begin with recognizing your strengths and accomplishments. You will always be more confident when you accurately realize — and honor — what you are good at. If you have a good idea of your strengths, then make a list, and put it where you can review it regularly. If you don't have a good sense of your strengths, you can get some help. Ask for feedback from those who know you well. Interview your mother. Build your list. Review the common elements of your past successes looking for clues. Think about the things that come easily to you, that you don't have to think twice about. All of these are clues and ways to develop your list of strengths. Add to it as you become aware of more. The process of building your list and reviewing it will make you more aware of your strengths and will help build your confidence. Pay attention to the positive feedback others give you. Add this to your list and review it frequently.

9. Are you so self-critical that it prevents you from creating a personal plan? Are you suffering from analysis paralysis about how to spend your time and energy? You have to learn how to turn down the internal volume and frequency of the self-critical voice. Chances are that this has been with you since childhood, which means it has staying power. At some point you have to ask, "What is the cost to my sense of effectiveness and my satisfaction of attending to this critical voice?" The usual first victim of this critical voice is self-confidence. One of the best ways to strengthen your self-confidence is to set goals and reach the goals you set — at home or at work. Keep a record of what your goals are and the progress you are making. Once completed, make a point to give yourself credit for accomplishing what you set out to accomplish. Write up a description of it. What actions did you take? What were the results, quantified, if possible? Who benefited? Each time you recognize that you are making things happen that you intend to make happen, you become more aware of your own effectiveness. Those are the building blocks of self-confidence. And obviously another outcome is building the capacity for intentionality.

10. Not convinced that being intentional matters? Create a top ten list of the most significant experiences of your life. Identify what happened and what the benefit has been to you in your life. Look at who and what was involved among these top ten experiences. Now make a list of the top ten experiences you want to have. While reflecting on the importance of the top ten so far, identify insights and lessons that can assist you in reaching the ten you want to have. Build on your lessons and insights of what you learned from the past to what you want to learn in the future. For example, if a top ten experience for you was coaching your kid's soccer team, think about how those coaching behaviors can help you coach your work team to greater success.

11. Avoiding making needed changes or dealing with important issues? Uneasy about the quality of your relationships at work or home? Know of conversations with your boss you need to have but don't? Each of these statements reflects an awareness that what you want to achieve and what is experienced are out of alignment. The distance between what you want and what is may seem like a journey of a thousand miles. All such journeys begin with the first step. An important first step is acknowledging that there is a gap between what you want and how things are. A second step begins with answering such questions as: How are you behaving that contributes to the status quo? What do others see about your behavior (which means asking) and the barriers to reaching your goal that you may unintentionally be generating? What is your current behavior in any of the situations listed above telling you, and what would be the tangible benefit of reaching the desired or preferred outcome? What are you deeply committed to that keeps things the way they are? How can you test if those commitments are on solid ground? Once these things are clear to you, identify specifically what you want to achieve and how you can get there.

Related Competencies

(18) Impulse Control   (34) Perspective-Taking   (35) Reality Testing
(36) Reframing   (39) Self-Actualizion

Learn from Experience

Work

❏ Create a change plan for an important organizational initiative. Thoroughly research change stages and key elements that must be implemented for the plan to be effective.

❏ Identify a long-standing conflict within your peer group and initiate a conversation for addressing the issue involved.

❏ Identify an individual who can discuss how to align intention, behavior, and impact on others. Make sure to select several behaviors where there are misalignments; if none are readily apparent, seek feedback to identify how what you intend and what others experience are aligned.

Personal

❏ Create a plan to develop skills that might help you be more effective as a parent, partner, or friend.

Resources

Books

Baldoni, John. *Lead With Purpose: Giving Your Organization a Reason to Believe in Itself.* New York: AMA, 2012.

Covey, Stephen. *The Seven Habits of Highly Effective People.* New York: Simon and Schuster, 2004.

Internet

www.healing.about.com. Search for "intention."

Classes and training

BeIntentional.com. Workshops and training on intentionality.
www.beintentional.com

The Center for Intentional Leadership.
www.centerforintentionalleadership.com

The Healing Vessel. Workshops on meditation, intentionality and related subjects. www.thehealingvessel.com

25 INTERPERSONALLY SKILLFUL

Definition

Using a wide range of skills to effectively communicate with, relate to, and get along well with others

> *The wonder is not that communicating is as difficult as it is, but that it occurs as much as it does.*
>
> —Reuel Howe

Talented

❑ Handles difficult situations with grace

❑ Uses influence skills, collaboration and negotiation as needed to successfully accomplish a goal

❑ Asserts self successfully with a wide range of people and situations

❑ Manages conflict effectively and addresses conflict to foster communication, build relationships and create positive outcomes

❑ Adeptly reads both nonverbal and verbal communication to foster understanding

❑ Shows interest and gives attention when meeting new people

❑ Engages others in conversation by asking thoughtful, open-ended questions relevant to the setting, listening for meaning, and sharing relevant personal information and experiences

❑ Uses humor well

Skilled

❑ Influences, collaborates and negotiates effectively but not at the same time

❑ Acts assertively in some situations with some people

❑ Establishes rapport by using good communication skills but not with all groups equally well

❑ Manages conflict if necessary, but avoids some difficult situations

❏ Recognizes when there is misunderstanding between people due to poor communication; follows up to clarify intentions

❏ Shows interest in people, asks appropriate questions, and listens

Unskilled

❏ Acts alone instead of collaborating and negotiating with others

❏ Avoids opportunities to interact with others; is somewhat withdrawn

❏ Bounces between unassertive and aggressive actions

❏ Creates confusion or lack of trust in relationships with unclear and inconsistent communication

❏ Creates a poor first impression due to poor communication skills

❏ Is sarcastic without realizing it is offensive

❏ Reacts impulsively, demonstrating a temper and irritability

Big Picture View

Interpersonal skills or social skills are an important part of emotional intelligence because they represent the ability to communicate, demonstrate leadership, build relationships, and work toward shared goals. Are there any among us who don't need to use these skills daily? Interpersonal skills affect your success and happiness in all parts of your life. Developing interpersonal skills is an expansive skill set and uses many building blocks from among the emotional intelligence competencies in *People Skills Handbook*, such as (27) Listening Generously, (29) *Reading* Nonverbal Communication, (2) Assertiveness, (11) Emotional Expression, (7) *Effective* Confrontation, (15) *Active* Empathy, and (4) Collaboration. These building blocks provide the groundwork for communicating and getting along well with others. While you may be more inclined to work alone, you can develop the skills necessary to be successful in your interactions with others.

Barriers to Effectiveness

❏ Over-focusing on interpersonal relationships at the expense of what you want or need to accomplish

❏ Hot buttons, emotional vulnerability, or extreme stress

❏ Lack of role models growing up

❏ Self-doubt or critical self-talk

❏ Hyper-critical about others

Quick Action Tips

1. Do you feel uncomfortable or find it difficult to join into conversations or discussions? Trying to join an energetic conversation can sometimes feel like intruding. Start by simply joining the group and listening until you understand the topic being discussed. Remember that people can listen in three ways:

- to gather information
- to empathize
- to try to solve a problem

Be sure to gear your listening style to fit the conversation. Make eye contact with the speakers and show interest by a nonverbal response such as smiling or nodding. When there is a break in the conversation, ask a relevant open-ended question addressing the last speaker by name or, if you have relevant experience or information, contribute that in a succinct manner. Soon you will fit in as part of the conversation.

2. So task focused that you damage relationships in your drive to get things done? While we all may have deadlines and urgent projects to accomplish, unless you show basic respect and appreciation for those who help you to be successful, your leadership or relationships will suffer. Engage others by providing information, asking for ideas, listening and considering suggestions that are offered, and using the talents and ideas of others whenever possible. Never cut someone else off, make deriding comments, or criticize someone behind his or her back. If you are under a tight deadline, be clear about a time frame and agree with those involved on how to reach it. Too often managers under pressure respond by taking over tasks or taking back responsibility from others instead of delegating with accountability around clear deadlines and goals. After a project is complete, debrief not only the success of the project, but also the process used, including the people management part. Ask yourself, "Would my colleagues want to work with me again?" Ask them for ideas to improve how people worked together to accomplish the goal. Ask for one suggestion that takes how you work with others to the next level. Confirm what you hear and try it out when you have an opportunity to do so.

3. Do you avoid dealing with difficult people? Who doesn't at times? But those who are skilled at using tact and diplomacy to handle difficult people or tense situations are more likely to be successful. Start by considering your part in a difficult relationship, because you may be part of the problem. Before you approach the other person, be prepared to learn about how you might appear to them. Ask to speak to the other person in private. Use these steps to talk with that difficult person:

- Start by specifying a situation that bothers you.

- Use "I" messages in which you take responsibility for your reaction. "When you refused to get the budget numbers for me on Friday, I was frustrated because Monday was my deadline to complete that proposal." "Saturday we had agreed to spend the day helping Habitat for Humanity. When you called that morning and backed out, I was disappointed and frustrated."

- Ask for input and listen to understand the other person's perspective.

- Confirm what you hear from your colleague, friend or neighbor.

- Ask how the two of you might communicate most effectively in the future.

- Try to problem-solve from a practical, big-picture point of view rather than individual personalities. Focus on your goal rather than who is at fault.

On the job you don't have to like difficult people; you just need to be able to work with them. With acquaintances and neighbors you may want to improve a relationship if possible.

4. Tend to dominate? No one likes being around someone who is overly forceful about taking air time or getting their way. Try using less dogmatic language to present your point of view. Use "I think...," or, "From my perspective...," instead of, "This is what we need to do...," or, "Obviously...." And remember that there are other points of view that you need to hear and consider in order to come up with the best possible decision or plan. Hold off immediate judgment of others and their ideas, especially if you have not fully heard them out.

If you still have reservations about a suggestion made by someone else after due consideration, try offering balanced feedback by first sharing what you like or appreciate about the idea or suggestion and then state the concern you have. Focus conversation around whether there a way to keep the positive part of the idea while addressing the concern.

Pace yourself to take only your fair share of air time in a discussion. Ask thoughtful questions based on what others say in addition to sharing your own ideas. Be sensitive to nonverbal signs that others want to say something, have heard enough from you or are ready to move on. If your goal is to be less domineering, the best feedback for you might be if no one remembers that your great idea was the one used.

5. Don't make a positive first impression? As the saying goes, you don't get a second chance to make a positive first impression, so those first few minutes are crucial. When you meet someone for the first time, make direct eye contact, smile, use their name and let them know you are glad to meet them. Establish ways that you might connect with them, such as identifying people in common, shared interests, hobbies, or professional goals.

If you are presenting to a group, be sure you can be clear, succinct and well informed. Find out from the person who invited you, if possible, what is most important to the group, and start with that part of your presentation. Arrive early to meet some of the attendees and find common ground. Practice your presentation ahead of time with colleagues or friends to get feedback for improvement, and be prepared for questions. Saying your presentation out loud is very different from simply reading it over or thinking about it. Use stress management techniques such as taking a deep breath, holding it for as long as you can and then slowly letting it out in order to go into the meeting calm and positive. Use humor as appropriate. Debrief your presentation for content and presentation style later with someone you trust who was present. Set one goal for improving the impression you make when presenting to groups.

6. Feel a bit overwhelmed by the people politics involved in accomplishing a major project? Often making progress on large initiatives demands as much focus on the people involved as the tasks involved. Start by identifying whom you need on your side to move forward. Set up a time to meet with each of these people to share your goals and information, request help and ask for input from them. Use good listening skills to understand their perspective, and incorporate their needs when possible into the project. Try to identify the tradeoffs you may need to make to ensure success. Seek out a mentor with understanding of how decisions are made in your organization or community and ask for insights or suggestions that may help you. Be sure you have a leader in the organization who actively and publicly supports your project. Keep lines of communication open with peers and colleagues so there are no surprises.

7. Find that you need to influence others without having direct control to accomplish your goals? Find ways to apply the three primary influence tactics described by Dr. Gary Yukl, a professor in the School of Business at the University of Albany.

- Inspirational: Appeal to the values and ideals of others. Create a compelling vision or picture of what you are trying to achieve. Use positive, exciting language to engage and inspire.

- Rational: Present clear facts and logic for what you want to accomplish. Explain your reasoning, show what advantages are in it for others, document why your proposal will work, explain how you will handle problems.

- Consultation: Invite others to participate, to support you and help you in meaningful ways. Ask for their ideas to improve your plan, listen to their suggestions, and address their concerns.

Many of us have a favorite strategy we rely on. Practice all three to expand your own influence skills and then take time to identify which strategy might be most useful in specific situations with certain people.

8. Does your humor tend toward sarcasm? Sarcasm is a risky kind of humor in that it usually implies criticism of the target. Even if those around you laugh, they may be put off by the negativity inherent in sarcasm or cynicism. Clean up your humor. Pause before that caustic humorous comment comes out, and choose your words more carefully. Find ways to voice the positive in the picture. Who uses humor in uplifting ways that you might learn from? If you want to use humor in presentations or speeches, consider using humorous anecdotes such as found in Bartlett's Book of Anecdotes.

Related Competencies

(2) Assertiveness   (4) Collaboration   (7) *Effective* Confrontation
(15) *Active* Empathy   (27) Listening Generously
(29) *Reading* Nonverbal Communication   (37) Relationship Savvy

Learn from Experience

Work

❏ Take on a work assignment which involves interacting with a wide variety of personalities and problems, such as adopting a new software package or reorganizing an office.

❏ Regain a customer who has cancelled your account by meeting with them to identify any problems and possible solutions.

❏ Meet with a potential client to build a relationship that might lead to working together.

❏ Build your network by setting up a meeting with a peer to better understand their goals and strategies.

Personal

❏ Volunteer to be on the board of a community organization.

❏ Go through training to become a volunteer mediator.

❏ Organize your neighborhood holiday party.

Resources

Books

Conger, Jay. *Winning Them Over*. New York: Simon & Schuster, 1998.

Fadiman, Clifton, and Andre Bernard (editors). *Bartlett's Book of Anecdotes*. New York: Little, Brown and Company, 2000.

Hoppe, Michael. *Active Listening: Improving Your Ability to Listen and Lead.* Greensboro, NC: Center for Creative Leadership, 2006.

McKay, Matthew, Martha Davis, and Patrick Fanning. *Messages: The Communications Skills Book.* Oakland, CA: New Harbinger Publications, 2009.

Patterson, Kerry, Joseph Grenny, Ron McMillan, and Al Switzler. *Crucial Conversations.* New York: McGraw-Hill, 2002.

Stone, Douglas, Bruce Patton, and Sheila Heen. *Difficult Conversations.* New York: Penguin Putnam, 2000.

Yukl, Gary. *Leadership in Organizations.* Upper Saddle River, NY: Prentice-Hall, 2009.

Internet

About.com Human Resources. Search for "Ten tips for dealing with difficult people at work." Susan M. Heathfield, 2010. humanresources.about.com

Cathy Bolger, 2009, "Using influence tactics." www.cathybolger.com

Classes and training

Dale Carnegie. "Effective communications and human relations." www.dalecarnegie.com.

25

26   INTUITION

Definition

Tuning in to your "gut feeling" or inner wisdom and checking it against something more tangible to help in decision-making and creativity

The intuitive mind is a sacred gift and the rational mind is a faithful servant. We have created a society that honors the servant and has forgotten the gift.

—Albert Einstein

Talented

❑ Trusts instincts and listens to that inner voice

❑ Checks out hunches against fact and previous history

❑ Demonstrates outstanding creative instincts

❑ Problem-solves well using all available resources including inner guidance

❑ Detects and deciphers underlying patterns in data or events

❑ Perceives beyond what can be experienced with the senses

Skilled

❑ Asks questions, listens well and thinks about possible outcomes

❑ Understands the need to focus beyond the observable

❑ Calls upon those who are gifted in intuition to assist in the creative or problem-solving process

❑ Tunes in to the body and pays attention to its signals (feeling in the pit of the stomach, itchy palms, gut instinct, etc.)

Unskilled

❑ Engages in wishful thinking, confuses fantasy with insight

❑ Guesses rather than spending time developing that inner knowing, leading to undisciplined, impulsive and rash decisions

❏ Projects opinions, thoughts and judgments onto others and calls it a "sixth sense" or intuitive knowing

❏ Avoids taking risks or takes too many; not sure what to trust

❏ Overly focuses on rational and fact-based thinking to the detriment of innovative process

Big Picture View

Intuition: The root of this word in Latin means "to see within" or "to contemplate." And both of those processes, to look within and to reflect, are important aspects of developing intuition. Using your intuition involves accessing your inner wisdom and checking it against something more tangible or concrete. It can often improve decision-making and increase your ability to understand people and situations. Intuition can provide that creative spark for a great idea or visionary inspiration. There is even evidence that intuition has the potential to save your life or prevent serious injury because you listen to that nagging voice inside saying, stop, or don't go there, or turn around, etc. However, benefiting from intuition requires the trust to listen to this inner guidance when there is often little logic to support it.

What is important about intuition and its value as an emotional intelligence competence? Those people who are able to access their intuitive skills are able to think in innovative ways. They can see patterns in events and are able to piece together a "big picture view" without the benefit of logical processing or all the data or information. This is often referred to as experiencing an "intuitive leap" and can be the difference between being stuck and finding a new, creative solution to a problem. And sometimes the answers come when you soak in what is known about a problem or issue and then put it on the back burner of your mind. At the least likely time, things fall into place with a new idea or direction, sparked by intuition.

26

Barriers to Effectiveness

❏ Rigid or narrow approach to problem-solving

❏ Inability to imagine or project into the future

❏ Cynical view of those who think outside the box

❏ Lack of trust in your ideas and creative inclinations

❏ Literal thinking, failure to see patterns or to make connections

❏ Little exposure to those who do use intuition with positive results

Quick Action Tips

1. **Are your creative and intuitive muscles weak?** Intuition requires use — meaning you need to engage those mental muscles that help to develop intuition through such practices as brainstorming sessions, journaling, building self-awareness and other activities that require you to pay more attention to your intuitive inclinations. Listen to your gut. Offer to serve on a task force or committee that is seeking to improve a product or process, learn what you can, and then give your mind time to digest it all. Put your intuitive muscles to work and watch for the results.

2. **Rely so much on your sensory perceptions and what you see that you tend to neglect your inner knowing or vision?** Everyone has the capacity to tune inward and tap into the intuitive way of knowing, but this ability is often obscured by sensory overload. We tend to seek out the expert opinion rather than depending upon our own internal guidance. We are bombarded daily with information that comes in multiple forms — mass media, social media, online data searches and a dozen other forms of information overload — all of which are great but tend to diminish our own capacity to intuitively learn. Learn to pay attention to that nagging thought, the idea pulling at the edge of your consciousness. Stop, listen, take it seriously. Give yourself a mental vacation from all the stimuli around you. Turn off the radio, TV, computer, smartphone, iPad, and try giving your inner radar time to pick up on what you are experiencing.

3. **Do you need to slow down and take your time?** The old adage "sleep on it" is good advice for developing intuition. Be careful not to act too quickly on an intuition. Sometimes people mistake impulsiveness for intuition. Let it sit for a while and maybe sleep on it. One good tip is to write down a problem you've been mulling over right before bed. The intuitive mind will work on it as you sleep, often providing real insight or direction in the morning. There is also ample evidence that, in order for our intuitive muscle to develop, we need to cultivate conditions like time for reflection. (See tip 2 above.)

4. **Do you have an instinctive reaction about something but don't trust yourself?** Many business leaders talk about the importance of following their instincts or intuition. Sometimes an idea flops, but sometimes it pays off. Elias Howe, the inventor of an important advancement in sewing machines, overcame a roadblock in his design through a dream. Had he not paid attention to the information that came through his dream, he never would have solved the problem of how to position the sewing needle in the machine. The husband of a friend trusted his intuition and stopped at an intersection although he had a green light. A car coming toward the same intersection on the cross street ran through the red light. Trusting his intuition saved him. Jot down

when you have a feeling about something and listen to it. How does your intuition work?

5. Do you listen to your dreams? Pay attention to your dreams just as Elias Howe did (see above, tip 4). Many people keep a dream journal to capture dreams as soon as they awake. Many times our intuitive mind works through our dreams. Listening to your dreams and taking them seriously is like learning another language — the more you speak the language the more sense it makes. Dream experts suggest that, before you go to bed at night, you remind yourself to remember your dreams. This conscious reminder to yourself to remember your dreams improves your ability to recall your dreams in the morning. Try this along with keeping a dream journal for a month or so and see what happens. If, after a few weeks of maintaining a dream journal, you notice a pattern or gain some insight into your life or a particular problem, then you are probably experiencing intuitive guidance.

6. Too uptight to let your intuition through? Intuition is something that responds well to playfulness and to your ability to relax and go with the flow. Relaxation or meditation practices are an excellent way to develop your intuition. Check into a course or class offering Mindfulness Meditation, take a Tai Chi class, or try a yoga class, which will help to increase your focus and concentration. And ... play! It takes your mind off of the serious stuff and lets your intuition come through. Play with your kids, your neighbor's kids or your grandkids. Laugh and watch how they follow their instincts to try things you never would. What ideas do you get from playing with them?

7. Looking for absolute answers? Great intuition is enhanced by the ability to accept and embrace ambiguity or paradox. Learn to enjoy the inconsistencies of a situation — have fun with them, play with the situation and let your mind enter the world of the absurd. Open yourself to the paradoxical elements of any decision or situation before you. Brainstorming is also an excellent tool for opening up this part of you. Make it a practice to begin every project or problem-solving session with brainstorming in order to help generate potentially creative solutions or ideas. Keep in mind the rules of the game: "Welcome new ideas, no criticism, nothing is too absurd to be shared." Let it rip! Anyone working in a marketing or advertising agency knows the value of this activity. At the very least it increases morale and team spirit.

8. Afraid of the worst-case scenario? Imagine it! By asking yourself, "What's the worst thing that can happen?" and following that chain of thought, you pin your fears down to realistic consequences. Or you find yourself laughing at absurd fears with no substance. Either way, you will set yourself free. It might also allow a new idea or way of looking at the situation to enter into your awareness. Don't be afraid to go off the grid and imagine the worst-case scenario. It might actually help you avoid it!

9. Ever heard of "going with the flow" and wondered how it might apply to you? The concept of "flow" is one that scientists coined to describe the state of mind or consciousness a person achieves when they lose themselves in their work, their art or in some highly challenging and engrossing activity. It is described as an intense experience, one in which you are so caught up in what you are doing that time stops, the world around you fades away and the only thing you are aware of is what is absorbing you in that moment. It is natural to think of those people who experience "flow" as being artists, musicians, and scientists. However, there is an abundance of evidence suggesting that work environments that create the right conditions for "flow" to occur have much higher worker satisfaction, greater creativity and more innovation in the workplace. And when you are in "the flow" you have more access to your intuition.

Experts say the proper conditions to create an environment where "flow" can occur are:

- There must be clear and concise goals established for the completion of the task. And the goal or activity should have personal meaning and intrinsic value (it must not be busy work!)

- The person engaged in the task, job or activity must have confidence in their perceived ability to accomplish the job and to believe that their skill is equal to the perceived challenge

- There must be adequate feedback provided to help the person assess their performance and how they are doing in relationship to the goal or assignment

- It is important that the activity be neither too easy nor too difficult

If you think about this from the point of view of yourself as a supervisor or parent, then you can make sure you provide each of these conditions. If you are approaching it as the person engaged in a job or activity, then work to make sure that you have clear goals to start, that you are engaged in an activity for which you believe you are well-qualified, one that holds your interest, and that you receive important and timely feedback along the way. If these are true for you, take action.

Related Competencies

(1) Adaptability   (10) Creativity   (13) Emotional Problem-Solving
(22) Insightfulness   (28) Mindfulness

Learn from Experience

Work

❏ Volunteer to lead a new project, however large or small. The beginning stages of a new project require a lot of "out of the box" thinking which will help you to learn to trust your intuition.

❏ As a part of your development plan, give yourself one challenging goal or problem to solve each year. When applicable, ask your team to work together toward its resolution.

Personal

❏ Keep a journal of the hunches you have in order to check their accuracy over time. This habit helps to develop your intuition by paying attention to it.

❏ What brings you peace of mind or deep emotional centeredness? Activities such as meditation, Tai Chi, yoga, prayer, journaling, mindfulness, and even gardening, cooking, or creative expression help to achieve a sense of deep knowing. Any of these practices will help you learn to trust your inner guidance. Try a few and see which fits your style.

Resources

26

Books

De Becker, Gavin. *The Gift of Fear.* New York: Random House, 1997.

Dyer, Karen, and Jacqueline Carothers. *The Intuitive Principal.* Thousand Oaks, CA: Corwin Press, 2000.

Gladwell, Malcolm. *Blink.* New York: Little, Brown and Co., 2005.

Goldburg, Philip. *The Intuitive Edge: Understanding Intuition and Applying It in Everyday Life.* Lincoln, NE: iUniverse, 1983, 2006.

Jing, Zhou, and Christina Shalley. *Handbook of Organizational Creativity.* New York: Lawrence Erlbaum Associates, 2008.

Klein, Gary. *The Power of Intuition: How to Use Your Gut Feelings to Make Better Decisions at Work.* New York: A Currency Book/Doubleday, 2003.

Sadler-Smith, Eugene. *The Intuitive Mind: Profiting From the Power of Your Sixth Sense.* West Sussex, U.K.: Wiley & Sons, 2010.

Von Oech, Roger. *A Whack on the Side of the Head.* New York: Warner Books, 1983, 1998.

Internet

Harvard Business Review article: "Don't Trust Your Gut." Go to www.hbr.org and search for the title of the article

www.ted.com. Wonderful web site with hundreds of fascinating presentations. Search for the presentation by Mihaly Csikszentmihalyi: Creativity, Fulfillment and Flow. Also found on YouTube.

Go to wikipedia.org/wiki/ and search for "flow"

Classes and training

New and Improved web site: Offers training in the development of innovation and creative problem solving: www.newandimproved.com

26

27 | LISTENING GENEROUSLY

Definition

Being completely attentive and accurately responding to what the speaker says and means, and also to what might be behind the words

You cannot truly listen to anyone and do anything else at the same time.

— M. Scott Peck

Talented

❑ Gives full attention when others are speaking

❑ Responds to speaker's message in such a way that the speaker indicates being heard and understood

❑ Articulates accurately the speaker's message, its meaning and why it's important to the speaker

❑ Verbally and nonverbally displays curiosity about and interest in speaker's message and the feelings behind it

❑ Sets aside prejudices, preconceived conclusions and judgments

❑ Demonstrates attentiveness through eye contact, facial expressions and body posture

Skilled

❑ Passively pays attention when others speak

❑ Waits until speaker is finished before responding, sometimes impatiently

❑ Reflects accurately most content heard but misses some nonverbal information

❑ Tempted to argue a position or talk about self, but able to resist most of the time

❑ Acknowledges content of message but misses the emotional content if left unstated

❑ Works to keep from interrupting others

Unskilled

❏ Concentrates on own agenda, tasks and thoughts at the expense of paying attention to anyone else

❏ Interrupts others when they are speaking

❏ Offers responses that are more about his or her own view, experience or situation than about speaker's

❏ Misses the point or important details when others speak

❏ Disinterested in the emotions behind the words when listening to others

Big Picture View

You already know how to listen. Right? You do it all the time. But how good are you at listening? What would your partner, child or best friend say? Listening generously takes listening to its highest level.

There are three key factors at the heart of generous listening: intention, attention and effort. Listening generously is setting aside anything else you would rather be doing or thinking about. It's being intentional about listening, paying close attention without distraction. The challenge is to remain present, curious and focused while someone else is talking. And it does take effort, especially initially, if listening doesn't come naturally to you.

Great listeners turn towards people, sometimes leaning in, when listening to them. They maintain eye contact, nod to indicate understanding and use facial expressions to match the speaker's emotions. What stops you from listening? Some common barriers to effective listening are rehearsing your response, judging, debating the content, or solving the problem.

"The greatest compliment that was ever paid me was when one asked me what I thought, and attended to my answer."

—Henry David Thoreau

Barriers to Effectiveness

❏ Talking. Rule No. 1 to become a better listener is to stop talking.

❏ Hearing things you don't want to hear

❏ Anticipating the content and filtering it

❏ Intense emotion or distress

❏ Complacency, taking people for granted

❏ Self-absorption

❏ Language differences

❏ Values differences or conflicts

Quick Action Tips

1. Lazy listener? Listening doesn't get the respect, or exercise, it deserves. Here are some quick tips to activate your listening muscle and improve any relationship you're in. Choose one to practice tonight or this week.

- Move to a space where you can more easily put aside potential distractions including any phone calls when talking with others.

- Take notes if needed to remember important points and for follow up (so you don't interrupt).

- Be open to views that differ from yours and opinions that change. Ask questions to better understand before offering your own opinion.

- Use open-ended questions that reach beyond a yes or no. (Examples: Can you tell me more about that? What do you mean by ... ? What about that did you find interesting? How did you react? What did you learn from that?)

Avoid:

- Anticipating speaker's message and planning your response while he or she is still speaking

- Finishing a speaker's sentence for him or her

- Hallway discussions on important topics

- Thinking about better uses of your time

- Shooting the messenger

2. Too busy to listen? "If speaking is silver, then listening is gold." (Turkish proverb.) Do you know how to listen effectively but lack the motivation to do it regularly? You may underestimate its value. You learn more from listening than talking. People are more likely to speak up and open up — offering potentially important information, creative ideas, concerns and opinions. It's the quickest and easiest way to warm up any relationship. Generous listening invites richer personal sharing, allowing you to better understand others (empathy). But generous listening takes some extra effort initially. You have to be intentional about it and practice it. Choose someone with whom to practice generous listening, for example, a partner or support staff, with whom you will practice (as described in the "talented" section above) for one week.

Watch and listen for the reaction.

3. Think you're a good listener, but others think differently? Test your assumptions:

- Journal daily your thoughts about people encountered and what you learned about them while interacting with them. Learn much?

- Observe people who model generous listening and identify at least three tactics they use. Are these tactics you use?

- Think of times when you feel compelled to listen (for example, if you're pulled over by a state trooper or meeting with a doctor giving you results of an important diagnostic test). How does this focused listening compare with your day-to-day listening?

- Wandering mind? Does your mind drift when others are speaking? Bored? Impatient? Something else catch your attention? Listening well can be hard work, harder than dieting and exercising for some. But to let your attention drift is to risk insulting the speaker. Can you afford to do that? There is probably nothing quite so off-putting as losing the attention of the person you're speaking to. People remember how they feel when they're with you far more easily than what you said or did. If you have ever felt dismissed while speaking, then you know the effect it can have. On the other hand, some people can focus their attention in ways that speakers are left feeling like there is no one else in the room, or in the universe, for that matter. One strategy for staying focused is to identify one or more things you need to know (or are curious about) that might emerge from this conversation. That will set you up to stay alert for it. Is this person or conversation especially important, and you want to leave a lasting favorable impression? Keep that outcome in mind — it will sharpen your attention. Practice focusing your concentration. Yoga and relaxation training can help develop your powers of concentration. Another strategy is to move the conversation to a space where distractions are less likely.

4. Interruptitis? Have you heard complaints that you interrupt others when they're speaking? Well, it only has to happen once or twice before you start reaping the negative consequences. Sometimes the reward for listening well is hearing things you don't want to hear, thus making the urge to interrupt almost irresistible. Consider the message your interrupting others sends. Do you think you and your thoughts are more important than the person you are interrupting? Do you have little or no interest in the thoughts of others? Do you believe the floor is yours for the taking any time you want it? Interrupting is a bad habit and one that can take some effort to break. It starts with a change in thinking — your thinking. What assumptions are you making when you chose to interrupt someone? What assumptions make it OK for you to interrupt others? Recall a time when you interrupted someone so that you can get a fix on just what your thought process was. You will probably discover some underlying values that either support the offending behavior or that are being violated by the behavior. In either case, revisiting your values will help drive a change in your behavior if this is something you want to work on.

5. "It's all about me, isn't it?" Do you find that your personal experience interferes with your hearing the speaker's experience? If your goal is to fully capture the other person's story, then find a way to put yours aside and redirect your attention back to the speaker. Specify a later time to capture or talk about your own experience and the feelings that go with it. You can write about it or find a generous listener to listen to you, but later. Process your experiences as they occur, freeing you up to be more attentive to others and their stories. Use the commonalities between the speaker's story and yours to tap into what you're naturally curious about, and redirect your attention back to the other person. Use questions. If you're asking questions, then you accomplish two things: you stop telling your story, and you return attention to the other person's story.

6. Mishear, misunderstand or mess up? Do you miss the speaker's point or their message entirely? Do you hear something different from what others hear, or understand what you hear differently? How could that happen? Some possible reasons: distraction, intense emotion, hearing impairment, language barriers, complicated or confusing information, different values, disinterest, or disagreement, to name a few. Determine the cause first, then you're half way to the cure. In general, however, consider using questions to confirm or improve your understanding of what has been said so far. Take notes to review later for clues to gaps in understanding. Ask others present for their perspectives on the information presented and on your understanding of it. Take a class on a subject about which you know nothing and use these tips.

7. Too emotional to listen? Your emotions may be distracting you. Reduce the intensity of your emotion, and its pull, by shifting your perspective. Reframe the situation that is causing the emotional intensity. Is there a potential silver lining? Reinterpret the meaning of the situation. Some examples: Instead of a positive diagnosis of shingles, it's a dodged diagnosis of appendicitis. Instead of a relationship lost, it's an opening for a more satisfying one. Instead of a perfect storm of personal challenges, it's a perfect time to reassess decisions made.

8. Miss the Listening 101 course? For those who need a basic overview of listening, here's the short version. Basic listening is focused on the content and accurately hearing what is being said. Active listening adds action to basic listening. The actions are behaviors that demonstrate to the speaker that listening is actually taking place. Such actions include restating, paraphrasing, acknowledging and asking related questions. Empathic listening takes listening to a whole new level. The listener now is listening with her eyes and ears for both the speaker's content and the emotions surrounding the content, as revealed by both verbal and nonverbal expressions. Attending to the speaker's message and feelings, and accurately reflecting both, triggers a feeling of being heard and understood in the speaker that is profound. Often a deepened connection emerges between the speaker and listener as a result. Generous listening is sustained empathic listening. In both empathic and generous listening, the speaker's emotions are accurately detected and confirmed. In generous listening, however, the listener seeks more information, encouraging the speaker to share more of their experience or story. Determine which listening skills you use regularly, and which would benefit from development. Decide which level you want to practice and with whom. Identify a situation that you think that person would like to talk about and a time convenient for you both. Afterwards, reflect on your effort. Did you demonstrate good listening at whatever level you targeted? What worked well? How could you have done better? What barriers did you encounter? What will you do differently next time?

Related Competencies

(15) *Active* Empathy   (18) Impulse Control   (25) Interpersonally Skillful

(29) *Reading* Nonverbal Communication   (54) Understanding Others

27

Learn from Experience

Work

❏ Do phone coaching. In coaching you will have to listen closely to establish and maintain rapport and to get the information you need to move the process forward.

❏ Conduct interviews by phone (hiring, 360 assessment, subject for article). Often you have only one chance, one call, to get the information you need. Good listening skills will make it easier to succeed.

❏ Interview several colleagues who are good listeners about what motivates them and why.

Personal

❏ Volunteer for service on a mental health hotline.

❏ Dedicate one conversation per week to listening generously to someone important to you.

❏ Take a class in a subject that you know nothing about.

❏ Identify one person who listens to you generously; describe how it feels and what they do that contributes to that feeling.

❏ Ask for feedback from a spouse, partner, or close friend about your listening skills and what would improve them.

Resources

Books

Covey, Stephen. *The Seven Habits of Highly Effective People.* New York: Free Press, 2004.

Donoghue, Paul J., and Mary E. Siegel. *Are You Really Listening? Keys to Successful Communication.* Notre Dame, IN: Sorin Books, 2005.

Davis, Martha, Kim Paleg, and Patrick Fanning. *How to Communicate Workbook: Powerful Strategies for Effective Communication at Work and Home,* New York: MJF/New Harbinger Press, 2004.

Hoppe, Michael. *Active Listening: Improve Your Ability to Listen and Lead,* Greensboro, NC: Center for Creative Leadership, 2007.

McKay, Matthew, Martha Davis, and Patrick Fanning. *Messages: The Communication Skills Book.* Oakland, CA: New Harbinger Press, 2009.

Internet

Mind Tools, "Essential Skills for an Excellent Career." Search for "communication skills." www.mindtools.com

Classes and training

The Training Registry. Search for "listening skills." www.trainingregistry.com

American Management Association. Search the web site for "communication skills training" or "dynamic listening skills." www.amanet.org

27

28 MINDFULNESS

Definition

Focusing on the present moment and suspending both internal chatter and also external distractions to allow clarity and composure

Do you have patience to wait till your mud settles and the water is clear? Can you remain unmoving till the right action arises by itself?

— Lao Tzu

Talented

❑ Savors the present moment with little to no self-consciousness

❑ Elevates an internal feeling of positive well-being through focus on perceiving experience rather than judging it

❑ Listens nonjudgmentally to interactions, seeking to understand content, intention, and emotions

❑ Cultivates a calm state of mind; capable of reflecting upon a situation before acting

❑ Creates an environment where preconceptions can be questioned and there is time to stop, reflect, and be receptive to new ways of doing things

Skilled

❑ Shows a capacity to self-monitor and keep quick judgments on hold

❑ Attends to information seeking to understand rather than judge value or merit

❑ Creates regular opportunities for reflection and meditation to reduce stress and fully enjoy the moment

❑ Demonstrates a curiosity about the way things are

❑ Engages in controlled breathing and body positioning exercises to boost awareness

Unskilled

❏ Exhibits very little interest on how to focus attention or direct personal ways of seeing things

❏ Judges situations without any self-reflection

❏ Seems to be in a frequent state of distress; feels that he or she has no way out of difficult situations

❏ Articulates being overwhelmed or unable to find time to meditate or reflect

❏ Is experienced as impulsive and reactive rather than thoughtful and responsive

Big Picture View

Mindfulness is an approach to living that allows us to be more present, to be less self-conscious and to accept ourselves and the events in our lives in a way that reduces stress and increases satisfaction. The research on mindfulness began in earnest in the 1970s. As a self-discipline practice, mindfulness has gained attention in medicine and psychology because of its effectiveness as a tool for lowering blood pressure and reducing other physiological and psychological aspects of stress. Mindfulness-based stress reduction courses are offered in medical schools and universities throughout the country and are used to teach people how to engage in nonjudgmental awareness of the present moment, helping to overcome the effects of negative thinking. Emotional intelligence is diminished when we over-engage in replaying or fearing the past or in anticipating or fearing the future. Mindfulness assists in overcoming this by asking you to focus on what is in front of you and to suspend judgment of your current experience. It is a way of calming the body and the mind in order to examine your present circumstance from a more detached or nonreactive position. By cultivating a calmer state of mind, you are able to make decisions that are thoughtful and responsive instead of reactive or overly emotional. This leads to greater EQ and well-being.

Barriers to Effectiveness

❏ Being too busy for reflection, focus, and relaxation

❏ Inadequate impulse control

❏ Judging interferes with focusing on what is

❏ Perception of mindfulness as too difficult or unusual

Quick Action Tips

1. **Forgotten how to relax and let go of that tension in your shoulders?** Not only is that tension and tightness in your body uncomfortable, but that tension is a sign of your stress. Use the discomfort as a signal that you need to more effectively manage what might trigger your stress. If your daughter's running late for school is frustrating, then how can you plan better tomorrow? If your mind starts racing when you can't find the numbers you need for a report at work, then who can you connect with to have those numbers available on time next month? Once you have considered how to better manage what triggers your stress response, add a mindfulness practice (meditation, yoga, Tai chi, prayer, etc.) to increase your resilience and maintain your calmness on an ongoing basis. Taking the time for regular reflection and relaxation may seem daunting given the complexity of most people's schedule. But developing a regular mindfulness practice can help you operate at your best, to have clarity of mind and to focus on what is essential and important. Not only will you be stress resilient, but you will be more able to respond in the moment to what matters the most.

2. **Never thought about the benefits of focusing on mindfulness and meditation?** Lower blood pressure, a greater feeling of purpose, and more engagement with others are outcomes of creating time for being more mindful. An important condition for mindfulness is the development of a calm, relaxed and meditative state of mind. By learning to reduce the internal chatter (all those thoughts racing around in your mind) and focusing your awareness on the present, you will be able to cultivate relaxation, which leads to a greater sense of inner peace. Start by taking a few minutes daily to go outside and sit quietly, tuning into the sensations around you — sounds, colors, shadows, physical sensations. Walking can become a form of meditation. It can be done slowly and deliberately by focusing your awareness on each movement in the body, savoring the physical sensation of walking. Regular practice of these exercises helps to cultivate a calmer mind and reduces stress, anxiety and tension. And no cell phones or loud or rhythmic music, because that can be distracting! Sometimes a headset with soothing music can lend itself to the process, but the best music is the silence of nature.

3. **Find that being quick to judge can turn others off?** Judgment is the enemy of mindfulness. When you are making fast judgments about a situation or information, you might be missing helpful information still available or ideas from others involved. In fact, when it comes to dealing with people, quick judgments rarely work out the way we expect. Create a cue (e.g. a piece of tape on your scheduler) to remind you to turn off judgment and turn on deep listening. Being open in the moment to really hear what a colleague or friend is saying may allow you to understand in a new way what matters to

that person. Being fully present, not only in body, but also mind, heart and soul, might open new avenues of communication in a relationship that you formerly dismissed.

4. Find it difficult to manage your negative reactions? Is being critical typical of the way you approach challenges? If you often see what is wrong with a situation first, you are setting yourself up to carry negative emotion around with you all day. Find a place for a few moments of total relaxation, then imagine that you are having a conversation with the people you talked with today. List in your head all of the positive and constructive things others did or said. The goal is to get you thinking more positively and less negatively so you can meditate without distractions.

5. Curious about the power of mindfulness, but not sure where to start? Consider the Six Steps of Mindfulness (adapted from the Psychology Today article listed in the resource section):

- Unselfconsciousness (not thinking about things too much)
- Savoring (not worrying about the future, more focused on the present)
- Breathe (inhabit the present)
- Flow (making the most of time, able to lose track of it)
- Acceptance (moving towards a problem rather than away from it)
- Engagement (know that you don't know, which makes you open to learning)

Which of these might be of most benefit to you at this point in time? Try out one of these steps this week, especially in combination with a mindfulness practice of being present in the moment, paying attention without judgment through meditation, Tai chi, yoga, prayer, or another mind-body approach. Use one of the "Guided Mindfulness Practices" available to listen to or for download at http://www.umsystem.edu/curators/mindfulness.

Benefits to mindfulness include increased ability to relax, better concentration and creativity, more energy and enthusiasm, reduced stress levels, and increased feelings of well-being.

6. Don't really know how many attention channels you can use? Studies of attention and focus inform us that there are four "channels" we move among all the time. The four channels include: scanning the environment, focusing on a specific item in the environment, internally analyzing options, and internally imagining scenarios. You cannot have more than one channel running at a time — your brain doesn't work that way. You can attend to details in your environment or to contextual scanning clues — but not exactly at the same time. You can internally analyze or shift the scope and focus of attention such that you are aware of all that is stimulating in your environment and in your head about your experience. Your goal should be to learn to use your attention for perceptions rather than to trigger judgments. Create an event log in which you identify how you use your attention and how your attentional focus contributes to how you behave. Being more mindful allows you to fluidly move among these channels to experience maximum awareness.

7. Have you forgotten how to relax, breathe and be in the moment? Every researcher who looks at the behavior of controlled deep breathing and relaxing reports the same results: healthier physical and mental conditions. Deep breathing — even just ten deep breaths — releases the kind of internal processes that produce relaxation, lower blood pressure, and increase stamina. Make it part of your routine to have three deep breathing sessions each day, and in a short period of time you will experience the benefits.

8. Are you constantly aware of time; feel like you are on a timetable that controls your life? "Time" is a funny word. You may attempt to measure it, control it, manage it, and fill it with more and more to-do's. Each day you are alive you get 86,400 seconds of time. You have to decide how to use those seconds. Only you can determine how to use the present and how to distribute those seconds for your well-being. Make a list of daily tasks that includes time for mindful reflection. Then learn to prioritize those tasks using the A, B, C method. "A" priorities are those things that are critically important to your success and reflect your highest values and goals. Thus they deserve more of your energy and time. "B" priorities are important and help you reach your goals. "C" priorities are those things that can wait, though often they get too much time because they are easier to accomplish than A or B priorities. Put time for being mindful on your "A" priority list. This might include time for a quiet, non-stressed daily walk, or sitting quietly and focusing on your breathing. Make cultivating the art of mindfulness an "A" priority!

Related Competencies

(12) Emotional Maturity   (14) Emotional Self-Control

(18) Impulse Control   (24) Intentionality   (34) Perspective-Taking

(41) Self-Awareness   (50) Stress Hardy

Learn from Experience

Work

❏ Attend a business or development meeting and sit back observing for a change. Open your mind to new possibilities or ways of doing things. Pay attention to where you focus and shift attention to see what you do not initially notice.

Personal

❏ Spend some observation time daily. Pick 10 minutes to simply observe what is going on around you. Pick a different sensation to focus on each day. For example, sit outside and let yourself notice all the sounds around you. Next, focus on smells, then what you see. Finally, walk slowly on the grass barefooted noting all the sensations in your feet.

❏ Try the experience of mindful eating. Take a nut or a raisin and eat it as slowly as possible. Note the texture, the taste, the way its consistency changes as you chew.

❏ Monitor your thoughts and reactions. Develop an observing eye that notices where your thoughts go when you're not paying attention. When you're driving, or walking, or falling asleep, does your mind dwell on successes or failures? Do you keep returning to instances of shame or humiliation? Are you afraid to think too deeply about the future? Use these prompters to remind you to relax and let go of negative emotions.

Resources

Books

Germer, Christopher, Ronald Siegel, and Paul Fulton. *Mindfulness and Psychotherapy.* New York: The Guilford Press, 2005.

Kabat-Zinn, Jon. *Coming to Our Senses: Healing Ourselves and the World Through Mindfulness.* New York: Hyperion, 2005.

Langer, Ellen J. *Mindfulness.* Boston: Norton Publishers, 1989.

Siegel, Daniel J. *The Mindful Brain: Reflection and Attunement in the Cultivation of Well-Being.* Boston: Norton Publishers, 2007.

Williams, Mark, John Teasdale, Zindel Segal, and Jon Kabat-Zinn. *The Mindful Way Through Depression: Freeing Yourself from Chronic Unhappiness.* New York: Guilford Press, 2007.

Internet

An Internet search on "mindfulness," or "mindfulness based stress reduction programs" will turn up many sites offering information on this topic. Many universities and medical schools have programs in mindfulness.

The University of Massachusetts put mindfulness on the map with the work of Jon Kabat-Zinn. www.umassmed.edu/cfm/stress

Mindful.net. Resources and tips for the use of mindfulness at work, in education and in other arenas. www.mindfulnet.org.

Psychology Today. "The Art of Now: Six Steps to Living in the Moment,"

by Jay Dixit, November 2008. On the web site, search for "mindfulness."
www.psychologytoday.com

Classes and training

Breathworks. Offers classes in mindfulness such as: "Living Well with Pain
and Illness" and "Living Well with Stress."
www.breathworks-mindfulness.org.uk

Mindful Awareness Research Center, UCLA. Offers classes and conducts
research related to mindfulness, both for enhancing general well-being and
treating ADHD. www.marc.ucla.edu/

Nashville Mindfulness Center. Offers Zen mindfulness classes in the methods
of Thich Nhat Hanh. www.nashvillemindfulness.org/

The Insight Center. Teaches mindfulness meditation to the general public
and provides mindfulness psychotherapy training to health professionals.
www.insightcenter.org

29   READING NONVERBAL COMMUNICATION

Definition

Observing and interpreting nonverbal messages expressed by body language and how a message is conveyed

The most important thing in communication is hearing what isn't said.

— Peter F. Drucker

Talented

❑ Listens with the eyes

❑ Notices consistencies and inconsistencies between a person's words and behavior

❑ Astutely notices unspoken messages and checks perceptions for accuracy

❑ Understands that nonverbal behavior speaks more accurately than verbal

❑ Accurately reads the collective reaction of a group

❑ Connects nonverbal behavior with the emotions people report at those moments

Skilled

❑ Considers nonverbal behavior when seeking to understand others

❑ Occasionally observes a speaker's behavior and considers its meaning

❑ Understands the importance of nonverbal behavior but doesn't always pay attention to it

❑ Senses, but may not interpret accurately, group reactions

❑ Notices but may misread nonverbal behavior

Unskilled

❑ Responds more to what is said than how it is said

❑ Rarely notices or reads nonverbal behavior

❑ Fails to pick up on inconsistencies between words and actions

❑ Overlooks emotional elements of communication

❑ Ignores nonverbal reactions of group

❑ Doesn't seem to recognize that nonverbal behavior sends messages too

Big Picture View

Nonverbal communication includes facial (e.g. smile) and physical gestures (e.g. hand waving) as well as para-verbal elements such as speed, volume and pitch of the spoken word. Nonverbal communication is the most telling when it reflects the speaker's emotion and attitude. So, it is especially important to read these signals accurately when you are relating to and communicating with others. But the implications of nonverbal communication are not limited to just reading others accurately. It is equally important to ensure that your own nonverbal communication is sending the message you intend. The impact of a message is shaped by the nonverbals accompanying the words. A common blind spot is failing to recognize when your nonverbal behavior is having a negative impact. Have you ever observed someone rock during a presentation or glance at their watch while talking to you? What impact did those nonverbal behaviors have? If you are the speaker and you get reactions from others that surprise you, then reflect on or get feedback about your delivery to get some insight. If you're a member of the audience, on the other hand, then notice when a person's words and behaviors don't line up. What does that do to the speaker's credibility?

29

Barriers to Effectiveness

❑ Lack of interest in, or curiosity about, people

❑ Lack of observational skills

❑ Overly analytical of content, missing behavioral reactions

❑ Distrusting intuitive skills

❑ Over-focusing on tasks or plans to the exclusion of noticing people

Quick Action Tips

1. **All ears? Listen with your eyes too.** Otherwise you may miss what is really important in what is being communicated. Watch facial expressions, eye contact, posture, and other hand, feet and body movement. Every gesture communicates something. Look for clusters of nonverbal behaviors that hang together for the most reliable way to read nonverbal behavior. Make it a prac-

tice to notice nonverbal communication and the emotions that accompany it. Your ability to read nonverbal communication will grow. A single gesture can mean any number of things, or nothing of consequence. If you place too much emphasis on just one signal out of many, you might come to the wrong conclusion about what a person is communicating. To develop this competency, systematically capture your observations, your speculations about them and your track record for accuracy. If you make this a practice, you will notice your skill growing over time.

2. Fearful of misreading nonverbal behavior? Ask questions about nonverbal signals. "I noticed you sat up when I made that suggestion. What are your thoughts about it?" Explore the meaning of those signals when you need facts or if you are skeptical. A person's nonverbal communication holds more significance than their words when they don't line up. If you are confused about another person's nonverbal signals, don't be afraid to ask questions. Start by describing the nonverbal behavior you observed and ask what it means. "You got quiet when I suggested that you become involved. What does that mean?" If the answer doesn't fit your perception or is evasive, you might mention what the behavior says to you. "When you get quiet, I wonder if you are disagreeing with what I'm saying." Note the person's reaction to this, both verbal and nonverbal. Continuing to ask about the nonverbal behavior can help draw someone out or get around evasion, but not always. If you see nonverbals that suggest an increasing negativity, then it's time to switch gears.

3. Suspect something is amiss but can't quite put your finger on it? Look for mismatches between people's words and their behavior. When words and behaviors don't line up and you want to know what the person is really feeling, focus on the person's nonverbal behavior. Words are the most easily controlled. Vocal features and gestures are less so. Facial expressions and other gestures are often out of a person's awareness and therefore are subject to the least control. They provide the clearest view into what a person is truly feeling. To someone skilled at reading people and their behavior, most of us are open books. Decisions and patterns of behavior over time are other forms of nonverbal behavior. Track both for additional evidence to test your hypotheses and gain insight into the motives of others.

4. Ever have a gut feeling that a person is being dishonest? Deception is unfortunate, and unfortunately deception is not limited to politicians. Trust your instincts. But investigate what is driving those instincts. Over time, make multiple connections between behaviors, emotions and the meaning you attach to them. Look for information that helps you refine your speculations and gives credibility to your instincts. The associations you are making take place more commonly at the unconscious level. Your past experiences make up a rich database of information, much of which you may not consciously remember. It's not uncommon for us to have a spontaneous reaction to someone or some event, a reaction that we cannot explain. You may be comparing your current experience with an earlier one that you don't consciously recall, but the comparison is alerting you in some way. Think of this as your inner expert on nonverbal messages. Treat it as data, mine it, and seek additional information to validate it.

5. How about your own nonverbal behavior and the impact it has? Everyone should have the opportunity to see themselves as others do. How you deliver your message shapes the meaning and impact of your words for your listeners. You can express the very same words in a variety of ways. Consider varying your delivery intentionally. What behaviors reinforce and support what you are saying? Notice the impact of your delivery. Use this information to adjust your behavior. Use it to emphasize the ideas that you want people to absorb and remember. Experiment with different styles and record yourself — audio or video. This can be especially useful when making presentations or when speaking to large groups of people. With practice you can use your delivery style for a variety of effects. Watch others' behavior for examples of what you might want to experiment with.

6. What's all the fuss about eye contact? Effective eye contact is one of those things that depends on who's on the receiving end. This is especially true when comparing different cultures. Failing to make eye contact may appear evasive or to indicate having something to hide in one culture, while it may be a sign of respect in another. On the other hand, fixed eye contact can seem confrontational, intimidating or flirtatious. At its most basic level, eye contact conveys attention and establishes a connection. Eye contact alone can communicate caring, undivided attention and attraction or disapproval. Eye contact is an important part of communication, but how much is enough, and how much is too much? Its effectiveness is situational — you have to be alert to how your audience is responding to gauge if it is being experienced as evasive, too intense, or just right. Some communication experts recommend intervals of eye contact lasting four to five seconds. At the group level, there is evidence suggesting a strong link between the amount of eye contact people receive and their degree of participation in group communications. Eye contact is known to increase a person's participation in a group conversation.

7. Wonder if your audience is listening? When leading a meeting or speaking to a group, nonverbal cues can tell you when you've talked long enough (people become restless), when someone else wants to speak (person leans forward) or the mood of the crowd and their reaction to your remarks (nodding heads). Pay attention to these cues and plan how you will respond to them. Some signs to look for are people who:

- look down instead of at you
- stare at the PowerPoint (TV, video, etc.)
- fidget, touch or rub their faces, hands or hair

29

- make copious notes (easily assumed to be about your key points)
- start reading (those copious notes on your key points?)
- stretch out and cross their arms
- stand or pace at the back of the room
- whisper to others quietly
- tap or spin their pens

8. Practice, practice, practice. Some people just seem to be naturally good at picking up on and correctly interpreting others' nonverbal communication. You too can build this skill by paying close attention to nonverbal behavior, speculating about the meaning behind it and confirming, when possible, the accuracy of your speculations. Remember, though, that nonverbal behavior also can be misread. What does a strong (or weak) handshake say to you? Strength of character and strength of handshake go together, don't they? Perhaps arthritis, gender or cultural implications affects how someone shakes your hand. What about crossed arms? Did you think "defensive" or "superior," or was the person cold or acting from habit? Develop hypotheses but look and listen for other data to confirm or refute them. Watch television with the sound off. Guess at what's going on based on the behavior alone. Turn the sound up and evaluate your guesses.

Related Competencies

(15) *Active* Empathy   (16) Flexibility   (26) Intuition

(27) Listening Generously (34) Perspective-Taking (46) Social Intelligence

Learn from Experience

Work

❑ Create success profiles and related interview questions for specific jobs. Identify which behaviors indicate matches with the profiles.

❑ Participate in group interviews for new hires where you can form impressions and compare them with those made by others on the interviewing team.

Personal

❑ Study film clips of people in the news, especially those without speech writers and coaches, and form impressions about their personalities, goals and values while you watch. Notice which overt behaviors are connected with which impressions. Research what information is available about these people to validate or correct your impressions.

❑ Notice the people around you. Make guesses about what's going on with them, beyond what they are disclosing. Watch, listen and wait for additional information to confirm or correct your speculations.

Resources

Books

Tieger, Paul D. *The Art of SpeedReading People: How to Size People Up and Speak Their Language*. New York: Little, Brown and Company, 1999.

LaBorde, Genie. *Influencing with Integrity*. New York: Crown House Publishing, 2003.

Ekman, Paul. *Emotions Revealed, Second Edition: Recognizing Faces and Feelings to Improve Communication and Emotional Life*. New York: Holt Paperbacks, 2004.

Gladwell, Malcolm. *Blink: The Power of Thinking Without Thinking*. New York: Little, Brown and Company, 2005.

Mckay, Matthew, Martha Davis, and Patrick Fanning. *Messages: The Communication Skills Book*. Oakland, CA: New Harbinger Publications, 2009.

Internet

Project Implicit, Harvard University. Blends basic research and educational outreach in a virtual laboratory at which visitors can examine their own hidden biases. www.implicit.harvard.edu

About.com. Web site to find tests, tips and additional information on nonverbal communication. www.about.com

Classes and training

F.A.C.E. Training by Paul Ekman. Training to improve your ability to "see" and "relate" to the world around us. Look for Ekman videos on YouTube. www.paulekman.com

29

30 | OPENNESS TO OTHERS

Definition

Being receptive to others' feelings, thoughts and ideas

You can't shake hands with a closed fist.

—Indira Gandhi

Talented

❏ Practices giving and seeking constructive feedback regularly to encourage ongoing learning

❏ Dedicates the time needed to hear and understand differences in ideas and opinions before moving forward with a decision

❏ Encourages others to use their own judgment and ideas as much as possible

❏ Regularly assesses the climate at work or home by asking what others are thinking and feeling; uses results to create improvements

❏ Suspends judgments in order to fully listen to and understand others and their ideas

Skilled

❏ Works at resisting temptation to justify and defend behavior

❏ Values what others say and sometimes adjusts own position

❏ In low-stakes situations, lets others use their own best judgment

❏ Listens to concerns about the work environment or family relationships

❏ Recognizes that judgments about others may not be true

Unskilled

❏ Avoids or is defensive about receiving feedback

❏ Justifies behavior rather than seeking to understand his or her impact on others

❑ Imposes authority or the power of position to influence others

❑ Inflexibility

❑ Fails to reach out to include those who disagree with him or her

❑ Micromanages; assumes there is only one best way

❑ Operates without questioning assumptions

Big Picture View

Developing receptiveness to others starts by believing that all people deserve respect and have a right to their own perspectives. This belief must be backed up with active listening skills, attending skills, good inquiry skills, and an interest in what matters to those around you. Openness to others also demands the maturity to realize that you are not always right, that there can be many "right" ways of doing things, and that sometimes there are more important things than being right. Being open to others is usually easier when you are rested, not under time pressure, don't feel stressed, and appreciate the individuals you are dealing with. Remaining open to others when these ideal conditions are not present means that you are progressing in developing this competency. Effective leadership and meaningful interpersonal relationships call for a balance of understanding and valuing others and their thoughts and also understanding one's own values and judgments.

Barriers to Effectiveness

❑ Early success or expertise which may lead to not valuing other perspectives

❑ Time pressure and stress which may close down discussion

❑ Openness to others overdone may convey a lack of leadership or self-doubt

❑ Unrealistic expectations about what others can do or should do

❑ Hyper-critical judgments about self and others

Quick Action Tips

1. **Tend to stick to your guns no matter what others say?** If you are unwilling to entertain other people's opinions or ideas, they will tend to avoid you. No one wants to talk to a brick wall. Before you disagree with another person's ideas, approaches or opinions, confirm what you are hearing to be sure you understand correctly what their point is. Sometimes disagreements are simply a matter of misunderstanding. If you do see things differently, consider how

important the difference is. Will it matter six months from now which approach was used? What is at stake? Choose your battles to allow others the feeling of success in order to ensure good relationships. Remember that the larger picture is not who is right, but whether the outcome is a success and all learn from it.

2. Find yourself dreading feedback from others? Take the initiative by asking for specific feedback about how you are perceived, what worked well during mutual endeavors and how you might improve. Seek to understand until you can identify specific behaviors of yours that others are responding to. Ask for specific examples of behavior to be sure you are getting the message they have for you. Confirm what you hear by stating a brief summary to let the other person know you got it. Ask for feedback from several sources since perspectives may be different. Remember that as you move up in an organization fewer people will give you honest feedback. No one likes to say the emperor has no clothes. Be sure to thank others for feedback and identify one new behavior you want to try as a result. If others see no changes in your behavior after giving you feedback, then they may not make the effort to give you honest feedback again.

3. Wish you had more time to listen to your colleagues? Do deadlines push you into being more directive than you like? While crisis situations call for a direct and quick response, too much is lost if that is your typical way of doing business. Not only might the best ideas get lost, but over time your co-workers will feel discounted and may look for other opportunities where they feel more respected for their abilities. Regroup and make sure you have time to engage with others, not just give directions. Listen to those around you and share responsibilities. Delegating more to others may just give you the additional time you need to plan ahead for that next deadline. Being directive at home or with friends also can alienate others. Use the same steps of asking for ideas, listening and including others at least 50 percent of the time.

4. Quick at sizing up people? Sure, sometimes this is an asset. However, too often you may take a few data points about what someone says in a meeting or how they look when you meet them and immediately begin adding your own meaning, assumptions, conclusions and beliefs about a person or what happened without recognizing that you may have left reality behind. The next time you find yourself forming a quick judgment about someone and what they have said or done, step back from your conclusion and hold it out away from you as interesting, as one explanation among many for what you think you perceive, but not necessarily the only one. Hold your judgments lightly until you get more data. Or, as William Isaacs suggests, suspend your judgment to see what more may emerge from that person or you. This may allow you to learn and partner in new ways with a wider range of people and to be more receptive to them. To learn more, read about "Dialogue and the Ladder of Assumptions" in *The Fifth Discipline Fieldbook*.

5. Which people or groups in your work life get your full attention? Family, friends, customers, direct reports, your boss, peers? Most of us tend to either manage up or manage down well. You may have time for your vice president, but not for your peers. You may throw a few words of direction to a direct report as you head out the door to spend hours with a customer. Who gets your full attention? Everyone in your business affects your effectiveness in different ways and deserves your full attention when you are with them. Don't unintentionally limit your success by discounting or taking for granted some of those you depend on. The same may hold true in your personal life. Consider whether you listen with the same openness to your spouse, children, friends and neighbors. Practice attending and listening fully to the person you are with.

6. Whom do you avoid? Is there anyone you fail to invite to the meeting, discussion or party? It is human nature to gravitate to those who agree with us or with whom we share common interests and ideas. While that is a comfortable way to work or live, you may be missing important perspectives or even information that could help you deal with problems or projects you are facing. That neighbor with the distressing political views may be glad to help you fix your mower. That colleague in accounting who holds you responsible for every penny may be quite willing to show you how to use the new business software needed for the budget process. Plus you might learn why every penny is important. By remaining open to people and their ideas even when you disagree, you may find unexpected value.

7. Anyone that you no longer speak to because you have had a bitter disagreement? Do you let your need to be right interfere with your important relationships? If I believe I am right and we disagree, then I am going to conclude that you are wrong. Openness to others means putting aside the need to be right in order to understand and respect differences in opinions, ideas and choices. You are not your differences; you are not your opinions. Who have you not spoken to, avoided, or stopped seeing because of a disagreement or difference of opinion about something you may not even remember? Seek out at least one such person in an effort to make amends. Listen with an open heart to those you care about rather than judging whether they are right or wrong.

Related Competencies

(15) *Active* Empathy   (27) Listening Generously   (32) Patience
(34) Perspective-Taking   (51) Tolerance

Learn from Experience

Work

❏ Take part in a cross-function task force that needs all involved agreeing in order to be successful. Practice listening for ways you might be discounting other perspectives and instead ask questions to better understand the thoughts of others.

❏ Identify someone with whom you tend to disagree on work issues. Arrange to have a lunch with that person and focus on learning more about him or her including background, experience, and job pressures. Understanding sometimes leads to appreciation of differences.

Personal

❏ With a spouse, close friend or family member practice seeking to understand what is important to them by asking open-ended questions and listening. Refrain from offering advice or making judgments about what they say.

❏ For a month, commit to spending five minutes each day alternating with another person, sharing for five minutes at a personal level about the day while the other simply listens and seeks to understand.

❏ Take a volunteer vacation in another country working with people you have never met on a project you find meaningful, such as building a school for children in Nicaragua.

Resources

Books

Senge, Peter M. *The Fifth Discipline*. New York: Doubleday, 1990.

Senge, Peter M., Charles Roberts, Richard B. Ross, Brian J. Smith, and Art Kleiner. *The Fifth Discipline Fieldbook*. New York: Doubleday, 1994.

Houston, Paul D., and Stephen L. Sokolow. *The Spiritual Dimensions of Leadership*. Thousands Oaks: Corwin Press, 2006.

Kirkland, Karen, and Sam Manoogian. *Ongoing Feedback: How to Get It, How to Use It*. Greensboro: CCL Press.

Covey, Stephen R. *The Seven Habits of Highly Effective People*. New York: Simon and Schuster, 1989.

Internet

CIO Update: Alan Carroll, (2010). "IT Leadership Is Listening." www.cioupdate.com

Stephen Covey. "Habit 5: Seek First to Understand, Then Be Understood." There are many clips on www.youtube.com. or www.franklincovey.com. Check for presentations featuring Covey himself.

Classes and training

Bell Leadership Institute, Chapel Hill. "Advanced Communication: Mastering the Seven Essential Skills of Effective Communication." www.bellleadership.com

DialogueWorks. Under training, look for "Collaborating for Results." www.dialogueworks.com

The Landmark Forum. www.landmarkeducation.com

31   OPTIMISM

Definition

Expecting that things will turn out well, that good will triumph; finding positive meaning or perspective in any situation

Few things in the world are more powerful than a positive push. A smile. A word of optimism and hope. A "you can do it" when things are tough.

— Richard M. DeVos

Talented

❏ Remains upbeat during stressful times

❏ Expresses confidence that an appropriate and constructive solution can be found

❏ Finds positive meaning or the silver lining in the majority of difficult situations

❏ Creates a positive organizational culture that supports risk taking, creativity and an entrepreneurial approach

❏ Assumes the best in others

❏ Promotes a "can do" environment

Skilled

❏ Communicates moderate confidence in self and others

❏ Solves problems and encourages others to solve problems with an expectation of success

❏ Exhibits an attitude that is more positive than negative

❏ Looks for the positive in situations more often than not

❏ Sustains effort to solve problems but only in areas of personal expertise and comfort

❏ Exhibits a general belief in the goodness of others

Unskilled

❏ Gives up after initial efforts to solve a problem

❏ Points out what is wrong instead of what is working

❏ Criticizes and judges others' intentions, ideas, and efforts

❏ Naively assumes a positive outcome without adequate investigation

❏ Demands assurance of success before agreeing to new venture

Big Picture View

Some people just seem to be born with more optimism than others, but it is a trait that can be developed. It begins with assuming that an answer or workable solution can be found in most situations. A second assumption is that everyone is doing the best they can. Finally, optimists believe that the skills needed to move forward and to find positive solutions are attainable by all. If you have a tendency to imagine the worst-case scenario and this approach to life is holding you back, then learn to challenge your negative assumptions and beliefs. Optimism involves the ability to view things from a different, more positive, point of view. Optimists are realists with an expectation of success. They can imagine a successful outcome and are able to inspire others to work towards that end. Indeed, success in many endeavors depends on a balance of optimism, which provides the "can do" factor; creativity, which fuels new insights and solutions; and reality testing, which puts feet on the ground with practical, concrete solutions. Being optimistic is directly related to both personal health and organizational vitality. Some researchers refer to optimism as the facilitator of behaviors that contributes to well-being. Numerous studies have shown that optimism is related to health, satisfaction, and a sense of achievement. While you may have learned a pessimistic approach to life, Dr. Martin Seligman in his "learned optimism" studies has identified ways to develop optimism and, in doing so, promises to change your life.

Barriers to Effectiveness

❏ Persistent critical mindset and focus on the negative

❏ Failure to align one's expectations with positive experiences

❏ Assumes no control, no ability to solve problems and no potential to develop the skills needed

❏ Failure to acknowledge personal strengths and previous success

❏ Lack of self-confidence

Quick Action Tips

1. Limited to one favorite approach to solve problems? To a hammer, everything looks like a nail. Hammers are useful, but not when faced with a screw. More tools are needed. There are many problem-solving strategies, often as many as there are people in a situation. Invite ideas and strategies from others involved in the problem you are facing. It is much easier to be optimistic about future outcomes if you believe you have a number of ways to tackle what lies ahead. Scan deBono's Six Thinking Hats® for ideas about different approaches. The point is that you need to recognize that you have options. If your "tried and true" way of solving problems isn't working, then it is easy to slide into thinking that a solution isn't possible. Investigate creative and divergent problem-solving methods and add a couple to your "backpack of ideas" so that you can optimistically report that there is more than one right answer.

2. Have an overly critical eye? While being a critical thinker is valuable, when overused, it can become a weakness. If all you see is the negative, it is difficult to motivate yourself, or others, to believe that a workable solution to a problem can be found. Add value by working to generate a number of possible solutions. Offering solutions builds confidence that an optimal solution can be found to a problem or a challenge. If you find yourself constantly identifying what is wrong, then trump your criticisms by finding twice as many good points. You might try experimenting with living a "negative-free or criticism-free" day (or morning, or hour, or minute!) in which you look for only the positive in all events or things. Make a game out of it by finding someone to partner with and see who can be the most positive.

3. Tend to be a skeptic, or to distrust the intentions of others? While there always are exceptions, experience suggests that people in most situations really want to find constructive outcomes. When observing and thinking about others' behaviors, consider that they may be doing their best and that their intent is constructive. Ask yourself what positive intentions others may have before assuming they are motivated negatively in some way. When you begin with the proposition of positive intent, your interpretation of information and events take on a completely different meaning. It is much easier to experience, and encourage, optimism when you begin with the question, "what is the positive intent?" behind the behavior, statement, or action of another person.

4. Have more self-doubt than confidence? Build your confidence by reminding yourself what you do well. Write down the competencies and abilities that you bring to your daily challenges. Life teaches many lessons, and sometimes you may forget just how to use those lessons successfully on a daily basis. Look for the talents you possess by listing five to ten challenges or projects (most recent or significant). Identify the skills that you used to succeed, and keep the list handy. Knowing your top talents and skills builds confidence. Use your learning journal or simply make a "top ten" list of things you are most proud of and why. Do a web search on the job competencies required for your various accomplishments and current projects to see the range of talents that you have at your disposal. The more you know about your own strengths, the easier it is to be optimistic about the challenges you are currently facing.

5. Hold back from sharing your perspectives and skills? Sharing ideas with others communicates an attitude that solutions can be found and that you are willing to look for them. Optimistic people often see possibilities and share those in the belief that doing so motivates and sparks creativity that may lead to better answers. Certainly it is important to choose when and how you share your ideas. However, if you hold back because you are afraid that others might criticize your ideas or because you are unsure of the merit of an idea, then you and everyone else loses. Keep in mind that your ideas and observations are grounded in experience and are worthy of consideration, even if only to stimulate further discussion or build on other ideas.

6. Don't take the time to celebrate? Optimistic people like to celebrate what is right, which helps provide the energy to fix what is wrong. Have there been recent achievements that you haven't celebrated? Why not? Are your expectations too high? Do you celebrate only those things that are "really, really big?" Is there so much on your plate that you move on to the next challenge before taking time to celebrate? Rethink when and how and with whom you celebrate the meaningful events of your life. Commit to bringing some family, friends or colleagues together to recognize and celebrate your achievements.

7. Believe optimism is a matter of personal traits or inheritance? There are some studies that show how some temperaments may be slightly more inclined toward optimism or pessimism; however, temperament is only one contributor to optimism. There is much greater evidence that when you change your thinking or behavior, you can change your mood, your perspective, and your future performance. For example, behaving *as if* you were optimistic about the future promotes your feeling of optimism, which helps you make choices that lead to a positive outcome. This is called a "self-fulfilling prophecy." Make a note that you can see on your desk, calendar, or computer that prompts you to envision hoped-for outcomes.

8. Do you tend to dwell on negative feedback and dismiss positive comments? Do you ever review the day as you are attempting to fall asleep at night and find that you think more about the negative events of the day than the positive events, that you focus more on your efforts that stumbled rather than those that succeeded — even when the favorable events far exceed the negative? Most people are drawn to focus on the negative, probably because they want to repair what went wrong and avoid a repeat experience. But you have a choice here; and if your goal is to fall asleep, then will thinking about what went wrong during the day help you do that? Not likely. More important, there's no benefit to giving the minimal negative events more thinking time than the many positive events. Consider identifying at least three hopeful, constructive, and positive things that occurred each day before you close your eyes.

9. Hang around optimistic people? Think about the individuals you spend a great deal of time with and consider whether these people are generally optimistic or pessimistic in their comments and outlook. Put them into two buckets: one for the optimists and one for the pessimists. Which group do you have more in common with? On balance, do you have enough optimistic people around you? Do you need to add some people to your circle whose outlook is more optimistic? Ask those in your circle who do tend to be more optimistic the secret to their attitude. What can you learn from their thinking that might enhance your outlook?

Related Competencies

(10) Creativity　　(24) Intentionality　　(33) Perspective-Taking

(35) Reframing　　(37) Resilience　　(41) Self-Confidence

(49) Stress Hardy　　(51) Trusting

Learn from Experience

Work

❑ Plan and execute a special team or department celebration.

❑ Identify an individual who is more optimistic than yourself and solicit his or her perspectives on the three most pressing issues in the organization.

❑ Make it a point to ask about the perspectives of the most optimistic people you work with.

Personal

❑ Volunteer to assist with a local Special Olympics event.

❑ Select a few key challenges you have encountered in your life and identify the capabilities you used. Now think of a personal or community challenge where those capabilities can be applied.

Resources

Books

Keller, Helen. *Optimism: an Essay.* New York: T.Y. Crowell, 1903. (Read online at www.archive.org)

Obama, Barack. *The Audacity of Hope.* New York: Random House, 2006.

Seligman, Martin E. P. *Learned Optimism: How to Change Your Mind and Your Life.* London: Vintage, 2006.

Internet

De Bono Thinking Systems. Look under "Tools for Six Thinking Hats®." www.debonothinkingsystems.com

Live Science. Pappas, Stephanie. March 2010. "Optimism boosts immune system." www.livescience.com/health

SelfGrowth.com. The Online Self-Improvement Community. Search for "positive thinking web sites." www.selfgrowth.com/positive

Classes and training

Business Training Works. Optimism and positive attitude training. Look for this course under "Onsite Training to Communications Skills Courses." www.businesstrainingworks.com

Pillars of Positivity. Customized programs to help develop strategies for developing your potential for success. www.pillarsofpositivity.com/pillars

31

32   PATIENCE

Definition

Waiting your turn. Enduring hardship, difficulty or inconvenience without complaint and with calmness and self-control; the willingness and ability to tolerate delay

Adopt the pace of nature: her secret is patience.

— Ralph Waldo Emerson

Talented

❏ Demonstrates equanimity, calmness and a reluctance towards anger when in the midst of a challenging project or situation

❏ Calmly waits for events to unfold

❏ Delays short-term gratification in the pursuit of larger goals

❏ Finds the silver lining in difficult situations and uses it to motivate self and others to stay the course

❏ Pays attention to the details, maintains focus, and demonstrates perseverance and thoroughness

❏ Proceeds in a steady, measured way, avoiding that frantic, stressed rush towards the finish

Skilled

❏ Curbs the inclination to push things through without due process

❏ Adjusts the pace of discussion to allow for sufficient integration of content

❏ Works at listening and being attentive

❏ Makes amends after losing temper or behaving with impatience

❏ Takes timeouts when needed to regain calm

❏ Waits for others to catch up when prompted

Unskilled

❏ Reacts with a hair trigger when annoyed; hot-tempered, easily irritated

❏ Moves rapidly without much regard to the pace of others

❏ Interrupts, finishes others' statements, tries to prod or push others along

❏ Wants answers or action now

❏ Loses focus when dealing with details and due process

❏ Gets frantic easily and rushes to get it done

Big Picture View

Sometimes our passion for efficiency and desire for immediate effective action produces the unintended consequence of being impatient. Reacting quickly in the moment can become a habitual style reinforced by seeming to get a lot done. We forget that what may seem slower (by taking time now to patiently listen) often results in a faster (more comprehensive and accepted) result. As impatience increases, approachability and influence tend to decrease. Patience tends to come more easily when we are confident and believe in the capabilities of others. When you find yourself feeling very impatient, check whether you are giving others the respect they deserve and whether you feel confident in managing difficult situations. Impatient people often have the "foot in mouth disease" of saying something they later regret. More important, impatience damages relationships and your personal credibility. Impatience can be improved by developing increased respect for others, impulse control and emotional self-control.

Barriers to Effectiveness

❏ Poor stress management skills which contribute to feeling rushed, frantic or reactive

❏ Judging and criticizing others; perceiving others as an obstacle

❏ Feeling pressured by tight deadlines

❏ Hot-tempered, easily irritated or annoyed

❏ Clueless as to how impatience affects others

❏ Poor impulse control

Quick Action Tips

I. **React so that others stop listening?** The words and tonality of your messages may reveal your impatience. Being reactionary often closes down conversation and prevents discussions from finding mutually satisfying solutions. To discover whether your impatience is a problem for others around you, ask them for honest feedback. The more you understand how your impatience affects those around you, the greater the chance that you will be motivated to learn what you can do to change. Ask people who know you well to tell you about your behaviors in specific situations that they experience as impatience. Choose one and practice a more patient behavior in its place.

2. Things moving too slowly for you? If you are in a hurry, you may jump in with answers before people really understand or are ready to buy into a possible solution. Most interactions have a beginning, a middle, and an end, and if you get to the end too quickly, then a great deal of content and understanding are lost. The unintended outcome is that others feel they didn't get to contribute, and so they don't buy into the decision moving forward. You need a pace that provides a baseline of understanding when interacting with others. Reflect on a recent conversation that didn't seem to go well or failed to reach a satisfactory conclusion. Create a conversation log and note how the conversation started, what was the primary give and take, and how the conversation ended. Now comes the important part: Note how you behaved. Were you offering solutions or critical observations before everyone was ready for phase two of the conversation — the give and take? Did you begin the conversation with a preset idea of what needed to happen? If so, then you may have set yourself up to assume that things were moving too slowly and that everyone else was behind. To help yourself be more patient, use active listening skills to stay engaged with others and their thoughts. Summarize what you hear to be sure that you are on the same page as the group. Ask for ideas from others to be sure that you are not moving ahead by yourself.

3. Can't believe others can be so consistently wrong? Impatient individuals tend to believe that they have the answers and that others are just waiting to hear them. You might consider making sure that you really understand the ideas others have offered. You can recap or paraphrase what another has shared before you respond. You might even probe a little by clarifying or building on a part of the idea presented. Otherwise, count to seven before responding, especially when you have a strong reaction to someone or what was just said. Although you may have a great deal of life experience or be exceptionally smart or creative, others also have experience and possible insights to offer. If your impatience shuts others down, then you may well lose out on important information or valuable ideas.

4. Listen only to find solutions? Solutions are important, but expanding your purposes for listening will expand your effectiveness. An active listener provides a continual feedback loop with the individual with whom he or she is interacting. The purpose of this loop is to double-check the meaning of the information being shared. When you paraphrase or confirm what you hear, new ideas or new perspectives often emerge. Practice listening more than you talk to increase your patience. Listening completely is hard work. It requires focusing attention, putting your tendency to judge in neutral, and making sure that you understand both words and associated emotions. As an exercise to enrich listening, take a sheet of paper and answer these questions about a recent conversation: What were the facts and opinions just expressed by the other person? What were the emotions underneath those opinions? What values, ideals, and world view were embedded in the conversation? There is a good chance that you can answer one of these questions, but not all three, unless you know the person very, very well. Use these three questions as a way to help focus your listening beyond solutions.

5. Confident you can do it better? When under time pressure, you may feel an urge to tell others how to do a task or to just do it yourself. While you may get the task completed, others miss the opportunity to learn on their own (especially if this involves a teenager and you are working on getting chores done). So while you may have the answers, you are likely to be more patient with others when you realize that, as they learn, you can spend your time on other things. Make a list of those on whom you depend to get things accomplished and identify at least one skill, competence, or aspect of their work you can delegate to them and then coach as needed. As they succeed, your urge to impatiently jump in to do the job yourself will diminish.

6. Do you enjoy giving others the "right" answer? Do you ever interrupt someone in mid-sentence and finish their thought? Ever interrupt someone brainstorming ideas to say that it is a waste of time? Have you ever told a colleague assigned a new project how to start it without being asked for help? While advice is useful at times (especially when it is specifically asked for), no one likes the "constant expert." Ask others for their thoughts and opinions before sharing yours. Explore why they may think and feel the way they do. Be generous about appreciating their good ideas. Recognize the expertise of others. When you share your ideas or give a suggestion, ask for a reaction. Engage others in a discussion without judgments before reaching a decision. Once you and the group hear all ideas and suggestions, ask what approach makes the most sense instead of telling everyone what to do with urgency and irritation in your voice.

7. Ever fire off a quick (impatient) email that you later regret? Who can't say yes to that? One survey suggests that we misunderstand the tone of electronic messages 50 percent of the time. This is largely due to a lack of nonverbal information, such as a smile or nod to help explain the emotion and intent behind the words, and the lack of opportunity to provide immediate feedback and get a reaction. A succinct and direct email message is open to all kinds of possible interpretations by the reader based on extraneous data, such as your

32

last interaction with the writer, your current emotional state, or the subject matter's importance. When you get a message and you find yourself writing an immediate, emotionally loaded response, do not hit send! If your reaction is negative, keep in mind that you may have misunderstood the message or its intention. Think about how well you know this person and consider that he or she probably had a constructive purpose in the email. Even if the email you received was emotionally loaded, you have a chance to move the conversation to a more productive level. Assume a positive intent. ("I want both of us to have input into this project and get credit for its success.") Provide a context for your message ("I know we both want this conference to be successful, so let me share a few concerns I have about how the planning is going.") Be sure you regularly communicate in person with those that matter to you to build personal credibility.

8. First to speak in a group? As you think about how you respond in a group, if you are usually the first to speak, then you may need to double-check your impulse control — that is, ask others if they feel you are a little quick on the draw. This behavior might be an indicator that you are impulsive in other areas of your life. Get more feedback to see if this is true for you, and solicit suggestions to help you wait for a few others to respond first. Often those who are quick to speak interrupt others and take up more then their share of air time. If you notice that you get impatient while awaiting your turn to speak, then listen more closely to what others are saying, enough to allow you to confirm what you are hearing. You might notice that your focus has shifted from you and your ideas to others and their ideas — very helpful as you learn patience.

9. Alienate people you care about? Often impatience results in others keeping their distance. No one wants to be around a blasting furnace all the time. Consider the number of times you have held your comments until others have finished theirs. Tell significant others that you realize you need to work on being more patient, and ask for help. Generally, those who care about you are willing to tolerate your interpersonal challenges; they will appreciate even more your willingness to work on what you say and how you say it when dealing with them. In addition, impatience that shows up as risky behavior such as drinking too much or driving too fast tends to push people away. If risky behavior is part of your pattern of impatience, then consider the costs. Make a decision to put the metaphorical tape over your mouth to listen more and talk less.

Related Competencies

(1) Adaptability	(16) Flexibility	(18) Impulse Control
(25) Interpersonally Skillful	(27) Listening Generously	
(34) Perspective-Taking	(54) Understanding Others	

Learn from Experience

Work

❏ Seek an opportunity to work with peers on a cross-functional team.

❏ Ask for feedback from individuals who can recognize your impatience so that you know the triggers and the impact of your behavior.

❏ Identify an important long-term project which by its very nature requires a careful, slow strategy (e.g. organizational culture change project).

Personal

❏ Take a class in an activity that is completely new and requires the use of skills you have not developed before.

❏ Volunteer for positions at an organization that has a long-term roll-out on projects and initiatives.

❏ Work with functional but disabled individuals who are slow at doing basic tasks.

Resources

Books

Easwaran, Enath. *Patience: A Little Book of Inner Strength*. Tomales, CA: Niligiri Press, 2010.

Ryan, Mary Jane. *The Power of Patience: How to Slow the Rush and Enjoy More Happiness, Success, and Peace of Mind Every Day*. New York: Broadway, 2003.

Internet

Essential Life Skills. Patience and tips on how to develop it. www.essentiallifeskills.net/patience

Ezine Articles. Paris, M. J. Nov. 7, 2008. "Patience, Perseverance, and Positive - P2P." www.ezinearticles.com/

Psychology Today. "Four Steps To Developing Patience, Four Steps to Decrease the Happiness Killer: Impatience," blog posted on Sept. 2, 2011, by Jane Bolton. www.psychologytoday.com/blog

Classes and training

Spirituality and Practice. E-courses. Once on the site search, for "patience builders." www.spiritualityandpractice.com

32

33 PERSONAL POWER

Definition

Demonstrating authority, control and confidence in ways that influence action, command attention or gain agreement on how to get something done

You are never given a wish without being given the power to make it true. You may have to work for it, however.

— Richard Bach

Talented

❑ Skillfully influences others to gain their commitment and agreement in ways that are beneficial to future actions

❑ Leads others in problem-solving and collaboration to meet goals

❑ Asserts ideas and objections persuasively and confidently

❑ Persuades and influences others through excellent communication skills

❑ Capably utilizes multiple influence tactics — subject matter expertise, reasoning, relationships, and authority

❑ Projects a presence that draws people to him or her

❑ Balances advocacy and inquiry when trying to persuade others

Skilled

❑ Leads some of the time, follows some of the time

❑ Listens carefully, sometimes facilitating group process

❑ Relies on authority or expertise to make things happen (less than being personally convincing)

❑ Advocates a point of view but may not encourage enough meaningful input from others

❑ Seeks to deal with issues, attempting to maintain enthusiasm and confidence

❑ Utilizes a limited range of influence tactics

Unskilled

❏ Overpowers others; appears inattentive and impatient with other's opinions

❏ Pushes personal views on others, failing to engage in collaboration

❏ Charges forward without eliciting insights, thoughts or knowledge of others

❏ Fails to recognize when others have shut down or tuned out

❏ May have good ideas but fails to express them well, or at all

❏ Influences using power, authority or threats, failing to gain the respect and loyalty of others

Big Picture View

Personal power is a type of influence that depends on how an individual presents himself or herself to others and how he or she manages relationships. Personal power begins with a confidence and strength that is demonstrated through a variety of behaviors. Personal power is evident with assertive, confident, forward-thinking statements that suggest competence, intelligence and ability. At times it may be seen as charisma or a striking personal presence. Another kind of power, position power, relies on the authority of position or title. While position power is often used in organizations to get things done, personal power is most useful when an individual lacks authority or wants to achieve cooperation and commitment, and not just compliance. When you work to help others get their needs met while accomplishing goals, when you are inclusive, open, and expressive about relationship expectations, and when you use interpersonal savvy to talk with and work with people from a variety of backgrounds, you develop confidence and relationship capital — personal power. Personal power is accessible to anyone. You do not need a title; you just need to recognize that as your confidence and relationships grow, so does your potential access to personal power.

Barriers to Effectiveness

❏ Hypercritical of, or disinterested in, ideas of others (but finds own ideas fascinating!)

❏ Over-reliance on a single source of influence (like authority or logic alone)

❏ Lacks confidence in own personal power, especially if there is no official title of authority

❑ Without direction — no vision or goal worth pursuing or advocating for

❑ Misunderstands and misuses personal power

❑ Fear of being seen as too directive or demanding, thus inhibiting influence and personal impact

Quick Action Tips

1. Not sure how to show authority and confidence? The words you use and the way you walk into a meeting or a conversation communicates authority and confidence. Use words that communicate that you will take action. Avoid tentative phrases unless there is good reason to use them. Be the first to shake hands, to initiate, and to solicit observations. It is important to know the difference between having influence, exerting authority, and being seen as an individual who demands compliance. Sometimes, when trying to communicate confidently about an issue, it may appear that you are more of a "know it all" than a true contributor to mutual problem-solving, so make sure to both advocate and inquire about perspectives and possible courses of action. Reflect on how you attempt to influence others, especially when something is important to you. Identify several people who can provide feedback about the effectiveness of your efforts to give a confident message and to leverage your method of influence (expertise, position, relationships). Is your style too pushy? Are you having the impact you intended?

2. Wondering how to strengthen commitment from others? Personal power is directly related to the depth of our relationships. And relationships are based in mutual regard and trust. Take the first step toward building shared commitment by showing an interest in others' concerns. Be willing to help them find a solution to their issues. As you do so, you are building relationships that may result in cooperation when you need help. At a minimum, be clear about what the benefit is for others when making a request. The more that individuals feel that you have their interests in mind and are willing to help them get their needs met, the greater will be your opportunity to influence them in the future. Identify someone you want to influence. Take the time to find out what matters to them and what their goals are. Do you have any goals in common? How might you encourage them to take ownership for the goals that matter to you?

3. Find it hard to get others on board? The greatest opportunity to influence others is when it is clearly in their self-interest to pay attention to your ideas. Have you taken time to communicate how your goals are linked to theirs? Have you looked at how to find common ground so that you and the other person feel that you are working toward common ends? Only when you've created an open area of mutual sharing will it become clear how to get needs met. Make a list of all of those on whom you rely to get things accomplished and identify their interests and motivations for working with you. If you don't know, ask. When your list is complete, identify how you actively show interest in helping them get their needs met.

4. Haven't considered yourself as someone with personal power? You have to begin to recognize that you have the potential for as much personal power as everyone else — you don't need a special title to assume you are personally significant. Your life experiences, your personal choices, and the path you have taken is a source of wisdom that you can tap and share with others. The sharing with others and connecting with their experiences increase your chances of demonstrating your personal power exponentially. How you think of yourself affects how you present yourself. Create opportunities to imagine your interactions with others as opportunities to exert personal power.

5. Do you fail to see how your experience could benefit others? Power can be used to make things happen — to influence others and their decisions, to accumulate wealth, to gain more control and to be seen as an authority. Power in any form is a double edged sword — it can be used to facilitate partnership or strictly for personal gain. A key aspect of having personal power is being confident in the value of your experience and the importance of your voice being heard when sharing your insights from those experiences. It may be that you all too often overlook the value of your experience to benefit others, thus failing to offer your insight and perspective when it could add value to their situation. Make a list of those things about which you know a good deal and how others could gain if they had the benefit of a relationship with you and you shared that knowledge.

6. Not making the impact you wish to make? Feel like others are not hearing you in a group? Ask for feedback from trusted friends or colleagues about why you might not be heard. Be sure you are using helpful nonverbal behavior such as a strong voice, good eye contact and gestures that fit your message. Speak to the dominant member of the group by name. If you get the attention of that person, others also will listen. Keep your comments clear and to the point. Be persistent. Build on the ideas of others. It is equally important to pay attention to the behavioral cues that tell you how others are reacting to you. Remain flexible; change what you are doing if what you are doing isn't working.

7. Do others seem to avoid you? Find that you are not included in casual conversations? It may be that you are behaving in an aggressive manner such as interrupting or talking over others, showing little interest in others' ideas, monopolizing air time, criticizing others, or demanding that it's your way or the highway. Consider that the demonstration of your authority may have gone too far resulting in a resistance to your ideas and influence. The adage that you can get more from others with honey rather than with vinegar is a good reminder. Stop and consider how you can show others as much respect as you want for yourself. Share air time, ask what others think, value the time of your friends and colleagues, be willing to take no for an answer, let others have their way. In the long run you will build relationships (a major source of personal power) by uplifting others.

8. Concerned that others will consider you overly directive or too confident? If you worry about what others think of you, then you've got lots of company. But here's what's interesting about that. How often do you actually know what others are thinking — really know? In the absence of actual data, what do you do? You make it up, right? If you're like most people, then you may create assumptions about what others are thinking. So, let's start there to fix this. If you're going to make up what others are thinking, make it positive. At least, then, you won't be sabotaging your self-confidence. But if you actually need to know how you're seen by others, talk with people. The best remedy, especially if you need a perspective that is different from yours, is to get the information from a source you trust, one whose opinion you value. Identify a trusted colleague and ask for feedback about your directness and how you demonstrate confidence. Depending on the feedback you get, vary your behavior to get the impact you intend.

Related Competencies

(2) Assertiveness   (4) Collaboration   (20) Influencing Others

(27) Listening Generously   (36) Reframing   (42) Self-Confidence

Learn from Experience

Work

❏ Ask for the responsibility to influence a group of employees who are resisting or complaining about a recent change or issue in the organization.

❏ Observe and record in a learning journal all of the behaviors demonstrated by the most personally power individuals you know in the organization. Identify which behaviors you could use more often.

Personal

❏ Volunteer for a role in a local nonprofit organization that uses your personal expertise.

❏ Offer to lead a United Way campaign for your organization.

Resources

Books

Robbins, Anthony. *Unlimited Power: The New Science of Personal Achieve-*

ment. New York: Free Press, 1997.

Roman, Sanaya. *Personal Power Through Awareness: A Guidebook for Sensitive People.* Tiburon, CA: H.J. Kramer, 1986.

Internet

AllBusiness.com. Once on the site, search for "communicating personal power" to find multiple articles. www.allbusiness.com

Executive Presence. Sign up for their Executive Presence e-tips or look into their Executive Presence workshops. www.executivepresence.com

Classes and training

Anthony Robbins. Look for "Personal Power II: 30 Day System" under products, personal achievement. www.anthonyrobbins.com

American Management Association. Once on the site, search for "creating and using personal power" and many courses and resources will be displayed. www.amanet.org

33

34 | PERSECTIVE-TAKING

Definition

Considering various points of view or assumptions about a situation; seeking alternative options and choices

I've always felt that a person's intelligence is directly reflected by the number of conflicting points of view he can entertain simultaneously on the same topic.

— Abigail Adams

Talented

❏ Seeks multiple and noticeably different views on situations

❏ Identifies and sets aside assumptions or judgments to approach people and situations freshly

❏ Quickly introduces different ways to see things

❏ Uses questions to help others shift and entertain different views on a topic

❏ Views situations through the eyes of others in order to better understand their behavior, positions or requests

❏ Shifts perspectives to shift emotional states when circumstances warrant it

Skilled

❏ Appears comfortable exploring different angles on a situation as long as it does not stray too far from conventional thinking

❏ Considers different views after the "tried and true" viewpoints fall short

❏ Displays patience with different perspectives but appears eager to settle on an approach

❏ Explores options within existing systems but tends to shy away from novel or conceptual possibilities

❏ Views situations on occasion with different eyes in order to better understand others' behavior, positions or requests

Unskilled

❏ Insists on the one right way to view a situation

❏ Seeks out those with similar views and avoids those whose views are different

❏ Acts as if exploring other perspectives slows down effective action

❏ Urges closure to avoid confusing the situation with too many perspectives

❏ Acts as if everyone is working with the same assumptions and perspective on an issue

❏ Tends to state facts or opinions while failing to explore the perspectives or viewpoints of others

Big Picture View

The willingness and ability to step back from a situation and consider another point of view can be developed. Stepping back to take perspective may be momentarily stressful, but it may open the door for creative thinking. Increasingly complex issues in life require multiple perspectives to fully work with them. If perspectives are limited, then so is the ability to understand the situation, thus limiting options. More important, if only one perspective is acceptable, then some people who feel differently may feel excluded and become disengaged, an undesirable situation, especially in organizations. Perspective-taking operates on the assumption that there is more than one point of view and that better thinking is possible only by exploring multiple angles on a situation.

34

Barriers to Effectiveness

❏ Using one way of thinking and never challenging it

❏ Avoiding those whose views are different from your own

❏ Being neither creative nor flexible in addressing complex challenges

❏ Avoiding new experiences, especially those that might challenge your way of thinking

❏ Assuming you are always right

❏ Rejecting ideas from people you do not know very well

Quick Action Tips

1. Find yourself defending your position more than listening to others' views? When you

are in conversations, do you disagree often with others and get a little agitated by their perspectives? Use this as a cue to step back and calm down. Deliberately restate the position of the other person in the conversation. This requires that you hear the other person and, at least momentarily, suspend your defensive thinking. Continuing to pursue your assumptions and reasons for the way things are in a situation cuts you off from new ideas or considering new ways of doing things. Become an active listener, especially when you find that you are reacting strongly and disagree. Before responding, confirm by restating what you think you have heard. Ask questions to be sure you understand the other's point of view and the reasons for it. Identify something that you can appreciate about the other person's point of view. Ask what other ideas and approaches might be helpful. Try to generate at least three different perspectives on a situation before you decide on the approach you want to take. When it comes to problem-solving, research suggests that the best ideas emerge between the second and third ideas.

2. Prefer to stay around those who think the way you do? You might find comfort by sticking around those who agree with your own perspective, but you are unlikely to learn anything new. Make it a point to seek out those whose views are different from yours and engage in a dialogue to tease out their ideas and what is behind them. While you don't need to become friends with those who have a different perspective, you probably will benefit from engaging in discussions with them. Their solutions might be as good as your own. When is the last time you engaged in an extensive conversation with someone whose views were 180 degrees different from your own? There is a good chance that engaging in such dialogues will broaden your own thinking and enhance your choices in the future. Identify someone at work or in your personal life who has a different take on things. Seek that person out for a conversation with the goal of learning about what is important to them and why.

3. Understand that what may feel slower is actually faster in the long run? Efficiency is a virtue much of the time, but oddly enough it can hinder effectiveness in human relationships. The benefits of considering other perspectives are better solutions and improved relationships. It may feel like taking the time to explore different assumptions and different frames of reference is unnecessary, if you think you know the best answer already. However, by taking time to explore, discuss, and challenge the thinking of those involved, you are likely to both educate them (assuming they are open to discussion) and deepen your own understanding of the situation at hand. This kind of give and take is fertile ground for creative thinking. Do you know multiple strategies for encouraging creative thinking? A core benefit of contrasting views is that it promotes more creative answers, which is a huge benefit to dialogue.

4. Convinced you are right? The conviction of being right is often in inverse portion to the quality of problem-solving applied to a situation. The more you are convinced you are right, the less likely it is that you've double-checked your assumptions or approached the situation from multiple perspectives. Often, being sure you are right is a good way to begin an argument, since no one likes to be considered wrong. Remember that right and wrong are ambiguous concepts. Cognitive research tells us that our brains naturally look for and find patterns and then create meaning in those patterns. These patterns become our beliefs and shape our picture of reality. We then seek out information that fits and confirms our beliefs and ignore information that contradicts them. Instead of "seeing is believing," the way our minds work is that we see what we believe. Part of perspective-taking is to realize that your beliefs aren't necessarily true or the only way to look at an issue. Identify assumptions you are making when you think you are right and list other possible assumptions or explanations for the same situation. Rather than talking about right and wrong, use language like, "The way I see it is ... because ...," and open up conversation by asking, "How do you see it?" After confirming other thoughts, agree on what is most useful in the given situation.

5. Brainstormed different views recently? A true brainstorming session with others means writing down every idea and thought that comes to mind without any judgment or evaluation. This is often hard to do, but with practice you can learn to do it more openly. If you don't brainstorm with others from time to time, then you will risk over-relying on the "tried and true." Brainstorming is a process that has a couple of key outcomes: lots of ideas, and divergent thinking. While the ideas may be useful in their own right, tapping into divergent thinking strategies may benefit you in many future situations. You are learning a new skill that you can use many times. In order to take perspective, you may need to think divergently about a problem or situation. Identify a couple of issues over the next month that could use a fresh perspectives and practice brainstorming as part of the process to get new ideas. Listen carefully to the way people think so you can hear the divergent mind at work.

6. Not sure how to use creative thinking methods to see multiple perspectives? The resources for learning creative thinking methods abound. Perhaps you need something to prompt you to see a situation from a new perspective. For example, a set of Creative Whack Pack cards from the creative thinker Roger von Oech, who wrote *A Whack on the Side of the Head*, can prompt different ways of seeing things from multiple points of view. The cards provide concrete and realistic ideas on how to see things differently.

7. Get too emotionally engaged to step back and take a different view? When you feel emotionally hooked or excited about an issue, it is difficult to step back and ask questions about what is actually happening. Learn to step back by asking yourself some basic questions such as, "What about this situation can I verify or is based on actual knowledge?" or, "If I view this situation from a different point of view, does it change my thinking or feelings?" Another question to

34

shift perspective is, "What is my emotional reaction telling me about myself?" By asking these and similar questions on a regular basis, you can make them habits of mind to broaden your perspective.

8. Find it difficult to approach relationship issues from multiple perspectives? Work-related issues are often about relationships. The emotional energy you invest in a relationship can reinforce patterns and perspectives. Making sure you actively create a dialogue and intentionally explore different points of view in relationships requires you to accept the possibility that your view is only a small slice of the whole picture. Patterns can become your prisons in relationships; you tend to see the relationship from a certain point of view that is regularly reinforced. To elevate the use of perspective taking in relationships, you need to be clear about your emotional reactions and why you are having them. Only when you own what you feel can you begin to recognize and possibly empathize with how others feel and with their point of view. Empathizing does not mean you agree with the new perspective; it just means you can see a different point of view. When you have achieved this, you are more open to other points of view. And by being open to these other views, an opportunity to synthesize the perspectives can lead to a more healthy and comprehensive look at a situation.

Related Competencies

(1) Adaptability   (10) Creativity   (15) *Active* Empathy

(22) Insightfulness   (30) Openness to Others (36) Reframing

(51) Tolerance

Learn from Experience

Work

❏ Engage in conversation with someone from an entirely different field or department. Volunteer to work with that person on a project.

❏ Ask to work with a group of individuals who have extensive expertise in a field you do not.

❏ Seek out a mentor in another field of expertise or from another culture.

Personal

❏ Engage in an activity that is new to you and reflect on your experience. For example, if you haven't watched a foreign movie in some time, rent one. If you haven't been to a museum of modern art, make a visit and reflect upon its impact on you.

❏ Converse with family members who have had a significantly different life experience from your own. Interview them to learn about how their experiences have affected their view of the world and how their views have changed over time. Identify factors that have influenced your world view and how it might have changed over the years.

Resources

Books

Rasley, Alice. *The Power of Point of View: Make Your Story Come to Life*. Palm Coast, FL: Writers Digest Books, 2008.

Senge, Peter, Rick Ross, Bryan Smith, Charlotte Roberts, and Art Kleiner. *The Fifth Discipline Fieldbook: Strategies and Tools for Building a Learning Organization*. New York: Doubleday, 1994.

Shermer, Michael. *The Believing Brain: From Ghosts and Gods to Politics and Conspiracies — How We Construct Beliefs and Reinforce Them as Truths*. New York: Times Books, Henry Holt, 2011.

Internet

McGraw-Hill Higher Education. Do an Internet search for "McGraw-Hill Higher Education — assessing your perspective taking." www.highered.mcgraw-hill.com

Six Thinking Hats®: This is an approach to looking at a situation from multiple perspectives. An online search will lead to many locations such as Mind Tools and Wikipedia.

Classes and training

The Creativity Workshop. Web site with multiple approaches to creativity as applied to many areas in life, including business. www.creativeworkshop.com

34

35   REALITY TESTING

Definition

Understanding and reacting to the way things are rather than responding to the way you wish, fear, imagine or assume them to be

> *If a person continues to see only giants, it means he is still looking at the world through the eyes of a child.*
>
> —Anaïs Nin

Talented

❏ Takes time to assess the facts of a situation from various points of view before proceeding

❏ Identifies one's own assumptions when interacting with others and tries to decide if they are useful and accurate

❏ Realizes that emotions affect perceptions (and vice versa) and takes time to check out those perceptions with other people

❏ Understands personal patterns of emotions and thinking that may interfere with accurately responding to certain situations

❏ Uses strategies to avoid emotionally over-reacting

Skilled

❏ Gathers information and facts before proceeding

❏ Identifies several ways to verify information

❏ Resists making major decisions or jumping to conclusions when in an emotional state of mind

❏ Knows and defuses hot buttons that may trigger an unwarranted emotional response

Unskilled

❏ Neglects gathering the facts about situations; jumps to conclusions

❏ Responds to situations based on assumptions; hears what one wants to hear

❏ Reacts based on emotions, hopes, or prejudices without recognizing that these reactions could be a result of distorted or inaccurate thinking

❏ Fails to identify consistent patterns of feelings such as fear, hurt, or anger that interfere with effective interpersonal behavior

❏ Lets personal concerns interfere with objectively dealing with others

Big Picture View

Reality testing depends on acknowledging that what we think is reality is often our opinion, based on our experiences and views about life rather than a concrete reality. Peter Senge and others describe how most individuals build a mental model of how the world works and think that it is reality. While such mental models or understandings of how the world works help us function, we need to remember that people with different experiences and backgrounds can have very different mental models. In any case, using good inquiry skills and having a willingness to check out assumptions with others is important to successful reality testing. Also important is grounding your perceptions in facts from various sources and points of view. Knowing yourself and understanding how your emotions affect your perceptions is important homework for successful reality testing. Sometimes your ability to assess a situation realistically is damaged by maintaining irrational beliefs and fears about yourself and others. This can include irrationally imagining worst possible outcomes and then worrying about them. Again, self-awareness is important to knowing whether you tend to over-worry about things. Learning about how to refute irrational beliefs can help with accurate reality testing. Only when you can clearly tune in to the immediate situation and size it up realistically can you go on to make good decisions and manage complex challenges.

Barriers to Effectiveness

❏ A strong need to defend your opinions and beliefs regardless of what other think or say

❏ Poor ability to notice nonverbal behavior and interpersonal dynamics

❏ Being self-absorbed because of fears and personal issues

❏ Lack of curiosity

❏ Being resistant to new information

❏ Emotionally volatile or reactive

35

Quick Action Tips

I. Are you concerned that you may be out of sync with office politics? After a meeting where important decisions were made, talk with a trusted colleague who also was there and whose opinion you value. Ask that colleague what factors he or she thinks influenced the decisions that were made. Compare your thoughts to theirs. What might you have missed or misinterpreted? Who else might you talk with to gain a better understanding of organizational politics? Seek out a mentor in the organization who might be willing to coach you around how to navigate within the channels of power.

2. Do your emotions sometimes get you in trouble? Think of a recent time when you were unhappy with an interpersonal interaction. Fill in:

- What happened? _____
- What were your assumptions about the reasons behind what happened? _____
- How did you feel? _____
- What else might account for what happened? _____

Next check out your assumptions to see if they were accurate by talking to the other persons involved. Change your assumptions (or correct them) and you may change your emotional response. Remember that our emotions are based on the assumptions and explanations we quickly create around an experience or interaction. Sometimes we are accurate, but other times we are off track.

3. Do fears keep you from taking meaningful risks? We all have fears of one sort or another, but when these fears prevent us from realistically assessing the value of taking calculated risks they are a hindrance to our professional and personal lives. Ask yourself if your fears stop you from speaking in public, making difficult decisions, changing jobs, (respectfully) disagreeing with someone in management or anything else that may be important to your success. Since risk taking is part of learning and developing, managing our fears is crucial. The next time you face a situation that calls for taking a risk, step back and objectively identify what your specific fears are and evaluate how likely it is that your worst-case scenario will happen. If it is hard to be objective about your fears, ask a trusted colleague or friend for realistic input. Build your confidence by finding a lower stakes risk-taking situation similar to what you are facing. For example, if you plan to run for the school board and will be interviewed by the media when you announce, gather a few friends and neighbors to try out your announcement and answer their questions. Debrief how you did to help you improve, and remember to feel good about what you did well to build confidence.

4. Do you tend to avoid problems until they get out of hand? Do others tell you that you tend to be too optimistic? Too pessimistic? If you tend to error on the side of pessimism, you may miss opportunities by worrying about issues that aren't relevant or that are unlikely to happen. If you are too optimistic, then you may not consider or address realistic problems ahead of time. Identify whether you have a tendency in either direction both by asking friends or colleagues how they see you and also by reflecting on your track record. Use that self-understanding to balance your approach in the future. Whom do you know that has a solid track record of judging opportunities realistically? Ask that person to share what criteria they use to evaluate opportunities.

5. Do you tend to jump to conclusions? It can be easy to notice water running down the window and assume it is raining … until someone says, "Thank goodness the windows are finally being washed!" If you tend to make quick leaps from a few facts to action, you may create unnecessary problems for yourself and others. Slow down to ask a few questions, talk to others who are involved in the situation, find out what else is relevant or related to the issue, and then plan your next steps. It is all part of being objective and realistic before taking action.

6. Unsure whether you have realistic expectations of yourself and others? There are many models to help people gain a clearer perspective and to assess a situation realistically. Mediators such as John Ford and Associates use many of the questions below to help clients assess a conflict situation. The questions have been modified to be applicable to your life and relationships with others. Identify a conflict that you are currently in and ask yourself these questions. Use any insights from your answers to move forward with a clearer sense of what a realistic outcome might include.

Reality testing questions:

- What do you see as the strength of your point of view?
- What do you see as the weakness of your point of view?
- What do you see as the strength of the other's point of view?
- What do you see as the weakness of the other's point of view?
- What is your best-case scenario if you don't resolve this issue with negotiation?
- What is your worst-case scenario if you don't resolve this issue with negotiation?
- What is the most likely scenario if you don't resolve this issue with negotiation?
- Is that better than the most likely negotiated decision?

7. Think you need to be competent in everything you do? Think everyone must like

35

you? You can't make a mistake? Of course it is admirable to aspire to walking on water, but very few people can do so. We all flub up at times, run into someone that just doesn't like us, and make mistakes. In fact we learn from such experiences and may become a bit more humble and appreciative of others. If you tend to have these or other unrealistic expectations of yourself, sometimes without even being aware of how they drive your behavior and thoughts about yourself, then it is time to look up "refuting irrational beliefs" on the web. Albert Ellis among other human behavior experts has identified a list of irrational beliefs that tend to set us up for unhappiness. With some awareness and practice, you can replace irrational beliefs with more reasonable ones: I am competent in many ways. I have many friends, colleagues and acquaintances that care about me. I make mistakes like everyone, but I make it a habit to learn so I do better next time. List several irrational beliefs you have about yourself and then list more reasonable beliefs next to them. Choose the rational beliefs that empower you to be your best, to learn and to grow.

Related Competencies

(17) Group Savvy   (34) Perspective-Taking   (40) *Accurate* Self-Assessment
(41) Self-Awareness   (45) Situational Awareness

Learn from Experience

Work

❏ Identify a mentor in your organization and meet with him or her regularly to gain insights into the top values of upper management, how decisions are made and strategic directions for the organization or your division.

❏ Take a temporary assignment to another related department or group to gain a better understanding of how colleagues there perceive issues that affect all of you.

❏ Ask to be part of a task force that includes colleagues from various departments that you interface with. Make a point of understanding their perspectives.

Personal

❏ Volunteer for an organization where you can interact with a wide variety of people with differing viewpoints such as a political action group, a community change group, or a church council. Seek to understand ideas and opinions that are different from yours.

❏ Compare your family expenses with total income. Involve adult family members in this process. Do you understand the reality of your personal financial situation? What changes do you need to make? How might family interactions improve with this shared reality testing?

Resources

Books

Dyer, Wayne. *Excuses Begone! How to Change Lifelong, Self-Defeating Thinking Habits.* Carlsbad, CA: Hay House, 2009.

Ellis, Albert, and Robert A. Harper. *A Guide to Rational Living.* Chatsworth, CA: Wilshire, 1997.

Jacobs, Charles S. *Management Rewired: Why Feedback Doesn't Work and Other Surprising Lessons From the Latest Brain Science.* London: Portfolio, 2009.

Jeffers, Susan. *Feel the Fear ... and Do It Anyway.* New York: Ballantine, 2006.

Pearman, Roger R. *Understanding Emotions.* Winston-Salem, NC: Leadership Performance Systems, 2007.

Senge, Peter. *The Fifth Discipline: The Art and Practice of the Learning Organization.* New York: Broadway Business, 2006.

Smalley, Susan, and Diana Winston. *Fully Present: The Science, Art, and Practice of Mindfulness.* Philadelphia: Perseus Books Group, 2010.

Internet

Mental Health.net. Mills, Harry. (2010). "Reality testing and anger management." www.mentalhelp.net

Resources for refuting irrational beliefs. There are many web sites offering information. Here are a few:

- www.Psychcentral.com
- www.livestrong.com
- www.ncsu.edu/counseling_center (go to resources and search for "refuting irrational beliefs")

Classes and training

John Ford and Associates. www.mediate.com/johnford

Mindful Living Programs. www.mindfullivingprograms.com/

35

36   REFRAMING

Definition

Seeing situations in a new light by considering different meanings, intentions or consequences to elicit more positive and productive responses

My barn having burned to the ground, I can now see the moon.
— Traditional Japanese Haiku

Talented

❏ Applies multiple perspectives on a situation to elicit more productive feelings and responses

❏ Asks others, "How could we look at this in another way?" to encourage creative thinking

❏ Recognizes that how you see things greatly influences how you feel

❏ Entertains different perspectives without changing the concrete facts in order to change evaluations, assumptions or emotions

❏ Looks for the opportunity in a problem, what's doable in what appears impossible and where or when a weakness might be a strength

❏ Enables others to see things from a new, more positive perspective through a comment or simple question

Skilled

❏ Offers a different perspective on situations from time to time

❏ Understands the value of shifting perspectives to enrich creative problem-solving

❏ Appreciates when others point out a different perspective, such as the glass is half full vs. half empty

❏ Moves to conclusions quickly and vacillates between considering various hypotheses about what may be going on

❏ Thinks about some things differently or in a variety of ways when encouraged to do so

Unskilled

❏ Sees things from a single perspective.

❏ Acts as if multiple perspectives on a situation are not worth considering

❏ Criticizes approaches that look at multiple options and views novel solutions as fuzzy or impractical

❏ Makes up mind about most things and can't be budged

❏ Resists considering anything other than his or her personal perspective to evaluate situations

❏ Struggles to see positive meaning in a challenging or difficult situation

Big Picture View

To reframe a situation is to think about the situation from different points of view. The potential benefits to reframing a situation include managing emotions, reducing stress, increasing mental flexibility, and discovering innovative solutions or ideas. There is always more than one way to look at a situation, and more ways than may initially appear. Expanding your assumptions and hypotheses about situations you face begins with recognizing that there are multiple factors or elements in a situation that you may not initially see. The ability to reframe situations is linked to your willingness to be flexible, to be somewhat independent, to keep your emotions in check (that is not get hooked), and to be open to new perspectives regarding the meaning of a situation. A drastic shift — such as in an individual diagnosed with a disease who sees it as an opportunity to prioritize rather than as a victim — is an illustrative reframe.

You have a frame of reference, or a set of beliefs, values, and experiences that you use to determine the meaning of any situation in which you find yourself. If you change the frame, you change how you see the situation and how you begin to see elements that you hadn't noticed before. Consider this analogy. You make a decision to buy a new frame for a painting that you've had for a long time. When you get the painting home in its new frame, you notice something in it you never saw before. Maybe the new frame brought out colors that had been previously muted or for the first time you notice something that had been there all along but never popped out until highlighted by the changed frame. This is the heart of reframing — it helps you to see things that you may have never considered before.

Reframing involves changing the assumptions you make without changing the facts of a situation (possibly a friend didn't return my call because he or she is mad or maybe out of town or very busy). Sometimes changing the

36

context of a situation changes your reaction. For example, owning and caring for a huge vacant lot can seem like a waste of time until someone wants to buy that property to build a new store. Another way to reframe is to change the content of a situation or what a situation means to you, such as reframing cleaning your home from a tedious chore to making your home attractive for friends coming to visit.

Reframing can help you see situations in a more positive or creative way. For example, getting critical feedback can be seen as disheartening or as an opportunity to develop needed skills; a flooded basement can be a major disruption or an opportunity to redecorate an old living space. Practice seeing difficult situations in productive or positive ways. It can help you manage your emotions, reduce stress, enhance your health, improve relationships, increase your productivity, and lead to creative solutions to difficult challenges.

Barriers to Effectiveness

❏ Impatience, wanting quick solutions

❏ Failure to seek different approaches when the current strategy isn't working

❏ Failure to learn from experience

❏ Inflexibility — can't see beyond own viewpoint

❏ Hooked by emotions, which limits perspective-taking

❏ Concrete, literal (even rigid) thinking

❏ Defensive when receiving feedback (even trying to avoid it altogether)

Quick Action Tips

1. See only one approach? It is difficult to consider reframing your thinking about a situation if you have only one approach or believe there is only one. To see more than one answer you have to find multiple ways to think about a situation. There are often many solutions in a problem situation, but to understand them you have to develop a variety of problem-solving approaches. Write down the three most common challenges you face in your work that seem never to get resolved. In a sentence or two, capture how you approach each situation. Go ask several others how they might approach similar situations and what their general frame of mind is about those situations. Which idea from these conversations is most different from your own? Take that idea and test it against what you know and what might be possible.

2. Want the perfect solution? There may be several good answers to a problem issue in a relationship but not a perfect solution. If you approach situations with the attitude that there is one right answer, then you are not in a mindset to even consider reframing or repositioning the assumptions in a situation. Ask others whom you trust to share with you their strategies for dealing with difficult situations. Ask them what they consider "best action in the moment" approaches and why these approaches are important. One of the ways to learn to reframe is to listen to different assumptions and expectations others have about situations like the one you find yourself in. There probably isn't a perfect solution, but there can be many good ones.

3. Quick to fire, then aim? If you have a made-up mindset about most things, you aren't likely to be open to the concept of reframing. Personal growth will occur for you when you are able to challenge the assumption that your perspective is the only one worth considering. At this point you will be able to open yourself to the ideas, viewpoints or possibilities offered by others before you jump to action. Try to practice listening behaviors, especially in emotionally charged interactions, which will enable you to get more information before you act. When you make up your mind before hearing all the facts in a situation, you risk others seeing you as condescending and having a disregard for their experience. That is surely something to avoid!

4. Have you failed to see how creativity might help you solve problems through reframing? Creative problem solving means trying out new assumptions, new strategies, and new perspectives. Interview others to learn about their problem-solving strategies. Identify the best problem-solvers you know and pick their brains. If you did this every month for a year, then at the end of that year you would have gained up to 12 different approaches to solving a problem! This will help you build your own stable of creative strategies. Investigate e-learning classes, especially in the area of creativity or innovation, to further extend your knowledge of creative reframing/problem-solving. Consider using one of these new techniques when facing problems that might respond well to a new and creative approach.

5. Prefer to stay around those who think like you do? You might find comfort by sticking around those who agree with your own way of thinking, but you are unlikely to learn anything new. Make it a point to seek out those whose views are different from your own and engage in a dialogue to tease out their assumptions and approaches. Listen to how others who have different perspectives frame their opinions and their observations. They probably frame the same facts differently from you, and you need to learn what that frame is if you are going to influence a reframe.

6. Convinced you were right the first time you spoke about or saw a situation? The conviction of being right either in your judgment or in what you believe you see in a situation is often in inverse proportion to the quality of thinking about underlying assumptions and the framing given to the problem. The more you are convinced you are right, the less likely it is that you've

36

double-checked your assumptions or approached the situation from multiple perspectives. Use your conviction as a flag — what else could you consider in a situation? How can you reframe this situation from another point of view? What assumptions are you relying on that are untested? Make sure that you can identify the primary assumptions that you have made and the primary assumptions of those who see things differently. Artful reframing takes the assumptions from multiple perspectives and seeks to find a perspective that is constructive. Reframing is at work when you begin with, "What if we consider some new assumptions about...."

7. Brainstormed different ways of saying things or framing things recently? A true brainstorming session with others means writing down every idea and thought that comes to mind without any judgment or evaluation. This is often hard to do, but with practice you can learn to do it more effectively. If you don't brainstorm with others from time to time, you might over-rely on the "tried and true" and be less open to repositioning your perspective. Brainstorming is a process that has a couple of key outcomes: lots of ideas and divergent thinking. While the ideas may be useful in their own right, tapping into divergent thinking strategies can benefit you in many future situations. In order to reframe well, you need to think divergently about a problem or situation. Identify a couple of issues over the next month which could benefit from fresh perspectives, then practice brainstorming as part of the process to get new ideas. Listen carefully to the way people frame their ideas so you can hear the divergent mind at work. Use this as a way to expand your way of saying things.

8. Feeling overwhelmed by challenges and problems? Hard to see your way out? Although solving your issues may take time and effort, changing your mindset to one of confidence and optimism may make a big difference in your ability to succeed. Remember when you have faced difficult challenges in the past and have overcome them. Review two or three issues you handled well. Acknowledge to yourself your ability to persevere. Imagine six months from now when you have met your challenges. As you look back, your challenges might be seen as exciting and intense, rather than overwhelming. Ask a few friends or colleagues who know you well what your strengths and talents are that can help you come out on top of problems. Make note of those. Now what can you say about your current challenges that emphasizes your strengths and how you are in control and will succeed? Write it down. When you change your mindset to be more positive, you lower your stress level and enhance your ability to succeed, whatever the problem.

9. Not sure how to help your team shift to a more optimistic perspective? Sometimes we all get discouraged by events such as cutbacks, layoffs, rejection by customers. Use these questions to get beyond discouragement:

- How might we feel about this in six months?
- How crucial will this seem in a year?
- What can we do now to get beyond this difficult time?
- What would someone who is upbeat and focused on the positive say about our situation?
- What is going well for us?
- When, in the past, we experienced a similar challenge, how did we overcome it?
- What might we learn from this situation?
- How might we think ahead to be better prepared for tough times?
- Is there a silver lining in what is happening?

Reframing doesn't change the challenges, but it may help us see the opportunities, even in hard times.

Related Competencies

(10) Creativity   (16) Flexibility   (22) Insightfulness

(31) Optimism   (34) Perspective-Taking

Learn from Experience

Work

❏ Ask for an opportunity to work with a project that needs to be renewed, re-established, or repaired in some way. Take on the role of communicating a new perspective on the project.

❏ Identify a communications or public relations specialist and solicit advice on how to approach a difficult situation with a positive perspective.

Personal

❏ Take a course in innovative or creative thinking with a focus on the use of language.

❏ Identify one problem or issue you are facing in your personal life. How could this be seen as an opportunity? Make up a plan on how to respond from the perspective of an opportunity.

36

Resources

Books

Bandler, Richard. *Reframing: Neuro-Linguistic Programming and the Transformation of Meaning.* Boulder, CO: Real People Press, 1982.

Chalofsky, Neal E. *Meaningful Workplaces: Reframing How and Where We Work.* Hoboken, NJ: Jossey-Bass, 2010.

Frankl, Victor. *Man's Search for Meaning.* Boston: Beacon Press, 2006.

Internet

About.com. Search on the site for "Reframing and Stress Management," by Elizabeth Scott, May 2011. www.about.com

Mindtools. Search on the site "The Reframing Matrix: Generating Different Perspectives." www.mindtools.com

Success Measures.com. Search on the site for "Reframing" by Robert L. Sandidge and Anne C. Ward. www.successmeasures.com

Classes and training

The Creativity Workshop. Web site with multiple approaches to creativity as applied to many areas in life, including business. www.creativeworkshop.com

PDI Ninth House. Extensive selection of online courses. Refer to "Reframing Change" with William Bridges. www.pdinh.com

New and Improved. Offers training in the development of innovation and creative problem solving. www.newandimproved.com

36

37 RELATIONSHIP SAVVY

Definition

Relating well and creating relationships with all kinds of people, even those you may not particularly like, to accomplish goals

The genius of communication is to be both totally honest and totally kind at the same time.

— John Powell

Talented

❏ Identifies common ground with others to jointly handle projects and problems

❏ Invests the time and energy to build effective relationships

❏ Gives clear and effective feedback; seeks feedback

❏ Manages differences and conflict to find the best outcome for all concerned

❏ Builds rapport easily with all kinds of people; uses diplomacy

Skilled

❏ Listens and shares well in conversations especially if interested in topic

❏ Relates well with most people in most situations

❏ Communicates with respect, tact and understanding

❏ Sees things from another's point of view when encouraged to

❏ Handles conflict well most of the time

❏ Involves people, even those not well known, to accomplish goals

Unskilled

❏ Narrowly interacts with only certain kinds of people or people at certain levels in the organization

❑ Tells others what to do, gives answers, acts the expert without making time to ask and listen

❑ Misunderstands or doesn't read others well; more focused on the task than relating to people

❑ Is unskilled and uncomfortable with differences and conflict

❑ Relies only on selected people; avoids others because of shyness or lack of confidence

Big Picture View

Relationships are an integral part of both our personal and work lives, so it is not surprising that being relationship savvy overlaps with many of the other 54 EQ Competencies. Research suggests that supportive, positive relationships lead to lower stress levels, better health, a greater sense of meaning, and a longer life. Skills in managing relationships are crucial to happiness, well-being and success. Getting along well with a variety of people, even those you disagree with or dislike, means appreciating that each person perceives the world differently based on their own life events and experiences. This calls for putting any quick judgments about others on hold and communicating respect and appreciation. It also means developing skills in communicating honestly, directly and kindly at the same time. It means spending time up front to develop relationships or, as Stephen Covey might say, putting emotional capital in your relationship bank. You may need that capital as you solve problems and manage differences with others. Developing the skills of active listening, using diplomacy and tact, giving constructive feedback, building on others' ideas for the greater good, and figuring out what matters to those with whom you live and work will help raise your emotional intelligence.

Barriers to Effectiveness

❑ Discomfort with people you don't know

❑ Technical orientation at the expense of relationships

❑ Valuing power and control more than relationships

❑ Overly critical, prickly, unapproachable

❑ Overly focused on relationships to the point of neglecting responsibilities

Quick Action Tips

1. **Uncomfortable with certain kinds of people?** Success at work or in your community

may mean broadening your relationship comfort zone. Identify when you feel uncomfortable. Is it with upper management, unfamiliar cultural groups, talkative people, sports addicts or hard chargers? Make a list of five people you tend to avoid or with whom you dislike spending time What qualities or characteristics do they have in common that might lead to your discomfort? If possible, spend time getting to better know someone with those qualities. Practice looking for similarities between you rather than differences. Notice your early judgments about people and hit the "hold" button until you know them better. Spending time getting to know someone on a personal basis can lead to greater understanding and appreciation of who they are beyond initial impressions.

2. Consider small talk a waste of time? Prefer to immediately focus on the task? Remind yourself that taking a few minutes to build rapport with a colleague will help the business part of a meeting or future interactions go smoother. Make yourself more approachable by sharing a few things about yourself. A couple of possibilities include something interesting you did last weekend, a new restaurant or recipe you tried and liked, something you recently enjoyed doing with your children, partner or a friend. Use open-ended questions and active listening (27 Listening Generously) to find out what matters to others and what their perspectives are on shared interests. Have they read any good books lately? Any plans to get away this summer? Any luck with a garden this summer? Knowing more about your colleagues may lead to a genuine interest in them. It will also increase your effectiveness.

3. Enjoy being the expert, the one with the "right" answers? Someone is starting a garden and you tell them what to plant. Someone likes watching television and you tell them why television is a waste of time. A colleague is assigned a new project and you tell them how to start it. While we all appreciate advice at times (especially when we specifically ask for it), no one likes being around the constant expert. While there may be some "right" answers in our lives, more often there are preferences for how we like to do things. Ask others for their thoughts and opinions before sharing yours. Use a reminder or cue such as a roll of scotch tape on your desk to help you remember to keep your mouth shut until others have shared. Seek to understand why they may think and feel the way they do. Be generous about appreciating their good ideas. Recognize the expertise of others. When you share your ideas or give a suggestion, ask for a reaction. Engage others in a discussion without judgment before reaching a decision. Once you and any others involved in a project hear all ideas and suggestions, ask what approach makes the most sense instead of telling everyone what to do.

4. Do you tend to misread people? Misinterpret comments? Take time to notice the expressions and tone of voice of others when you are talking with them. Do people seem relaxed and comfortable with you, or are they quick to leave?

Practice listening to others. Confirm what you think you are hearing or seeing to be sure you are correct by summarizing key points. Who do you know who does read people well? Talk with that person after a meeting to compare impressions to sharpen your skills.

5. Have you damaged a relationship by an unfortunate email? Who can't say yes to that? One survey suggests that we misunderstand the tone of electronic messages 50 percent of the time for two reasons: one, a lack of nonverbal information such as a smile or nod to help explain the emotion and the intent behind the words and, two, the lack of immediate feedback, since no person is present to immediately give a reaction. A brief and direct email message is open to all kinds of possible interpretations by the reader based on extraneous data such as whether the writer was friendly the last time you interacted or how confident you are feeling. When you have to send an important message by email or text, write it and save it until later. Then reread your message to check whether you have said what you wanted to say, knowing that only your words will be seen. Put the positive intention you might be thinking and assuming into the message ("I want both of us to have input into this project and get credit for its success"). Provide a context for your message ("I know we both want this conference to be successful, so let me share a few concerns I have about how the planning is going"). Be sure you regularly communicate in person with those that matter to you to build personal credibility so that any confusion via email tends to be interpreted in a positive light.

6. Do you tend to avoid conflict in relationships? If you are uncomfortable with conflict, you are not so different from most people. Developing conflict management skills can improve relationships and boost your career. Be objective about the issue rather than making it personal. Ask open-ended or clarifying questions to really understand what is important to the other person. Examples might include:

- What is important to you in this situation?
- How do you want to approach this challenge?
- What might be a successful outcome from your perspective?
- Is there anything I may not have considered?
- How might we work most effectively going forward?

Confirm what you hear and the reasons behind what is said. Once the other person knows you understand, share your needs and what matters to you without trying to win or overwhelm the other person. Look for common ground and build on that. Reaching a win-win means that both parties will be willing to solve problems jointly in the future.

7. Are you shy? Reserved? Lack social confidence? Practice meeting people in settings outside of work such as neighborhood get-togethers, volunteer work, or your children's activities. Take the initiative to introduce yourself to new people with three sentences explaining who you are. "Hi, I am Josie Smith and have been a volunteer with Habitat for Humanity now for three years. I live in Ardmore, so I enjoy fixing up my home as well as helping build first homes for people who need them. During the week I am a receptionist for Williams Associates." Greet people you know by open-ended inquiries into how they have been or what they have been doing. Questions you can ask anyone include:

- Tell me a bit about yourself.

- Where do you live? How did you happen to locate there?

- What do you enjoy doing in your free time?

- Any particular goals you have for this year?

Watch more socially comfortable people around you to learn how they engage others. Notice the specific things they say and do. Practice what you see.

For other ideas go to: www.towerofpower.com.au/101-conversation-starters

8. Do you have a few favorite "go-to" people? Ask yourself if you tend to go to the same people for help and ideas. How can you expand your social network? Who might you get to know better by stopping by their desk, setting up lunch or talking with them before a meeting? Make it a goal to talk to one new person each month. Get to meetings five to ten minutes early and talk to whoever is there. Look beyond your immediate group for individuals who might give you a broader perspective about your organization and its initiatives. Call up a peer you may not see often and ask for his or her thoughts about a project you are working on. Find ways to get to know new colleagues, and include them on your team. Asking for help (especially if you are specific about what you need) is a wonderful way to enlarge your network. Most of us enjoy sharing our expertise and are happy to help others if we can do so.

Related Competencies

(6) Conflict Management   (15) *Active* Empathy

(25) Interpersonally Skillful   (27) Listening Generously

(30) Openness to Others

Learn from Experience

Work

❏ Attend a work-related social function you might tend to avoid and interact with at least two people you don't know well. Prepare by listing three to five open-ended questions you can use to start conversations such as:

- How long have you worked here? How did you decide to work here?
- Which department do you work in?
- Any interesting projects or initiatives going on there?
- What kinds of things do you enjoy doing in your spare time?

❏ Offer to plan a department retreat or event for team-building.

Personal

❏ Be part of a volunteer project such as a Race for the Cure fund-raiser and talk with other volunteers about how they decided to volunteer.

❏ Ask your spouse or a close friend for feedback after a social situation about the positive steps you took to get to know others better.

Resources

Books

Baber, Anne, and Lynne Waymon. *Make Your Contacts Count: Networking Know-How for Business and Career Success*. New York: AMACOM, 2007.

Lowndes, Leil. *How to Talk to Anyone: 92 Little Tricks for Big Success in Relationships*. New York: McGraw-Hill, 2003.

Paul, Maria. *The Friendship Crisis: Finding, Making, and Keeping Friends When You're Not a Kid Anymore*. Emmaus, PA: Rodale, 2004.

Roane, Susan. *How to Work a Room, Revised Edition: Your Essential Guide to Savvy Socializing*. New York: Harper, 2007.

Wiskup, Mark. *The It Factor: Be the One People Like, Listen to, and Remember*. New York: AMACOM, 2007.

Internet

HRM Today. "Ten Simple Ways to Improve Your Interpersonal Savvy," by Jason Seiden, 2009. www.hrmtoday.com

Classes and training

Total Awareness Coaching. Under the "training" link, look for "interpersonal skills training." www.totalawarenesscoaching.com

37

38   RESILIENCE

Definition

Bouncing back from difficult events and stressful situations by employing effective strategies to maximize well-being

The test of success is not what you do when you are on top. Success is how high you bounce when you hit bottom.

—General George Patton

Talented

❏ Approaches life and its challenges with a sense of personal control and commitment

❏ Adapts very well to adversity and emerges from challenges stronger

❏ Reframes negative events in a way that make them manageable

❏ Maintains optimism by looking for "silver lining in the clouds" and turning "lemons into lemonade"

❏ Fosters resilience and inner strength by living a balanced, harmonious and healthy lifestyle

❏ Maintains a strong network among friends, family, and spiritual connections

Skilled

❏ Recognizes the need to respond to a problem and sometimes seeks help from others

❏ Stumbles when stressed but adjusts, adapts and rebounds quickly

❏ Inconsistent with lifestyle and health choices; cycles in and out or does well in some areas but lousy in others

❏ Handles routine problems relatively well but becomes overwhelmed with major life challenges or crises

Unskilled

❑ Stresses out when crisis or challenge appears

❑ Engages in unhealthy life choices such as poor diet, exercise and stress management strategies

❑ Avoids problems and crisis when possible

❑ Freezes in a crisis, unable to initiate an intervention or solution

❑ Becomes demoralized by problems and feels powerless to thwart their negative impact

❑ Struggles to find meaning and purpose in life, leading to possible despair or cynicism

Big Picture View

Resilient people are more capable of managing stress and crises as well as managing the day-to-day decisions of life. Resilience combines innate traits with habits that strengthen your emotional, spiritual and physical self. When you are stressed or unhealthy, your ability to respond to stress is compromised.

Resilience is enhanced by a healthy lifestyle. We know that those who exercise, maintain a healthy weight and diet, and who have a spiritual system that provides life with meaning and purpose, are more capable of managing stress, crisis and day-to-day challenges. Those people who demonstrate high self-awareness and who feel in charge of their lives are better able to respond to the stresses of life's challenges.

The Mayo Clinic conducts regular resilience seminars, and their research demonstrates that the following practices are necessary to developing resilience.

- Fostering acceptance
- Finding meaning in life
- Developing gratitude
- Addressing spirituality
- Retraining one's attention

Resilient people are positive, adaptable, flexible and optimistic in their approach to life; they address problems rather than avoid them.

Conversely, if your health is affected by poor self-care (lack of exercise, unhealthy eating habits, lack of sleep, etc.) then your ability to respond well to demanding situations will be compromised. A big step in building resilience is to take control of your life by making healthier choices.

38

Barriers to Effectiveness

❑ Poor health habits — lack of exercise, poor diet, too little or too much sleep

❑ Negative attitude; attitude of defeatism

❑ Lack of goals or meaningful purpose in life

❑ Inadequate social support

❑ Projecting responsibility for self onto others — not taking personal responsibility

Quick Action Tips

1. Don't have any idea of how to build resilience? One of the resources below (*Resilience* by Clarke and Nicholson) lists ten steps to develop resilience. Notice how many of these you find listed among the EQ competencies in this book. Pick one and get started!

- Visualize success
- Boost your self-esteem
- Enhance your self-efficacy
- Take control
- Become more optimistic
- Manage your stress
- Improve your decision making
- Ask for help
- Deal with conflict
- Learn to be yourself

2. What inspires, energizes and engages you? Do you know what it takes to become fully engaged in your daily activities? Spending time examining these issues is important to establishing resilience. In the book *The Power of Full Engagement* a comprehensive system is presented to help you to achieve greater energy and well-being. It includes these four key principles:

- Mobilize four key sources of energy — physical, emotional, mental and spiritual
- When you expend energy, you need to replenish and renew that expenditure — don't let it get out of balance!
- You must train yourself to be stronger and more resilient, just as

athletes train in a systematic way, to build your mental, emotional, spiritual and physical capacity

- Create highly specific, positive, energy-management rituals. You must have a plan, and you must find a way of making it work for you!

3. Lack energy — easily exhausted? Join a gym, start an exercise program, work with a trainer. Use available resources to help you stay on track. SparkPeople. com was started by a young man who was inspired by his own health makeover and wanted to help others reach their health goals. There are dozens of online apps now to assist those who wish to develop better diet and exercise habits. But the simplest thing you can do is to make a plan, put it on your calendar, and then follow through. The benefits of improving your health, exercising regularly and eating a healthy diet cannot be emphasized enough as a way to help you build immunity to stress.

4. Insomnia a problem? No energy during the day because of poor sleep habits? Commit to getting a good night's sleep. Cut out caffeine after 2 p.m., begin a nighttime pattern of slowing down in the evening, avoid TV that is too stimulating before bed. Too much sleep is also a problem. Try to strike the balance of seven to eight hours a night. If necessary, do some research on healthy sleep habits. Look up sleepeducation.com.

5. What is depleting your energy? Too much clutter, life disorganized? A cluttered home or office contributes to a cluttered mind! There is some evidence that our energy is drained by having disorganization and clutter around us. Start small and begin to go through the disorganized areas of your office or home and sort out what to keep and what to throw out. Create a system for keeping it that way. Use storage bins, cabinets or other storage options to find a place for all of your keepable stuff. If need be, hire a professional organizer to get started in the right direction.

6. Not aware of how stress affects you or whether you are suffering from stress problems? Keep a diary in order to monitor your stress, mood or energy during the day to increase your self-awareness. The TARP system found on the eHealthMed. com site offers a system for identifying and analyzing your stressors.

> **T** = Tune in to the habit of recognizing and identifying stress
> **A** = Analyze the source of your stress
> **R** = Respond to the stress and deal with the cause
> **P** = Prevent stress by developing good stress reduction habits

Awareness is the key here. You would be surprised at how many people are unaware that they are experiencing high levels of stress. A diary or system for identifying stressors and recognizing your particular response to stress is very helpful.

38

7. Do you know how food affects your health, energy and mood? Nutritional research is clear that sugary foods are energy drains and that certain other foods create a sluggish metabolism. Clean out your pantry of junk food and buy healthy, more nutritious foods to keep at home. Do your own research on food and mood! To begin with, substitute a healthy food for a food you wish to cut back on or eliminate from your diet. For a longer list of energy drains, check out eMed Experts and their top 15 Energy Zappers.

8. No sense of purpose or meaning in your life? Taking action to identify and clarify meaning in your life means aligning values and purpose with what you do from day to day. Go to the Franklin-Covey web site and use their Mission Statement Builder tool. The quest to finding greater meaning or purpose is a lifelong journey. It requires that you exhibit emotional self-control, that you take the initiative to make positive changes, and that you make choices that benefit you in body, mind and spirit! Having the intention to change is a great beginning.

Related Competencies

(14) Emotional Self-Control   (21) Initiative   (31) Optimism

(41) Self-Awareness   (42) Self-Confidence   (49) Stamina

(50) Stress Hardy

Learn from Experience

Work

❏ Become part of a task force designed to increase health in the workplace.

❏ Work to get a gym at work or to start a Weight Watchers group, a yoga class, etc., in the workplace.

Personal

❏ Begin an exercise program. Hire a personal trainer to keep you motivated, or have a group of friends agree to meet at the gym or to run or walk together. Keep track with an exercise log.

❏ Get a good night's sleep. Write out your goals for sleep and begin to keep a sleep journal. Start your sleep preparation an hour or two before retiring — no high intensity TV or activity beforehand as it makes it more difficult to go to sleep.

❏ A meditation, centering prayer or mindfulness practice is a great antidote to stress, which increases resilience. Resolve to start such a practice today!

Resources

Books

Benson, Herbert, and Eileen Stuart. *The Wellness Book: Comprehensive Guide to Maintaining Health and Treating Stress-Related Illness*. New York: Fireside, 1992.

Clarke, Jane, and John Nicholson. *Resilience: Bounce Back From Whatever Life Throws at You*. Crimson, 2010

Davis, Martha, Elizabeth Eshelman, and Matthew McKay. *The Relaxation and Stress Reduction Workbook*, Oakland, CA: New Harbinger, 2000.

Elkin, Allen. *Stress Management for Dummies*. Foster City, CA: IDG Books Worldwide, 1999.

Kabat-Zinn, Jon. *Arriving at Your Own Door: 108 Lessons in Mindfulness*. New York: Hyperion, 2007.

Luskin, Fred and Kenneth Pelletier. *Stress Free for Good: 10 Scientifically Proven Life Skills for Health and Happiness*. San Francisco: HarperCollins, 2005.

Loehr, Jim, and Tony Schwartz. *The Power of Full Engagement: Managing Energy, Not Time, Is the Key to High Performance and Personal Renewal*. New York: The Free Press, 2003.

McKay, Matthew, Martha Davis, and Patrick Fanning. *Thoughts and Feelings: Taking Control of Your Moods and Your Life*. Oakland, CA: New Harbinger Publications, 1997.

Internet

Instant Stress Management. Site describes 21 stress management and meditation techniques, and tips on relaxation breathing and visualization. www.instantstressmanagement.com

Mayo Clinic — Food and Mood. Search web site for "health, food, mood" www.mayoclinic.org

Myfitnesspal.com and Livestrong.com have great tools for starting a health and fitness program.

PeopleSkillsHandbook.com. Resources and further material for the benefit of personal, physical and mental health. www.peopleskillshandbook.com

Positive Psychology Center. www.ppc.sas.upenn.edu/positiveeducation

Sleep Health. www.sleepeducation.com

38

Classes and training

The Benson-Henry Institute for Mind Body Medicine. Nonprofit scientific and educational organization dedicated to research, teaching, and clinical application of mind/body medicine. www.massgeneral.org/bhi

Mindfulness Based Stress Reduction (MBSR®) Training Program. UMass Medical School: Center for Mindfulness founded by Jon Kabat-Zinn. www.umassmed.edu/cfm/stress

Mayo Clinic Resiliency Training. www.mayoclinic.org/resilience-training

39 | SELF-ACTUALIZATION

Definition

Pursuing activities that lead to a personally meaningful life; becoming more of your best self

What man actually needs is not a tensionless state but rather the striving and struggling for some goal worthy of him. What he needs is not the discharge of tension at any cost, but the call of a potential meaning waiting to be fulfilled by him.

— Victor Frankl

Talented

❑ Exhibits ability to think and act with autonomy

❑ Energetically pursues personally meaningful activities; sets challenging goals and meets them

❑ Reacts with spontaneity and enthusiasm to people, places and ideas

❑ Readily accepts responsibility for self and actions

❑ Demonstrates healthy acceptance of self and others; lacks prejudice

Skilled

❑ Accepts day to day life as it comes rather than pursuing dreams

❑ Enjoys work and gets satisfaction from it

❑ Acts comfortable with self and others

❑ Pursues modest goals and meets expectations; has tendency to accept the status quo rather than push self

Unskilled

❑ Exhibits low self-esteem and self-confidence

❑ Lacks ambition, motivation and focus

❑ Hesitates to pursue goals because of self-doubt

❏ Motivated more by a desire to please others and less by an inner drive

❏ Approaches goals, achievement and interests passively

Big Picture View

Abraham Maslow was the first to coin the phrase self-actualization, and his work has inspired many others to expand upon the subject. Management experts have borrowed from his writings to encourage organizations to create work environments that help their employees achieve in a personally meaningful way, meeting their own needs as well as the needs of the company. In recent years the Human Potential Movement has encouraged people to reach for the untapped potential within themselves and to help others achieve their potential. Such people are valued additions to any organization and contribute positively to their communities and families.

Self-actualization is important in a discussion about emotional intelligence because the process of becoming self-actualized involves many of the qualities discussed in this book. Self-actualized people are confident, they respect and get along well with others, they lack prejudice, they are open-minded and creative, and they have a passion for life. Two common characteristics of those on the pathway toward self-actualization are, first, their ability to be honest with themselves and to examine their personal motives, values and emotions and, second, their motivation to take action on their goals and desires. Achieving self-actualization means that you have identified your primary needs in life, that you have largely met them, and that now you are concentrating on what gives you joy and what ignites a passion within you to achieve and create at a higher level. And to do so helps to bring about positive changes in the world around you.

Barriers to Effectiveness

❏ Externally motivated, lacks personal convictions

❏ Acts more from fear of failure than a passionate desire to achieve or learn something new

❏ Overly conforming; needs to fit in

❏ Inertia, lack of energy, motivation or initiative

❏ Takes on the victim role

❏ Blames others for failures or disappointments

❏ Lack of self-confidence and self-regard

Quick Action Tips

1. Don't get around to setting goals? Research and experience tells us that those people who set realistic goals and commit publicly to them are more likely to be successful in accomplishing those goals with resulting high self-esteem. Try setting a simple goal each day such as, "I will walk twenty minutes during lunch," or, "I will sign up for that painting class." Having the intention to succeed, picturing what it will look like when you do, writing down or publicly committing to a goal, and evaluating the results are all great ways to help you succeed in your intention.

2. Overlook reflection or regular self-review? People who take the time to reflect on themselves and their experiences with the intent to learn and grow are more successful. Peter Bregman, a well-known leadership consultant, recommends that at the end each day we ask ourselves the following questions.

1. How did the day go? What success did I experience? What challenges did I manage?

2. What did I learn today? About myself? About others? What do I plan to do — differently or the same — tomorrow?

3. Whom did I interact with? Anyone I need to update? Thank? Ask a question? Share feedback?

3. What gives your life meaning, purpose and fulfillment? When you allow yourself to ponder questions such as these and their answers, you are engaging in an inquiry that helps lead toward self-actualization. Sit down and make a list of the things that most matter to you. For example, list ten key events in your life, the ten most important people in your life, the ten most (you fill in the blank) in your life. Or, ask yourself, "If I had just one year to live, how would I want to live my life?" Knowing that you are connected to something larger than yourself brings purpose and fulfillment to your life and is an important component of self-actualization. Committing part of yourself to a greater good or higher purpose is also linked to improved health, both physical and mental.

4. What brings you joy? Consider the things that bring deep joy to you or that inspire a passion to pursue a personal goal. What traits of character evolve in you when engaged in these pursuits? What is it about these activities that make you a better person or improves the quality of your life? By reflecting on these things, you are determining what motivates and nurtures you.

5. Whom do you admire? Think of the two or three people you really admire, and tease out the qualities that you admire most. Reflect on how you exhibit these same traits or character qualities. What values do these character traits suggest you embrace? Do these values line up with how you see yourself and how you want to see yourself? How do they motivate you in your life? Self-actualization is about reaching for your dreams. It's also about becoming the person you're capable of being. An interesting way to explore this line of thinking is to read biographies of successful or interesting people.

6. Avoid pushing yourself or aiming for the next step? A great beginning is to ask your boss for a more challenging work assignment, or to work out with a fitness trainer who will motivate you to the next level. It can be helpful to engage the services of a life or leadership coach to help you identify areas in which you want to develop and excel. Even small challenges that yield results have value and are the building blocks to further success. And success begets success.

7. Undermined by low self-esteem or self doubts? With whom do you spend time? Are they the kind of friends or colleagues who encourage you and point out your strengths and potential? Having people in your life who help build your self-esteem is important. Find ways to spend time with them and talk about what's important to you. Ask for help in identifying strengths and achievable goals that can help you succeed. By the same token, it might be helpful to identify those people who seem to bring you down, always pointing out your faults and shortcomings. Perhaps it's time to limit your interactions with them.

Related Competencies

(3) Authenticity   (21) Initiative   (23) Integrity

(40) Accurate Self-Assessment   (41) Self-Awareness

(42) Self-Confidence   (44) Self-Regard

Learn from Experience

Work

❏ Explore a voluntary assignment at work for which you feel a passion or excitement, such as leading the United Way campaign, or serving on the board of a nonprofit that has personal meaning for you.

❏ Try writing a mission statement that applies to your work or professional goals. The Franklin-Covey web site has a mission statement builder that you can use to get going. www.franklincovey.com/msb/

Personal

❏ Expand your personal mission statement to your total life mission statement using www.franklincovey.com/msb

❏ Take the results generated above in Quick Action Tip 3 and imagine one or two goals or activities that would enrich your life. Then pursue one or both. This kind of self-examination can be energizing.

39

Resources

Books

Covey, Stephen. *Seven Habits of Highly Effective People*. New York: Free Press, 1989, 2004.

Dalai Lama. *The Art of Happiness*. New York: Riverhead Books, 1998, 2009.

Hudson, Russ, and Don Riso. *The Wisdom of the Enneagram*. New York: Bantam, 1999.

Katie, Byron. *Loving What Is: Four Questions That Can Change Your Life*. Three Rivers Press, 2002.

Frankel, Victor. *Man's Search for Meaning*. Boston: Beacon Press, 1959, 2006.

Maslow, Abraham H. "A Theory of Human Motivation." *Psychological Review*. 1943, 50, 370-96.

Moss, Richard. *The Mandala of Being: Discovering the Power of Awareness*. New World Library, 2003.

Internet

Franklin Covey web site. Search "Mission Statement Builder" and "Habit 2 — Begin with the End in Mind." www.franklincovey.com/msb/

Classes and training

Self-Actualizating.org. The Ultimate Process for Unleashing Your Potential. www.self-actualizing.org/

Enneagram Institute: Courses such as "The Wisdom of the Enneagram, A Map to Your True Essence." www.enneagraminstitute.com

40 | ACCURATE SELF-ASSESSMENT

Definition

Knowing your strengths and limits

There is no freedom like seeing myself as I am and not losing heart.
— Elizabeth J. Canham

Talented

❏ Leverages strengths and compensates for weaknesses

❏ Reflects on and learns from experience

❏ Seeks and is open to candid feedback, new perspectives, continuous learning and self-development

❏ Views self from different perspectives, even when they're not favorable

❏ Demonstrates excellent self-awareness; aware of how behavior affects self and others

Skilled

❏ Seems generally aware of own strengths and weaknesses but less aware of their impact on others

❏ Examines experiences to better understand strengths and weaknesses when confronted with failure

❏ Listens to but doesn't proactively seek feedback

❏ Acts on feedback when development is needed

Unskilled

❏ Seems to be unsure of strengths, weaknesses and impact on others

❏ Repeats behaviors that have triggered negative consequences — doesn't seem to make the connections or learn from experiences

❏ Avoids opportunities for feedback and appears unreceptive when it is offered

❏ Misreads others' perceptions and reactions

Big Picture View

Accurate self-assessment is about viewing yourself accurately. This includes your strengths and weaknesses and the impact you have on others. Understanding your strengths and weaknesses, whether through formal or informal means, allows you to assess the fit between yourself and the requirements of the job you have or the job you want. This knowledge prepares you to address any gaps proactively. Seeking feedback from others gives you insight into how others see you and react to you. This allows you to adjust what you're doing in order to have the impact you want. Self-assessment is a major contributor to self-awareness, which plays a major role in job success, effective relationships and life satisfaction.

Accurate self-assessment is an essential step toward developing greater emotional intelligence. There is considerable research demonstrating that people who engage in active self-assessment and who challenge themselves to continue learning enjoy a high degree of success and personal satisfaction in their lives. Set yourself up to succeed. Build on your strengths, and, where possible, neutralize your weaknesses. But first you need to know what they are. And seek feedback early and often.

Barriers to Effectiveness

❏ Failure to seek or learn from feedback

❏ Unrealistically high or low self-esteem or self-confidence

❏ Faulty assumption that you already know everything that you need to know

Quick Action Tips

1. Know thyself. Do you? It is hard to work on what you don't know needs work. Accurate self-assessment is critical to success, both personally and professionally. Here are some questions that can start you on that path.

- What has shaped you so far? Make a list of your characteristics and where they came from (genetics, childhood, learned later).

- What are your emotional buttons? Common buttons include public speaking, confronting people, asking for help or a date.

- Which aspects of your life excite, disappoint, satisfy or bore you? (Substitute the emotions that matter to you.) Are there patterns here that provide insight? What is under your control?

40

- How open are you to others? How does that vary? For example, do you behave differently at work and at home?

- Do some people push your buttons? Your reactions to others often reveal more about you than about them. What are the triggers, and how might they be important?

- From a work perspective, consider these questions: What am I doing well? How do my strengths match the needs of my job? Where do I need to improve? How do my behaviors affect others? How do others view me? Do I have work goals? What, and how, am I doing with those goals?

2. Impatient with self-reflection? Action-oriented people are known for their productivity. They are the go-to people if you want something done. If this describes you, then you might be less inclined to be reflective, less likely to spontaneously consider the questions listed in Quick Action Tip 1 above. Mix it up — go against the grain and learn something about yourself. Getting results is important. But how you get results matters too. Understanding yourself, what you offer and what you need from others helps you get the job done right, the first time. Before jumping into a task, examine the approach you plan to take. Consider alternate approaches (at least two more, which research shows will improve your choices and overall decision-making). Get input from others with relevant experience. Teams generate better ideas than individuals. All these ideas ask you to take the time to reflect — not easy if you are action-oriented. What did you learn about yourself?

3. Do you keep pushing forward, overlooking the need to do something different? Common barriers to change are lack of motivation, lack of a better idea and discomfort with uncertainty. People are creatures of habit; they do what comes automatically, out of habit, sometimes without thinking. It is human nature to repeat behaviors that have worked in the past. But, do you notice when and whether those behaviors have stopped working? People see what they expect (or hope) to see more readily than what actually is. Set up feedback loops, early warning systems and other triggers to stop and look with fresh eyes. Ask the people around you to give you regular feedback, positive and corrective, on your impact.

4. Burned by feedback in the past? Has your experience with getting feedback in the past been negative? Unfortunately, not all feedback is fun to hear, nor are all people who give feedback skilled. For most people, getting feedback is anxiety producing. If you have had a painful experience with feedback, you might display defensive behaviors that discourage others from approaching you with useful informal feedback. If so, you risk being surprised by feedback when you do get it. It is very difficult to have an accurate view of yourself without the objective perspectives of those around you, updated frequently.

Multi-rater assessments that are done professionally are careful to ask the right people the right questions to get a clear picture of a person's effect on others. It is important that this "snapshot" be delivered to you in a way that you can hear, understand, value and use. If you are interested in an assessment to help you better understand yourself and to receive feedback on your strengths and weaknesses, then investigate various leadership development programs that include a serious assessment process or try engaging the services of a qualified executive or leadership coach. Contact your human resources department to learn whether or not your organization offers multi-rater assessments. In most cases they can provide a coach to help you better utilize and understand your results.

5. Think feedback and self-assessment is fluff? If you're skeptical about the value of feedback, then there's a good chance that we won't change that opinion in the space we've got here. But it's worth a try. Consider this: 70 percent of those failing to get and to act on feedback derail in their careers, far short of their potential. Worse still, 90 percent of these folks suffer impaired relationships, sometimes seriously impaired. If you're having an unintended, negative impact, one that has negative implications for you personally or professionally, then would you want to know? Blind spots can be fatal. Some people believe they've already learned what they need to know to be successful, that there's little left to learn or little of value that others can tell them. If this describes you, then look for a seasoned coach who has experience working with tough-as-nails personalities. This journey will be worth every penny, but it needs a highly expert escort.

6. Where to begin? Don't know how to get started with assessing yourself? Just like the annual review offered by your boss, conducting your own routine assessment could yield helpful results, maybe in time to improve before your formal review. This also is a great strategy to keep you challenged and open to personal and professional growth. Use these questions to start assessing yourself:

- What do I do well?
- What does my job require?
- Where do I need to improve?
- How do my actions affect other people?
- How do others view me?
- What motivates me?
- What matters to me?
- Do I live according my goals and values?

This process, accompanied by feedback (from boss, colleagues, friends and family), can move you closer to knowing more about yourself and how you come across to others.

7. So, you know yourself pretty well. Now what? Success is a moving target. "What got you here won't get you there." (Marshall Goldsmith, author, coach.) "Success isn't permanent, and failure isn't fatal." (Mike Ditka, NFL coach.) Any way you cut it, you either stay in "learning" gear or you risk running off the road. Stay alert to changing demands to keep your self-assessment current. Take a look in this book at the chapter on development planning (Chapter 4). Use the ideas found there to consider opportunities that will prepare you to meet emerging demands. But keep in mind that your greatest room for growth is in the area of your strength. There is a temptation for people to over-focus on weaknesses and on fixing them while ignoring the potential of their strengths. That would be an unfortunate mistake.

8. Can you laugh at yourself? People who have a sense of humor and a perspective about themselves stay grounded, even in the face of difficult feedback. Getting bad news is never fun. But it is almost never as big a deal as it feels like in the moment of getting it. Having a sense of humor keeps the negative impact from becoming demoralizing without losing sight of its value. Use your sense of humor to make it easier to take feedback in stride. Learning more about your strengths and weaknesses should be an ongoing effort throughout your lifetime. Tempering it with your humor makes the journey easier and more pleasant.

9. Believe in guardian angels? Well, many people don't. But mentors, coaches, managers, parents, spouses, partners and close friends often serve such a role. These are the people close to you who have invested in you, either at a moment in time or over the course of your life and maybe your career. They provide you with valuable feedback, and sometimes guidance, that you use to improve. If you have one or more of these "angels" in your life, then thank them. And pay attention to what they tell you. They have your best interest at heart, and they have a perspective that you do not have.

Related Competencies

(12) Emotional Maturity   (22) Insightfulness   (27) Listening Generously

(30) Openness to Others   (41) Self-Awareness   (46) Social Intelligence

Learn from Experience

Work

❑ Seek an assignment at which others in the past have failed (requires recognizing limitations and assessing what expertise is needed).

Personal

❏ Volunteer for a committee or organization whose focus is unfamiliar to you (requires you to learn about the group's focus from ground up, and fast).

Resources

Books

Adams, Kathleen. *Journal to the Self: Twenty-Two Paths to Personal Growth — Open the Door to Self-Understanding by Writing, Reading, and Creating a Journal of Your Life.* New York: Warner Books,1990.

Boyatzis, Richard E. *The Competent Manager: A Model for Effective Performance.* Hoboken, NJ: John Wiley & Sons, 1982.

Hayes, Charles D. *Self University: The Price of Tuition Is the Desire to Learn: Your Degree Is a Better Life.* Wasilla, Alaska: Hayes Autodidactic Press,1989.

Keirsey, David, and Marilyn Bates. *Please Understand Me: Character and Temperament Types.* Del Mar, CA: Prometheus Nemesis Book Company, 5th edition, 1984.

Internet

The Riley Guide. Go to the navigation bar and select "Before You Search," then look for "Self-Assessment" links. www.rileyguide.com

Find Articles.com. Do an onsite search for "How to Conduct Self-Directed 360 — Employee Assessment" by Kate Ludeman (July 2000). www.findarticles.com

Classes and training

Center for Creative Leadership. Leadership Development Program (LDP®), Maximizing Your Leadership Potential (MLP), Women's Leadership Program (WLP) and many other programs offering self-assessment. www.ccl.org

Qualifying.org. Offers training in the certification of 360-degree feedback assessments as well as provide a qualified coach to assist you in your own self-assessment. www.qualifying.org

Board Certified Coach (through Center for Credentialing and Education). Find a certified coach to help provide you with 360-degree feedback. www.cce-global.org/

40

41 | SELF-AWARENESS

Definition

Knowing your own emotions, thoughts, motives, tendencies to react and their impact on others

The most fundamental aggression to ourselves, the most fundamental harm we can do to ourselves, is to remain ignorant by not having the courage and the respect to look at ourselves honestly and gently.

— Pema Chödrön

Talented

❑ Accepts responsibility for own emotions and how they influence behavior in self and others

❑ Understands how personal behaviors affect others

❑ Demonstrates knowledge of own strengths, weaknesses and personal qualities

❑ Expresses emotions skillfully and appropriately

❑ Seeks and welcomes feedback as an opportunity to learn more about self

❑ Behaves consistently with personal values and guiding purpose

Skilled

❑ Gains insights by reflecting on experience

❑ Responds openly to feedback when it is offered

❑ Makes amends when behaviors offend others

❑ Recognizes basic feelings but not subtle distinctions

❑ Expresses emotions, but sometimes awkwardly

Unskilled

❑ Appears unaware of how one's behavior is affecting others

❏ Expresses thoughts about self that are too self-critical and possibly too self-revealing

❏ Shares views about self that are inaccurate — either over-inflated or under-inflated

❏ Fails to recognize or understand own feelings — emotional illiteracy

❏ Reacts defensively when feedback is provided

Big Picture View

Self-awareness is an essential building block to many EQ skills. Without awareness of your motivations, thoughts or feelings, you may act like a loose cannon, buffeted about by your emotions, reacting impulsively to the events around you. Common descriptors such as "clueless," "out of touch" and "bull in a china shop" reflect a general lack of self-awareness. When people overestimate their abilities or are blind to weaknesses it can interfere with effectiveness at work and at home. On the other hand, underestimating one's own abilities and achievements can lead to fear of failure and low self-esteem.

Self-awareness is fundamental to self-development — knowing your starting point allows you to set goals for development and effectively use your strengths to help get you there. Self-awareness includes being sensitive to how you affect others, which allows you to be more intentional about your behavior. A bonus of gaining a better understanding of yourself is a deeper understanding of human nature in general. Staying open to feedback illuminates blind spots and provides the opportunity to change self-defeating patterns of behavior. As a tool, self-awareness improves your ability to listen accurately, to empathize, to resolve conflict and to mentor or coach others. Since the Age of Enlightenment humans have sought to better understand themselves. Achieving that understanding is a lifetime journey that depends on openness to feedback, observation, reflection and accepting responsibility for your actions and choices.

Barriers to Effectiveness

❏ Disinterest in understanding self or others

❏ Too busy to reflect on thoughts and feelings

❏ Self-centeredness, little empathy

❏ Low self-esteem

❏ Defensiveness, especially in the face of objective feedback

❏ Competitiveness; feeling driven

41

Quick Action Tips

1. **"I don't know what got into me!"** Ever find yourself trying to excuse thoughtless behavior with these platitudes? "I'm sorry, I don't know what got into me," or, "I didn't mean it that way." But, unless the apology is accompanied by a significant effort to change the behavior, it becomes meaningless. Lasting behavior change requires understanding what's driving the behavior in the first place. Make it a point to use these occasions to dig a little deeper into what is going on with you. Ask yourself, what motivated your behavior? Or what was interfering with your better self? Hopefully, you want to operate out of conscious choice rather than a potentially thoughtless, unconscious one. Keep a journal in which you describe these kinds of experiences and what you're learning from them. As you gain some insights, consider discussing them with a trusted friend, mentor or coach, to build on what you are learning. Another practice self-aware people engage in is conducting daily self-reviews. (See tip 8 below.)

2. **Can you describe yourself and your personality?** Don't know? Personality assessments are used for all kinds of purposes and are widely available. Take one or more and use the results as a springboard for learning more about yourself and your motivations. Many employers offer such assessments. There also are many Internet sites that offer simple personality assessment tools to get you started thinking about what makes you tick. Or work with a professional who is trained to administer and interpret assessments. Two things to remember about personality assessments: One, you decide how well the results describe you. Although most valid and reliable personality assessments are enlightening (if you are open to new information), there is always some margin of error. Two, if you use online assessments, they will vary in their validity and reliability. The goal is to get you thinking about yourself, to expose blind spots in your awareness and to increase self-knowledge.

3. **Are there times when you feel out of control?** Do you react emotionally instead of responding thoughtfully to a challenging situation? Sometimes people react impulsively, giving in to their emotions, rather than making a choice or decision informed by reason. Research indicates that we have thousands of thoughts and impulses a day. Knowing yourself well enough to know when to act and when to slow down and think through a challenging situation is important. Some people find it helpful to sleep on an important decision or to talk it over with a trusted confidant before responding. In any case, being aware of the thoughts and feelings motivating you can help prevent unfortunate decisions. The Stop — Breathe — Reflect — Choose model is a stress management tool that helps prevent impulsive or self-destructive behavior that can occur when caught in the snare of negative thinking. When faced with a thought that threatens to run out of control, try these four steps:

- *Stop*: Say the word "stop," either out loud if alone or to yourself if in a crowd, to get your attention.

- *Breathe*: Take four or five deep abdominal breaths or until you feel yourself relaxing and calming down. Maintain this pattern of deep and slow breathing for the duration of the exercise.

- *Reflect*: As you become more relaxed, seek to cultivate a sense of detachment from the tense situation. Ask yourself some questions designed to offer you greater perspective: "Am I overreacting?" "Is there a more rational way I can look at the situation?" "What's the worst thing that could happen? Can I handle it?"

- *Choose*: After asking yourself these questions, does another choice emerge that makes more sense for you? Does a change in your perspective suggest different choices? Challenge the rationality of any negative thoughts or fears. Continue to practice relaxing or whatever helps to calm and center you. (Adapted from *The Wellness Book* by Herbert Benson, M.D.)

4. Have trouble realistically assessing your strengths and weaknesses? It is important to be realistic about your strengths and shortcomings. What do you consider to be your five best qualities (strengths) and your five worst qualities (weaknesses or areas for development)? Ask a select group of family, friends and co-workers the same question. Compare your answers, and use what you learn to create a plan for your development. Identify a strength that you want to build upon and any weakness you need to work on to prevent possible derailment. If your company offers a multi-rater assessment, elect to take it. Discuss the results with a HR professional or a leadership coach.

5. Do you have trouble admitting your mistakes? Being able to admit that you are at fault or that you are lacking in knowledge is, ironically, a sign of self-knowledge. Humility is an important quality in handling your emotions. Be willing to admit your weaknesses, and, if there are consequences, learn to accept them. You can begin immediately if you have a situation in which an apology or an admission of wrongdoing would benefit you and your relationship. Accept responsibility for your part in the problem and do your best to rectify the situation.

6. Has a sheltered or narrow life experience limited your self-awareness? Have you been limiting yourself to the same experiences, people, places and challenges? Self-awareness can be gained through travel, reading about other cultures, religions or world views, participating in a reading club or discussion group, and by being open to new experiences or opportunities. Commit to stepping outside your routine with films, books, people and experiences. Reflect on your reactions and what you are learning about yourself. Choose someplace completely different for your next vacation. If feasible, travel to another

41

country or take a service vacation, in which you work on a volunteer project while on vacation. Again, reflect on your reactions and what you are learning about yourself.

7. Find yourself going in circles at times, or lacking focus? Lack of focus can scatter your attention, making it difficult to engage in an honest self-assessment. A common malady of modern day life is the tendency to multi-task, to stay overly busy and to cram in as many experiences as possible, leaving little time for reflection or rejuvenation. The 21st century's array of technology has inserted itself into our lives in marvelous and, at times, troubling ways. The miracle of the electronic and technical age can have the negative side effect of diverting us from the ability to tune in to and know ourselves. If you find yourself feeling stressed, distracted or unfocused, then try one of the disciplines below to increase your power to focus and concentrate. Such disciplines or practices as mindfulness, meditation, centering prayer, yoga, Tai Chi or even gardening can bring you into the present moment and help you to become more focused and grounded. An additional benefit is that they are effective at relieving stress.

8. Do you ever think about how your day went, or wonder about how others reacted to your actions, your choices or your impact on them? You will be surprised at what taking the time to reflect on recent experiences will reveal to you. It may prompt you to make a well-advised correction or addition to an earlier interaction. Such a revisit, in turn, may invite input that further increases your self-awareness. Peter Bregman, a well-known leadership consultant, recommends that at the end of each day we ask ourselves the following set of questions:

- How did the day go? What success did I experience? What challenges did I endure?

- What did I learn today? About myself? About others? What do I plan to do — differently or the same — tomorrow?

- Who did I interact with? Anyone I need to update? Thank? Ask a question? Share feedback?

Exercises such as these improve relationships and provide opportunities to better understand the impact your behavior has on others. This is must-have information if you want to build upon your strengths and seek improvement where needed.

Related Competencies

(3)Authenticity   (8) Congruence   (28)Mindfulness

(39) Self-Actualization   (40) *Accurate* Self-Assessment

(43) Self-Disclosure

Learn from Experience

Work

❏ Participate in a leadership development program that involves personal one-on-one feedback by a skilled coach.

❏ Ask your boss or colleagues to provide you with feedback on your behavior or work performance.

❏ Consider an experiment in which you swap jobs with a colleague, share your experiences and give each other feedback that will increase both empathy and self-awareness.

❏ Take a personality assessment and use it as a springboard to greater self-awareness (for example, MBTI,® FIRO-B,® Workplace Big 5, to mention a few).

Personal

❏ Think of two or three events or circumstances in your life that have shaped you (for better or worse) and write about them in a journal or blog over the course of several weeks. Use this process to help you become more insightful about the reasons these experiences had such an impact in your life.

❏ Take a course, class or workshop designed to help you better understand yourself. Many are offered through church, work and community organizations.

Resources

Books

Arbinger Institute. *Leadership and Self Deception: Getting Out of the Box*. San Francisco, Berrett-Koehler, 2010.

Benson, Herbert, and Eileen Stuart. *The Wellness Book: The Comprehensive Guide to Maintaining Health and Treating Stress-Related Illness*. New York: Simon and Shuster, 1992.

Dalai Lama, and Paul Ekman. *Emotional Awareness: Overcoming the Obstacles to Psychological Balance and Compassion*. New York: Holt, 2008.

Frankel, Victor. *Man's Search for Meaning*. Boston: Beacon Press, 1959, 2006.

Katie, Byron. *Loving What Is: Four Questions That Can Change Your Life*. New York: Three Rivers Press, 2002.

Hudson, Russ, and Don Riso. *The Wisdom of the Enneagram: The Complete*

Guide to Psychological and Spiritual Growth for the Nine Personality Types. New York: Bantam, 1999.

Pearman, Roger R., Michael M. Lombardo, and Robert W. Eichinger. *You: Being More Effective in Your MBTI Type.* Minneapolis, MN: Lominger International: A Korn/Ferry Co., 2005.

Pearman, Roger R., and Sarah Albritton. *I'm Not Crazy, I'm Just Not You.* Boston: Nicholas Brealey Publishing, 1997, 2010.

Internet

People Skills Handbook web site: Many additional resources for increasing EQ and self-awareness. www.peopleskillshandbook.com

Help Guide. Video on "Roadblocks to Awareness." www.helpguide.org

Livestrong.com: Search the site for "Getting in Touch With Feelings" article. www.livestrong.com/search

The Enneagram Institute. Training and resources for development through self-awareness. www.enneagraminstitute.com

Classes and training

The Center for Creative Leadership. Leadership Development Program (LDP®). A five-day program with self-assessment tools, including a 360-degree instrument for the purpose of increased self-awareness through feedback.
www.ccl.org.

"Getting the Love you Want" workshop for couples.
www.imagorelationships.org

Center for Mindfulness in Medicine, Healthcare and Society. Courses in Mindfulness Leadership Programs and other mindfulness resources on their web site. www.umassmed.edu/cfm

Landmark Forum Education. Programs and workshops to increase self-knowledge. www.landmarkeducation.com

42   SELF-CONFIDENCE

Definition

Believing in your worth — your abilities, qualities and judgment — and behaving accordingly

A man cannot be comfortable without his own approval.

— Mark Twain

Talented

❑ Walks and talks with self-assurance and willingness to take risks

❑ Expresses belief in ability to achieve goals

❑ Takes unpopular stands and goes out on limbs for what is right when necessary

❑ Makes timely decisions despite uncertainties and pressures

❑ Admits mistakes

❑ Shares credit

Skilled

❑ Speaks as if mostly free from self-doubt

❑ Expresses realistic self-evaluations

❑ Takes risks but seeks support when doing so

❑ Stands alone, reluctantly and not comfortably

❑ Admits mistakes tempered with explanations

Unskilled

❑ Hesitates to speak up or reach for challenging goals

❑ Expresses self doubt or self-criticisms that others would not support

❑ Worries about what others might think

❑ Tends to brag, drop names or show off

❏ Over-reacts to perceived slights, rejection or failure.

❏ Competes inappropriately or takes credit due others

Big Picture View

While childhood experiences shape self-confidence, genetics and later experiences play even greater roles, and you can leverage both. Many seek therapy to shorten that journey. Self-confidence develops over time and in response to having the impact you intend to have. Whether you set out to make a friend, make money or make progress toward a degree, it almost doesn't matter what your goal is. Making a plan to achieve something, then following through to completion, creates a feeling of mastery that fuels self-confidence. Success leads to greater confidence and willingness to take risks and set bigger goals in the future. Success breeds success. But no one is good at everything. Confident people set themselves up to succeed by choosing achievable goals that matter to them. They incorporate people and strategies that help them get there. Almost as important, they can accurately describe what they have achieved, the challenges they have overcome and the problems they have solved. They appreciate their strengths and manage their shortcomings.

Barriers to Effectiveness

❏ Negative self-talk and constant self-criticism

❏ Being unaware of thought patterns

❏ Hypersensitive to feedback

❏ Unwilling to take risks

❏ Overly concerned about pleasing others

❏ Failure to set goals or has a fear of failure

Quick Action Tips

1. **Hesitant to speak up?** If yes, do you fear making mistakes, risking failure, exposing incompetence, being rejected or appearing foolish? They are all a part of life. Without taking some risks, there is no learning. You cannot learn without making mistakes. Failure is not fatal. Rejection is more about the other person than you. Fear of exposure or making a fool of yourself is common, but how often does it actually happen? Rarely. The best protection against being hijacked by negative emotion, including fear, is challenging the irrationality of it. Switch perspectives. Imagine putting someone you care about in your chair. Imagine listening to this person describing your situation as if it were their own. Hear what they are saying. How does it look and

42

sound now from this other perspective? What advice would you offer? What is a more rational way of thinking about this? Now incorporate that thinking into your self-talk.

2. Are you your own worst critic? Do you doubt or criticize yourself in ways others would not support? Do you find the one thing that you could have done better rather than the things you did well? Most experiences are neutral, but others contain positive elements as well as negative. Too often, though, the temptation is to focus on the negative. If this is you, especially after you've climbed into bed at night, then where does that leave you but awake and miserable? If this is your custom, then challenge yourself to shift your attention to the high points — especially compliments and positive feedback — one day at a time. You might as well focus on and enjoy the best parts of your day and make it easier for sleep to come. It sure gets the next morning off to a much better start.

3. Too concerned about what others think? If yes, then you've got lots of company. But here's what's interesting about that. How often do you actually know what others are thinking — *really* know? In the absence of knowing, for a fact, what do you do? You make it up, right? If you're like most people, when guessing what others are thinking, it usually is not favorable. So, let's fix that first. If you're going to make up what others are thinking, make it positive. At least, then, you won't be sabotaging your self-confidence. But if you actually need to know how you're seen by others, talk with people. The best remedy, especially if you need a perspective that is different from yours, is to get the information from a source you trust, one whose opinion you value. Like most things, balance is important. Balance your self-perspectives with input from others. Balance what others tell you with what you know about yourself. Trusted advisors are important relationships to cultivate.

4. Fragile self-esteem, maybe since childhood? Do you tend to be self-critical, sensitive to perceived slights or defensive when receiving corrective feedback? Self-confident people are less likely to report any of these experiences. If, however, these experiences are common to you, your self-confidence needs work. One of the best ways to strengthen your self-confidence is to set goals and reach the goals you set — at home, school or at work. Keep a record of what your goals are and the progress you make. Once completed, make a point to give yourself credit for accomplishing what you set out to accomplish. Write up a description of it. Tell someone about it. What actions did you take? What were the results, quantified, if possible? Who benefited? Each time you recognize that you are making things happen that you intend to make happen, you become more aware of your own effectiveness. Those are the building blocks of self-confidence.

5. Name drop? Boastful? If you feel the need to prove yourself or your worth, then ask yourself, "To whom? Why?" Being tempted to recite your successes, drop names or demonstrate your importance is a tip-off that your self-confidence needs some care and strengthening. Self-confident people rarely boast. In fact, they tend to focus on others and their accomplishments. They are often humble. Situations may cause this to vary. Interviewing, especially in a competitive job market, is a common example. In these situations, you put your best foot forward by citing your positive attributes and giving examples. But if poor performance, perceived personal failures or an overly critical self-view are compromising your confidence, determine the specific cause. Compare notes with a trusted observer to assess your objectivity. If there's good reason for the negative assessment, then a plan of action to correct the cause is the next step. But if your view is faulty, then correcting your self-assessment is the next step. In neither case will you need to drop names or brag inappropriately.

6. Over-focused on criticisms and overlook the compliments? Many people review their days and the feedback they received as they lie in bed attempting to fall asleep. If you are among them, do you tend to think more about criticisms than compliments, efforts that stumbled than those that succeeded — even when the favorable events far exceed the negative? Most people are drawn to focus on the negative, in part because they want to repair what went wrong and avoid repeating the experience. But you have a choice here. Your goal is to fall asleep. Will thinking about what went wrong during the day help you do that? Not likely.

Some ideas to help you (or someone you are coaching) build self- confidence:

- Keep self-talk upbeat. Stay focused on what's right and working well.

- Recognize your strengths and accomplishments. Pay attention to what you are good at. Make a list. Review and add to it regularly.

- Pay attention to the positive feedback others give you. Thank them, repeating (yes, out loud) what they just said.

- Identify a role model of self-confidence that you can emulate. What do they do or say that makes you think they are confident? Which of those behaviors will you do more of or add to your repertoire?

- Confront self-doubt. Avoid social events? Fear speaking up in groups or, worse, public speaking? Go against the grain. Attend a meeting with a focus you're interested in. Express your opinion. Did it go better than you expected? What worked? Look for ideas of what to do more of or less of the next time.

- Build on past successes. Survey your successes and what makes you proud. Make a list and keep it close. Add to it.

42

- Build your competence. Learn a new skill, or strengthen one you already have. Practice. Competence grows confidence.

- Recall that confident feeling. Remember past successes and the confidence triggered by them. Use those mental images to trigger that confidence any time, anywhere.

- Monitor your thinking. Notice any self-talk that causes self-doubt and challenge it. Your thoughts are under your control; redirect them to your list of accomplishments.

- Set goals. Work the plan. Confidence comes from accomplishing what you set out to accomplish. It almost doesn't matter what that is, as long you follow through on it. Don't just think or talk about it — take action.

7. Do the opinions of others trump yours too quickly or too often? This is similar to dwelling on criticisms of others, in that you value what others think more than you value what you think. Do the paradoxical: Use this thinking to change yours. Would others agree with you that your thinking is of less value than that of others? Probably not. So, align your thinking to theirs this time. And use the suggestions given in Action Tip 6 to achieve objectivity and greater balance in how you value your views against others'.

Related Competencies

(2) Assertiveness   (33) Personal Power   (38) Resilience

(39) Self-Actualization   (40) *Accurate* Self-Assessment   (44) Self-Regard

Learn from Experience

Work

❑ Make speeches for your organization.

❑ Lead a task force of inexperienced or low competency people.

Personal

❑ Teach someone something that you're good at and they are not.

❑ Volunteer expertise or experience to a nonprofit that needs it.

❑ Observe people you regard as self-confident. Identify the behaviors that they exhibit that reflect their confidence. Which behaviors, already in your repertoire, can you demonstrate more often?

❑ Periodically ask for feedback. Keep track of what you hear. And pay special attention to the positive feedback that you receive.

Resources

Books

McKay, Matthew, and Patrick Fanning. *Self-Esteem: A Proven Program of Cognitive Techniques for Assessing, Improving, and Maintaining Your Self-Esteem*. Oakland, CA: New Harbinger Publications, 3rd edition, 2000.

Seligman, Martin E. P. *Learned Optimism: How to Change Your Mind and Your Life*. New York: Vintage, 2006.

Alberti, Robert E. and Michael Emmons. *Your Perfect Right: A Guide to Assertive Living*. Atascadero, CA: Impact Publishing; 25th anniversary edition, 1995.

Internet

Mindtools — Essential Skills for an Excellent Career. Once on the site, search for "self-confidence." www.mindtools.com

Classes and training

Fred Pryor Seminars and CareerTrack. Search on the site for "Assertive Leadership Skills: A One-Day Seminar" and "self-esteem." www.pryor.com

Dale Carnegie. Search on the site for "Confident, Assertive, In Charge: Developing the Attitudes of Leadership." www.dalecarnegie.com

Toastmasters International. Search on the site for "public speaking" and "leadership." www.toastmasters.org.

The Leader's Institute®. Search on the site for "overcoming the fear of public speaking." www.leadersinstitute.com

42

43 SELF-DISCLOSURE

Definition

Sharing information about yourself with others, appropriately and in the face of risk or vulnerability

When the heart is at ease, the body is healthy.

— Chinese proverb

Talented

❏ Shares self-awareness gathered from personal insights — spontaneously and appropriately

❏ Responds to personal questions when appropriate — even tough ones — in a relaxed, nondefensive manner

❏ Appears trusting and confident when talking with new people, regardless of position

❏ Balances self-disclosure with expressed interest in others

❏ Makes good choices about depth of personal information to disclose

Skilled

❏ Responds openly to routine personal questions but may not initiate self-disclosures spontaneously

❏ Responds cautiously to questions involving risk or vulnerability

❏ Focuses more on others than self during interpersonal exchanges

❏ Discloses personal information but only when others do

Unskilled

❏ Acts as if personal questions are an invasion of privacy

❏ Criticizes others for sharing personal information

❏ Observes a strict separation between work and personal life (for example, doesn't share or ask about personal lives at work)

❏ Appears uncomfortable when questions get personal or deal with emotions

❏ Exercises poor judgment when choosing when, to whom or how much to share when disclosing personal experiences or reactions

Big Picture View

Opening up to others may include but is not limited to thoughts, feelings, aspirations, goals, failures, successes, fears and dreams as well as your likes, dislikes, and favorites. By sharing personal information, you foster an intimacy with others. It's a way of letting your guard down. Your willingness to be transparent builds not just understanding but trust. And trust plays a major role in motivating and influencing others. In short, self-disclosure is a useful strategy for strengthening interpersonal relationships. It also is useful in learning more about yourself. Being open with others invites others to talk more frankly with you. Like so many other things, self-disclosure is best exercised with balance and good judgment. While it is likely that you are more apt to be too restrained in sharing about yourself, you can also share too much or inappropriately. Balancing self-disclosure and self-restraint is governed by factors related to you, your desired outcome and the situation you're in. For example, if you learned that your dog and steady sidekick was just found after having disappeared two weeks ago, you would be naturally excited and jubilant. But sharing your joy in the approaching staff meeting might be out of step with your organization's culture. Might be better to wait and celebrate with friends and other dog-lovers.

Barriers to Effectiveness

❏ Distrust

❏ Low self-esteem

❏ Immaturity

❏ Being overly assertive

❏ Unclear boundaries

❏ Being self-absorbed

❏ Inability to read situational cues

❏ Lack of self-awareness

Quick Action Tips

I. **Are you knowable?** Are you willing to risk the vulnerability of sharing what you know about yourself with others? Self-disclosure is more than sharing general or routine information with another person. It is sharing information that others would be unlikely to know or discover on their own. Self-disclosure can involve risk and vulnerability, and it depends on self-awareness. A popular exercise that explores how much information you know about yourself and how much others know about you is the Johari Window. It maps various combinations of what information about you is known to you and open to others, what is hidden to others, and what is blind to you. The goal of this exercise is to expand the "open" window, that is, to increase the information about you that is known to you and others. You can do this several ways: sharing more of what you know about yourself but that you keep hidden, learning more about how others see you, and by exploring some of the areas outside of your awareness. An Internet search of Johari Window will generate multiple sites offering information, assessments and activities, should you have an interest in exploring this further.

2. Do you think of personal questions as an invasion of your privacy? Do you sidestep questions or give vague answers to evade personal disclosure? Is this fairly typical for you or more situational? In general, sharing information fosters trust in relationships. People who are willing to share private information, when appropriate, are generally seen as confident and willing to trust others. As such, it generates increased respect for and willingness to trust in them. Effective self-disclosure is a balancing act: knowing when to share what information and with whom. Practice first in low-stakes situations, if self-disclosure is new or uncomfortable for you, and pay attention to how you and others respond. Look for clues that will help you make good choices around the "when," what" and "who" as you engage in self-disclosure.

3. Is it nosy to ask others personal questions? Relationships grow through time spent together and the gradual exchange of information. Your willingness to disclose information about yourself and to express interest in knowing others will directly affect the quality of your relationships. Reluctance might be well founded if confined to specific situations. Otherwise, it might be an issue of self-esteem or of trust. What assumptions are you making and what are they based on? Sharing personal information creates some vulnerability; the greater the vulnerability the greater the trust needed. Ironically, it is the sharing of personal information that builds trust. Think about a close relationship you are currently in. Notice how self-disclosure and trust move together in a two way interaction?

4. Do you maintain a strict separation between work and personal life? Is this necessary because of your role at work, or is this self-imposed? Boundaries and barriers describe how people come together or keep their distance. In common parlance, a personal boundary defines one person as emotionally distinct from another. The invisible space where two people come together with mutual respect, sensitivity and appreciation for what distinguishes each from the other forms the boundary. Healthy boundaries are clear and permeable, and they foster rewarding relationships. Barriers keep others at a distance, sometimes causing problems in relationships, and sometimes because of problems in relationships. As people share their personal and emotional selves, their personal boundaries ease and relationships grow. Conversely, when communication closes down, barriers emerge. Are you currently in any relationship, personal or professional, where you feel either crowded or isolated? Either would suggest an issue with boundaries or barriers. Think through, either alone or with a sounding board, what in your relationship might indicate either a boundary being run over or a barrier keeping you at arm's length emotionally. Sometimes just becoming aware of their existence puts you on a path to address this relationship difficulty. Be honest with yourself and open with others; it pays off.

5. Prefer to stay at arm's length? When a discussion gets personal or emotional, do you become uncomfortable? Often when a discussion ventures toward personal or emotional content, people become uncertain, sometimes tense. They may fear losing control, being exposed or being judged … unfavorably. Or, worse, some people might use the information against them. Realistically, how often in your experience do any of these scenarios actually occur? What is at risk? What could be gained? Keep in mind, self-disclosure is around information that is yours to share. It's about you, your opinions, values, emotions, decisions, etc. Sharing information about yourself can be an investment in a goal that matters to you. There also are occasions where you don't want to share. For example, you don't want to disclose information that could damage others or impair people's respect for you.

6. Have you ever wondered if you've said too much, too soon or at the wrong time? If you suspect that this might be the case, it is important that you explore further. Poor judgment or faulty brakes can damage reputation, trust or regard very quickly. Assess regularly the responses you get and the circumstances surrounding them. If a reaction is unfavorable, was there anything about the context that might explain it? Ask someone who was present for their opinion about what you said, how you said it and any suggestions for improvement. You can describe what took place to a mentor and get his or her opinion. Survey a number of people whose opinions you trust about your general approach to self-disclosure. One way to ask the question is, "I would like to become more effective when I talk about myself and my feelings. What suggestions do you have that might help me do that?"

7. Limited experience internationally or with cultural diversity? Self-disclosure and frank discussions with others have to take into account prevailing cultural norms. Some cultures are open and accepting of self-disclosure and direct feedback. Others aren't. Dealing with issues directly or asking for feedback can cause of-

43

fense or discomfort when dealing with someone who's not used to it or where it is regarded it as rude behavior. Get expert advice, be sensitive to how others behave and react to you, and go slowly.

Related Competencies

(12) Emotional Maturity   (22) Insightfulness   (45) Self-Awareness

(42) Self-Confidence   (48) *Managing* Social Space   (52) Trusting

Learn from Experience

Work

❑ Lead a task group where others in the group have the necessary expertise and you do not.

❑ Be a loaned executive.

❑ Work for short periods in other departments where sharing your experience is important to your success.

Personal

❑ Make peace with an enemy.

❑ Join a support group in an area where you would like some help. It could deal with any of a number of topics, such as public speaking or networking.

❑ Work with a psychologist, social worker, counselor or coach on some personal or professional goal. The potential benefits to you are directly connected to how open you are.

❑ Identify someone you know whom you respect and regard as appropriately open and relaxed about who they are. What do they do that makes you think they are good at self-disclosure? Which of these behaviors can you do more of?

Resources

Books

Adams, Kathleen. *Journal to the Self: Twenty-Two Paths to Personal Growth — Open the Door to Self-Understanding by Writing, Reading, and Creating a Journal of Your Life.* New York: Grand Central Publishing, 1990.

Lerner, Harriet. *The Dance of Intimacy.* New York: Harper Paperbacks, 1990.

Pennebaker, James W. *Opening Up: The Healing Power of Expressing Emotions*. New York: The Guilford Press, 1997.

Rich, Phil and Stuart A. Copans. *The Healing Journey: Your Journal of Self Discovery*. Hoboken, NJ: John Wiley, 1998.

Internet

HealthyPlace.com. Search the site for "How to Open Up and Reveal Yourself to Others." www.healthyplace.com

Classes and training

The Leadership Trust.® Offers personalized engagement focused self-awareness. www.leadershiptrust.org

43

44   SELF-REGARD

Definition

Behaving in ways that reflect how good you feel about yourself; accepting yourself, warts and all

No one can make you feel inferior without your consent.

— Eleanor Roosevelt

Talented

❏ Expresses feelings, requests and opinions comfortably and appropriately

❏ Views self realistically and favorably, building on strengths

❏ Pursues own goals and interests but with sensitivity to those of others

❏ Enjoys successes and graciously accepts compliments as deserved

❏ Reaches out to others for help and favors when needed but not as if entitled; responds in kind

❏ Challenges disrespectful behavior and asserts personal rights to security and liberty

Skilled

❏ Expresses feelings, requests and opinions — some of the time

❏ Views self realistically and favorably but seeks reassurance from others

❏ Speaks to personal goals and interests but sometimes place others' interests before own.

❏ Appears embarrassed by public accolades

❏ Discusses rather than confronts disrespectful behavior unless blatant

❏ Asks for help when needed, reluctantly

Unskilled

❏ Slow to stand up for self or ask for help

❑ Discounts or dismisses compliments

❑ Fails to seek professional growth or advancement

❑ Underestimates strengths; compares self with others unfavorably and unrealistically

❑ Routinely attributes failures to self and successes to luck

❑ Puts others and their needs and wants first, often at the expense of own emotional state

Big Picture View

Self-regard arises from, contributes to and shares properties with self-worth, self-respect, self-confidence and feelings of adequacy. These terms are often used interchangeably. Positive self-regard frees up considerable mental and emotional energy to focus on higher-level interpersonal and personal experiences. If you are feeling pretty good about yourself, then it is much easier to interact with others even if they are behaving negatively in some way; you experience less need to be defensive. It is easier for you to express yourself authentically — your feelings, needs, wants, opinions, you name it — when it seems appropriate to you for you to do that. You also are in a much better position to see yourself more accurately and to use that knowledge to grow. This again arises from the fact that you are less "defended." The capacity to be yourself and interact with others honestly, irrespective of the emotional tensions, raises your EQ. Positive self-regard grows with maturity and emotional wisdom. As we interact with others, we gain experience that builds, clarifies and confirms our self-perceptions and, therefore, our self-regard. If you want to strengthen your self-regard, it is important for you to look at, and to get feedback on, your level of self-awareness, pessimism or perfectionism, your breadth of experience, your current feedback channels, and your early experiences with significant others.

Barriers to Effectiveness

❑ False or inaccurate self-assessment

❑ Overly self-critical

❑ Paying more attention to what's not working than to what is

❑ Limited appreciation, resources or time for assessment

❑ Feeling compelled to get to the next task before reflecting on and enjoying successes

44

Quick Action Tips

1. Think asking for help is a character weakness? Some people think that asking for help is a character flaw, or, worse, that help is undeserved. The irony here is that asking for help actually indicates strength. People with positive self-regard comfortably acknowledge that they don't have all the answers. Their self-regard often comes from having reached out to others for the expertise they needed to succeed. People who enjoy positive self-regard emphasize their strengths and compensate for their weaknesses. They value and share freely their own perspectives. They trust their instincts and know when to defer to others. As a result, others hold them in similar regard, which further reinforces their self-regard. Size up your strengths and leverage them, intentionally. Develop trust in your instincts by acting on them and evaluating the results. Ask for help, expertise and ideas from others when you need it. Reflect on situations where you sized them up and acted. Were your instincts right more often than wrong? You are creating a rational basis to trust your instincts. Build up that trust — yours and others '— and you will build up your self-regard.

2. Tend to overuse skills already acquired rather than stretching to learn new ones? Successful people (and those with positive self-regard) value and pursue ongoing development. They believe in themselves and understand that success depends on keeping their skill sets fresh. They stay alert to changing demands and seek experiences that will develop the skills necessary to meet them. They ask for feedback and input to confirm their perceptions and plans. By continuously investing in yourself, you affirm your own value and build greater self-regard. It is a continuous loop. Schedule discussions with those who can help you see the horizon clearly, those who have the skills that you will need to be successful tomorrow. Identify people who can give you honest and informed feedback on your strengths and weaknesses today. Look for new assignments and volunteer opportunities that will help you continue to develop your skills for tomorrow.

3. Mismatched in your job? Self-regard is affected by the fit between your skills and interests and the job you're in. There is a bias in the business world that says you are successful if you move up through the organization and take on leadership roles. But not everybody is cut out to be a leader. Just recently I (one of your authors) was talking with a very successful scientist who was struggling to lead a team. Like some others I've coached, he is uncomfortable with conflict and having to get the job done through others. Every day is an ordeal — and exhausting. He has stepped completely out of what is a natural fit for him professionally. He may succeed, eventually, but at what cost — to him, to the organization and to the team he's trying to lead? Life is short. Do what you love and what you are good at. You will get better at doing it and enjoy positive self-regard.

4. What impact do you have on the people around you? Moods are contagious. So is positive self-regard. People who have it tend to induce positive self-regard in those around them — family, friends, teams. This is an important factor in the ability to lead. Pride motivates. Sam Walton, founder of Walmart, once observed, "Outstanding leaders go out of their way to boost the self-esteem of their personnel. If people believe in themselves, it's amazing what they can accomplish." Study people you know with positive self-regard and the impact they have on others. How do they communicate, motivate and get things done? Which of their behaviors can you adopt? When, where and with whom can you practice those behaviors?

5. Uncomfortable with praise or recognition? Maybe you are modest, self-conscious or skeptical. Positive self-regard makes it easier for you to see yourself objectively and to accept favorable reviews when offered. And it shows up in the way you interact with others. You accept compliments graciously and criticisms with a degree of circumspection. Periodically, run a check on your objectivity. Gather additional evidence and input to validate, and possibly correct, any critical assumptions about yourself.

6. Perfectionistic? Are you realistic about what you expect of yourself? Do you expect the same of others that you expect of yourself? If your answer is yes, you know that you feel better, accomplish more and inspire others as a result. If your answer is no, then you may be applying a double standard to yourself. That's neither rational nor useful. There are some things that you can change and some that you cannot — or maybe don't want to. It is important that you are reasonably comfortable with who you are, warts and all. But if there is some factor impairing your self-regard, do something about it, for your sake.

What would you advise someone else with a similar flaw? Ask yourself if someone you cared about asked you for advice about this same issue. What would you advise? Then take your advice.

7. Your fault, their success? How does it happen that what goes wrong is your fault and what works well is because of their genius? It's called attribution theory. How you explain your experiences and what happens around you (successes and failures) has big implications for how you feel about yourself, not to mention what others think of you. Humility (often encouraged in women) is expressed in terms of others' success, not yours. And yet mistakes or failures are more readily taken on as personal responsibilities. While you don't want to steal credit or throw others under the bus, you can acknowledge your role in successful outcomes and learn from failures without always naming names. How you explain successes and failures often occurs just outside of conscious awareness. As events unfold, explore what succeeded, what didn't and why.

Look for patterns in your thinking. Are you being objective in your attributions? Compare notes with someone else. With this information in mind, look for opportunities to own your successes, however small. And pause before you assume failures are your fault, to give them an objective evaluation.

Related Competencies

(2) Assertiveness   (12) Emotional Maturity   (39) Self-Actualization

(40) *Accurate* Self-Assessment   (41) Self-Awareness

(42) Self-Confidence

Learn from Experience

Work

❏ Lead a task force charged with improving results with limited resources.

❏ Attend a leadership development or self-awareness seminar.

Personal

❏ Volunteer to consult with an agency on a problem or issue.

❏ Become active in a professional organization with a plan to serve in a role that stretches you.

❏ Interview people who have demonstrated self-regard. Ask them how they use their strengths to address their weaknesses.

Resources

Books

Seligman, Martin E. P. *Learned Optimism: How to Change Your Mind and Your Life*. New York: Vintage, 2006.

Alberti, Robert E., and Michael Emmons. *Your Perfect Right: A Guide to Assertive Living*. New York: Impact Publishing; 25th Anniversary edition, 1995.

Ursiny, Tim. *The Confidence Plan: How to Build a Stronger You*. Naperville, IL: Sourcebooks, Inc., 2005.

Internet

MindTools.com. Search the site for "high personal effectiveness," "good leadership," "career success." www.mindtools.com

More Self-Esteem. Search for articles, tips, courses, books and downloads on self-esteem. www.more-selfesteem.com

Classes and training

Outward Bound. www.outwardbound.org/

Center for Creative Leadership. Leadership Development Program (LDP®). www.ccl.org

44

45   SITUATIONAL AWARENESS

Definition

Being alert and informed about your environment; reading patterns of interactions among individuals and observing what may be unique about the setting

Awareness is empowering.

— Rita Wilson

Talented

❏ Pays finely attuned attention to what's going on

❏ Observes events and circumstances to better understand people and make decisions

❏ Observes people's body language to discern their emotional meaning

❏ Accurately anticipates and predicts how other people (team members, family, groups) will respond

❏ Communicates awareness of situations in clear, concise ways, allowing others to better understand them

Skilled

❏ Recognizes different social expectations across situations

❏ Scans situations to anticipate next steps or reactions

❏ Shows awareness about the emotional climate of situations and interactions

❏ Solicits multiple perspectives from others about the dynamics in a situation

❏ Identifies some needs of others but doesn't necessarily act to address them

Unskilled

❏ Focuses on the irrelevant, missing the most important interactions or information in a situation and among people

❑ Communicates observations vaguely or inaccurately

❑ Fails to read body language, or emotional expressions, or interactions among people

❑ Seems disinterested or unaware of the opinions, thoughts or feelings of others

❑ Discredits own ability to read others, so doesn't try to do so

Big Picture View

Situational awareness is the valuable skill of being attuned to what is happening around you. By allowing your awareness to go beyond your own skin, you pick up on information, events, dynamics and emotions that might influence decisions and lead to greater effectiveness and possibly even greater physical safety. At work and at home, the person who can size up what is going on around him is better able to respond appropriately, whether by offering support, calming tensions, providing information or even celebrating a success or positive event. Situational awareness involves the ability to listen, to notice and to observe the interactions among people, allowing for insights about the situation and the people involved. At times situational awareness can even be an important survival skill, alerting you to potential dangers in the environment. The situationally tuned-in leader, teacher, parent, or colleague is better able to relate to a constituency, demonstrate empathy or speak to common goals and interests.

Barriers to Effectiveness

❑ Inability to track multiple layers of interaction

❑ Unobservant of surroundings and what's going on

❑ Self-centered; failing to pay attention to the interpersonal dynamics among people in a group

❑ Does not value the emotional elements in interactions

Quick Action Tips

I. **Don't notice what is going on around you?** Do others pick up on the social cues before you do? Emotional intelligence, by definition, involves the ability to tune in to and relate well to others. By paying attention to your environment, the people in it and the way they are relating to one another, you are better able to influence a group process in a productive and meaningful way. There

45

are two primary approaches to focusing on or attending to events and people in your environment.

- Broad or narrow focusing: When you do a broad scan of the environment, you notice who is there and the basic feeling in the room. This provides the big picture, but it doesn't tell the whole story. Narrow your focus by tuning into the specific details of the environment, such as where people are sitting in relationship to one another, who is talking to whom, who is avoiding whom, what is being said and the information obtained from observing body language.

- Internal or external focusing: Make distinctions between what is going on inside you and what seems to be happening with others. Distinguish between your own feelings and reactions to events and what you are noticing in other people. Internal focus is important because it informs you of your own reactions to a situation. By focusing outwardly on others, and, by carefully observing their behaviors, reactions, words and interactions, you are demonstrating situational awareness.

You might want to assess your own way of attending to the circumstances and events around you. Do you tend to use one method of focusing over another? Try doing a daily review for a week. At the end of each day, think about the key interactions and events in your day and assess them from the perspective above. Were you too broad or too narrow in your focus? Did you focus inwardly, taking into account only your own reactions? Or did you tune in to the behaviors and reactions of others in the group? If you find yourself using one aspect of focusing more than another, then make an effort to expand your way of paying attention to the events around you.

2. Tend to be stuck in a behavioral or emotional rut, approaching situations in the same way again and again? Often situational awareness requires that you let go of old patterns and focus on your environment in a more adaptive or flexible way. If you tend to react to situations in overly emotional ways, then that limits your ability to accurately assess what's going on around you. First, take the time to focus internally, becoming aware of your reactions to events around you. Are you feeling angry, scared, disappointed, upset? Are you judging the people and situation before you have all the information? If so, then these internal states and filters will limit your ability to accurately tune in to what is going on around you. Flexibility means being able to adjust to circumstances, depending upon the changing demands of each situation. Another factor that decreases flexibility is negative thinking, resulting in low self-esteem, stress and anxiety. Such negativity is an inhibitor to flexibility. To increase flexibility, you need to reduce the anxiety or stress that you are dealing with on events around you (see tip 1 above). Are you being too inwardly focused, or do you primarily attend to the needs of others, ignoring your own? Being able to flex back and forth as needed is an acquired habit.

3. Not sure what body language might mean? Or what to do with it? Body language reflects when you — or those you are with — are feeling comfortable, safe, energized or anxious. Begin by paying attention to facial expressions of those whom you are observing. Notice how others shift from leaning forward or backwards during conversations. Watch when an individual folds his or her arms during discussions. When paying attention to body clues, you will have reactions to others' behavior. Give credence to your reactions, but check them out with others. From time to time, think about how these kinds of clues can help you read the emotional climate in a meeting or program. When you scan the room and read the nonverbal behavior, you add power to your ability to communicate with others. You can see body language examples on YouTube to illustrate the kinds of behavior you need to pay attention to. Choose a meeting that you will be in this week and observe the body language of one person. What do you notice? Check out your observations and impressions with a trusted colleague or friend at the meeting. If you are comfortable with the person you observed, ask that person whether a couple of your impressions fit.

4. Fail to note the emotional elements in interactions? All interactions have emotional elements to them — pleasure, agitation, interest — and if you don't tend to pay attention to the emotions in the room, try doing so. It is important in this process to include reading the emotional climate when scanning a room or a large meeting so you can respond in a way that helps the situation move forward. When you scan, you are looking for details about the physical setting, the people involved, and the emotional energies that others are sharing. Keep a log for a couple of weeks that captures the emotional climate of the interactions you have with those with whom you work. This will help you notice emotions in various situations so you can respond in helpful ways.

5. Realize after an important meeting that you missed some of the discussion? Surprisingly enough, one common reason we tend to miss important data or information in a group setting is that we stop to analyze what is being said. Research shows that it simply isn't possible to be focused on analyzing something while at the same time being open to information that is being shared while you are with other people. Analysis takes us inward, with a focus in our mind, but awareness of current reactions, discussions or events call for external awareness. No one can be aware of internal analysis and external happenings at the exact same moment. So be conscious of the tradeoff you may be making: To take a point being made in a meeting and analyze it may prevent you from really hearing and seeing what else is going on in the meeting. Choose a meeting that you plan to attend this coming week and attend with the goal of hearing and seeing what is said and what is happening. Save your analysis for later.

45

Discuss the meeting with a colleague to determine whether you were more aware of what took place in the meeting than when you also try to analyze what is being said.

6. Are you out of sync with office politics? Have you ever been caught by surprise by a decision that was made in your organization? You were present during discussions and didn't see the decision coming? After such an event, talk with a trusted colleague who also was there and whose opinion you value. Ask that colleague what factors they think influenced the decisions that were made. Ask what behaviors they saw — who talked to whom most often and about what topics? Compare your thoughts to theirs. What might you have missed or misinterpreted? Who else might you talk with to gain a better understanding of organizational politics?

7. Too rushed to notice how your customer is responding to you? When meeting with a new client group or person that you want to influence, remember to pay attention to the responses you get, especially the nonverbal cues that may or may not be congruent with the words you are hearing. The information conveyed in nonverbal behavior is less intentional or consciously driven, so it may be more accurate than the words being spoken. Is your client saying that he or she will consider your product or service, but not looking at you while speaking? Is he or she moving toward the door while thanking you for coming? On the other hand, your client nodding, smiling and being attentive may suggest that he or she appreciates what you are saying. Use all of the reactions you get to take the next step in your conversation or presentation. If he or she is not attentive, then pull out some impressive information or make a more attractive offer. Another source of information as you attune to the environment is what you see in the office or room where you are meeting. Is it a basic design with functional furniture? Maybe you need to keep your presentation to the basics. How did your customer interact with colleagues as you walked to the room? If he or she was warm and friendly, can you show that side of yourself? Do you see family photos on the desk? Asking about them might be a good way to deepen your understanding of that person and build rapport. If he or she was serious and direct, be sure you get to the point of what you have to offer. Do you see charts and graphs on the walls or an easel? Make sure you cover the data you brought to demonstrate the value of your service or product. Being aware of your environment may mean the difference between success and failure when influencing others.

Related Competencies

(15) *Active* Empathy   (16) Flexibility   (17) Group Savvy

(26) Intuition   (29) *Reading* Nonverbal Communication

(34) Perspective-Taking   (35) Reality Testing

Learn from Experience

Work

❏ Become an observer of nuance in meetings with others. Note the alignment between how things are said and what is said with what eventually happens. Pay careful attention to the emotional expressions of others.

❏ Seek an opportunity to work with individuals from another culture. Notice their behavior when they are trying to influence and communicate.

❏ Spend time with the best salesperson in your organization. Go with this individual on customer visits to find out what they pay attention to.

Personal

❏ People watch. Go to a public place to watch how people walk, talk, and engage with their environment and others. Look for patterns that give you future clues about others' behavior.

❏ Notice the differences in the homes of neighbors and friends. Can you see personality differences reflected in the décor and design of their homes?

Resources

Books

Banbury, Simon. *A Cognitive Approach to Situation Awareness: Theory and Application*. Farnham, Surrey, UK: Ashgate Publishing, 2004.

Corey, Marianne S., Gerald Corey, and Cindy Corey. *Groups: Process and Practice*. Belmont, CA: Brooks Cole, 2010.

Goleman, Daniel. *Emotional Intelligence: Why It Can Matter More Than IQ*, 10th anniversary edition. New York: Bantam, 2006.

Internet

Situational awareness: Psychology wiki. www.psychology.wikia.com/

Classes and training

American Management Association. "Developing your emotional intelligence." www.amanet.org

Leadership Performance Systems. Leadership web courses: "Emotional intelligence: What it is and what you can do about it." www.leadership-systems.com/ecourse.aspx#EQ

Talent Smart. EQ training certification. www.talentsmart.com/eqcert/

45

46 SOCIAL INTELLIGENCE

Definition

Sensing, understanding and reacting effectively to others' emotions and the interactions with and between people; getting along well with others and getting them to cooperate with you

Never underestimate the power of very stupid people in large groups.

— Unknown

Talented

❑ Understands people, their emotions and how they interact

❑ Observes and reflects on interpersonal dynamics

❑ Is sought after for wisdom in dealing with people

❑ Acts wisely in human relations

❑ Engages with people in ways that inspire their cooperation and commitment

❑ Uses good timing and empathy in emotionally sensitive situations

Skilled

❑ Notices how people respond in different situations but does not always connect the dots

❑ Recalls and applies lessons from past social observations

❑ Demonstrates adequate levels of social acumen

❑ Recognized as socially skilled but not as a role model

❑ Attempts to motivate others but is not always successful

❑ Senses but occasionally misunderstands others' emotions

Unskilled

❑ Ignores people's emotional reactions in different situations

❑ Draws a blank if asked to anticipate how others might react

❑ Serves as role model for what not to do in the realm of interpersonal relations

❑ Discounts the importance of relationships in most circumstances

❑ Fails to engage others when initiating efforts

Big Picture View

Do you find people's behavior difficult to understand? Do you think of company politics as distasteful? Social intelligence helps to navigate company politics, especially when they become complex and rife with intrigue, as it can within families and other social groups. Multiple interactions driven by varied motivations among people within a group are also known as group dynamics. All groups experience social interplay — you see it at neighborhood gatherings, family holidays and staff meetings. Social intelligence is the ability to read the political, emotional and power currents among people. Developed over time, social intelligence helps with motivating and dealing with different personalities and with detecting the often unwritten rules within a group.

Social scientists Karl Albrecht and Daniel Goleman proposed models of social intelligence that broadly include the following elements: confidence in social situations, genuine interest in others, skill at reading and responding to others, appropriate assertiveness, and understanding social dynamics. Sounds a lot like emotional intelligence, doesn't it?

Barriers to Effectiveness

❑ Low self-confidence

❑ Preoccupation with negative emotions

❑ Self-consciousness (and anxiety in general)

❑ Being self-absorbed, arrogant or disinterested in others

❑ Lack of curiosity

❑ Being more task-focused than people-focused

❑ Little interest in what emotions may be in the background, driving behavior

❑ Concrete or literal mindset

Quick Action Tips

1. Feel out of place or disconnected from others? Would you like to feel more confident

in social situations? People who lack social confidence tend to go "inside," so their attention is drawn to their own thoughts and (usually) discomfort. They miss valuable social cues that could help them connect with others. And they may appear disinterested, further discouraging social connections. To create greater comfort and self-confidence, start by paying attention to what is positive about you. At the end of the day, write down any social experiences that went well, any positive comments that came your way and anything you did that you feel good about. Keep these lists handy, add to them, and review them regularly. As you enter social activities, think about these positive experiences. If you are approaching an occasion that is especially important or new to you, try this strategy: Think of a previous experience in which you distinctly remember feeling pride, confidence or success. Step back into that earlier experience as fully as you can so that you can re-engage that feeling of confidence. Then step into today's important occasion and carry that feeling with you.

2. Feel less confident in social situations than you'd like? Would you like to feel more confident generally? Thinking is like behavior. Many thoughts and assumptions that we have about ourselves are merely thinking habits and, as such, can be changed. If you don't like what you think about yourself, then you can change it. Yes, you can! Try this. Identify three beliefs that you would like to have about yourself but that you do not yet have. Write them down and rate how much you believe each one on a ten-point scale — zero if you don't believe it at all and ten if you believe it fully. If you're rating a belief four or higher, then choose another belief that you would like to have about yourself that you do not yet have. For the next two weeks, each morning and night, repeat these beliefs out loud to yourself, preferably in front of a mirror. Rate these beliefs again at the end of each of the next two weeks. Notice how much more you actually believe them at the end of week one, then week two. Notice how you are feeling different!

3. "Enough about you. What do you think of me?" Is your interest in others self-serving, situational, or 24/7? A genuine interest in others builds social intelligence while building relationships. A genuine interest in others goes beyond just those times when you are engaged with them to those times when you are alone. It involves caring about others, anticipating their needs, whether or not you're with them, whether or not they asked you for something they need. Thinking about others and anticipating their needs takes time and effort. While some do this naturally, it is a habit that can be developed. Either way, this is a habit that pays huge dividends.

4. Do people baffle you? Are you perplexed and sometimes surprised by other people's emotional reactions in different situations? People can be confusing at times — saying one thing and doing another, for example, or abruptly changing direction for no apparent reason. The solution is simple, but surprisingly few people do it. Ask questions. Describe what is confusing you and ask for help in understanding the behavior in question. As people share what they're feeling and what's driving their behavior, track it. Write or talk about your observations as a way of consolidating what you are learning. As you make connections between people's reported internal feelings and their external behavior, you become better able to "read" people and your impact on them. Connecting external behavior (cues) to internal emotions is called "calibration" in NeuroLinguistic Programming (NLP), a model of communication. If you are interested in learning more about calibration, then do an Internet search for NLP and calibration.

5. Can you read people? Reading people skillfully starts with paying attention to others. Intuitive people are attentive people. While some people come by being intuitive more naturally than others, it is learnable by anyone. It comes with practice and by being fully present with others. Notice other people's facial expressions, body language and voice qualities. Connect these signals to how people are feeling and, eventually, learn to read them. As you observe people, their actions and reactions, exercise your intuitive muscle by speculating about the emotions they may be feeling, what matters to them, and what they are likely to do next. Track these speculations, because that's all they are until you get some confirming data. Continue to observe and stay on the lookout for information that might relate to your speculations, either to confirm or refute your hypotheses. You also have the option of checking out your ideas about the person with the person. Notice how many of your guesses prove accurate. Being attentive to others and connecting your observations over time will make you more socially intelligent and intuitive.

6. Expressing your feelings — no problem, right? Or do you find it difficult to express your feelings — much less to express them clearly, appropriately and assertively? Put simply, assertive behavior is saying what you want to say, when you want to say it, in a nice way. There are some occasions where people commonly find this difficult — delivering bad news, confronting someone, fearing a negative reaction, and requesting help. There are generally two blocks to being assertive and expressing your feelings: anxiety and not knowing how. Overcome anxiety by first identifying, then challenging, the rationality of your fear. Name it. Is there any evidence to support it? What are the odds that what you fear will actually happen? Next, practice assertive behavior. Try the empathic assertiveness model:

- First, speculate about the other person's feeling and position: "I understand that you (think, or feel, or want)…"
- then state your own feeling and position: "However, I (think, or feel, or want)…"
- and assert your intention or request: "Therefore, I …"

46

Example: I know you are swamped with extra work and this might be tough for you to do. However, I have only this weekend to finish my project. So, is there any chance you could help me by ... ?

Socially intelligent people are typically less vulnerable to emotional blocks and more practiced in assertive behavior. Practicing assertive behavior adds to your social intelligence. See competency (2) Assertiveness for more tips.

7. People's reactions ... do they matter? Do you take the time to think about how others might react in a given situation? Or do you think it takes too much time or effort? Or, worse, is of little value? Having an interest in how others feel and react is fundamental to social intelligence. Being interested will motivate you to pay attention — to people and what they say and do. Over time, you will collect enough information to see patterns of behavior and when those patterns connect with internal emotional states. Keep a personal journal of your observations, tentative questions, analyses, and interpretations, with details of your accuracy along the way. Write a few words every day or so. This isn't a diary or a biography — it's a place to record your observations and your interpretation of them. Use it as a place to ask yourself questions. In the process, you are more likely to notice faces, names, eye color and other details, and eventually you will be better able to spot subtle changes that often allow you to predict what that person is experiencing internally. Journal your observations; you will be more likely to remember them. The implications of this are probably pretty obvious. Being alert to this information prepares you with what you need to know to respond effectively and powerfully in social situations.

8. How knowable are you — will the real you please stand up? How well do you know yourself and how others see you? Before talking with others, describe your personality as you think it is today. Use any assessment data you've taken over the years. Just for the fun of it, read through a few astrological descriptions for your birth sign on the Internet. You don't need to accept what they say, but what do you agree with? Add to your description. This is your "self-view." Now ask friends, colleagues or people who see you from a distance for honest feedback. Family can be helpful here. Although your family's observations might not be very objective (after all, they contributed to the way you are, right?), they are insiders, and their perspective can be invaluable. This is your others view. How similar or different these views are reflects how knowable you are. Do you fit the "what you see is what you get" profile or the "imposter syndrome"? Being authentic, self-disclosing and open to others builds social intelligence. See competencies (3) Authenticity, (43) Self-Disclosure and (30) Openness to Others.

9. What makes you the way you are? Understanding the impact of your early life experiences offers insight into what might be driving your choices today. Understanding yourself and what motivates your behavior also provides insight into the behavior of others. Understanding other people's behavior allows you to avoid taking it personally, to exert influence more effectively, and to help others make better choices for themselves. Back to you. Make a list of your characteristics. Look back over your life and ask yourself where these characteristics might have come from. Traits, preferences, etc., are either genetic or learned (many in childhood). What might account for who you are today? For instance, if you feel that you are shy, when did you first feel this way? Were you always shy, or was there a significant life event associated with it? Also important to consider: growing up in certain economic conditions, with unique siblings, parents with strong personalities or values or circumstances that you might not have recognized as exceptional or unique at the time. Reflecting on who you are and how you got here can unravel mysteries and give you choice about who you want to be today.

10. Distractible? Does your attention wander when you're talking with others? Some people are more easily distracted than others. What is the impact of distractibility on social intelligence? Aside from missing potentially important information, wandering attention can be offensive. Most people are offended when, mid-sentence, they see the listener's eyes drift away. Remember how you felt that time you were speaking with someone and their eyes left you to follow someone walking by? How about the blank, fixed stare that says, "It may look like I'm listening because I'm making good eye contact, but I've tuned you out and I'm thinking about something else." How about the exact opposite? Let's go from feeling abandoned to feeling heard and understood. There's no feeling quite like the one that comes from talking with a person who stays fully present, making eye contact, appearing interested, and listening generously. See competency (27) Listening Generously.

11. Charming and inspirational but emotionally distant? Emotional intelligence and social intelligence cover much of the same ground, but they are not the same thing. Socially intelligent people work well with other people. They understand them and "get" them. They are aware of their motivations, their goals, and their stated and unstated intentions. Emotional intelligence is broader and includes emotional competencies that allow for emotional intimacy as well. Ronald Reagan, especially during his tenure as President of the United States, earned the affection of many Americans and those around the world. After he left office, the affection felt by many toward him, regardless of their politics, only grew. Yet Reagan's closest associates readily acknowledged the paradoxical contradiction between his emotional and social personas. While he was charming and inspirational, many of Reagan's relationships with close family members were distant and strained. People who worked closely with him reported that he showed very little interest in them as individuals. These observations would suggest that Reagan was a man of remarkably high social intelligence while low in some traits of emotional intelligence. Study examples of social intelligence for additional insights. Some personalities you can study are Larry King, Oprah Winfrey, and Princess Diana.

Related Competencies

(2) Assertiveness   (3) Authenticity   (15) *Active* Empathy

(17) Group Savvy   (25) Interpersonally Skillful   (27) Listening Generously

(29) *Reading* Nonverbal Communication   (30) Openness to Others

(42) Self-Confidence   (43) Self-Disclosure

(45) Situational Awareness

Learn from Experience

Work

❑ Handle a negotiation with an unhappy customer.

❑ Lead a task force responsible for launching a new process or system across several units.

Personal

❑ Work with a nonprofit in crisis.

❑ Mediate between two conflicting parties.

Resources

Books

Albrecht, Karl. *Social Intelligence: The New Science of Success*. San Francisco: Pfeiffer, 2005.

Flaxington, Beverly. *Understanding Other People: The Five Secrets to Human Behavior* (Volume 1). Medfield, MA: ATA Press, 2009.

Goleman, Daniel. *Social Intelligence: The New Science of Human Relationships*. New York: Bantam, 2007

McIntyre, Marie G. *Secrets to Winning at Office Politics: How to Achieve Your Goals and Increase Your Influence at Work*. New York: St. Martin's Griffin, First edition, 2005.

Pfeffer, Jeffrey. *Managing With Power: Politics and Influence in Organizations*. Boston: Harvard Business Press, First edition, 1993.

Vaknin, Shlomo. *The Big Book of NLP Techniques*. Prague: Inner Patch Publishers, 2001.

Internet

Personality Zone. Explore your personality type. www.keirsey.com

Classes and training

Center for Creative Leadership. Programs in personal and leadership development, including the Leadership Development Program (LDP®). www.ccl.org

Dale Carnegie Institute. Courses and training designed to increase individual and interpersonal effectiveness. www.dalecarnegie.com

Ken Blanchard Companies. Training in trust and leadership. www.kenblanchard.com

46

47 SOCIAL RESPONSIBILITY

Definition

Cooperating with and contributing to the common good of your community or social group by acting out of a basic concern for others and putting them first

Teach this triple truth to all: A generous heart, kind speech, and a life of service and compassion are the things which renew humanity.
— The Buddha

Talented

❏ Demonstrates commitment to the community's welfare through action and community involvement

❏ Collaborates with others to identify the needs of the group and group members

❏ Acts upon the belief that what is good for the whole community is better than acting in self-interest

❏ Places as much value in the well-being of the community and group as in personal concerns

❏ Stands up for the rights of the minority as well as for the stated values and goals of the group or community

❏ Consistently acts from the principle of caring for others and "doing no harm"

Skilled

❏ Accepts others' perspectives and works to alleviate concerns

❏ Assists others in a group when it may not be convenient

❏ Appreciates others' needs and expectations but may not act on it

❏ Invests time in community affairs and activities

❏ Fits volunteer work into the schedule

Unskilled

❏ Invests little in group or community unless it's convenient

❏ Insists on specific rigid roles before participating in groups

❏ Demonstrates a social consciousness only when personally expedient

❏ Acts out of personal gain with little regard for community needs

❏ Shows a lack of awareness of the underlying needs of others in a group and how his or her behavior affects the group

Big Picture View

Community and society are built on the proposition that each member of the community needs to be aware of and protective of the needs of the whole. Showing concern and acting responsibly toward others and the communities in which you work and live means taking time to understand how you might make a difference using your particular talents, interests and connections. Organizations also can be good citizens in their community by identifying a cause or needs that have meaning for them and provide a structure for employees or members to contribute with broader impact than individuals alone could have. Socially responsible individuals understand through experience that their generosity in time and effort is more than repaid by their sense of satisfaction and personal connections with those they meet. Individuals who demonstrate a commitment to their communities generally are more satisfied and more fulfilled personally. In a number of studies, individuals with greater social responsibility exhibit more emotional intelligence than the average individual. In our virtual age, many "communities" are not necessarily neighbors, but they can be part of our social responsibility.

Barriers to Effectiveness

❏ Failing to grasp the importance of community values and goals of the groups or affiliations you are part of

❏ Insisting on having your agenda addressed regardless of pressing priorities of the group — for example, "I don't have time to recycle; they can do it"

❏ Assuming that someone else will step up

❏ Failing to understand the multiple ways that you can be a socially responsible community or group member

❏ Self-centeredness; more concerned with own needs that those of the community

47

Quick Action Tips

1. **Find yourself thinking "someone should do something about that?"** And then forget that someone could be you? A well researched issue in community behavior is the "tragedy of the commons," which is simply that everyone sees a problem but no one feels empowered to fix it. Interestingly, when one individual stands up to say that he'll work toward a solution, others are willing to pitch in and help. Even if you do not have all the answers or resources to address an issue you feel is important, a small initiative can have a big consequence later on. Think of that one small thing that you can do to address a community related issue that you feel needs to be addressed. An excellent example is an individual who created a read-to-ride program at a local elementary school. The deal was simply that if the kids read a certain number of books in a semester and had parental approval, they would get a motorcycle ride through her riding club. So, once a semester, 600 kids get a ride through the Texas countryside. Reading comprehension scores have doubled.

2. **Is your plate too full to add a volunteer activity?** It's time to evaluate what is reasonable to do in the time you have available for volunteer work within the organizations to which you belong. Prioritize those things that are most important given your values and where you might have the most impact with your particular interests and skills. Let others know what still remains to be done, and encourage those with interest, commitment and the talent needed to also consider helping. Offer to meet with and brief anyone who is willing to help. Share with them how rewarding your volunteer work has been to you. Remember, even if those you talk with are not willing to help the cause you believe in, you are not responsible for solving all of the world's problems. Do what you can and others will show up.

3. **Do you sometimes feel things are so bureaucratic that it is not worth the effort to try to help?** Rules guide and facilitate decision-making. Talk with other community members about their interpretation of the community rules and decision-making processes so you get a better understanding of the various perspectives on how to get the group to take action to fix a community problem. It is a socially responsible action to point out the spirit and intentions of the rules and guidelines a group or community may have created. If group members over-reply on "laws and rules," then people tend to hide problems. The consequence is that community issues may not get the attention they deserve. List the barriers you feel are in place, and start asking how some of them can be removed so more solutions can be implemented.

4. **Does social responsibility extend only as far as it meets your own needs?** In just about any setting in which you live and work, there are consequences to your be-

havior for all those present. Everything from how you manage your work or living space to how you share responsibilities for a community project has an outcome for which you are responsible. Shared roles help glue community and group members to common goals. To get a taste of how powerful your contribution can be, identify a not-for-profit organization that could use your talents, then volunteer. Make sure the mission of the organization is focused on elevating the community's increased awareness on a project or needed change.

5. Not clear what is in it for you? Sometimes you might wonder why you should invest time and effort in the community. A basic sense of reciprocity should be sufficient to engage your commitment. Your selected communities bring a great deal of comfort and care to your life and well-being, so giving something back only seems fair. Take time to evaluate what your community contributes to the quality of your life and then start investing in what you can do to give some of it back. In other words, "paying it forward" has many benefits to you personally and to the communities in which you engage.

6. Overwhelmed by all the needs you see in the community? It may be hard to choose one or two volunteer opportunities when so many need help. Start with the organizations you may be part of such as where you worship, a school your children attend (or one in your neighborhood), or a local scout group. Identify someone you know who is connected to those organizations and talk with them about volunteer opportunities. Or ask yourself what you currently consider the most serious problem in your community: hunger, homelessness, overflowing animal shelters, poor high school graduation rates, polluted rivers? Seek out an organization that is working to improve that situation and attend a meeting. Speak to people there and offer to help. Or talk to friends of yours. Ask them how they might see you contributing to the community, given what they know of you — what talent or gift they see in you that could make a difference. Follow up on one of their ideas to learn more. Take a step to help in one of these ways; you can't solve every problem or need that you see in your community, but you can make a difference to someone and feel the satisfaction of helping.

7. Feel out of place or disconnected from others? Feeling disconnected from others may be due to a lack of social confidence which feeds distance from others. Or difficult behavior such as being rude, interrupting, or talking over others leads to others disconnecting from you! Social confidence helps when asking for and accepting volunteer responsibility. People who lack social confidence tend to go "inside," so their attention is drawn to their own thoughts and (usually) discomfort. They miss valuable cues and may appear disinterested. To create greater comfort and self-confidence, start with paying attention to what is positive about you. Do this early and often! At the end of a day, write down social experiences that went well, positive comments that came your way and what you did that you feel good about. Keep these lists handy, add to them and review them regularly. As you enter social activities, think about times in the past when you experienced social success. If this occasion is especially important or new to you, try this strategy: Think of a previous experience in which you distinctly remember feeling pride, confidence or success. Step back into that earlier experience as fully as you can so that you can re-engage that feeling of confidence. Then step into today's important occasion and carry that feeling with you. If you think your behavior is pushing people away, then consider asking for feedback and adjusting your interpersonal style.

8. See ways to help in your community, but not sure you have the ability? Would you like to feel more confident generally? Thinking, like behavior, falls into habits. Many of the thoughts and assumptions that you have about yourself are merely habits and, as such, can be changed. If you don't like what you think about yourself, you can change it. Yes, you can! Try this. Identify three beliefs that you would like to have about yourself as a community volunteer but that you do not yet have. Write them down and rate each one on a ten-point scale according to how much you already believe it — zero being "don't believe it" and ten being "believe it fully." For the next two weeks, each morning and night, repeat these beliefs out loud, preferably in front of a mirror. At the end of the two weeks, rate how much you believe each of them. Notice how much more you *do* believe them today. Notice how you feel different and more willing to volunteer your services.

9. Never really thought about the importance of being socially responsible? Sometimes you are so immersed in just getting through everyday life demands that it is easy to forget the larger context of social relationships on which you depend. Taking care of self and family are crucial. Contributing to your community organizations (for example, volunteer fire department, free tutoring clinics, chess club, etc.) increases the well being of many others. If contributing to the community feels like a new idea, it might seem overwhelming. Whatever you offer to do makes a difference. Even a small act combines with the small acts of your neighbors to make the world around you a little more like the place you want it to be.

Related Competencies

(5) Compassion   (8) Congruence   (21) Initiative

(39) Self-Actualization   (46) Social Intelligence (52) Trusting

(54) Understanding Others

Learn from Experience

Work

❏ Ask to be part of the corporate social responsibility committee that examines organizational policies and chooses a commitment that fits with the corporation values.

❏ Ask to serve on your company's United Way campaign, or ask to be given a special assignment to the community involvement committee in your organization.

Personal

❏ Volunteer for a citizens committee that makes decisions or recommendations for social programs with your local government.

❏ Get a list of all the volunteer opportunities in your community, look through it, and pick one that speaks to you (most local United Way offices have a list posted on their web site).

Resources

Books

Kotler, Philip. *Corporate Social Responsibility: Doing the Most Good for Your Company and Your Cause.* Hoboken, NJ: Wiley and Sons, 2005.

Vogel, David. *The Market for Virtue: The Potential and Limits of Corporate Social Responsibility.* Washington: The Brookings Institution, 2006.

Werther, William, and David Chandler. *Strategic Corporate Social Responsibility: Stakeholders in a Global Environment.* London: Sage Publications, 2011.

Internet

Harvard Kennedy School. Search for "Corporate Social Responsibility Initiative." www.hks.harvard.edu.

Classes and training

University business schools (MBA programs and some undergraduate programs) often have courses or a concentration in the area of corporate social responsibility (for example, the University of California, Berkeley, and Southern New Hampshire University).

47

48 MANAGING
SOCIAL SPACE

Definition

Recognizing and maintaining the physical and emotional distance needed to interact comfortably with others

No person is your friend who demands your silence, or denies your right to grow.
— Alice Walker

Talented

Recognizing physical social space:

❑ Demonstrates awareness of and respect for physical space and the needs of self and others

❑ Educates self on personal space customs and practices of those from another culture or background

❑ Adjusts social distance, taking into account social etiquette between intimates, friends, new acquaintances, co-workers and strangers

Recognizing emotional social space:

❑ Identifies and respects the needs of others, creating a safe, inviting space

❑ Confidently requests or creates the time and space to accommodate personal emotional needs

❑ Respects the privacy of others

❑ Strikes the right emotional balance in relationships — neither becoming too involved nor too detached

Skilled

❑ Creates private space and mental renewal time to maintain personal health

❑ Reads basic social cues but may miss the more subtle cues outlining emotional boundaries

❏ Cues into the cultural, religious or international differences in how people relate to one another, but more exposure or knowledge would improve overall effectiveness

❏ Sets limits but often feels the need to defend them

Unskilled

❏ Allows others to move uncomfortably close, unable to establish personal space

❏ Displays indifference to others' need for time and space

❏ Intimidates others by intentionally violating their comfort zones

❏ Fails to take into account the differing backgrounds, cultures or nationalities of others when interacting with them

Big Picture View

Have you ever had the experience of being extremely uncomfortable when talking to someone who is standing so close you can smell their shampoo or the gum they are chewing? Or they punctuate each sentence with a touch to your arm or shoulder? Or they ask overly personal questions, or disclose too much information? These are examples of the poor management of social space. Some causes: widely different cultural, religious or national backgrounds; being clueless about your impact on others; undervaluing how others feel; or overvaluing your own agenda. There's actually a science built around this — it's called proxemics, the study of the invisible space around us and how it affects communication between people. But it doesn't take much to know when someone pushes up against that space in a way that feels uncomfortable and inappropriate.

Skillful management of social space with others depends on staying aware of the nonverbal messages sent by other people. If you step forward and others step back, what message does that send? If you ask a personal question and it is deflected, then you might want to drop your question or redirect the conversation. Skillful management of social space also honors your own boundaries and space. Be clear about where your comfort limits are — social space and privacy — and, when appropriate, request that others respect these limits. Skillful management of interpersonal or social space includes saying no with confidence (and without guilt), handling intrusive and overly personal behavior in others, and creating safety and comfort for others.

Emotionally intelligent people educate themselves about different cultures, customs and nonverbal cues so they can build rapport and avoid inadvertently offending others. The world is small enough now that we all benefit by

48

understanding cultural differences and learning to communicate appropriately based on those differences.

Barriers to Effectiveness

❏ Disabled radar for other people's comfort zones

❏ Neediness leading to being overly eager to connect with others

❏ Discounts differences among cultures and implications for interpersonal space and communications

❏ Assumes superiority of own standards of propriety at the expense of reading the other person's signals regarding personal space

❏ Oblivious to or dismissive of what others are thinking or feeling

❏ Lack of self-confidence and assertiveness

Quick Action Tips

1. Unsure what violates privacy or personal space? Privacy and personal space are, well, personal matters. So there is lots of gray area here. But, some general behaviors to avoid are:

- Physical Space: standing or sitting too close, unwanted touching or sexual advances

- Emotional space: asking overly personal or private questions, telling someone how they feel, telling someone they are wrong for feeling a certain way, making excessive demands of another's attention and energy (being high maintenance!)

- Thoughts and beliefs: Telling someone how to think or believe, criticizing their thoughts (politics, religion, choice of major, job, etc.), pressuring someone to your point of view or decision

2. Fail to notice others' reactions to you? Have you ever noticed that when you are talking with people that they tend to back away from you? If your style is too close for comfort, then you will notice the person with whom you are talking begin to create distance or space by stepping back or turning away as they attempt to create a more comfortable boundary or space between you. It is important to become more self-aware and to tune in to the nonverbal behavior of those around you by noticing how they react in your presence. To increase your awareness of this dynamic, pick a specific time, place and person and pay special attention to the interactions between you.

3. Inexperienced with different cultures? If you expect to interact with people from a different culture or country, then it would be both gracious and smart of you to educate yourself about their social and communication habits. For example, when Americans shake hands, they stand close enough not to have to step forward to accomplish the handshake (about 2.5 feet) while in Asian cultures the distance is greater. In Latin and Middle Eastern cultures it is close enough to be able to feel the breath of the other person on your face. For most Americans or Northern Europeans this would be way too close for comfort. But when interacting with people from South America or the Middle East it is important to know and understand their cultures or risk offending them. They are, hopefully, doing the same.

Look around where you work, worship or volunteer and notice others who may have come from other cultures. Go online and research information about their customs. Ask if this person would be willing to spend some time with you helping you to learn about them and their culture. Some questions you might ask are: What are some observable and underlying elements that distinguish your culture? How is meaning conveyed beyond words? Any taboos or things a first-time visitor should know? How would I need to adapt if I were to live in this culture? What other things would you like to know? Did you learn anything not reflected in your questions?

4. Clueless when it comes to setting appropriate limits? If you need help setting limits, then try this response: "Let me think about it, and I'll get back with you." This gives you time to assess your availability, needs and preferences before agreeing to something that you may not really want to do. If you are unsure of whether or not you have the right to say no or establish limits or boundaries, then identify and challenge your assumptions. Is your belief system self-limiting? Rational Behavior Therapy suggests that you use the DIBS (Disputing Irrational Beliefs) format for examining self-defeating thoughts.

- What irrational belief do I wish to refute or surrender?
- What makes this belief irrational or inaccurate?
- Does any evidence exist to prove the truth of my belief?
- What is the worst thing that could happen if I surrender this belief?
- Can I make something positive happen out of not getting what I expected or thought I should?

Here are some examples of typical irrational beliefs that are commonly held by many people: *I must be perfect and thoroughly competent in all that I do. Everyone must like me, and if they don't my life will be a failure.*

5. How are you at reading nonverbals? Some people are uncomfortable being touched, which requires that we "read" them and then respond accordingly. Just as some people like broccoli and others don't, some people are more comfortable with physical touch or personal sharing than others. Your interests are better served if, when interacting with others, you read the situation to guide the choices you make when interacting with them. If you are confused or uncertain, then ask! This will bring clarity to the situation. Watch for groupings of behaviors that may indicate a pattern. Does the person avert their eyes, turn away and avoid answering your questions directly or pretend that they didn't hear you? Chances are these behaviors are clearly communicating a message, even if not through words.

6. Need some help creating space around you? Some practices that might help you protect your space include: holding or reading a book, newspaper, computer, iPad or cell phone, choosing a seat on the end of a row or table, and avoiding eye contact. Averting your eyes or turning away is a way of saying "back off," or, "not interested." If someone is engaging in a conversation that you don't wish to have, then learn to change the subject or display disinterest through the tone of your voice. Or if none of this works you may have to go with a hammer type response (see tip 7 below).

7. To use a hammer or a feather? Sometimes the difficulty in managing personal space is a result of either overdoing it (over-reacting) or under-doing it (not speaking up). The chapters on (2) Assertiveness, (7) Effective Confrontation, and (25) Interpersonally Skillful all have excellent resources and tips to help choose between a "feather" or "hammer" and how to use both. For now think of a situation in which you want to set better limits to protect your personal space or boundary. Perhaps a good starting point is to assume goodwill or intent on the other person's part. In this case you can demonstrate understanding and adaptability (a feather). If that does not work, then you may have to escalate to a stronger response such as creating a diversion or even providing feedback regarding the objectionable behavior of the person in question. If the person turns out to be difficult or unresponsive to your efforts, then you may have to escalate further by asking him or her to leave you alone (more like using a hammer).

Is there anyone you have encountered in the last few weeks with whom you can practice? Is there someone in your life who tends to impinge upon your personal space? If so, anticipate the next interaction and be prepared to set limits with that person.

8. Do you know the spatial zones that are typical for your culture? The study of proxemics is about the distance humans generally use in their interactions with others depending upon the nature of the relationship. For Americans, intimate relationships (lovers, close friends, children with parents) have a distance of 0 to 18 inches. Personal relationships (friends, close associates) have a distance of 1½ to 2½ feet, which is close enough to talk privately together. Social distance for business transactions or interactions with people who are working in your home is generally 4 to 12 feet. When in the public zone, the preferred distance is greater, 12 to 20 feet, and involves strangers in public or the distance a teacher might use in the classroom or a boss addressing a group of employees.

Try doing a double observation:

Observe yourself interacting with others and notice the distance you tend to maintain with the various people in your life. Then observe the distance people maintain with you. Is the distance you maintain appropriate for the relationship? Are you creating distance or aloofness, or are you encroaching upon the private space of another, creating discomfort or embarrassment? Is the space others create around you appropriate to the relationship? Do your colleagues step too closely into your space or sit on your desk? Does your boss use the power of his position to enter your space unwelcomed? Does your next-door neighbor hug you or stand closer than you want? Does your partner maintain a greater distance than you desire, leading to tension or hurt feelings? Note your observations, and ask yourself if any of your interactions could use some adjustment. If yes, make a plan to adjust your behavior.

Related Competencies

(2) Assertiveness   (11) Emotional Expression   (17) Group Savvy

(22) Insightfulness   (25) Interpersonally Skillful

(29) *Reading* Nonverbal Communication   (45) Situational Awareness

Learn from Experience

Work

❏ Serve on a task force regarding establishing policies related to sexual harassment in the workplace.

❏ Serve on a project that involves international travel or considerations, such as building a plant in another country, or an international acquisition.

❏ Be the first person to a meeting and carefully observe how people greet one another (and you) as they enter the room. Observational learning is an excellent way to see what behavior works and what doesn't.

Personal

❏ Volunteer at a youth detention center or a minimum-security prison. The in-service training will be instructive in developing the skills of setting limits and learning to recognize manipulative or unacceptable behavior.

❏ Attend a local festival or event that is offered by a group representing another country or culture. Observe members of that group to see if

48

you can assess their traditional way of greeting and interacting with one another.

Resources

Books

Alberti, Robert, and Michael Emmons. *Your Perfect Right: Assertiveness and Equality in Your Life and Relationship*s. Atascadero, CA: Impact Publishers, 2008.

Back, Ken, and Kate Back. *Assertiveness at Work: A Practical Guide to Handling Awkward Situations.* Berkshire, U.K.: McGraw Hill, 2005.

Burns, David. *The Feeling Good Handbook.* New York: Penguin Putnam, 1999.

Ellis, Albert. *How to Control Your Anxiety Before It Controls You.* New York: Citadel Press, the Kensington Publishing Group, 2000.

McKay, Matthew, Martha Davis, and Patrick Fanning. *Messages: The Communication Book*, Oakland, CA: New Harbinger Press, 2009.

Morrison, Terri, and Wayne Conaway. *Kiss, Bow or Shake Hands.* Avon, MA: Adams Media, 2006.

Swallow, Deborah, Phillip Khan-Panni. *Communicating Across Cultures: The Key to Successful International Business Communication.* Oxford, UK: How To Books, 2006.

Internet

Rational Emotive Behavior Therapy. www.rebt.org

Intercultural Communication Institute. www.intercultural.org/

KissBowShakeHands.com: Check the online learning tool to increase global awareness. www.kissbowshakehands.com

Ezinearticles.com. Go to the home page and search for "setting healthy boundaries,"or "assertiveness." www.ezinearticles.com

Classes and training

American Management Association. Search for "assertiveness training." www.amanet.org

Ed2go. Search "assertiveness training." www.ed2go.com

48

49 STAMINA

Definition

Persisting in the face of difficulties, obstacles or disappointments

Energy is the essence of life. Every day you decide how you're going to use it by knowing what you want and what it takes to reach that goal, and by maintaining focus.

— Oprah Winfrey

Talented

❏ Demonstrates fortitude by seeing challenges as opportunities to learn and succeed

❏ Uses problem solving strategies, seeks support, and trusts own abilities to persist

❏ Recognizes that failure isn't a permanent condition; analyzes events to make needed changes

❏ Manages personal energy ups and downs in order to meet challenges successfully

❏ Uses a sense of humor as one means of defusing tense situations and keeping focus on the goal

❏ Maintains vitality and a high energy level by living a healthy lifestyle

❏ Shows backbone and endurance under pressure

Skilled

❏ When efforts don't succeed, seeks to bounce back and try again

❏ Recognizes when energy levels are fluctuating and takes positive action to re-energize

❏ Shows more staying power and toughness than many

❏ Maintains high energy and reasonable stress levels although they may fluctuate

Unskilled

❏ Gets discouraged and gives up easily when facing difficult challenges or setbacks

❏ Uses poor coping skills when faced with disappointments or failure

❏ Criticizes and acts impatient with self when stressed

❏ Shows low or variable energy levels

❏ Deals with stressful situations by blaming others, emotional outbursts, withdrawing or negative self-talk

❏ Overuses substances like nicotine, alcohol, caffeine or drugs to increase energy and manage disappointments

❏ Gets sick easily or frequently

Big Picture View

Persevering in the face of challenges and difficulties builds the muscle of emotional stamina. Psychological hardiness is a term often used when talking about stamina, and it is characterized by three primary qualities or attitudes.

- Commitment: having a personal and meaningful commitment to what you are doing in life

- Control: feeling you have the ability to control and influence events in your life

- Challenge: seeing challenges and new experiences as exciting opportunities to learn and develop

A person with stamina is not impervious to setbacks but is strongly resilient in responding to a range of stressful conditions. He or she also tends to manage disappointments better, perform better under stress and remain healthier. Physical energy is an important component of stamina. Partner with your physician to be sure you are in top physical shape. Build your physical endurance by regular exercise that you enjoy. Your vitality and toughness to stick it out when it counts means balancing the demands and activity in your life with rest and relaxation. Recognize those people and situations that drain your energy. If you must interact with energy drainers, limit your contact. Say no when you need to. Take control of your calendar by scheduling time to recharge your batteries, even if it is thirty minutes for a short walk at lunch or twenty minutes to plan your day before interruptions begin. Understand your level of mental, emotional and physical stamina and use it well.

49

Barriers to Effectiveness

❑ Irrational beliefs that undermine energy and well-being

❑ Overdoing it; failing to rest and rejuvenate

❑ Neglecting physical health

❑ Thinking you should be able to do it all

❑ Social isolation

❑ Mental stagnation (lack of stimulating activities can sap motivation and energy)

❑ Negative thinking or adhering to a "victim" mentality

Quick Action Tips

1. Do you find yourself feeling depleted and overwhelmed by present problems? Ask yourself how much these current difficulties will matter in three hours, three months, or three years. By putting current issues in perspective, you may regain the energy needed to meet your challenges. Talk to a close friend or colleague who may be able to remind you that you are more than this current challenge and that you have often succeeded in the past. Remind yourself that, even when you didn't, your world didn't end. What strategies have you used in the past to overcome the feeling of being overwhelmed and exhausted? Try them again. List your challenges in order of priority and deal with them one at a time. Getting a few things off your plate can help create the energy you need to continue to manage additional challenges. Remember to ask for help; colleagues and friends may be glad to pitch in. Finally, if you are getting beat up by circumstances at work or in life (as we all are at times), then stop and consider how you might be compassionate to yourself. You are your own best friend.

2. Feel overwhelmed when under a lot of stress? Wish you had more energy? Ongoing stress affects us in two primary ways: physical tension and mental anxiety. Both are energy drains. One of the best ways to deal with physical tension is a regular exercise program. Join a gym or nearby health club and find out what kind of exercise works for you. Revisit sports you enjoyed in the past such as tennis or basketball. Take up a new hobby such as golf. Try an activity like yoga to clear your mind and increase your flexibility. If nothing else appeals to you, then start with a 20- or 30-minute walk each day outside. If you are feeling low energy in the middle of your day, try a few slow deep breaths, a short walk around the office, or tightening, holding and releasing your fists. Deal with your anxiety by listing your concerns and worries. Identify one action step that you can take to make progress with each concern. One way we create anxiety is by catastrophizing, or imagining the worst possible outcome to a situation. Ask a friend to help you be realistic about whatever is bothering you. Creating better balance in your life with time for family, friends, personal interests, and volunteering can lead to a healthier perspective about work challenges and difficulties.

3. What problems have you been avoiding? Avoiding problems is actually a hidden energy drain. Because you aren't dealing with a problem, it continues to sap your energy whenever it comes back up or you think about it. List the key issues which you have been avoiding. Consider the emotional cost of not doing anything and the benefits of now addressing the issue, even if it is initially uncomfortable to do so. Take a deep breath and act. Analyze what your options are, enlist the support and resources you need, and take the first step. Often, brooding over your worries and concerns is worse than actually doing something to solve that nagging issue. You will build confidence and emotional stamina by acting on these initial suggestions.

4. How well do you know your own energy cycles? Are you a morning person? Early afternoon? Use your best time of day to work on difficult or important assignments. Plan a protein or fruit snack mid-day for a boost of energy to help you concentrate on that report due at the end of the day. Tune in to your body and energy level to know what you need to move ahead full throttle. Sometimes a short walk is the best way to reboot for the rest of the afternoon.

5. Are you in good health? Good physical health is a vital part of stamina. Schedule a physical exam each year and use the results with your doctor's advice to set goals to improve your physical condition. Control your cholesterol level and blood pressure through healthy habits or medication if needed. Know your family history of heath risks by asking key family members to fill you in on medical issues. Better eating habits, regular exercise, getting enough sleep each night, and a reasonable weight can improve your ability to concentrate and persist in the face of obstacles.

6. Do you take things too seriously? If it has been weeks since you have laughed at yourself, maybe you are taking yourself too seriously. Your staying power depends on moments of lightness and breaks from the pressure of life's challenges. Find the fun in your day, or make some time for laughing. If you rarely step back from your serious side, perhaps you need to make some changes to gain perspective. What did fun look like for you ten years ago? Twenty years ago? Take a trip back in time to rekindle that self that played more often.

7. Feel like you are always playing catch up? Part of building stamina is being prepared so you can use your energy efficiently. Take a few moments to consider what may be walking in your door tomorrow. If your boss manages the budget and you haven't learned the ins and outs of that process yet, then set up time to meet with someone in finance to learn how it is done. Ask your

49

boss if you can attend a high level meeting with him or her to better understand how your responsibilities fit in a larger scheme. When change comes, you will be better able to move with it. Inventory your home for what fix-ups need to be done in the coming year, then plan for them. Budget for painting if the outside of your house is beginning to look worn. Set aside a Saturday to take junk to the dump. Your satisfaction at making progress will energize you and will be worth the effort.

8. Who is the captain of your ship? Sometimes it may feel like your calendar, boss, spouse, clients, a special project, and even your smartphone and email are running your life. When you feel overwhelmed by technology and responsibilities, it is hard to maintain energy and enthusiasm. Put yourself back in command of your own ship. Are you being realistic about what you can accomplish? Make a list of your top five commitments. Are they reasonable? Would you be comfortable asking a colleague to do them all? If not, set priorities among them, delegate something, or drop something for now. Learn how to say no when asked to take on new projects that are not in your best interests or not a priority for your organization. If saying no is hard, then start by saying, "Thanks for thinking of me; let me consider that and get back to you." Then reflect and get back with a polite "no" if you need to set boundaries for yourself. Manage the technology rather than let it manage you. Limit the times you check your messages. Respond to them in order of criticalness. Set up systems with those you work with so that you don't need to constantly check messages. Turn off your electronic devices so you can enjoy family or personal time. Feeling in control will increase your feeling of stamina.

Related Competencies

(1) Adaptability	(2) Assertiveness	(21) Initiative
(31) Optimism	(36) Reframing	(38) Resilience
(41) Self-Awareness	(50) Stress Hardy	

Learn from Experience

Work

❑ Identify a challenge that seems daunting but has a meaningful payoff for you, then take it on. That might mean running the United Way Campaign for your company, putting together a task force to decide on new software for the division, or talking to two direct reports about an underlying conflict situation. Step back afterwards and note times you may have wanted to quit and how you helped yourself persevere.

❑ Who do you know who shows vitality and endurance at work? Set up time to talk to that person and ask how they maintain their stamina. Identify one or two strategies that might be beneficial and try them.

Personal

❏ Note how you respond to low energy at home. Anything you want to do differently? Ask your partner or children for suggestions.

❏ Reflect on times in your life when you had a lot of vitality, stamina, and endurance. What was happening? Any differences between then and now (other than being younger)? Any habits or activities you can bring forward in your life?

Resources

Books

Kersey, Cynthia. *Unstoppable: 45 Powerful Stories of Perseverance and Triumph From People Just Like You.* Naperville, IL: Sourcebooks, 1998.

Marshall, Joseph M. III. *Keep Going: The Art of Perseverance.* New York: Sterling Ethos, 2009.

Seldman, Marty, and Joshua Seldman. *Executive Stamina: How to Optimize Time, Energy, and Productivity to Achieve Peak Performance.* Hoboken, NJ: Wiley, 2008.

Internet

Squidoo.com. Developing perseverance. www.squidoo.com/develop-perseverance

Hardiness-Resilience.com. Click on "free downloads" for many interesting articles on resilience and hardiness. www.hardiness-resilience.com

Classes and training

American Management Association. Search for "leadership and team development for managerial success." www.amanet.org/training/seminars

SkillPath seminars. Search for "managing emotions." www.skillpath.com

49

50   STRESS HARDY

Definition

Maintaining performance, positive mood and commitment to goals in spite of adversity

When you find yourself stressed, ask yourself one question: Will this matter five years from now? If yes, then do something about the situation. If no, then let it go.

— Catherine Pulsifer

Talented

❑ Responds with optimism and energy when faced with challenges

❑ Interprets events in ways that maintain momentum

❑ Views adversity as opportunity for learning and growth

❑ Raises performance level under stress

❑ Bounces back quickly from adversity and frustration

❑ Exhibits well-rounded coping strategies (physical, mental, emotional)

Skilled

❑ Loses enthusiasm but not momentum when facing challenges

❑ Relies on just one or two strategies to cope with stress

❑ Struggles but maintains performance under stress

❑ Diffuses negative responses to stress most of the time

❑ Bounces back when thwarted … eventually

Unskilled

❑ Fails to shift perspective or strategy when coping efforts aren't working

❑ Appears exhausted instead of energized when faced with challenges

❑ Becomes withdrawn, anxious, or depressed under stress

❏ Takes longer than most to bounce back from adverse events

❏ Loses sight of the bigger picture when things don't work out as expected or wanted

Big Picture View

Stress hardiness is significantly influenced by how a person views the world, himself and the interaction between the two. Susan Kobasa studied executives under considerable stress and found a number of personality traits that protected them from the negative effects of stress. The executives who had these stress hardy personality traits decreased their risk of developing a stress related health problem by a massive 50 percent. The traits included commitment (to something or someone), internal sense of control, and seeing negative events as challenges versus threats.

Barriers to Effectiveness

❏ Inflexibility

❏ Strict performance standards

❏ Unassertive behavior

❏ Reluctance to ask for help, risk rejection or confront conflict

❏ Pessimism

❏ Learned helplessness

❏ Limited repertoire of coping strategies

Quick Action Tips

1. Are you easily overwhelmed by challenges? Those who practice multiple strategies for managing stress tend to be the least overwhelmed. The following practices inoculate people against stress:

- Being perceptive — sizing up people and situations insightfully, thereby avoiding unwanted surprises and sidestepping potential stress

- Being an active learner — learning from experience and applying the lessons to avoid repeating what is stressful

- Being optimistic — expecting the best, even if preparing for the worst

- Staying motivated — exhibiting personal energy and initiative

50

- Being spiritual — experiencing personal faith in something greater than yourself

- Persevering — keeping at it in spite of difficulty

- Shifting perspective — taking alternate points of view to manage emotions

- Internal compass — developing trust in your own judgment when evaluating choices and making decisions. As confidence in your own judgment goes up, second-guessing yourself goes down.

Which stress busters do you use? Are there any that you would like to add, do better or do more of? Identify someone who stays above the fray and observe how they do it. Interview them for their strategies and add to this list.

2. Does self-care come last? Those who fail to practice self-care get exhausted by the unexpected and experience more ill effects — both physical and mental — from stress than others do. One common stress trap is overwork. It can creep up on you without you realizing it. In Japan, there was a time when people worked until they dropped, literally. They actually have a word for "death from overwork" — karoshi (kah-roe-she). Once it had a name and its symptoms became better known, it quickly became apparent that Japan was experiencing an epidemic. Self-care is a habit that needs to be practiced on a continuous basis. Regular exercise, good nutrition, adequate sleep and a network of supportive relationships are consistently correlated with good health. While obvious, it is still worth stating: You are better able to meet challenges head on when you feel good and have stamina than when you're exhausted or off your game mentally.

3. Reluctant to change course when what you're doing isn't working? Newton's first law of motion, in part, states, "An object in motion stays in motion with the same speed and in the same direction...." That's true for most people, too. Once started on a path, there's an emotional investment in it, and it takes more effort to change course than to stay the course. Changing perspective or approach, however, might be the better choice. But flexibility, unless practiced regularly, doesn't come easy. Experiment with changing your perspectives and strategies when you're not under stress as a way to increase your comfort and skill with it. It is much easier to practice and adopt new and healthier habits during periods of low stress. Then, when stress increases, it will be easier for you to objectively assess your choices and make needed changes.

4. Set up to succeed? Do you view external events as being out of your reach to control? What can you control? It is important that the outcomes you want are under your control. Much frustration, disappointment and failure can be avoided if, at the outset of any action, you are clear about your outcomes and you have confirmed that they are under your control. If not, alter your outcome until you can pursue it on your terms. If you determine that a stressor is out of your control, then shift your attention to some aspect of it that you *can* control. Then do something about it.

5. Are you a regular on the best stressed list? Do you become withdrawn, anxious, and or depressed under stress? You may be vulnerable to stress either because of a negative outlook or because you have too few strategies for dealing with stress. Review the strategies below and identify which ones you rarely or never use. Commit to changing that by choosing several to practice.

- Relationships — Build and maintain healthy relationships that reinforce your value and offer support when needed. Distance yourself from dysfunctional relationships that drain your energy or cause you self-doubt.

- Self-worth — Recount and appreciate your accomplishments and positive attributes. Name your accomplishments and the strengths you used to secure them. As you remind yourself of your strengths, you make them more available to you for solving life's current challenges. While you're at it, identify other personal assets — important lessons learned, virtues, talents, skills, capabilities, what makes your life meaningful, how you help or serve others, all the best things about being who you are.

- A larger purpose — Choose a cause or purpose to commit or re-commit to. Being charitable, doing good for others, giving back or just working at something that benefits something or someone other than yourself triggers positive emotions. Positive emotions make you more resilient and able to bounce back from hard times.

- Competence — Be intentional about being good at something. Having a talent or skill that you have worked to develop excellence in creates a feeling of being special. It serves as a source of pride and can offset difficulties in other areas.

- Reframing the situation. It's not the event that is stressful but how you perceive it. And that determines your response to it. Different people can have the very same experience but report very different emotional reactions. Speaking to a group is no big deal for one person, while another avoids it if at all possible. Same situation, just different reactions. You can learn to think differently about an event, thereby changing how you feel and lowering your stress. Think of a current, or recent, stressor. How can you talk to yourself about it differently? Try different perspectives and notice how your feelings change. Other examples: See change as normal, or inevitable, or as a stimulating, healthy

50

challenge, not as a threat. See problems as part of the journey and the future as an opportunity to learn from and surmount problems.

- Humor — Practice finding the humor in everyday situations. Not only will life become much more pleasant for you and those around you, but also, when you're faced with a major difficulty, your skill at seeing the lighter side will help you keep your head while dealing with the issue.

- Flexibility — Develop multiple options for thinking about and responding to events, and cultivate the flexibility to exercise those options. Practice thinking and doing things in new ways. Develop comfort with variety and change.

- Creativity — Find new ways to do things and to express yourself. The Law of Requisite Variety holds that he who has the most choices wins. The more choices a person has, the more likely it is that she or he has the one that will work best in a given situation. The logical extension of this is that the person who has the most strategies for dealing with stress is likely to have the ones that work the best.

Which of these strategies above could work for you? Together with other strategies you use, write them on index cards, one per card. The next time you're feeling overwhelmed, immensely frustrated or emotionally drained, commit to pulling out your deck of strategy cards and practice at least two. Rotate the strategies you try so that you practice all at least twice within some reasonable length of time.

6. Take longer than most to bounce back from adverse events? You may be dealing with stress that is constant but not obvious, and that is leaving you vulnerable to, and less able to deal with, adverse events. Unremitting low levels of stress can be exhausting. Repeated restructuring or layoffs at work, for example, can leave everyone worried about when the next shoe is going to drop. Conduct an assessment of the key areas of your life: health and self-care, relationships, work, spiritual, community and financial. What do you have control over? Which areas do you feel good about? Is there one area that needs attention or has some constant factor that concerns you? Keep what is going well clearly in your sights and commit to talking with a friend, counselor or trusted advisor to get some ideas for improving the part of your life that concerns you.

7. Glass half empty? Focus on what you have and what's working instead of on what's missing or broken. For example, list what you appreciate in your life and are proud of accomplishing. Some refer to this as a Gratitude Journal. At the end of each day, jot down what you are grateful for: for example, achievements, good health, simple pleasures, contentment. Focus more on what you have done and less on what you haven't yet accomplished. Researchers have discovered that experiencing positive emotions in a 3 to 1 ratio with negative emotions moves people to a tipping point beyond which they naturally become more stress hardy and more resilient to adversity, allowing them to more easily achieve what they once only imagined.

Related Competencies

(2) Assertiveness	(13) Emotional Problem-Solving	(16) Flexibility
(31) Optimism	(34) Perspective-Taking	(36) Reframing
(38) Resilience	(42) Self-Confidence	(49) Stamina

Learn from Experience

Work

❑ Lead a task force charged with improving results with reduced resources.

❑ Manage a group of balky people.

Personal

❑ Volunteer to serve a nonprofit agency providing help to those upended by economic downturn.

❑ Raise funds for a charity and set stretch targets.

❑ Interview people who have demonstrated resilience in the face of adversity for their strategies; choose three strategies that you can put into action.

Resources

Books

Seligman, Martin E. P. *Learned Optimism: How to Change Your Mind and Your Life*. New York: Vintage, 2006.

Reivich, Karen, and Andrew Shatte. *The Resilience Factor: Seven Keys to Finding Your Inner Strength and Overcoming Life's Hurdle*s. New York: Broadway, 2003.

Altman, Donald. *The Mindfulness Code*. Novato, CA: New World Library, 2010.

Kabat-Zinn, Jon. *Full Catastrophe Living: Using the Wisdom of Your Body and Mind to Face Stress, Pain, and Illness*. McHenry, IL: Delta, 1st edition, 1990.

Stahl, Bob and Elisha Goldstein. *A Mindfulness-Based Stress Reduction Workbook*. Oakland, CA: New Harbinger, 2010.

50

Internet

PositivityRatio.com. Search for Dr. Barbara Fredrickson and "positive emotions." www.positivityratio.com

Hay House Radio. Search for Michael Neill and "how to succeed." www.hayhouseradio.com.

Classes and training

Franklin Covey web site. Search for "Seven Habits Training," especially "Put First Things First" and "time management." www.franklincovey.com

The Silva Method. Programs to increase mental calmness and well-being. www.silvalifesystem.com

51   TOLERANCE

Definition

Listening to and appreciating differing perspectives and ideas; valuing diversity

We meet naturally on the basis of our sameness and grow on the basis of our differentness.

— Virginia Satir

Talented

❑ Recognizes the limits of one's personal perspective and seeks to learn from others

❑ Uses a diversity of thought and experience to leverage the best possible decisions and plans

❑ Creates a culture of valuing diversity by acknowledging the contribution and importance of differing perspectives

❑ Demonstrates valuing diversity for key roles in a team or project group; promotions and hiring decisions reflect cultural diversity

❑ Communicates respect and appreciation for widely divergent perspectives

❑ Accords respect and dignity to people of differing race, religion, appearance, sexual orientation and background

Skilled

❑ Open to experiences with various cultures and people with backgrounds different from oneself.

❑ Seeks out differing points of view; listens with an open mind

❑ Is comfortable with, though not fully accepting of, a diversity of backgrounds in others

❑ Presents ideas and thoughts in a way that allows others to comfortably disagree ("I think…," or, "In my opinion…," instead of, "The only way is…," or, "Obviously…")

Unskilled

❏ Shows discomfort around those from different backgrounds

❏ Demonstrates prejudices or stereotypes, either knowingly or unknowingly, in behavior

❏ Makes very few attempts to seek diversity for a work group or project

❏ Judges others' ideas too quickly, cuts off discussion and pushes for premature closure before everyone has shared their ideas or opinions

❏ Acts out against or blames innocent people due to their origins, race, homeland or appearance; judges groups of people based on the actions of a few

Big Picture View

Most of us initially tend to be more comfortable around those who look like us, share the same values and come from a background we understand. Some find diversity more naturally interesting and seek to understand and incorporate novel ideas from others into work projects or personal activities. For others, it is necessary to consciously seek out those from culturally diverse backgrounds in order to listen and learn that different is not good or bad, but can enrich what we do together. History shows that deep intolerance only causes harm. Some of our country's darkest moments have resulted from prejudice and intolerance for our own people of diversity because individuals acted out of fear. Guard against repeating such mistakes by rejecting inappropriate treatment of minority groups. Being respectful of all, using good listening skills, developing self-awareness, making yourself approachable, following a policy of treating others fairly, and being aware of the diversity policies of your organization are all important components to building your tolerance and the appearance of tolerance. Get to know those you work with as individuals rather than whatever first impressions or stereotypes you may initially have. The quiet person in your meeting may have the answer you need if you just ask and listen. Set a standard of listening with an open mind to those within your work group. Seek out neighbors and people you may meet at worship, community organizations or volunteer events that may have a different background, appearance or set of experiences from you. Get to know them in ways that can enrich your understanding of life.

Barriers to Effectiveness

❏ Limited exposure to different people, traditions, nationalities and cultures

51

❑ Close-minded; not open to different perspectives

❑ Lack of self-confidence

❑ Fear of the unknown

❑ Raised in a family with prejudices and a poor understanding of different ethnicities and cultures

❑ Failing to recognize and test assumptions about differences

Quick Action Tips

1. Uncomfortable with people of certain backgrounds or ethnicity? Recognize your lack of comfort and find ways to get to know individuals that fit those categories. Talk to someone after a PTA meeting, join a group for lunch, or ask to be part of a cross-functional task force that includes people you don't know. Building a personal relationship will help you get beyond your discomfort and may break down any negative stereotypes that you might have.

2. Surround yourself with others that look and sound like you? Research shows that diverse groups are more innovative than homogeneous groups. Take a look at your work group and identify two or three types of diversity that you might seek out to expand your group's perspective. Invite a marketing person, a sales person who travels in Latin America, or a quality control expert to join your meetings, and solicit their input. Listen for value added that is different from your usual perspective. Seek out opportunities in your community to meet others from a different culture. Attend a Black History Month or Cinco de Mayo event at your library or community.

3. Impatient with the ideas others bring to the table? Slow down to make time to understand the perspectives of all in the discussion. Ask yourself who with "skin in the game" is not represented in the faces you see present. As you approach issues, be inclusive instead of exclusive. Involve those who will take action and implement decisions in the decision-making process, and listen to them. Be sure you talk less than you listen. Practice separating out a time for generating possible approaches or solutions from the actual decision making; engage everyone in coming up with ideas. It costs less to listen up front before decisions are made than to redo poorly-thought-out decisions later.

4. Who me, intolerant? I get along with everyone! Yes, and most of us have a blind spot or two. Sometimes we are not aware of how we appear to others. Ask a trusted friend or colleague for feedback about ways you might appear intolerant either about the ideas of others or about specific types of people. Listen and confirm what you hear and set a goal for how you might increase your tolerance based on that feedback. Maybe what you think is decisiveness is seen by your colleagues as lack of appreciation for their perspective. Perhaps what you think is logical seems judgmental to others. You are simply trying to save time by making decisions about vacation plans, but your son feels excluded and feels that his ideas don't count. Perhaps you are worried about violence in another country, but your comments seem to be blaming a certain religious or cultural group for what is happening. Your intentions may be good, but you might not be conveying appreciation and tolerance for differences.

5. Do you find yourself snapping at others? Irritated at small things? Get a grip on yourself and remember that others are also usually trying their best. Take time both to listen fully to those around you and to patiently explain your own ideas so that everyone is on the same page. Maybe your colleagues are missing the big picture or the reasoning behind what you are trying to accomplish. Maybe you are the one missing some data points or a helpful perspective that your co-workers are trying to bring to the table. If you are just tired, take a break and come back with more patience. You need everyone's enthusiasm to make a project successful. The same can be true at home. If you find yourself short on patience with your family or close friends, then slow down, take a deep breath, and be present to what is happening. Stop worrying about that meeting at the office tomorrow and read to your son or daughter. Life goes by quickly.

6. Find yourself at times joining in conversations critical of specific cultural, racial or religious groups? In times of unrest or violence among different groups or nations, it is easy to want to blame a group that seems associated with perpetrators of terrorism through a common religion, race, homeland or appearance. Step back and remind yourself that groups of people cannot rightly be judged by the actions of a few. People of all ethnicities are hurt by terrorism and other acts of senseless violence. Choose to speak up and remind others that we are all in this life together and need to find ways to protect against the horrific actions of a few without pigeon-holing any one group. Highlight facts that go against stereotypes, such as Moslem firefighters and first responders to 9/11. Encourage others to resist random blaming. Respond to the concerns and fears of others, especially children, in positive ways without blaming groups of people.

Related Competencies

(1) Adaptability   (5) Compassion   (15) *Active* Empathy

(18) Impulse Control   (27) Listening Generously   (34) Perspective-Taking

(36) Reframing

51

Learn from Experience

Work

❏ Work on a project that involves travel to a variety of geographical areas. Build relationships with people you meet while there.

❏ Identify a person you tend to criticize. Observe that person for a few weeks, looking for the positive contributions they make. After a meeting including that person, list what positive intentions they may have had for behavior you tend to criticize. Some of your criticalness may be about you, not them.

❏ Identify someone with a different style. Are there ways that person is different from you that might add value to a project? Seek that person out to work with you on a project to make use of their talents and perspective.

❏ Look for a community project that your organization can sponsor that promotes appreciation of a diverse culture.

Personal

❏ Model tolerance and compassion in how you speak about various racial, ethnic or religious groups around your children, colleagues, friends and neighbors.

❏ Volunteer in a school and help debunk myths about other cultures by having children share information about their family or cultural customs to reinforce that all people have special beliefs and rituals.

❏ Find books to read to your children that may address prejudice, tolerance and hate in ways that help children think about and define their feelings about these issues. Ask your school librarian for suggestions that are age appropriate.

❏ Get involved with your school system supporting ways to reduce harassment or bullying of any students.

Resources

Books

Bucher, Richard D., and Patricia L. Bucher. *Diversity Consciousness: Opening Our Minds to People, Culture, and Opportunities.* Upper Saddle River, NJ: Prentice Hall, 2009.

Page, Scott. *The Difference: How the Power of Diversity Creates Better Groups, Firms, Schools, and Societies.* Princeton, NJ: Princeton University Press, 2008.

Thomas, R. Roosevelt, Jr. *Building on the Promise of Diversity: How We Can Move to the Next Level in Our Workplaces, Our Communities, and Our Society.* New York: AMACOM, 2005.

Internet

Association of American Colleges and Universities. Diversity Web: A resource hub for higher education. www.diversityweb.org/

Classes and training

Diversity University. "Edge advantage." www.diversityuniversity.com/edge

51

52   TRUSTING

Definition

Believing that an individual or entity will do the right thing and act in the best interest of others

He who does not trust enough will not be trusted.

— Lao Tzu

Talented

❑ Articulates that people are interdependent and therefore mutually responsible for building trusting relationships

❑ Demonstrates confidence in others' willingness to achieve constructive goals; readily gives others the benefit of the doubt

❑ Shows confidence in others that they will do the right thing and communicates a belief that others will protect confidential information

❑ Seeks to understand why someone acts in ways that cause discomfort or confusion

❑ Builds trust by taking initiative and reasonable risks in relationships

❑ Understands that there are differences in who may be trusted for what

Skilled

❑ Shares ideas and feelings selectively with others; is sometimes seen to have favorites

❑ Discloses reactions and perspectives when asked, but with caution

❑ Acknowledges when others occasionally share information "out of school"

❑ Acts out of the expectation that people generally will do the right thing

❑ Expresses occasional cynicism but tends to give others a chance to prove themselves

❑ Gives others second chances when encouraged by others to do so

Unskilled

❏ Keeps others at arm's length.

❏ Expresses doubt that others will keep confidences so fails to share ideas and information that might build support for his or her plans

❏ Expects that others will be inconsistent and unreliable

❏ Shares personal observations on rare occasions, expressing the belief that others will use the information negatively

❏ Suspects that others are out to get him or her; puts the worst interpretation on questionable actions of others

❏ Fails to build meaningful relationships because of an unwillingness to open up to others

Big Picture View

Trusting others implies that you begin with an assumption of positive intention in others' behavior. Communicating that you are trusting creates some vulnerability — the trust you offer could be abused. Yet the benefits lead to a deep, lasting relationship. Trust is the foundation of relationships. Without trust, you invite fear, suspicion, doubt, and a constant defense mode. Building trust is based on consistency of action and congruence of behavior with stated beliefs, values, and perspectives. Showing that you are trusting of others creates an opportunity for others to trust you back. Do you communicate that you expect a fair and open dialogue between you and others? If not, what is stopping you? What needs to change for you to expect a fair and open dialogue? Is the power in the relationship shared? If not, you need to make sure that the other person knows how much you value and appreciate them if you want trust to develop. Trusting others helps establish the glue that holds relationships, communities, and nations together. Trusting others creates a positive social context; otherwise, cynicism, negativity, and selfishness take root.

Barriers to Effectiveness

❏ Saying you trust others while looking for reasons not to

❏ Pushing to win at all costs; trying to beat them before they beat you

❏ Assuming that, if given the chance, others will abuse confidences shared.

❏ Creating cliques where some feel "special" and others are uninvited

❏ Being hurt or deceived in the past

❏ Being overly trusting, ending in disappointment.

52

Quick Action Tips

1. **Want to increase your trust in those around you?** Build trusting relationships by openly discussing what you and the other person bring to the relationship. Make sure to outline needs, wants, and expectations on how to deal with issues, conflicts, and information. Prepare before having these conversations to clarify individual needs by making a list of all of those who are important to you. Speculate on what they want from you and what they need in order to build a productive and trusting relationship. Be prepared to share what you perceive their contribution is to the quality of your life and work. Ask for what you want and need from them. Be specific and use examples. Let them know how much their help, time and attention means to you.

2. **Need to show more trust in others?** Communicating trust is not a one-time thing. You need to be consistent in sending the message that you are trusting of others. Trust begins with the perception that you are consistent, that you can be counted on to do what you say you are going to do, and that you communicate that you expect the same from others. Most important, you need to communicate your confidence that others will attempt to meet their commitments. Discuss how and when you want to know if they will be unable to meet their commitments to you. Consistency in perspective, positive mood, and constructive action are usually identified by others as key to building trust. Think about times when you have not been consistent and what you did to re-establish equilibrium with others. See if you can identify various situations in which you are not as consistent as you would like in sending a trusting message. Create a plan to tackle those situations

3. **Clear about your expectations of behavior?** When there is a misalignment between what you say is important and how you act, others begin to doubt your word. And in a context of doubt, communicating that you are trusting of others is nearly impossible to create. Make time to get feedback from others to see how they view the alignment between your values and your choices related to showing your trust of others. Make sure to ask people what they think you feel is most important. What do they believe are your top five assumptions about others' motives? As you learn about others' perceptions of your motives, you are more likely to identify ways or areas where you may not have been as consistent. Make sure to check in with those on whom you depend to find out how aligned your talk and walk is in your day-to-day activities. Clarify how to communicate a basic trust of others.

4. **Need to be more open with your reactions and perspectives?** The body never lies. Your interpretations of body language can lead you to be suspicious. When you are having a reaction to something or some comment, it shows in your face, your hands, and your posture. It is best to share your reactions in a constructive

way, because if you don't then others will read you as being suspicious. It is OK to say, "I'm really puzzled," or, "I'm finding myself annoyed" by a situation as long as you point out your responsibility to move through it and find a constructive outcome. Are you reading them accurately? Although nonverbal expressions tell you a lot, sometimes you misinterpret them. Checking out your impressions before taking action can be useful. A way to show that you are trusting is to share your observations and ask for clarification.

5. Find that you have lost your trust in people that are important to you and have drifted away from them? Sometimes it is easier to drop relationships or avoid people when they seem to let you down or disappoint you. You no longer believe them or trust their sincerity. One approach that may allow you to keep those relationships is to give that person the benefit of the doubt. Perhaps their intentions were good although their actions disappointed you. Maybe they didn't understand what you expected from them. In any case, give them the benefit of a doubt and take the risk of talking to them. Let them know that you value your relationship with them and want to talk about something that troubled you. Use this model:

- Describe factually what happened and when it happened

   Last week we had agreed to meet for dinner. You called me just before I was going to leave for the restaurant and said you had changed your mind and didn't want to go.

- Express how you felt

   I was disappointed and hurt.

- Check out any assumptions that you might be making

   I wondered if you didn't enjoy being with me for some reason.

- Ask for their reaction

   What happened?

- Listen and seek to understand

   So you were sick and embarrassed to tell me?

- Ask for what you need from them to rebuild trust

   So next time you need to change our plans, please let me know as soon as possible and tell me why.

Use your judgment about whether there is a pattern to the behavior of others that is uncomfortable for you. Decide how much you can trust others after being open about your reactions to their behavior. Not everyone deserves your trust, but most deserve a chance to discuss your expectations of them and your reactions to their behavior.

6. Aren't clear about what is shared in confidence? Assume that when individuals are

52

sharing information with you that it is to be held in confidence unless they tell you it is OK to share or unless you ask. Explain that being trusting of others implies a mutual commitment to keeping confidences. If you find that you simply share information because you forget who told you what or the conditions under which they shared the information, then create a memory prompt (such as a piece of tape on your journal, calendar, etc., to remind you to tape your mouth closed). It is essential that you model the trusting behavior you wish to assume about others. Remember to be explicit when you share sensitive information with others if you want them to keep it private. For you to trust others, you need to be clear about what matters to you and what you expect of them.

7. Have you trusted someone recently and been disappointed? Do you find it hard to trust now as a result of that experience? It is tough to be let down by someone you thought you could rely on. The lesson might be that reading others well and keeping communication open are important to ensuring your trust is well placed. If you let one unfortunate event get in the way of trusting others then everyone loses — you and those reliable friends and colleagues whom you are unwilling to trust. Draw a diagram with four concentric circles. In the smallest circle in the middle, put the initials of the individuals in whom you put most trust. In the next circle, just outside the inner circle, put the initials of those you trust but not as much as those in the center. Make a note why these individuals are not in the inner circle. What would need to change for them to be in the inner circle? Repeat until you come to the outer circle. Put outside the circle the initials of individuals on whom you need to depend but whom you are reluctant to trust. Note what your current reason is for not trusting these individuals. Indentify one individual at each level with whom you are willing to extend more trust. Identify how you will spend time with or engage with these individuals to test out your assumptions about trusting them.

8. How open are you with others? Trusting others means taking a risk, sharing responsibility, and working collaboratively with them. One way to communicate your trust in others is to directly and in a timely way communicate your goals, aspirations, hopes, and mistakes. Take stock of the challenges you face and those individuals on whom you depend to meet those challenges. Identify how you can communicate your confidence in these individuals and how you trust their abilities and efforts to help you and them be successful. You can achieve this by asking their opinions, sharing your own opinions, creating a transparent way to deal with issues, and making sure that you appreciate their efforts.

9. Are there few people you really trust when you need to get things done? One way to expand your network of trusted colleagues and friends is to create opportunities to talk with others about what they want to achieve, things they would like to do, or interests that motivate them. Use these conversations to learn about the ambitions and hopes of others and communicate your own. This kind of personal discovery can help to establish a trusting relationship with others and to give you a clearer picture of the positive intentions of others. By building trusting relationships and gaining comfort with the intentions of others, you increase your network of people who can help you meet your goals. If you find you are feeling skeptical or cynical about someone's intentions, then check whether you've had a conversation with the individual that was substantial enough to deepen your relationship with them. If not, then create the time to have a conversation with them soon.

10. Are you guarded when talking with others or taking on commitments because you don't trust those involved? This is the interpersonal "Catch 22." If you aren't trusting of others, they probably don't trust you. Whether you intend to communicate a lack of trust by being guarded or it is just your style, the outcome is the same: a trustless interaction. Chances are that the more you open up and ask their opinions and share your perspectives, the more likely it is that others will do the same. This creates a much larger arena of information which increases the opportunity for trust to develop among those involved. When in doubt about taking on a commitment, air your concerns with the relevant parties. Ask for what you need from them to be comfortable taking on the commitment. When working with someone, let them know as soon as you sense a problem and ask for their help in solving it. Being guarded means that communicating, trusting, and working with others has very little opportunity to grow. In a sense, it prevents the "trusting muscle" from stretching and being used. Open up and exercise your trusting muscle; the more you flex it, the more strength you have.

Related Competencies

(4) Collaboration	(8) Congruence	(14) Emotional Self-Control
(24) Intentionality	(31) Optimism	(34) Perspective-Taking
(51) Tolerance	(53) Trustworthy	(54) Understanding Others

Learn from Experience

Work

❏ Identify a relationship that needs repair. Deliberately reach out to reinitiate and work on rebuilding trust.

❏ Talk with the most trusting member of the senior leadership team in your organization about how to be more trusting of others.

52

Personal

❏ Work with teenagers in trouble.

❏ Write letters to the leaders of organizations important to you to express your confidence in their work and to ask how you can help.

Resources

Books

Bracey, Hyler. *Building Trust: How to Get It! How to Keep It!* Taylorsville, GA: HB Printworks, 2003.

Covey, Stephen M. R. *The Speed of Trust: The One Thing That Changes Everything.* New York: Free Press, 2008.

Fukuyama, Francis. *Trust: The Social Virtues and the Creation of Prosperity.* New York: Free Press, 1996.

Internet

Buzzle.com. Search the site for "Building trust in the workplace: A valuable topic for leadership training." www.buzzle.com

All Business.com. Search the site for "A crash course in trust-building," R.D. Ramsey, and G. MacDonald, (2009). www.allbusiness.com

Classes and training

Franklin Covey web site. Search for the workshop "Leading at the Speed of Trust." www.franklincovey.com

53 | TRUSTWORTHY

Definition

Behaving so that a large and diverse circle of people respond to you with belief and confidence

Trust is an emotional strength that begins with the feeling of self-worth and purpose that we're called to extend outward to others, like the radius of a circle, eventually reaching everyone on our team, and in our department, division, or entire company.

— Robert K. Cooper and Ayman Sawaf

Talented

❏ Tells the truth with candor, diplomacy and tact

❏ Consistently acts respectfully, openly, sincerely, and candidly

❏ Embraces differences and disagreements openly as opportunities for constructive dialogue and valuable connections

❏ Is always there in good and in difficult times

❏ Delegates real responsibilities to others, thereby demonstrating confidence in them

❏ Demonstrates that he or she can and will fulfill commitments; keeps confidences

❏ Creates and maintains partnerships with others to achieve mutually satisfying goals

Skilled

❏ Keeps commitments and follows through with promises most of the time

❏ Walks the talk and delivers on promises

❏ Demonstrates concern for others and seeks to provide support

❏ Delegates or shares control with others; no withholding of information

❏ Keeps confidences

❑ Openly seeks out others' perspectives to build relationships

❑ Seeks to understand rather than to blame others when mistakes occur

Unskilled

❑ Spends the majority of time with a select few; is not readily available

❑ Fudges on ethics or principles when it seems expedient

❑ Fails to keep commitments

❑ Communicates impatience, distraction or disinterest with others when they are talking

❑ May manipulate and use others for his or her own purposes

❑ Succumbs to unreliable, dishonorable, or corrupt actions at times

Big Picture View

You can increase your trustworthiness among the people that you interact with by being honest, open, reliable, and credible. People who express and act on their principles are generally seen as trustworthy; they can be trusted to do the right thing. Be sure that when you make a commitment you keep it. If circumstances interfere with being able to keep a commitment, then take the initiative to explain the issue and what you are able and not able to do. When the going is tough, have the courage to do the right thing. It takes a consistent record of doing the right thing, being loyal, and being reliable to build a good reputation. That reputation can be destroyed by one thought-less action or failure to deliver. Research suggests that trust leads to increased group effectiveness because people more openly express their feeling and ideas and are less defensive. To expand your radius of trustworthiness, reach out to those beyond your immediate circle of trusted colleagues and friends to take advantage of the opportunity that others provide. It means making time to meet and get to know others. It means demonstrating that you appreciate differences and view disagreements as a source of learning. Teamwork and cooperation among members of an organization are evidence of trustworthiness in a system.

Barriers to Effectiveness

❑ Sticking to yourself

❑ Being suspicious and doubtful of others' intentions

❑ Holding strong judgments about others and what is "correct behavior"

❑ Having too many "close friends" or "trusted colleagues" contributes to the

53

appearance of being overly involved

❏ May act impulsively, raising doubts about reliability

❏ Being unrealistic or having a tendency to over-commit may mean a failure to keep commitments

Quick Action Tips

1. Do you find yourself not really listening to that colleague or friend? Do you wish that others would cut to the chase? Making time for others to express themselves is an important way to build trust. Slow down and really listen to what is being said. Sit down and invite your colleague to sit down. That shows that you are interested in what they have to say. Move away from your computer screen, don't answer your phone, make good eye contact, and don't check your watch. If your time is limited, then say so and sincerely add, "If we need more time, we can meet again." Accessibility is a cornerstone of trustworthiness. Give your spouse or children the same respect. Turn off your cell phone during dinner. Open your laptop after your children are in bed, if then. Create quality time with your spouse and good friends. For others to trust you, they need to know that you are interested in them and what they think. Avoid gossip or passing along secondhand information.

2. How large is your circle of trusted people in your life? Draw a circle and put inside it the names of individuals that you fully trust. Check with each of them about whether they consider you a trusted friend or colleague by asking questions such as: Have there been instances when I let you down? Have I ever disappointed you? Failed to follow through? Over-promised and under-delivered? Implied that I would help you and then didn't show up? Use their responses to consider what you might do more of or stop doing to be more fully trusted by others. Without intending to be untrustworthy, most of us at times can do or say things that can seem that way to others. Consider who else you would like to add to your circle, and make the time to connect in a meaningful way with at least one additional person in the next month. Ask that peer you work with occasionally to have lunch with you. Stop by the desk of a colleague who works on another floor to find out what they think about a change at work. At your next neighborhood get-together, sit down by someone you rarely talk with and find out what they enjoy doing in their free time.

3. Do you have a broken trust with someone in your life or office? Of course there may be very legitimate reasons to not trust someone, but often we lose trust because of differences in perception or expectations about how people should act or treat us. Seek that person out and ask about what it might take to begin rebuilding trust between the two of you. Seek to understand their perspective, and then share yours. Find out if they had expectations of you that you didn't meet. Apologize for any failure to follow through even if you didn't intend to create a problem. Ask for what you need going forward to avoid miscommunication. Look for mutual benefits to building trust. Be sure that you only make commitments and promises that you can keep. Confirm any commitments so you both understand what they are.

4. Do you find it difficult to ask for help? To admit a mistake? Both are meaningful ways to expand your circle of trust. Sincerely asking a colleague or neighbor for help communicates that you value them, their expertise or experience, and their judgment. You are indicating trust and confidence in them, which encourages them to do so with you. Similarly, admitting a mistake is being honest and open with another person at an emotional level; it communicates that you trust them enough to show a small vulnerability of yours, that you aren't perfect. It may seem counter-intuitive that showing ways you need others leads to deeper relationships, but authenticity builds trustworthiness.

5. Are you reluctant to delegate meaningful responsibility? Do you over-organize a task before you let others get involved? When you keep control or closely manage someone, your basic message is that you don't trust him or her. Even though you may have more experience and can handle a responsibility quicker than a colleague, now is the time to show your trust by delegating. Let that direct report show you what he or she can do. Your confidence will energize that person and increase their productivity and learning curve if you provide an environment where you both can be respectful, open, honest and free to discuss any concerns. This trusting attitude is especially important if you manage over long distances or work in a matrix organization without authority and want to show trustworthiness. This willingness to let others do things their way is just as important at home. Allow your son to take the garbage out when and how he chooses (unless the house is beginning to smell).

6. Trying to make headway with a client who is reluctant to meet with you? Take some time to analyze what problems your client has that you might help solve, over and beyond your initial reason for seeking him or her out. The client may be more open to spending time with you around issues that are central to him or her. As you provide helpful consulting, you will raise your credibility and have an opportunity to build a trusting relationship. That relationship can then naturally lead to the partnership and business you initially wanted.

7. Find it difficult to create an organization where people are trustworthy and respect each other? Often the reward systems in organizations promote competition and individual achievement. The salesperson who makes the sale gets the commission. If you want trust to be built into the value system in your organization, then cooperation and synergy need to not only be appreciated, but also rewarded. How can you reward not only the salesperson, but also the office worker who creates resource materials for the salesman, the customer service person who troubleshoots the new product, and the product research efforts that may lead to product improvements? Both individual efforts and team

53

achievements are important for most organizations to work. Consider what your compensation and rewards system foster and what you want them to foster.

Related Competencies

(3) Authenticity	(8) Congruence	(12) Emotional Maturity
(30) Openness to Others	(35) Reality Testing	(43) Self-Disclosure
(51) Tolerance	(52) Trusting	

Learn from Experience

Work

❏ Take on a project or task force that involves interacting with other departments or business units; create an environment based on trust, openness and valuing differences of opinion.

❏ Create a partnership with an organization outside of your own.

Personal

❏ Volunteer with an organization that puts you in contact with people you have not interacted with often before. Take time to get to know at least two new people. Finding common ground with them can lead to an added degree of comfort and trust.

❏ Identify a friend that you have not talked with in years. Contact that person and connect with them in a meaningful way.

Resources

Books

Covey, Stephen M. R., and Rebecca Merrill. *The Speed of Trust*. New York: Free Press, 2008.

Csorba, Les T. *Trust: The One Thing That Makes or Breaks a Leader*. Nashville, TN: Thomas Nelson, 2004.

Goldratt, Eliyahu M. *It's Not Luck*. Great Barrington, MA: North River Press, 1994.

Reina, Dennis S. and Michelle L. Reina. *Trust and Betrayal in the Workplace: Building Effective Relationships in Your Organization*. San Francisco: Berrett-Koehler Publishers, 2006.

Internet

Demand Media. Livestrong.com. Search for "building trust."
www.livestrong.com/search

Classes and training

Booher Consultants. Communication skills training.
www.booher.com/programs/

Edge-Leadership Consulting. Workshop on building organizational trust.
www.edge-leadership.com/publicworkshops/

54　UNDERSTANDING OTHERS

Definition

Being curious about and understanding the motivations, feelings and moods that underlie behavior — yours and others'

When I get ready to talk to people, I spend two thirds of the time thinking about what they want to hear and one third thinking about what I want to say.

— Abraham Lincoln

Talented

❏ Appears interested in others; seems to know what will motivate and persuade others

❏ Makes psychologically insightful observations about self and others

❏ Sees connections between others' thoughts, feelings and actions and how they play out over time

❏ Asks questions to anticipate and better understand feedback

❏ Explores the political dynamics occurring in groups of people

❏ Predicts people's reactions accurately

Skilled

❏ Uses immediate data to understand people rather than observations over time

❏ Responds to people's behavior but with less attention to what might be behind it

❏ Predicts behavior of others when external factors prompt it

❏ Confirms with others what matters when attempting to motivate them

❏ Makes effort to understand own behavior, to be self-aware

Unskilled

❏ Judges rather than seeking to understand others

❑ Appears disinterested in what makes people tick

❑ Reads situations but overlooks the human component.

❑ Appears confused by people's behavior; seems baffled when behavior doesn't seem logical

❑ Underestimates the impact that emotions and values have on behavior

❑ Expresses disdain for organizational politics

Big Picture View

Understanding others is not the same thing as empathy, nor are the two mutually exclusive. Understanding others is a thinking process; it is driven by curiosity and a basic interest in human nature, and it develops over time. Empathy is a feeling process, tapping into the emotions that you think others are experiencing. Observations accumulated over many and varied experiences with people lead to speculations about people, then rules of thumb and, eventually, finely honed instincts. In a dynamic workplace, people come and go ever more rapidly. Understanding others contributes to forming workplace relationships quickly and to a more friendly work environment. Understanding others helps to diffuse emotional reactions when others behave in unexpected ways — a form of stress-hardiness. Such are the benefits for family and personal relationships too, leading to fewer misunderstandings and greater harmony.

Barriers to Effectiveness

❑ Self-consciousness

❑ Apathy

❑ Being oblivious

❑ Being overly task-focused

❑ Lack of curiosity about or interest in people

❑ Being a concrete or literal thinker

❑ Self-focused, more concerned with own point of view

Quick Action Tips

I. **Little interest in people?** Do you notice what drives behavior — yours or others? Lack of interest or curiosity, in general, blocks learning. And learning is essential to success. Curiosity, if it doesn't occur naturally, can be encouraged. Some action tips that can prompt your curiosity are:

54

- Ask lots of questions. Questions are the handmaidens of curiosity. Don't accept things at face value too quickly. Go deeper, or below the surface, with follow-up questions. Question things that you think you already know. Ask about things that you don't know. One or more of the answers might stimulate your interest.

- Suspend judgment. Keep your mind open to new possibilities, to learning, unlearning, and relearning. Be prepared to change your mind.

- Practice reframing. See challenges and obstacles, especially with people, as opportunities to get new information. Speculate about what you see. When the unexpected occurs, probe for underlying causes. Speculate again. Make curiosity fun.

- Read diverse subject matter. Exposure to widely different topics and views may spark your interest in exploring them further. Pick up a book or magazine on a topic that you normally would ignore. Scan TV listings for programs on topics that are new to you. Look for information that is new to you. Look for ways to connect new information to what you already know, and expand your view.

- Find the sweet spot. When encountering a new person or situation, look for what innately interests you. When you actually make the effort to look, you will often find several points of interest that can spark your curiosity.

2. Baffled by people? As you attempt to size up situations, do you ignore the human component? Perhaps people are confusing to you. Interacting well with others matters — personally and professionally. Invest time here and it will pay off for you in both worlds. Begin by studying the people around you. Be fully present in conversations with them — listen to them attentively. Notice facial expressions, body language, and vocal tones along with the words spoken, then put these clues together. Speculate about what these clues mean. Eventually, these speculations will firm up into rules of thumb and, eventually, instincts. Your confidence as a people reader will take off.

3. Over-focused on task while overlooking people ... people, what people? Are you more focused on getting the job done than on the people doing it? Work gets done by people. Understanding what makes them tick can be very helpful. Some believe that understanding yourself is the best way to understand others. Strengthen your self-understanding by developing a habit of reflecting on your experiences as you have them. That's simple enough, and it gets easier as you get into the routine of it. Create a practice where you take time to think about your experiences. What are your first impressions and reactions?

What do the experiences mean to you? What do you want to remember or do differently in the future? Discuss your experiences with someone whose perspective you value. Over time, you will make connections between your past experiences and later behavior, and between your emotional states and their effect on relationships. The enhanced self-awareness and self-understanding will help you explain behavior — yours and others'.

4. Overlook the impact of emotions and values on behavior — yours and others'? People have emotional needs and deeply held values that are very powerful. Such emotions and values drive behavior. Some connections include:

- Fear of conflict, therefore avoid difficult conversations
- Valuing loyalty, therefore avoid giving even constructive criticism
- Feeling confident, therefore take greater risks
- Believing in being honest, therefore admit mistakes
- Feeling accepted or valued and showing vulnerability

To see more clearly how thoughts, emotions and behavior interact, map a recent emotional experience.

- What happened? What specifically triggered the emotion? (For example, after stressing the importance of communication during transitions, a manager learned that his supervisors had not held a weekly meeting in more than two months.)
- What did you say to yourself about what happened? (In this example, "I told them what they needed to do, and they still didn't do it. I don't have time to baby-sit them!")
- What was your emotional reaction, and what did you do next? (In this example, anger, frustration. "I threatened to replace them with new supervisors because they needed baby-sitters.")

Notice the connection between how an event is interpreted and what happens next — the emotions triggered and the behavior that follows.

- How else could you have thought about the situation? (For example, this manager realized that his supervisors were behaving exactly as their previous boss wanted them to behave.)
- How would that change your feelings? (With greater understanding, this manager went back to the supervisors reporting to him, acknowledged his error and asked for their ideas on how to make the necessary changes.)

How can you use greater understanding to think more rationally and manage your emotions and behavior to everyone's benefit? Are you facing a challeng-

54

ing situation right now? (Who isn't?) Want to handle it differently, more effectively? Use the questions above to consider alternative ways to think about it. See what happens.

5. Do you find organizational politics distasteful? Politics are a reality, but they are not always dysfunctional. Ignore them at your own risk. You'll be out of the loop at best, or on the losing end at worst. Organizational politics can benefit operations. But research has found that while most people have the ability to engage in productive politics, they don't use it. If office politics are unavoidable and if practicing positive politics is potentially very beneficial, then what would it take for you to step up to political activity? Success lies in reading the political dynamics accurately through keen observation, in gaining understanding by interacting with different groups of people, and in using this information and these relationships to guide your efforts. Look for indicators of the political climate, like general job satisfaction at different levels, responsiveness to innovative ideas, what gets rewarded, how decisions get made, who makes them and the speed of their implementation. What key practices in your organization reflect the political climate? Understanding others and the systems in which you operate offers insight with which to make good decisions and to protect yourself should there be some unsavory elements.

6. Do you find that some people are just plain illogical? Emotion and logic are not mutually exclusive. Research suggests that most decisions are made emotionally, then justified logically. People make decisions and choices for many reasons, many that may not be apparent. Understanding what motivates people to make the choices they make enhances your ability to interact with others effectively and, when appropriate, to be persuasive. Many assume that most people are motivated by money. Maslow's hierarchy of needs, Hertzberg's two factor theory (1959) of job satisfaction, and the research of Rewick and Lawler show otherwise. Other factors influencing work-related behavior and where they rank include:

- Chance to do something that makes you feel good about yourself. (#1)
- Opportunity to develop your skills and abilities. (#4)
- Amount of information you get about your job performance. (#9)
- Taking part in making decisions. (#10)
- Amount of pay you get. (#12)
- Amount of fringe benefits you get. (#16)
- Physical surroundings of your job. (#18)

Source: Rewick & Lawler (1978).

What is one people-related challenge that you are facing? What motivates those involved? Do you give thought to what motivates you and what motivates the people around you? Where and how do you see these motivations play out? How might this information help you work with that approaching people-related challenge?

Related Competencies

(20) Influencing Others   (22) Insightfulness   (25) Interpersonally Skillful

(29) *Reading* Nonverbal Communication   (46) Social Intelligence

Learn from Experience

Work

❏ Run an "assessment for development" center or assist HR in setting up a Career Resilience Center. Both provide assessment services for employees to manage their careers, whether they stay with or leave the organization.

❏ Consult with HR or an organizational development professional to plan a team-building event that includes an assessment.

❏ Conduct an employee satisfaction survey. Learn what affects morale and productivity.

Personal

❏ Volunteer to work a job fair. Many job seekers are unemployed. The competency (54) Understanding Others not only helps to match people to positions but also brings sensitivity to what might be a difficult situation.

❏ Work with a nonprofit organization that is about to recruit board members or volunteers. Understanding what talents a board needs or what makes a good volunteer can strengthen both.

❏ Ask to serve on a grievance committee, interviewing people to better understand their concerns and grievances.

❏ When your family member arrives home, or at dinner, or later, ask open-ended questions designed to understand more about his or her day and the emotions he or she experienced.

Resources

Books

Hertzberg, Frederick. "One more time: How do you Motivate Employees?"

54

Harvard Business Review 46(1), 1968.

Keirsey, David. *Please Understand Me II: Temperament, Character, Intelligence.* Del Mar, CA: Prometheus Nemesis, 1st edition, 1998.

Pink, Daniel H. *Drive: The Surprising Truth About What Motivates Us.* New York: Riverhead (Penguin Group), First edition, 2009.

Renwick, Patricia and Edward E. Lawler. "What You Really Want from Your Job." Psychology Today, May 1978.

Tieger, Paul D. *The Art of SpeedReading People: How to Size People Up and Speak Their Language.* New York: Little, Brown and Company, 1999.

Internet

Ted Talks. Search for "Dan Pink" and "the puzzle of motivation." www.ted.com

LifeHack.com. Search for "Four Reasons Why Curiosity Is Important and How to Develop It." www.lifehack.com

Dilbert.com. Search for blog entry by Scott Adams, "Curiosity is one of the most underrated phenomena." www.dilbert.com

Classes and training

Center for Creative Leadership. Maximizing Your Leadership Potential (MLP) and Leadership Development Program (LDP). Programs built around self-awareness and understanding differences. www.ccl.org

The New Curiosity Shop Online College. Online tutor-supported learning courses. www.newcurioshop.com/

Part 3

Toolboxes: Tools for Applying EQ Competencies

TOOLBOX I
The 54 EQ Competencies

❏ 1. Adaptability	❏ 28. Mindfulness
❏ 2. Assertiveness	❏ 29. *Reading* Nonverbal Communication
❏ 3. Authenticity	❏ 30. Openness to Others
❏ 4. Collaboration	❏ 31. Optimism
❏ 5. Compassion	❏ 32. Patience
❏ 6. Conflict Management	❏ 33. Personal Power
❏ 7. *Effective* Confrontation	❏ 34. Perspective-Taking
❏ **8**. Congruence	❏ 35. Reality Testing
❏ 9. Constructive Discontent	❏ 36. Reframing
❏ 10. Creativity	❏ 37. Relationship Savvy
❏ 11. Emotional Expression	❏ 38. Resilience
❏ 12. Emotional Maturity	❏ 39. Self-Actualization
❏ 13. Emotional Problem-Solving	❏ 40. *Accurate* Self-Assessment
❏ 14. Emotional Self-Control	❏ 41. Self-Awareness
❏ 15. *Active* Empathy	❏ 42. Self-Confidence
❏ 16. Flexibility	❏ 43. Self-Disclosure
❏ 17. Group Savvy	❏ 44. Self-Regard
❏ 18. Impulse Control	❏ 45. Situational Awareness
❏ 19. Independence	❏ 46. Social Intelligence
❏ 20. Influencing Others	❏ 47. Social Responsibility
❏ 21. Initiative	❏ 48. *Managing* Social Space
❏ 22. Insightfulness	❏ 49. Stamina
❏ 23. Integrity	❏ 50. Stress Hardy
❏ 24. Intentionality	❏ 51. Tolerance
❏ 25. Interpersonally Skillful	❏ 52. Trusting
❏ 26. Intuition	❏ 53. Trustworthy
❏ 27. Listening Generously	❏ 54. Understanding Others

The 54 EQ Competencies and Definitions

1. Adaptability (page 54) Responding effectively to multiple demands, ambiguity, emerging situations, shifting priorities, and rapid change

2. Assertiveness (page 60) Standing up for your rights; expressing your feelings, thoughts and beliefs in ways that respect yourself and others

3. Authenticity (page 68) Being honest with yourself and transparent with others, even when it is difficult to do so

4. Collaboration (page 74) Working with others toward shared goals — willingly

5. Compassion (page 80) Understanding, caring about, and responding to the needs of others

6. Conflict Management (page 86) Identifying tension or disagreement within yourself or with others and promoting solutions that are best for all

7. *Effective* Confrontation (page 94) Addressing behaviors or decisions that are negatively affecting you or others in ways that are understood and lead to action

8. Congruence (page 102) Behaving in ways consistent with your feelings, values, and attitudes as demonstrated by decisions and actions; walking your talk

9. Constructive Discontent (page 108) Expressing dissatisfaction, frustration or displeasure in a way that others can hear and respond to; finding a creative way to bridge differences

10. Creativity (page 114) Generating, envisioning and getting excited about ideas that depart radically from current thinking

11. Emotional Expression (page 120) Recognizing your emotions and expressing them directly, appropriately, timely, and thoughtfully

12. Emotional Maturity (page 126) Choosing how you react to your emotions so that your responses are both appropriate and productive

13. Emotional Problem-Solving (page 132) Understanding a problem and its possible causes while taking emotional components into consideration, then generating the best possible solutions

14. Emotional Self-Control (page 138) Controlling and restraining your emotionally based actions; demonstrating self-restraint

15. *Active* Empathy (page 146) Understanding how and why others feel the way they do and conveying it effectively

16. Flexibility (page 154) Remaining open and responding effectively to new, different or changing information or circumstances

17. Group Savvy (page 160) Reading and adjusting to group dynamics to promote an intended impact or to motivate the group to act

18. Impulse Control (page 166) Recognizing emotional triggers as a signal to slow down, think before acting and choose a constructive response

19. Independence (page 174) Thinking for yourself and making decisions based on personal values and beliefs while considering, but not being overly influenced by, the feelings, needs and desires of others

20. Influencing Others (page 180) Conveying a message in a manner that moves people towards commitment to it

21. Initiative (page 188) Taking a proactive, action-oriented approach

22. Insightfulness (page 194) Seeing beyond the obvious and discerning the true nature of a situation or the hidden nature of things

23. Integrity (page 202) Behaving consistently with your values, principles and motives; being trustworthy, truthful and candid; doing the right thing even when no one is looking

24. Intentionality (page 208) Acting with purpose, direction and clear will toward a specific outcome or goal

25. Interpersonally Skillful (page 216) Using a wide range of skills to effectively communicate with, relate to and get along well with others

26. Intuition (page 224) Tuning in to your "gut feeling" or inner wisdom and checking it against something more tangible to help in decision-making and creativity

27. Listening Generously (page 232) Being completely attentive and accurately responding to what the speaker says and means, and also to what might be behind the words

28. Mindfulness (page 240) Focusing on the present moment and suspending both internal chatter and also external distractions to allow clarity and composure.

29. *Reading* Nonverbal Communication (page 248) Observing and interpreting nonverbal messages expressed by body language and how a message is conveyed

30. Openness to Others (page 254) Being receptive to others' feelings, thoughts and ideas

31. Optimism (page 260) Expecting that things will turn out well, that good will triumph; finding positive meaning or perspective in any situation

32. Patience (page 266) Waiting your turn. Enduring hardship, difficulty or inconvenience without complaint and with calmness and self-control; the willingness and ability to tolerate delay

33. Personal Power (page 272) Demonstrating authority, control and confidence in ways that influence action, command attention or gain agreement on how to get something done

34. Perspective-Taking (page 278) Considering various points of view or assumptions about a situation; seeking alternative options and choices

35. Reality Testing (page 284) Understanding and reacting to the way things are rather than responding to the way you wish, fear, imagine or assume them to be

36. Reframing (page 290) Seeing situations in a new light by considering different meanings, intentions or consequences to elicit more positive and productive responses

37. Relationship Savvy (page 298) Relating well and creating relationships with all kinds of people, even those you may not particularly like, to accomplish goals

38. Resilience (page 304) Bouncing back from difficult events and stressful situations by employing effective strategies to maximize well-being

39. Self-Actualization (page 312) Pursuing activities that lead to a personally meaningful life; becoming more of your best self

40. *Accurate* Self-Assessment (page 318) Knowing your strengths and limits

41. Self-Awareness (page 324) Knowing your own emotions, thoughts, motives, tendencies to react and their impact on others

42. Self-Confidence (page 332) Believing in your worth — your abilities, qualities and judgment — and behaving accordingly

43. Self-Disclosure (page 338) Sharing information about yourself with others, appropriately and in the face of risk or vulnerability

44. Self-Regard (page 344) Behaving in ways that reflect how good you feel about yourself; accepting yourself, warts and all

45. Situational Awareness (page 350) Being alert and informed about your environment; reading patterns of interactions among individuals and observing what may be unique about the setting

46. Social Intelligence (page 356) Sensing, understanding and reacting effectively to others' emotions and the interactions with and between people; getting along well with others and getting them to cooperate with you

47. Social Responsibility (page 364) Cooperating with and contributing to the common good of your community or social group by acting out of a basic concern for others and putting them first

48. *Managing* Social Space (page 370) Recognizing and maintaining the physical and emotional distance needed to interact comfortably with others

49. Stamina (page 378) Persisting in the face of difficulties, obstacles or disappointments

50. Stress Hardy (page 384) Maintaining performance, positive mood and commitment to goals in spite of adversity

51. Tolerance (page 392) Listening to and appreciating differing perspectives and ideas; valuing diversity

52. Trusting (page 398) Believing that an individual or entity will do the right thing and act in the best interest of others

53. Trustworthy (page 406) Behaving so that a large and diverse circle of people respond to you with belief and confidence

54. Understanding Others (page 412) Being curious about and understanding motivations, feelings and moods that underlie behavior — yours and others'

TOOLBOX 2
Career Stallers and Interpersonal Problems

If you have received any of the following messages in feedback, then you may find these competencies useful to remedy the issue. Key competencies for each issue are provided.

FEEDBACK	Key Competencies to address these issues
"Too blunt"	(14) Emotional Self-control; (15) *Active* Empathy; (18) Impulse Control; (25) Interpersonally Skillful; (32) Patience
"Sarcastic"	(5) Compassion; (14) Emotional Self-control; (15) *Active* Empathy; (18) Impulse Control; (25) Interpersonally Skillful; (32) Patience; (53) Trustworthy
"Too close to the vest"	(3) Authenticity; (4) Collaboration; (11) Emotional Expression; (43) Self-Disclosure; (52) Trusting
"Standoff-ish;	(25) Interpersonally Skillful; (27) Listening Generously; (37) Relationship Savvy; (43) Self-Disclosure; (48) *Managing* Social Space
"Too judgmental"	(15) *Active* Empathy; (27) Listening Generously; (30) Openness to Others; (34) Perspective-Taking; (52) Trusting
"Not clear"	(2) Assertiveness; (11) Emotional Expression; (20) Influencing Others; (32) Patience; (35) Reality Testing; (41) Self-Awareness
"Manipulative"	(2) Assertiveness; (3) Authenticity; (11) Emotional Expression; (20) Influencing Others; (23) Integrity; (53) Trustworthy
"Arrogant"	(3) Authenticity; (12) Emotional Maturity; (15) *Active* Empathy; (25) Interpersonally Skillful; (30) Openness to Others; (51) Tolerance; (52) Trusting
"Defensive"	(12) Emotional Maturity; (27) Listening Generously; (34) Perspective-Taking; (46) Social Intelligence

"Like personal ideas too much"	(4) Collaboration; (27) Listening Generously; (30) Openness to Others; (34) Perspective-Taking
"Not a team player"	(4) Collaboration; (25) Interpersonally Skillful; (30) Openness to Others; (34) Perspective-Taking; (46) Social Intelligence; (47) Social Responsibility
"Overly Aggressive"	(2) Assertiveness; (6) Conflict Management; (18) Impulse Control; (25) Interpersonally Skillful; (37) Relationship Savvy; (41) Self-Awareness; (48) *Managing* Social Space
"Don't seem to like other people much"	(5) Compassion; (15) *Active* Empathy; (27) Listening Generously; (30) Openness to Others; (32) Patience; (37) Relationship Savvy; (46) Social Intelligence; (52) Trusting
"Discounts others' ideas"	(23) Integrity; (27) Listening Generously; (30) Openness to Others; (34) Perspective-Taking
"Devious"	(2) Assertiveness; (3) Authenticity; (8) Congruence; (11) Emotional Expression; (12) Emotional Maturity; (23) Integrity
"Not insightful about yourself"	(3) Authenticity; (8) Congruence; (23) Integrity; (39) Self-Actualization; (40) *Accurate* Self-Assessment; (41) Self-Awareness;
"Too emotional"	(11) Emotional Expression; (12) Emotional Maturity;(13) Emotional Problem-Solving; (14) Emotional Self-Control;(18) Impulse Control; (41) Self-Awareness
"Selfish or too Self-focused"	(5) Compassion; (15) *Active* Empathy; (27) Listening Generously; (30) Openness to Others; (47) Social Responsibility
"Overly sensitive"	(12) Emotional Maturity; (14) Emotional Self-Control; (34) Perspective-Taking; (35) Reality Testing; (37) Relationship Savvy
"Insensitive"	(5) Compassion; (15) *Active* Empathy; (27) Listening Generously; (51) Tolerance
"Too serious, too heavy"	(25) Interpersonally Skillful; (30) Openness to Others; (31) Optimism; (34) Perspective-Taking; (35) Reality Testing; (37) Relationship Savvy; (41) Self-Awareness

"Unfocused"	(21) Initiative; (24) Intentionality; (28) Mindfulness; (40) *Accurate* Self-Assessment
"Intimidating"	(15) *Active* Empathy; (25) Interpersonally Skillful; (41) Self-Awareness; (46) Social Intelligence; (51) Tolerance
"Don't know where you stand"	(2) Assertiveness; (3) Authenticity; (11) Emotional Expression; (20) Influencing Others; (39) Self-Actualization
"Not trusting"	(25) Interpersonally Skillful; (34) Perspective-Taking; (52) Trusting; (53) Trustworthy
"Steps on too many toes"	(5) Compassion; (25) Interpersonally Skillful; (37) Relationship Savvy; (41) Self-Awareness; (51) Tolerance
"Not good at influencing"	(20) Influencing Others; (24) Intentionality; (33) Personal Power; (34) Perspective-Taking; (37) Relationship Savvy;
"Pushy"	(2) Assertiveness; (14) Emotional Self-Control; (27) Listening Generously; (32) Patience; (46) Social Intelligence; (48) *Managing* Social Space
"Doesn't listen"	(15) *Active* Empathy; (27) Listening Generously; (29) *Reading* Nonverbal Communication; (32) Patience; (51) Tolerance
"Interrupts"	(14) Emotional Self-Control; (18) Impulse Control; (25) Interpersonally Skillful; (27) Listening Generously; (32) Patience
"Too narrow focus"	(10) Creativity; (16) Flexibility; (33) Personal Power; (34) Perspective-Taking; (35) Reality Testing
"Unpredictable"	(3) Authenticity; (8) Congruence; (14) Emotional Self-Control; (18) Impulse Control; (43) Self-Disclosure
"Overly critical"	(5) Compassion; (15) *Active* Empathy; (25) Interpersonally Skillful; (30) Openness to Others; (31) Optimism; (54) Understanding Others
"Too controlling"	(4) Collaboration; (25) Interpersonally Skillful; (27) Listening Generously; (30) Openness to Others; (52) Trusting

| **"Moody" or "emotional swings"** | (11) Emotional Expression; (12) Emotional Maturity; (14) Emotional Self-Control; (18) Impulse Control; (28) Mindfulness |

TOOLBOX 3

Personal and Work Challenges

An array of personal and work challenges often require us to think about our strategies to address those demands. The following table lists the competencies most useful for each issue.

Personal Challenges	Associated EQ competenciess to address these challenges more successfully
Extended conflict with family or significant others	(5) Compassion; (6) Conflict Management; (25) Interpersonally Skillful; (9) Constructive Discontent; (41) Self-Awareness
Difficulty communicating with teenagers	(2) Assertiveness; (27) Listening Generously; (32) Patience; (35) Reality Testing
Difficulty communicating with aging parents	(5) Compassion; (15) *Active* Empathy; (27) Listening Generously; (32) Patience; (35) Reality Testing
Fostering closer relationships with friends	(3) Authenticity; (11) Emotional Expression; (15) *Active* Empathy; (27) Listening Generously; (30) Openness to Others
Feeling disconnected with others	(15) *Active* Empathy; (25) Interpersonally Skillful; (27) Listening Generously; (30) Openness to Others; (41) Self-Awareness; (43) Self-Disclosure
Managing a life transition	(13) Emotional Problem-Solving; (16) Flexibility; (35) Reality Testing; (38) Resilience
Managing a divorce — personal and family issues	(6) Conflict Management; (12) Emotional Maturity; (18) Impulse Control; (27) Listening Generously; (38) Resilience; (46) Social Intelligence
Building confidence	(2) Assertiveness; (3) Authenticity; (31) Optimism; (39) Self-Actualization; (41) Self-Awareness; (42) Self-Confidence
Meeting new people	(21) Initiative; (25) Interpersonally Skillful; (27) Listening Generously; (31) Optimism; (44) Self-Regard

Taking better care of yourself	(2) Assertiveness; (13) Emotional Problem-Solving; (19) Independence; (35) Reality Testing; (38) Resilience
Feeling "blue" or disappointed	(8) Congruence; (13) Emotional Problem-Solving; (31) Optimism; (35) Reality Testing; (50) Stress Hardy
Moodiness (personal)	(12) Emotional Maturity; (22) Insightfulness; (31) Optimism; (35) Reality Testing; (38) Resilience
Moodiness (others)	(13) Emotional Problem-Solving; (15) *Active* Empathy; (27) Listening Generously; (54) Understanding Others
My partner is jealous	(2) Assertiveness; (7) Effective Confrontation; (25) Interpersonally Skillful; (27) Listening Generously; (34) Perspective-Taking
Becoming less intimidating	(25) Interpersonally Skillful; (27) Listening Generously; (30) Openness to Others; (41) Self-Awareness; (53) Trustworthy
Letting go of anger and other negative feelings	(11) Emotional Expression, (12) Emotional Maturity; (25) Interpersonally Skillful; (35) Reality Testing; (41) Self-Awareness; (53) Trustworthy
Dealing with passive aggressive people	(2) Assertiveness; (6) Conflict Management; (7) *Effective* Confrontation; (25) Interpersonally Skillful
Dealing with crises and emergencies	(1) Adaptability; (12) Emotional Maturity; (18) Impulse Control; (45) Situational Awareness; (50) Stress Hardy
Work Challenges	**Associated EQ Competencies to address these challenges more successfully**
Conflict with boss that has gone on over six weeks	(6) Conflict Management; (7) *Effective* Confrontation; (14) Emotional Self-Control; (25) Interpersonally Skillful
Team work is lagging and team members seem unmotivated	(4) Collaboration; (17) Group Savvy; (20) Influencing Others; (34) Perspective-Taking; (45) Situational Awareness; (54) Understanding Others

Cross departmental co-operation is non-existent and collaboration with other departments is important to getting your work done	(4) Collaboration; (20) Influencing Others; (45) Situational Awareness; (46) Social Intelligence; (53) Trustworthy; (54) Understanding Others
Influencing others where you have no direct control	(4) Collaboration; (20) Influencing Others; (25) Interpersonally Skillful; (33) Personal Power; (54) Understanding Others
Delegating more effectively	(2) Assertiveness; (20) Influencing Others; (24) Intentionality; (25) Interpersonally Skillful; (27) Listening Generously
Dealing with complexity	(1) Adaptability; (13) Emotional Problem-solving; (22) Insightfulness; (26) Intuition; (45) Situational Awareness
Managing diversity, working with differences	(1) Adaptability; (16) Flexibility; (23) Integrity; (30) Openness to Others; (51) Tolerance; (52) Trusting
Fostering creativity	(10) Creativity; (16) Flexibility; (20) Influencing Others; (26) Intuition; (28) Mindfulness
Becoming more politically savvy	(17) Group Savvy; (22) Insightfulness; (45) Situational Awareness; (46) Social Intelligence; (54) Understanding Others
Standing alone	(2) Assertiveness; (3) Authenticity; (19) Independence; (23) Integrity; (33) Personal Power; (42) Self-Confidence
Working cross culturally	(16) Flexibility; (25) Interpersonally Skillful; (30) Openness to Others; (34) Perspective-Taking; (51) Tolerance
Leading others during significant change	(1) Adaptability; (16) Flexibility; (27) Listening Generously; (36) Reframing; (37) Relationship Savvy; (51) Tolerance
Leading resistant teams	(6) Conflict Management; (17) Group Savvy; (20) Influencing Others; (34) Perspective-Taking; (53) Trustworthy
Leading a virtual team	(4) Collaboration; (25) Interpersonally Skillful; (27) Listening Generously; (46) Social Intelligence; (53) Trustworthy

Boss is a micromanager	(2) Assertiveness; (7) *Effective* Confrontation; (25) Interpersonally Skillful; (32) Patience; (34) Perspective-Taking
Influencing up	(2) Assertiveness; (20) Influencing Others; (25) Interpersonally Skillful; (42) Self-Confidence; (46) Social Intelligence;

TOOLBOX 4

If You Don't Find What You're Looking for, Look Here

Some terms carry multiple meanings or have synonyms. The following table provides some terms or items you might be looking for but did not find in Part 2.

If looking for the following...	...Then review these competencies
Appreciative inquiry	(19) Independence; (27) Listening Generously; (30) Openness to Others; (34) Perspective-Taking; (51) Tolerance
Approachability	(5) Compassion; (25) Interpersonally Skillful; (27) Listening Generously; (30) Openness to Others; (46) Social Intelligence
Being centered	(3) Authenticity; (8) Congruence; (23) Integrity; (28) Mindfulness; (41) Self-Awareness
Caring for others	(5) Compassion; (15) *Active* Empathy; (27) Listening Generously; (30) Openness to Others; (47) Social Responsibility; (50) Stress Hardy
Change management	(1) Adaptability; (10) Creativity; (31) Optimism; (35) Reality Testing; (36) Reframing; (53 Trustworthy
Commitment	(3) Authenticity; (8) Congruence; (19) Independence; (23) Integrity; (24) Intentionality
Communication skills	(2) Assertiveness; (7) *Effective* Confrontation; (15) *Active* Empathy; (20) Influencing Others; (25) Interpersonally Skillful; (27) Listening Generously; (29) *Reading* Nonverbal Communication
Community service	(5) Compassion; (30) Openness to Others: (45) Situational Awareness; (47) Social Responsibility; (54) Understanding Others
Composure	(11) Emotional Expression; (12) Emotional Maturity; (14) Emotional Self-Control; (18) Impulse Control; (25) Interpersonally Skillful

Cooperation	(4) Collaboration; (30) Openness to Others; (37) Relationship Savvy; (46) Social Intelligence; (47) Social Responsibility; (53) Trustworthy
Curiosity	(10) Creativity; (22) Insightfulness; (26) Intuition; (30) Openness to Others; (34) Perspective-Taking
Dialogue	(4) Collaboration; (25) Interpersonally Skillful; (27) Listening Generously; (30) Openness to Others; (54) Understanding Others
Developing others	(13) Emotional Problem-Solving; (20) Influencing Others; (21) Initiative; (27) Listening Generously; (32) Patience; (52) Trusting; (54) Understanding Others
Initiating change	(20) Influencing Others; (21) Initiative; (24) Intentionality; (33) Personal Power; (53) Trustworthy
Inspiring others	(10) Creativity; (11) Emotional Expression; (20) Influencing Others; (24) Intentionality; (33) Personal Power; (42) Self-Confidence
Interdependence	(2) Assertiveness; (16) Flexibility; (19) Independence; (22) Insightfulness; (30) Openness to Others; (34) Perspective-Taking; (42)Self-Confidence; (51) Tolerance
Interest in others	(5) Compassion; (15) Active Empathy; (27) Listening Generously; (32) Patience; (52) Trusting; (54) Understanding Others
Good judgment	(12) Emotional Maturity; (13) Emotional Problem-Solving; (19) Independence; (22) Insightfulness; (23) Integrity; (35) Reality Testing; (45) Situational Awareness
Managing perceptions	(8) Congruence; (14) Emotional Self-Control; (17) Group Savvy; (25) Interpersonally Skillful; (37) Relationship Savvy; (46) Social Intelligence
Motivating self and others	(20) Influencing Others; (24) Intentionality; (31) Optimism; (33) Personal Power

Negotiating	(2) Assertiveness; (6) Conflict Management; (20) Influencing Others; (27) Listening Generously; (36) Reframing
Partnering	(4) Collaboration; (25) Interpersonally Skillful; (27) Listening Generously; (46) Social Intelligence; (53) Trustworthy
Perceptiveness	(22) Insightfulness; (26) Intuition; (28) Mindfulness; (29) *Reading* Nonverbal Communication; (45) Situational Awareness
Personable	(3) Authenticity; (11) Emotional Expression; (25) Interpersonally Skillful; (27) Listening Generously; (30) Openness to Others; (37) Relationship Savvy
Political awareness	(17) Group Savvy; (22) Insightfulness; (45) Situational Awareness; (46) Social Intelligence; (54) Understanding Others
Reading people	(15) *Active* Empathy; (22) Insightfulness; (29) *Reading* Nonverbal Communication; (46) Social Intelligence; (48) *Managing* Social Space; (54) Understanding Others
Receptivity	(15) *Active* Empathy; (27) Listening Generously; (30) Openness to Others; (34) Perspective-Taking; (51) Trusting
Self-control	(12) Emotional Maturity; (14) Emotional Self-Control; (18) Impulse Control; (28) Mindfulness; (32) Patience
Self-management	(12) Emotional Maturity; (13) Emotional Problem-Solving; (14) Emotional Self-Control; (18) Impulse Control; (24) Intentionality; (38) Resilience
Social skills	(15) *Active* Empathy; (17) Group Savvy; (25) Interpersonally Skillful; (27) Listening Generously; (37) Relationship Savvy; (46) Social Intelligence
Sustainability	(10) Creativity; (23) Integrity; (24) Intentionality; (45) Situational Awareness; (47) Social Responsibility

Team building	(4) Collaboration; (17) Group Savvy; (25) Interpersonally Skillful; (37) Relationship Savvy; (46) Social Intelligence; (54) Understanding Others
Team leadership	(4) Collaboration; (17) Group Savvy; (20) Influencing Others; (21) Initiative; (24) Intentionality; (33) Personal Power
Work/life balance	(2) Assertiveness; (38) Resilience; (39) Self-Actualization; (41) Self-Awareness; (44) Self-Regard

TOOLBOX 5

Linking EQ Competencies to Assessments

This toolbox links various assessment inventories with the 54 competencies in Part 2.

Whether you have been exposed to these assessments as a learner or as a coach, you will find these scale-competency links useful in identifying the areas essential to your effectiveness.

EQ Based Assessments

EQ-I 2.0 (Formerly the BarOn EQ-i)

Published by MHS, Toronto, Canada   www.mhs.com

Scale	Associated People Skills Competencies
Self-Regard	40, 41, 42, 44
Self-Actualization	3, 8, 39
Emotional Self-Awareness	12, 14, 41
Emotional Expression	11, 12, 14
Assertiveness	2, 11, 21, 33
Independence	19, 24
Interpersonal Relationships	2, 21, 25, 37
Empathy	5, 15, 27
Social Responsibility	23, 47
Problem-Solving	2, 13, 35
Reality Testing	34, 35
Impulse Control	12, 18, 31, 50
Flexibility	1, 16
Stress Tolerance	38, 49, 50,
Optimism	31, 38, 39

MSCEIT (Mayer-Salovey-Caruso Emotional Intelligence Test)
Published by MHS, Toronto, Canada   www.mhs.com

Scale	Associated People Skills Competencies
Understanding emotions	12, 15, 27, 41, 46
Managing emotions	14, 18, 25
Perceiving emotions	14, 45, 46, 48
Facilitating thought	34, 36, 37

EQ Map by Robert Cooper
Published by ESSI Systems, San Francisco, CA
www.essisystems.com

Scale	Associated People Skills Competencies
Emotional self-awareness	40, 41
Emotional expression	11, 18, 43
Personal power	3, 14, 20, 33, 42
Optimal performance	2, 21, 20, 33, 35, 39
Qualify of life	8, 28, 39, 42, 44
Emotional awareness of others	46, 54
Compassion	5, 30, 34
Interpersonal connections	25, 27, 46
Relationship quotient	25, 30, 37, 51
Trust radius	52, 53
Life pressures	38, 49, 50
Intentionality	24, 33, 44
Constructive discontent	9, 15, 22, 34
Intuition	22, 26
Resilience	38, 49, 50
Outlook	31, 34
Life satisfactions	39, 44, 50

Creativity	10, 13, 26
Integrated self	3, 8, 12, 39
General health	28, 36, 38, 49, 50

ECI (Emotional Competence Inventory 2.0)
Published by Hay Group, Philadelphia www.haygroup.com

Scale	Associated People Skills Competencies
Emotional awareness	11, 12, 14, 41
Accurate self-assessment	35, 40, 41
Self-confidence	39, 42, 44
Emotional self-control	12, 14, 32
Transparency	3, 32
Adaptability	1, 49
Achievement	2
Initiative	21, 33
Optimism	31
Empathy	5, 22
Organizational awareness	45, 46, 47
Service orientation	5, 10, 21, 47
Developing others	22, 25, 32, 54
Inspirational leadership	2, 4, 8, 19, 21, 23, 24, 25, 30, 37
Change catalyst	3, 7, 9, 25, 26, 33
Influence	2, 4, 20, 33
Conflict management	2, 6
Teamwork and collaboration	1, 2, 25, 32, 37

Non EQ Based Assessments

Hogan (Hogan Potential Inventory)
Published by Hogan International, Tulsa, Oklahoma
www.hogan.com

Scale Name	Associated People Skills Competencies
Adjustment	11, 31, 42, 47, 49
Ambition	2, 21
Sociability	2, 17, 30, 46
Interpersonal Sensitivity	1, 20, 25, 27, 37, 51
Prudence	18
Inquisitive	10, 22, 26
Learning Approach	19, 21, 35

Personality Big Five Model
(Various tools cover these dimensions)

Scale Name	Associated People Skills Competencies
Neuroticism, Emotional Stability, Emotional Reactivity	12, 13, 18, 39, 49
Extraversion	2, 21, 17, 20, 25, 46
Openness or Originality	10, 16, 22, 30, 34, 36
Accommodation	4, 25, 30, 32, 51, 54
Conscientiousness	18, 21, 23, 35, 47

CPI 260® (California Psychological Inventory)
Published by CPP, Inc., Mountain View, California
www.cpp.com

Scale Name	Associated People Skills Competencies
Dominance	2, 21, 20, 33
Capacity for Status	2, 17, 20, 25
Sociability	2, 4, 17, 25, 31, 37
Social Presence	2, 17, 33
Self-Acceptance	8, 40, 42
Independence	19, 34
Empathy	15, 27
Responsibility	35, 53
Social Conformity	35, 46, 47
Self-Control	11, 14, 18
Good Impression	8, 12, 33
Communality	35, 39, 40, 41
Well-Being	12, 39, 44, 50
Tolerance	27, 34, 36, 51
Achievement via Conformance	8, 35
Achievement via Independence	8, 19, 24
Conceptual Fluency	10, 22, 26, 46
Insightfulness	22, 54
Flexibility	16, 30, 32, 54
Sensitivity	5, 27, 36
Managerial Potential	2, 14, 18, 25
Work Orientation	25, 39, 53
Creative Temperament	9, 10
Leadership	2, 4, 20, 23, 37,46
Amicability	4, 6, 12, 15, 25, 27, 30

TOOLBOX 6

EQ Development Opportunites for the 16 Personality Types

ISTJ	ISFJ	INFJ	INTJ
10, 11, 12, 15, 16, 25, 27, 30, 34, 46, 54	2, 3, 9, 13, 19, 21, 33, 42	2, 6, 7, 9, 20, 33, 35	5, 11, 15, 25, 27, 30, 37, 43, 46, 52, 54
ISTP	**ISFP**	**INFP**	**INTP**
4, 5, 11, 15, 17, 18, 27, 32, 36, 46	2, 6, 7, 9, 11, 19, 20, 21, 33, 37, 38, 42	2, 6, 7, 20, 25, 35, 37, 49	5, 11, 15, 17, 25, 27, 30, 32, 37, 41, 46, 54
ESTP	**ESFP**	**ENFP**	**ENTP**
9, 11, 15, 18, 27, 28, 29, 33, 32, 51, 53	13, 14, 18, 22, 24, 26, 32, 34, 45	7,14, 18, 20, 21, 28, 35, 40, 53	5, 8, 14, 15, 18, 27, 28, 30, 32, 34, 35, 51, 54
ESTJ	**ESFJ**	**ENFJ**	**ENTJ**
1,5, 10, 11, 12, 15, 16, 25, 27, 28, 32, 34, 37, 43, 46, 54	1, 6, 7, 9, 10, 16, 22, 28, 32, 34	6, 7, 9, 16, 20, 35, 40, 43	5, 11, 15, 27, 43, 30, 32, 25, 37, 41, 54

TOOLBOX 7
Identifying Emotions
Identification leads to understanding and more personal control.

Pleasant Feeling Words

Adequate	Affectionate	Befriended	Bold
Calm	Capable	Considerate	Challenged
Charmed	Cheerful	Clever	Comforted
Confident	Content	Delighted	Determined
Eager	Ecstatic	Enchanted	Enhanced
Energetic	Enjoyed	Excited	Fascinated
Fearless	Free	Fulfilled	Generous
Glad	Gratified	Happy	Honored
Impressed	Infatuated	Inspired	Joyful
Kind	Loved	Peaceful	Pleased
Proud	Refreshed	Relaxed	Relieved
Rewarded	Safe	Satisfied	Warm

Unpleasant Feeling Words

Abandoned	Agony	Angry	Annoyed
Anxious	Betrayed	Bitter	Bored
Cheated	Cold	Confused	Defeated
Despair	Destructive	Different	Diminished
Distraught	Disturbed	Divided	Dubious
Empty	Envious	Exasperated	Fatigued
Fearful	Flustered	Foolish	Frustrated
Guilty	Intimidated	Irritated	Isolated
Jealous	Judged	Lonely	Low
Mad	Melancholy	Miserable	Nervous
Overwhelmed	Pain	Panicked	Persecuted
Pity	Quarrelsome	Rejected	Sad
Shocked	Sorrowful	Strained	Stupid
Tenuous	Tense	Threatened	Trapped
Troubled	Unsettled	Vulnerable	Weak

TOOLBOX 8: EQ Action Plan

Start with what behavior changes you want to make, what challenges you are now facing, or what feedback you want to address to determine your goal. Use the 54 EQ Competencies in Part 2 as a resource for ideas to help you design your personal EQ Action Plan with this form. The Quick Action Tips for each competency can be used along with any behavior changes you may already be considering. The Resource section found in each competency will provide additional ideas for your action plan.

State what behavioral goal you wish to achieve

1. What specific behaviors are you doing, not doing, or overdoing that you wish to change?

_____

_____

_____

2. What is the EQ goal or outcome that you wish to achieve?

_____

_____

_____

3. How will achieving this goal benefit you?

_____

_____

_____

Make it happen: Action steps

4. List any of the 54 EQ Competencies that might be related to your goal.

_____

_____

5. Read the competencies you listed above. Use the *Quick Action Tips* and *Learn from Experience* sections to identify action steps that are most relevant and useful for achieving your goal. Later, star (*) the ones that work best for you, and continue to use those.

_____

_____

Action step 1 _____

_____ Target date _____

Action step 2 _____

_____ Target date _____

Action step 3 _____

_____ Target date _____

Action step 4 _____

_____ Target date _____

6. Who might be a role model you can learn from?

_____

_____

7. List at least three resources (books, courses, web sites, etc.) that you will investigate to better understand the skills needed to reach your goal. Later, star (*) the most helpful.

_____ Target date _____

_____ Target date _____

_____ Target date _____ .

8. How will you get ongoing feedback about your progress?

_____

_____

9. Who will you ask to be an accountability/learning partner as you work on your goal?

_____

_____

Notes

Chapter 1

1. "Leadership Skills and Emotional Intelligence," Center for Creative Leadership, Research Synopsis Number 1, 2001.

2. Harvard Business Review List: "Breakthrough Ideas for Tomorrow's Business Agenda," Reprint r0304g, 2003.

3. Goleman, Daniel P. *Emotional Intelligence: Why It Can Matter More Than IQ for Character, Health and Lifelong Achievement.* New York: Bantam Books, 1995.

4. David Rock, "Managing with the Brain in Mind," from Strategy + Business, issue 56, Autumn 2009.

Chapter 2

1. Statistics reported in numerous journals and popularized in Buckingham, Marcus and Curt Coffman. *First, Break All the Rules: What the World's Greatest Managers Do Differently.* Simon & Schuster, 1999.

2. 2009 National Business Ethics Survey® of the Ethics Research Center. See www.ethics.org.

3. Darwin, Charles. *The Expression of the Emotions in Man and Animals.* New York: Norton & Company, 1872.

4. Salovey, Peter, Marc A. Brackett, and John D. Mayer. *Emotional Intelligence: Key Readings on the Mayer and Salovey Model.* New York: National Professional Resources, 2004.

5. Ledoux, Joseph. *The Emotional Brain: The Mysterious Underpinnings of Emotional Life.* New York: Touchstone Press, 1998.

6. Mayor, John, Peter Salovey, and David Caruso. *The Mayer-Salovey-Caruoso Emotional Intelligence Test (MSCEIT) Manual.* Toronto: MHS, Inc., 2006.

7. Goleman, Daniel. *Emotional Intelligence and Emotional Intelligence at Work*. New York: Random House, 1995.

8. Pearman, Roger R. *Understanding Emotions* and *Emotions and Health*. Winston-Salem, North Carolina: Leadership Performance Systems, Inc., 2008.

Chapter 3

1. Harvard Management Update. *Hiring (Emotionally) Smart*. Boston, MA: Harvard Business Publishing Newsletters, Volume 5, Number 9. September 2000.

2. Covey, Stephen. *The Seven Habits of Highly Effective People*. New York: Free Press, 2004.

3. Leatherwood, Jim. *Facing the Future Together: Forming Successful School-Business Partnership*s. Riverside, CA: The Brooke Press, 2007.

4. Johnson, Spencer. *Who Moved My Cheese?* New York: G.P. Putnam's Sons, 1998.

5. Bullock, Sandra, in "Miss Congeniality." Warner Brothers, 2000.

6. *Kolb Learning Style Inventory* (LSI). TRG Hay/McBer. www.haygroup.com

7. Learning Tactics Inventory. The Center for Creative Leadership (CCL®). www.ccl.org

8. Choices Architect®. Lominger International — a Korn/Ferry Company. www.lominger.com

Chapter 4

1. Locke, Edwin A., Latham, Gary P., (September 2002), "Building a Practically Useful Theory of Goal Setting and Task Motivation," American Psychologist, Vol. 57.

2. "Improve Productivity With Goal Setting." Center for Management and Organizational Effectiveness. Retrieved March 8, 2011 from http://www.cmoe.com/blog/improve-productivity-with-goal-setting.htm

3. Campbell, David. *If You Don't Know Where You Are Going, You'll Probably End Up Somewhere Else*. Notre Dame, Indiana: Sorin Books, 2007.

4. Clifton, Donald O., and Harter, James K.. "Investing in Strengths." In A.K.S. Cameron, B.J.E. Dutton, & C.R.E. Quinn (Eds.), *Positive Organizational Scholarship: Foundations of a New Discipline* (pp. 111-112). San Francisco: Berrett-Koehler Publishers, Inc., 2003.

About the authors

Judy Aanstad, Ph.D.

Judy Aanstad, Ph.D., is a consultant, coach and trainer working with individuals and organizations in the areas of leadership, effective communication, career management, and team development. She earned her B.A. from Macalester College and her Ph.D. from the University of Florida. Judy began her career in higher education working at Virginia Tech and then Salem College, where she served as the Director of the Lifespan Center for Women. She also worked in market research before starting her own consulting business. Her clients include managers and executives in settings including community leadership programs, government agencies and a variety of businesses and industries. Judy has been an adjunct executive coach and faculty at the Center for Creative Leadership for over 20 years. She is a Board Certified Coach who enjoys helping clients develop the people skills needed to be as effective and happy as possible.

Pamela Corbett, M.A.

Pamela Corbett, M.A., psychologist and owner of Spectrum Psychological Services in Winston Salem, N.C. She was educated at Pennsylvania State University, Indiana University of Pennsylvania and Wake Forest University, where she also taught. Before graduate school, Pamela worked in the business sector negotiating insurance settlements, co-founding a veterinary hospital and producing live television for a local cable station. She also earned a Master Practitioner Certification in Neuro-Linguistic Programming. Appointed adjunct faculty at the Center for Creative Leadership, she has focused on leadership and executive effectiveness for more than 20 years. She combines practical business experience with academic training in human behavior to help clients, teams and organizations set and reach their goals. Community leadership and mental health advocacy contribute to her ongoing learning.

Catherine A. Jourdan, MA.Ed.

Catherine A. Jourdan, MA.Ed., is a Licensed Professional Counselor and Board Certified Coach who has a career spanning more than three decades in which she has developed her emotional intelligence skills in positions such as a senior staff member at the Wake Forest University Counseling Center, where she also taught in the department of Psychology, as the Executive Director of a nonprofit organization and as a counselor in private practice. Since 1977 she has worked as adjunct staff at the Center for Creative Leadership providing coaching, feedback and facilitation in their leadership development programs. She earned her B.A. in Psychology from East Carolina University and her master's degree in counseling from Wake Forest University. She spent a year studying at the C.G. Jung Institute in Zurich, Switzerland. When she is not working, writing or traveling she enjoys singing in the choir, spending time with her family and with her canine companions.

Roger R. Pearman, Ed.D.

Roger R. Pearman, Ed.D., President of Leadership Performance Systems, Inc., and Qualifying.org, Inc., is an award winning researcher and writer of numerous books and articles on leadership development. He earned both his B.A. and M.A. from Wake Forest University and his Ed.D. from the University of North Carolina-Greensboro. His career extends from higher education as faculty and staff, corporate leadership as a chief operating officer, to his current entrepreneurial endeavors. As a senior adjunct associate for the Center for Creative Leadership, he serves as an executive coach, program designer and trainer, and researcher. He has authored or co-authored a number of books including, *I'm Not Crazy, I'm Just Not You* (2010); *Emotions and Health* (2008); *Emotions and Leadership* (2008); *You: Being More Effective With Your MBTI Type* (2006); *Introduction to Type and Emotional Intelligence* (2002). Roger is a contributing writer to Inc.com, Talent Management, and Training. His adult children are in the Marines and Peace Corps. He lives with his wife in Winston-Salem, N.C.